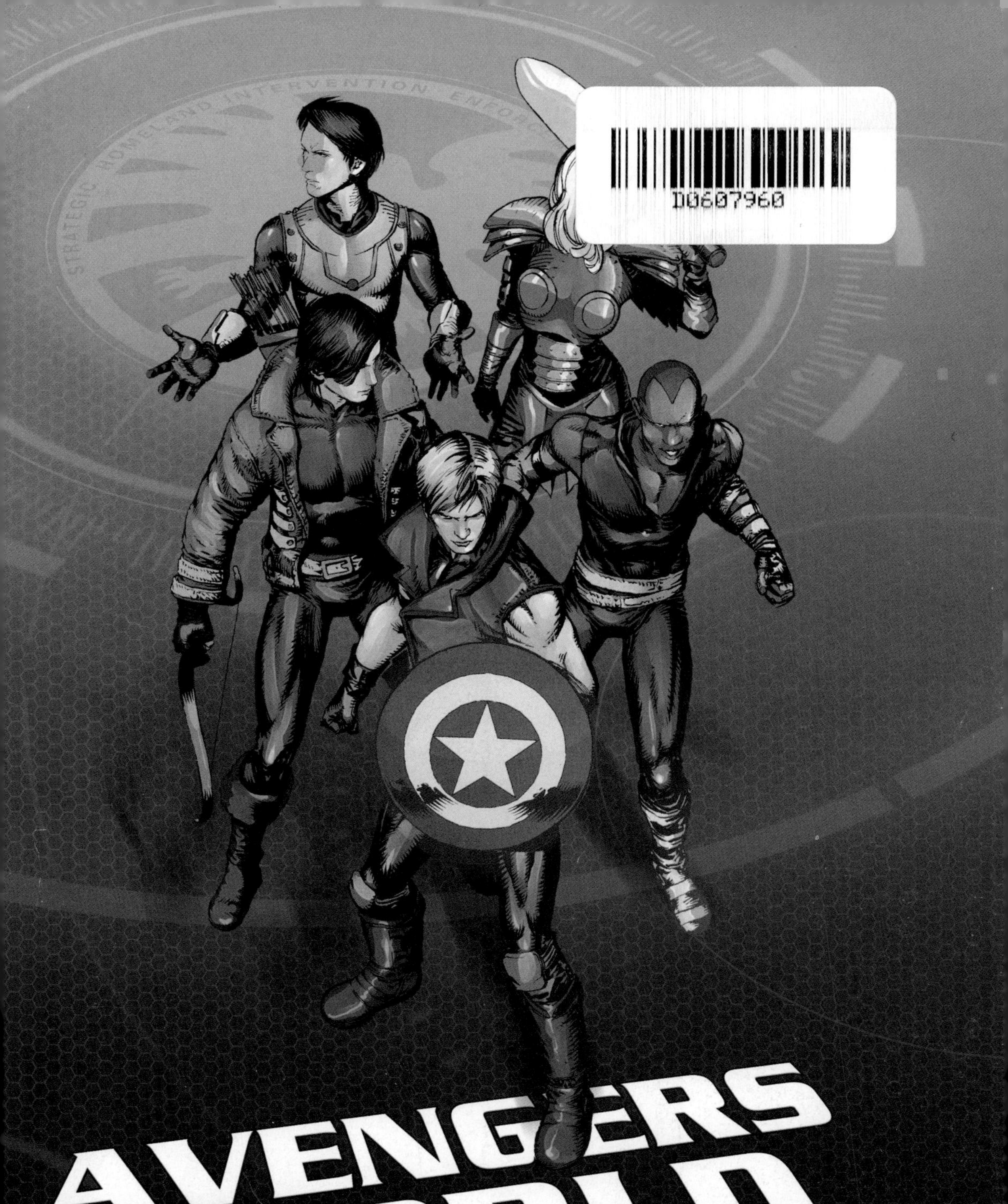

AVENGERS WORLD
NEXT WORLD

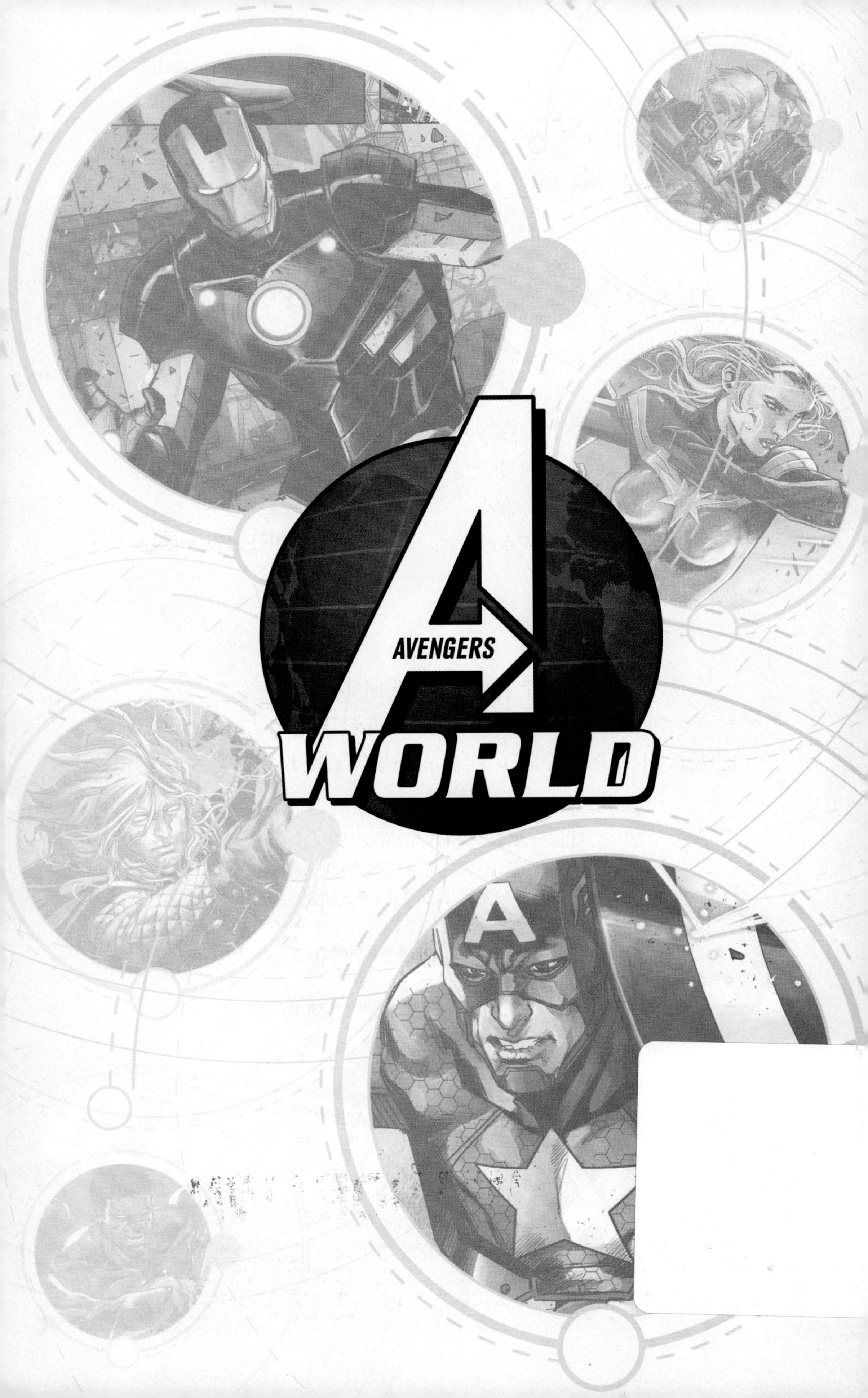
AVENGERS
WORLD

NEXT WORLD

WRITERS
NICK SPENCER WITH **FRANK BARBIERE** (#15-16)

Avengers World
#10, #12, #14-16
ARTISTS: **MARCO CHECCHETTO** WITH **RAMON ROSANAS** (#16)
COLOR ARTIST: **ANDRES MOSSA**
COVER ART: **SIMONE BIANCHI** (#10),
JORGE MOLINA (#12, #14) & **KALMAN ANDRASOFSZKY** (#15-16)

Avengers World
#11, #13
ARTIST: **RAFFAELE IENCO**
COLOR ARTIST: **ANDRES MOSSA**
COVER ART: **PAUL RENAUD** (#11) & **JORGE MOLINA** (#13)

LETTERERS: **VC'S JOE CARAMAGNA** (#10-15)
AND **TRAVIS LANHAM** & **JOE SABINO** (#16)
ASSISTANT EDITOR: **JAKE THOMAS**
EDITOR: **WIL MOSS**
EXECUTIVE EDITOR: **TOM BREVOORT**

AVENGERS CREATED BY **STAN LEE** & **JACK KIRBY**

Collection Editor: **Jennifer Grünwald** • Assistant Editor: **Sarah Brunstad** • Associate Managing Editor: **Alex Starbuck**
Editor, Special Projects: **Mark D. Beazley** • Senior Editor, Special Projects: **Jeff Youngquist**
SVP Print, Sales & Marketing: **David Gabriel** • Book Design: **Nelson Ribeiro**

Editor in Chief: **Axel Alonso** • Chief Creative Officer: **Joe Quesada**
Publisher: **Dan Buckley** • Executive Producer: **Alan Fine**

WITHDRAWN

GERS WORLD VOL. 3: NEXT WORLD. Contains material originally published in magazine form as AVENGERS WORLD #10-16. First printing 2015. ISBN# 978-0-7851-9251-0. Published by MARVEL WORLDWIDE,
a subsidiary of MARVEL ENTERTAINMENT, LLC. OFFICE OF PUBLICATION: 135 West 50th Street, New York, NY 10020. Copyright © 2014 and 2015 Marvel Characters, Inc. All rights reserved. All characters featured
s issue and the distinctive names and likenesses thereof, and all related indicia are trademarks of Marvel Characters, Inc. No similarity between any of the names, characters, persons, and/or institutions in this
zine with those of any living or dead person or institution is intended, and any such similarity which may exist is purely coincidental. **Printed in the U.S.A.** ALAN FINE, EVP - Office of the President, Marvel Worldwide,
nd EVP & CMO Marvel Characters B.V.; DAN BUCKLEY, Publisher & President - Print, Animation & Digital Divisions; JOE QUESADA, Chief Creative Officer; TOM BREVOORT, SVP of Publishing; DAVID BOGART, SVP of
ations & Procurement, Publishing; C.B. CEBULSKI, SVP of Creator & Content Development; DAVID GABRIEL, SVP Print, Sales & Marketing; JIM O'KEEFE, VP of Operations & Logistics; DAN CARR, Executive Director
blishing Technology; SUSAN CRESPI, Editorial Operations Manager; ALEX MORALES, Publishing Operations Manager; STAN LEE, Chairman Emeritus. For information regarding advertising in Marvel Comics or on
el.com, please contact Niza Disla, Director of Marvel Partnerships, at ndisla@marvel.com. For Marvel subscription inquiries, please call 800-217-9158. **Manufactured between 12/19/2014 and 1/26/2015 by**
DONNELLEY, INC., SALEM, VA, USA.

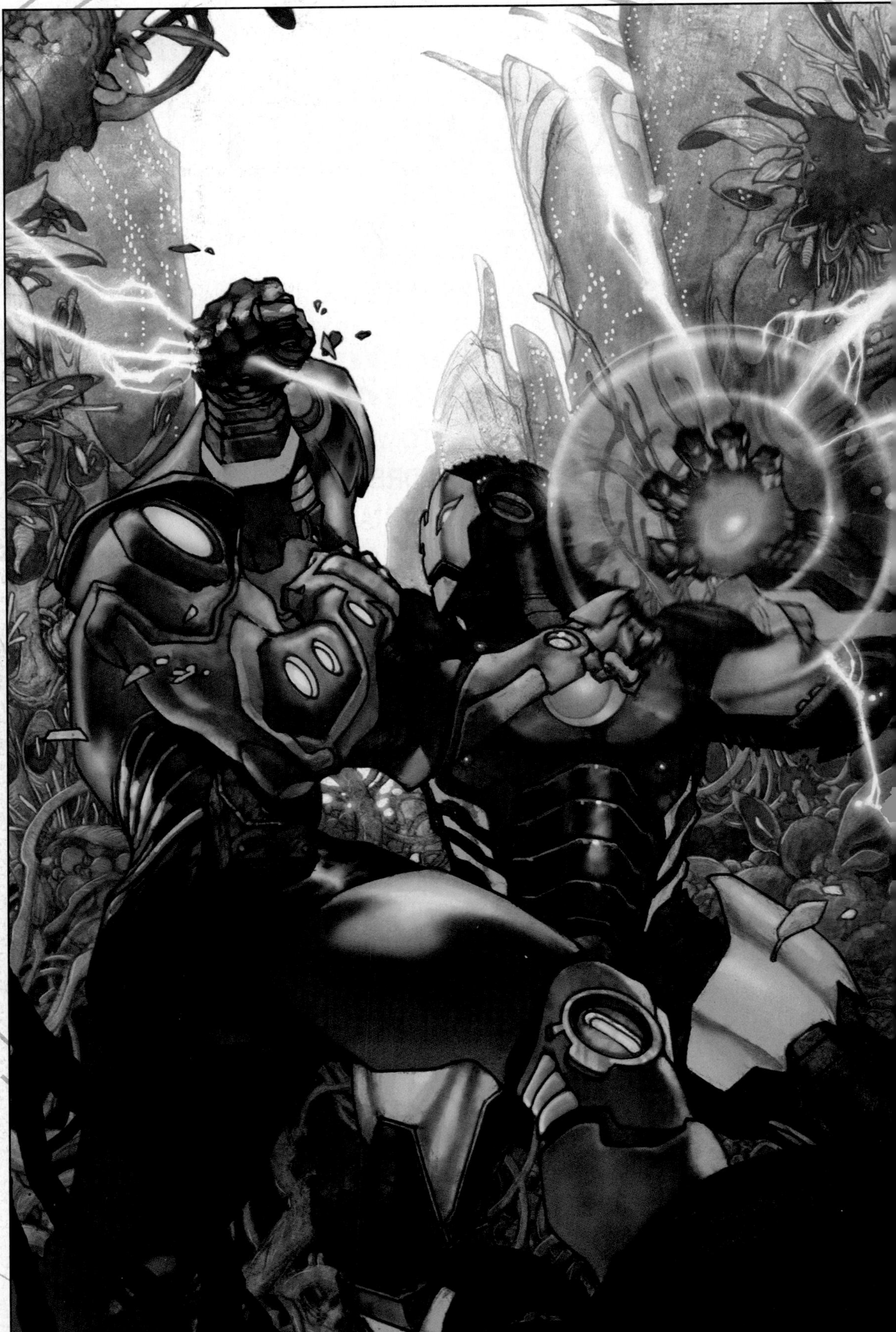

MISSION CONTROL

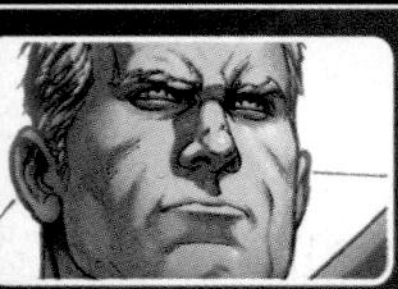

CAPTAIN AMERICA

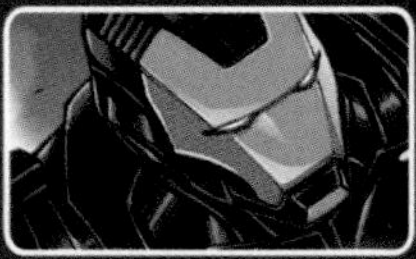

IRON MAN

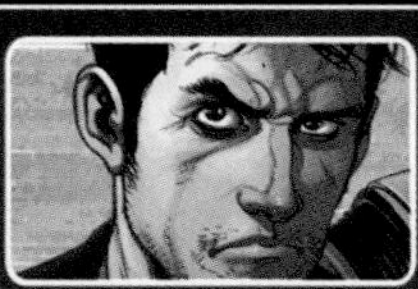

BRUCE BANNER

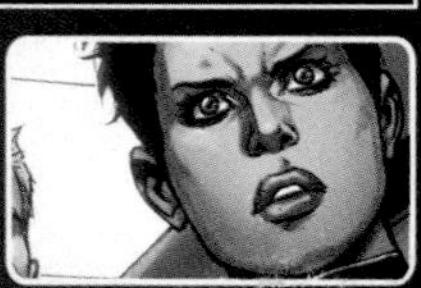

S.H.I.E.L.D. DIRECTOR MARIA HILL

CAPTAIN AMERICA, IRON MAN and BRUCE BANNER (a.k.a. The Hulk) joined with S.H.I.E.L.D. to be Avengers liaisons in creating response teams for large threats the world over. On their first day, three crises exploded around the globe:

TROUBLE MAP/LOCATION CHARLIE: MADRIPOOR

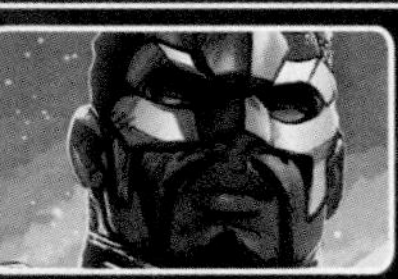

FALCON

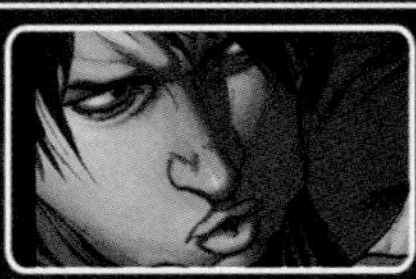

SHANG-CHI

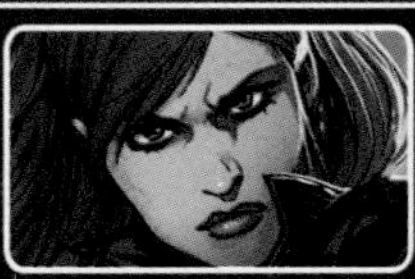

BLACK WIDOW

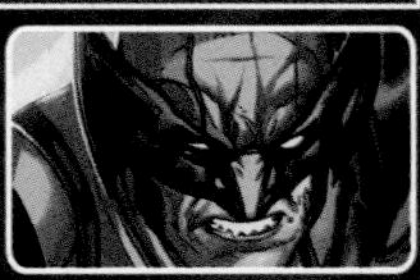

WOLVERINE

The island crime haven of Madripoor erupted in violence (moreso than usual). The villain GORGON completed a mystical ceremony, raising the slumbering dragon upon whose head Madripoor rested. As the dragon neared the Chinese mainland, China's intelligence agency S.P.E.A.R. sent its mobile base The Circle and its super hero team The Ascendant to combat the threat.

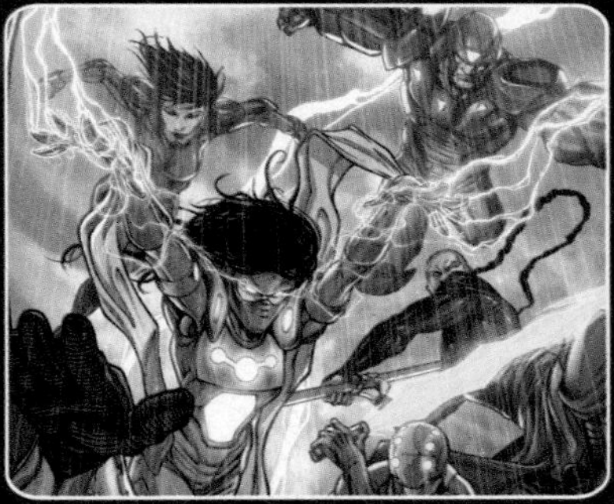

THE ASCENDANT

TROUBLE MAP/LOCATION BRAVO: VELLETRI, ITALY

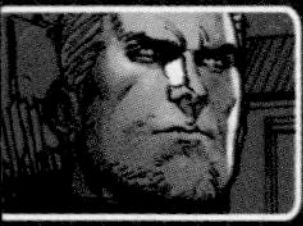

HAWKEYE

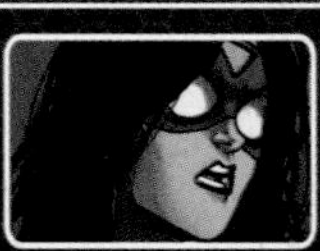

SPIDER-WOMAN

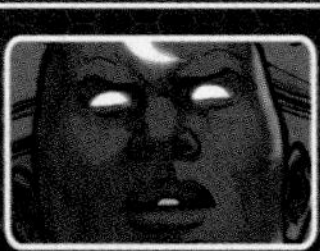

NIGHTMASK

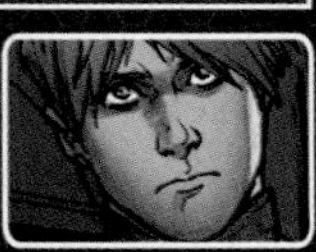

STARBRAND

Underneath a number of European cities are CITIES OF THE DEAD, places that trap tormented souls. Powerful sorceress MORGAN LE FAY infiltrated one underneath Velletri, Italy. Despite the intervention of the super hero team Euroforce, Le Fay used the power of the tormented souls to launch an army of the undead from all of the Cities of the Dead.

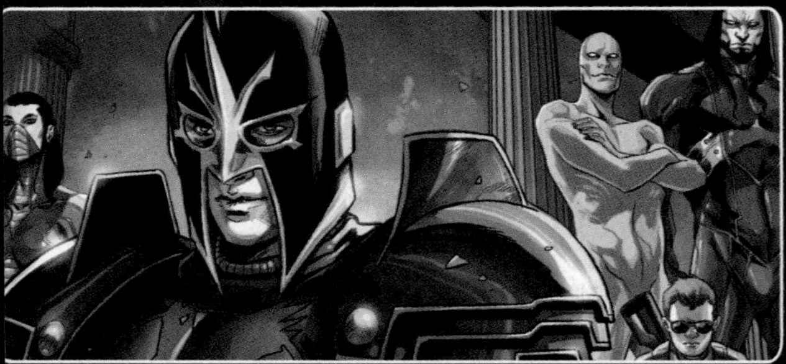

EUROFORCE

TROUBLE MAP/LOCATION ALPHA: BARBUDA (A.K.A. A.I.M. ISLAND):

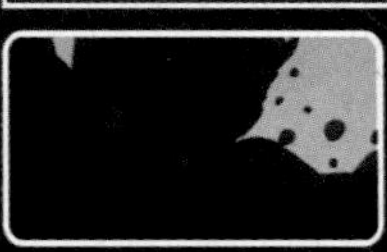

SUNSPOT

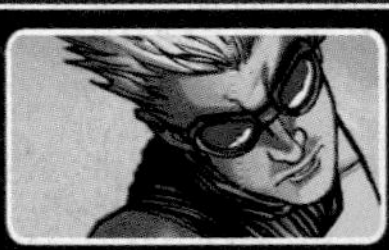

CANNONBALL

A.I.M.'s island nation of Barbuda began rapidly advancing, pulling technology from the future. CANNONBALL and SUNSPOT used Barbuda's technology to jump into the future, where a version of Jocasta told them of Maria Hill's secret mind-wiping "Reverie" program and introduced them to the Next Avengers, a group made up of the future children of current Avengers.

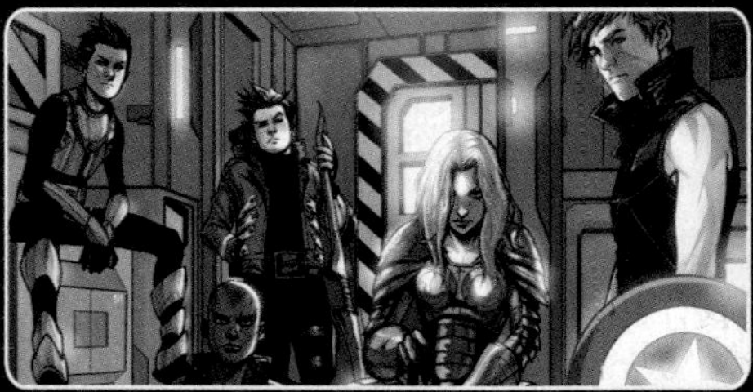

NEXT AVENGERS

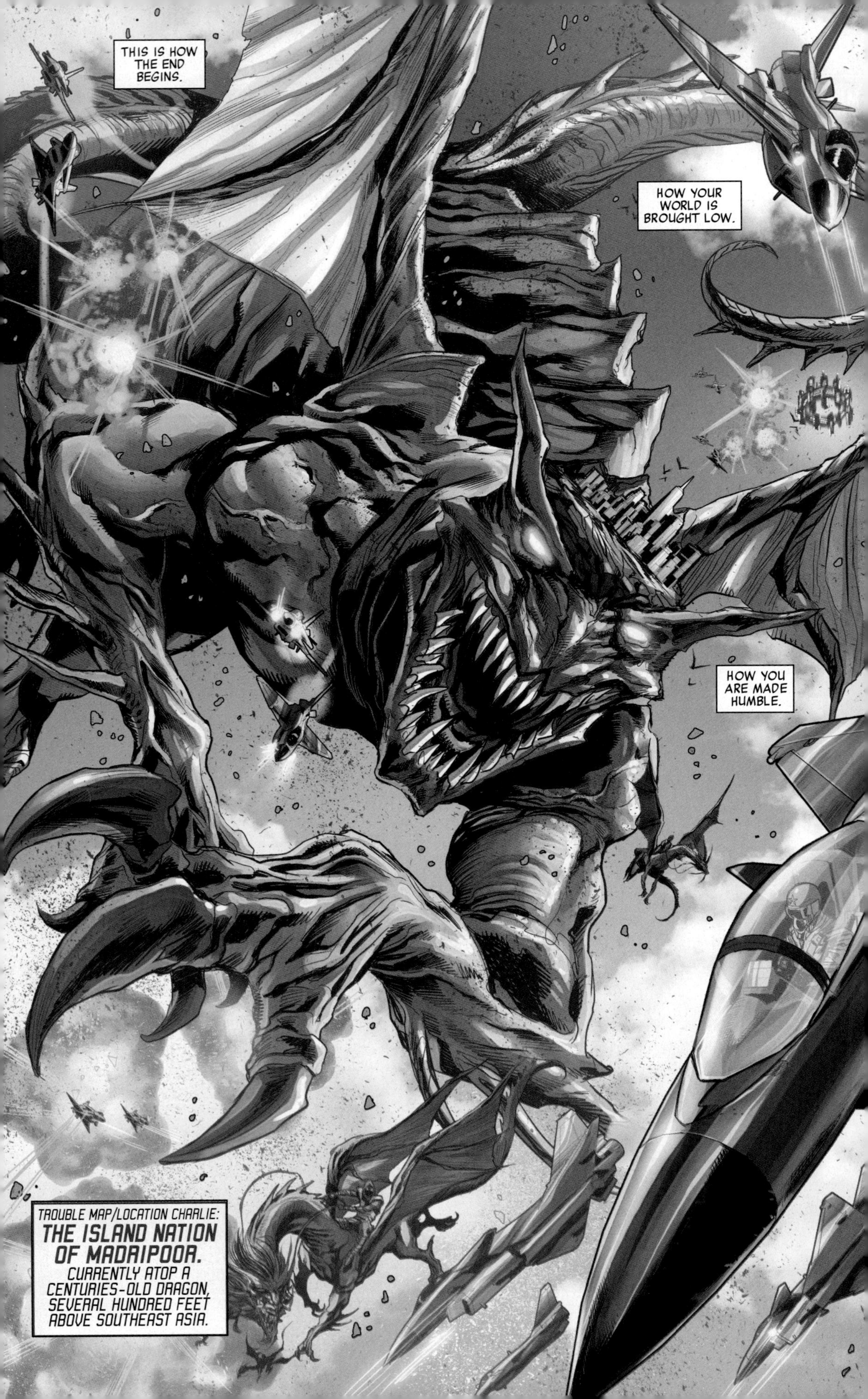
THIS IS HOW THE END BEGINS.
HOW YOUR WORLD IS BROUGHT LOW.
HOW YOU ARE MADE HUMBLE.
TROUBLE MAP/LOCATION CHARLIE:
THE ISLAND NATION OF MADRIPOOR.
CURRENTLY ATOP A CENTURIES-OLD DRAGON, SEVERAL HUNDRED FEET ABOVE SOUTHEAST ASIA.

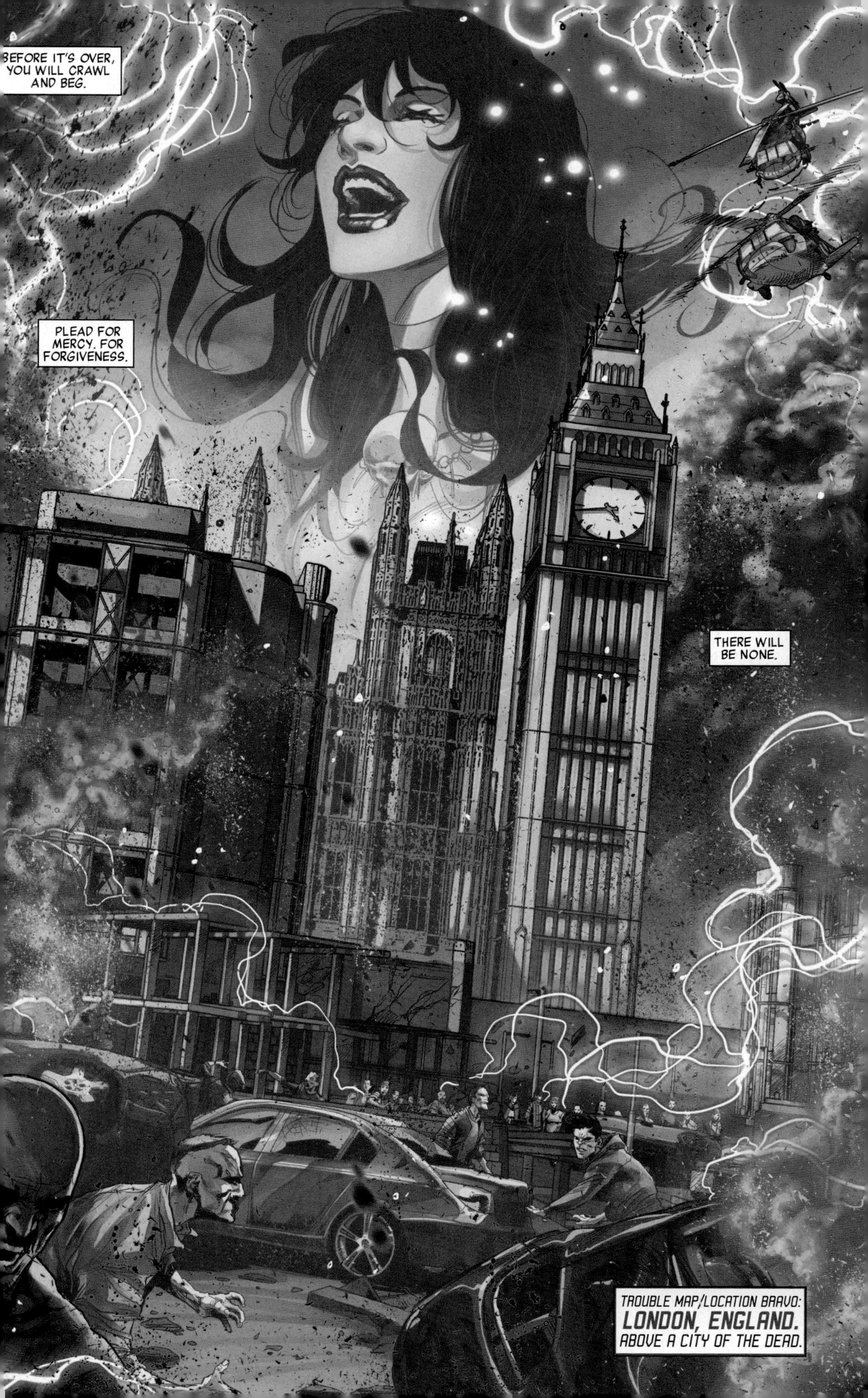
BEFORE IT'S OVER, YOU WILL CRAWL AND BEG.
PLEAD FOR MERCY. FOR FORGIVENESS.
THERE WILL BE NONE.
TROUBLE MAP/LOCATION BRAVO:
LONDON, ENGLAND.
ABOVE A CITY OF THE DEAD.

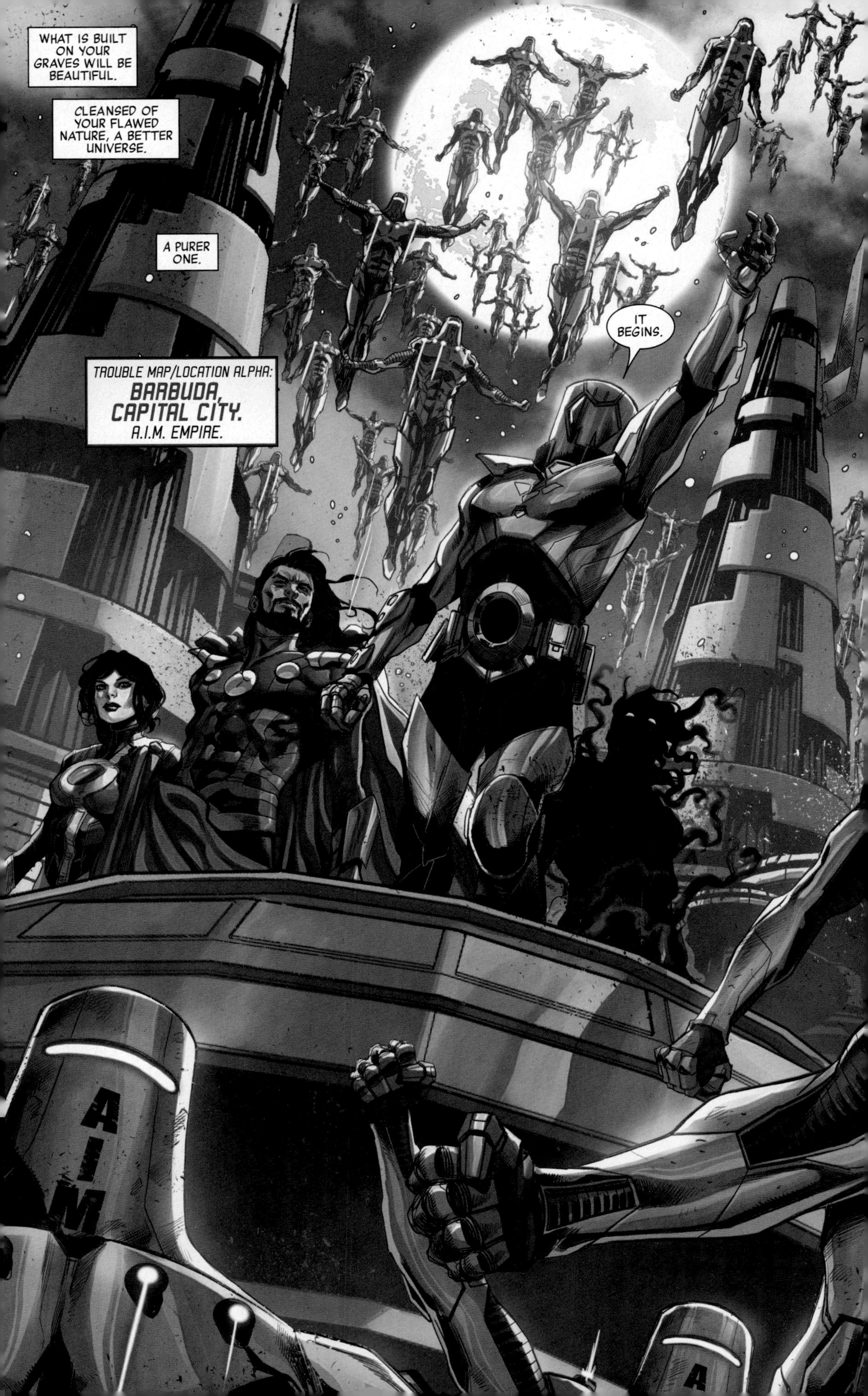
WHAT IS BUILT ON YOUR GRAVES WILL BE BEAUTIFUL.
CLEANSED OF YOUR FLAWED NATURE, A BETTER UNIVERSE.
A PURER ONE.
TROUBLE MAP/LOCATION ALPHA: BARBUDA, CAPITAL CITY. A.I.M. EMPIRE.
IT BEGINS.
AIM
A

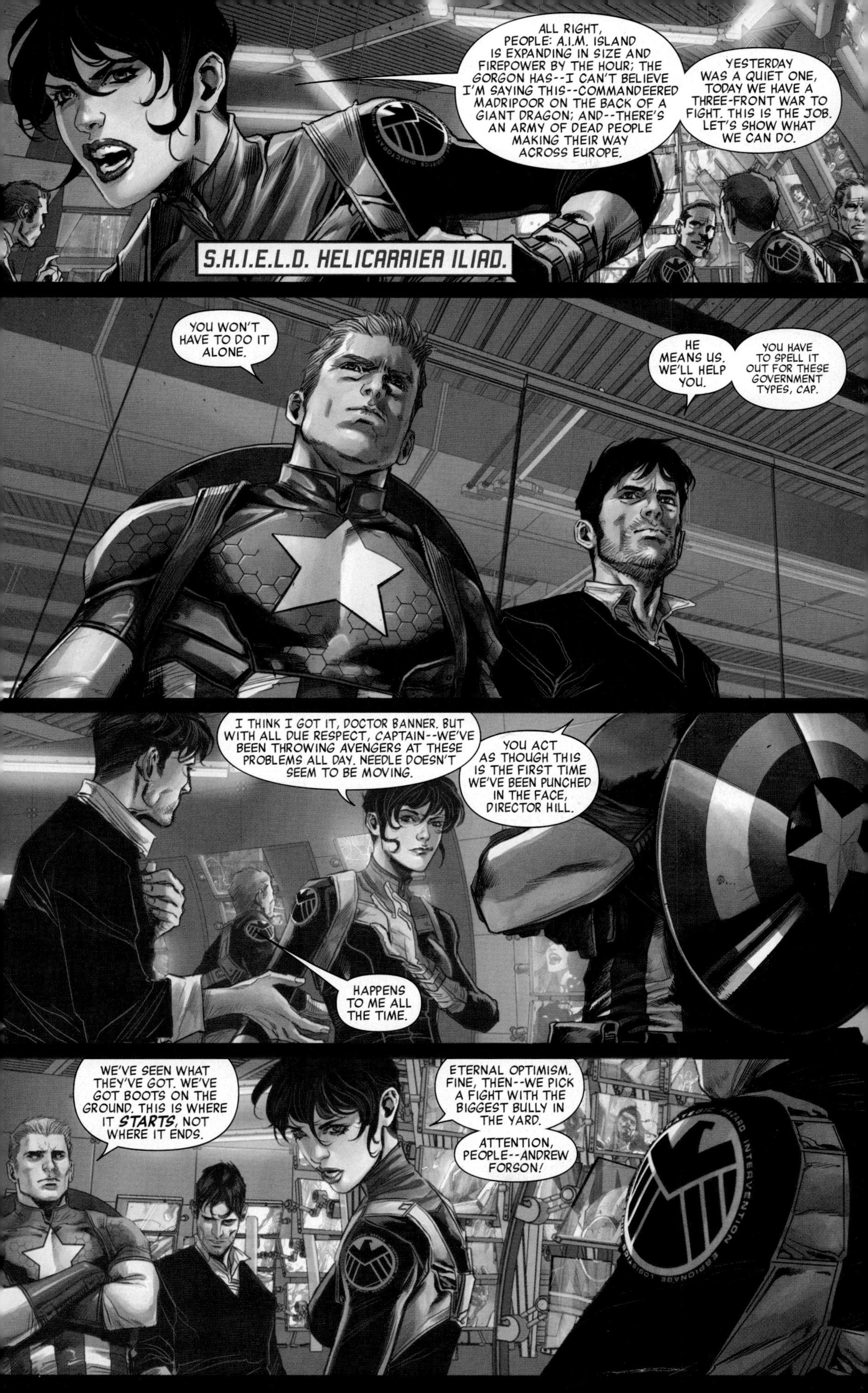
ALL RIGHT, PEOPLE: A.I.M. ISLAND IS EXPANDING IN SIZE AND FIREPOWER BY THE HOUR; THE GORGON HAS--I CAN'T BELIEVE I'M SAYING THIS--COMMANDEERED MADRIPOOR ON THE BACK OF A GIANT DRAGON; AND--THERE'S AN ARMY OF DEAD PEOPLE MAKING THEIR WAY ACROSS EUROPE.
YESTERDAY WAS A QUIET ONE, TODAY WE HAVE A THREE-FRONT WAR TO FIGHT. THIS IS THE JOB. LET'S SHOW WHAT WE CAN DO.
S.H.I.E.L.D. HELICARRIER ILIAD.
YOU WON'T HAVE TO DO IT ALONE.
HE MEANS US. WE'LL HELP YOU.
YOU HAVE TO SPELL IT OUT FOR THESE GOVERNMENT TYPES, CAP.
I THINK I GOT IT, DOCTOR BANNER. BUT WITH ALL DUE RESPECT, CAPTAIN--WE'VE BEEN THROWING AVENGERS AT THESE PROBLEMS ALL DAY. NEEDLE DOESN'T SEEM TO BE MOVING.
YOU ACT AS THOUGH THIS IS THE FIRST TIME WE'VE BEEN PUNCHED IN THE FACE, DIRECTOR HILL.
HAPPENS TO ME ALL THE TIME.
WE'VE SEEN WHAT THEY'VE GOT. WE'VE GOT BOOTS ON THE GROUND. THIS IS WHERE IT **STARTS**, NOT WHERE IT ENDS.
ETERNAL OPTIMISM. FINE, THEN--WE PICK A FIGHT WITH THE BIGGEST BULLY IN THE YARD.
ATTENTION, PEOPLE--ANDREW FORSON!

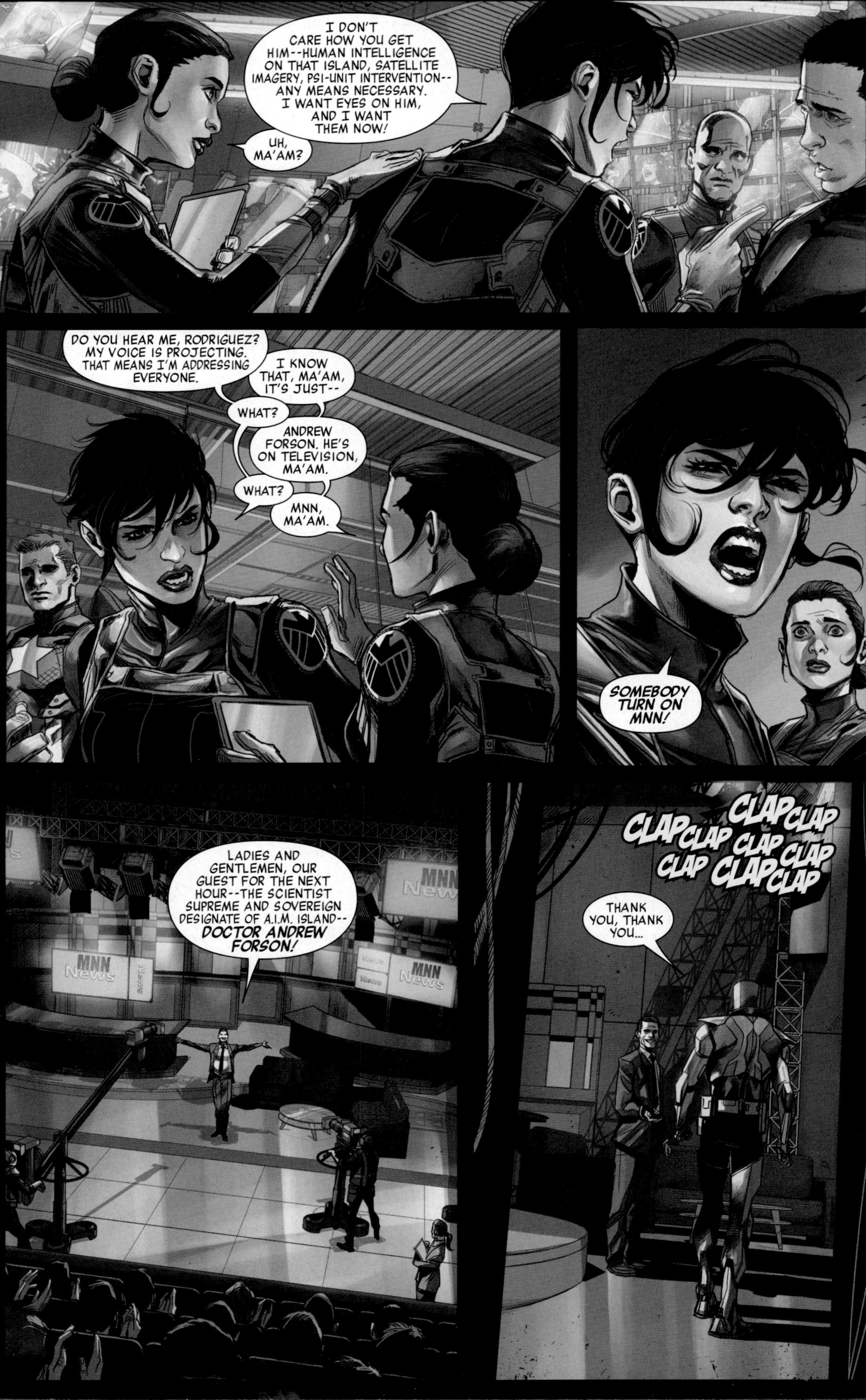
I DON'T CARE HOW YOU GET HIM--HUMAN INTELLIGENCE ON THAT ISLAND, SATELLITE IMAGERY, PSI-UNIT INTERVENTION--ANY MEANS NECESSARY. I WANT EYES ON HIM, AND I WANT THEM NOW!
UH, MA'AM?
DO YOU HEAR ME, RODRIGUEZ? MY VOICE IS PROJECTING. THAT MEANS I'M ADDRESSING EVERYONE.
I KNOW THAT, MA'AM, IT'S JUST--
WHAT?
ANDREW FORSON. HE'S ON TELEVISION, MA'AM.
WHAT?
MNN, MA'AM.
SOMEBODY TURN ON MNN!
LADIES AND GENTLEMEN, OUR GUEST FOR THE NEXT HOUR--THE SCIENTIST SUPREME AND SOVEREIGN DESIGNATE OF A.I.M. ISLAND--DOCTOR ANDREW FORSON!
CLAP CLAP CLAP CLAP CLAP CLAP CLAP CLAP CLAP
THANK YOU, THANK YOU...

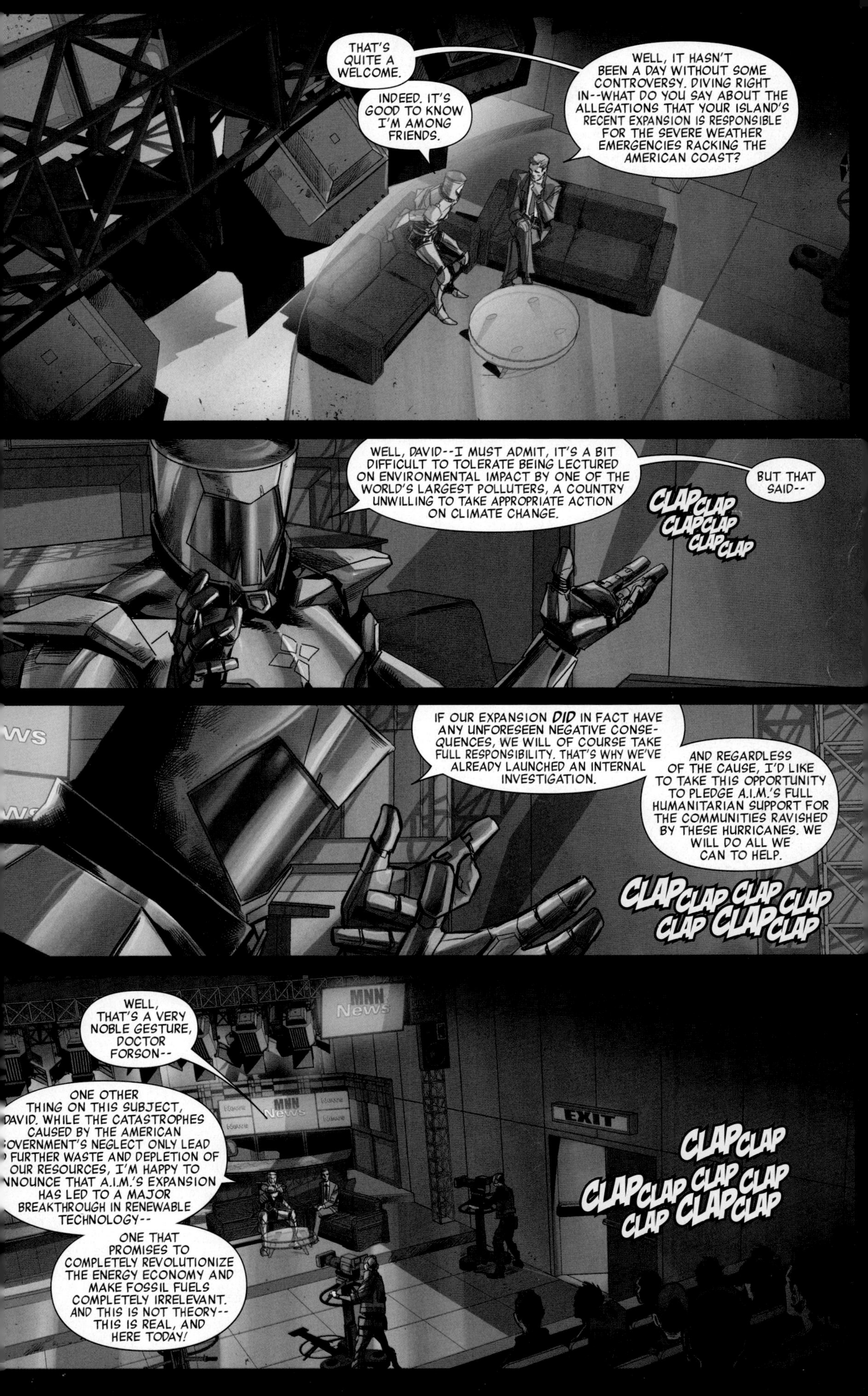
THAT'S QUITE A WELCOME.
WELL, IT HASN'T BEEN A DAY WITHOUT SOME CONTROVERSY. DIVING RIGHT IN--WHAT DO YOU SAY ABOUT THE ALLEGATIONS THAT YOUR ISLAND'S RECENT EXPANSION IS RESPONSIBLE FOR THE SEVERE WEATHER EMERGENCIES RACKING THE AMERICAN COAST?
INDEED. IT'S GOOD TO KNOW I'M AMONG FRIENDS.
WELL, DAVID--I MUST ADMIT, IT'S A BIT DIFFICULT TO TOLERATE BEING LECTURED ON ENVIRONMENTAL IMPACT BY ONE OF THE WORLD'S LARGEST POLLUTERS, A COUNTRY UNWILLING TO TAKE APPROPRIATE ACTION ON CLIMATE CHANGE.
BUT THAT SAID--
CLAP CLAP CLAP CLAP CLAP CLAP
IF OUR EXPANSION *DID* IN FACT HAVE ANY UNFORESEEN NEGATIVE CONSE-QUENCES, WE WILL OF COURSE TAKE FULL RESPONSIBILITY. THAT'S WHY WE'VE ALREADY LAUNCHED AN INTERNAL INVESTIGATION.
AND REGARDLESS OF THE CAUSE, I'D LIKE TO TAKE THIS OPPORTUNITY TO PLEDGE A.I.M.'S FULL HUMANITARIAN SUPPORT FOR THE COMMUNITIES RAVISHED BY THESE HURRICANES. WE WILL DO ALL WE CAN TO HELP.
CLAP CLAP CLAP CLAP CLAP CLAP CLAP
MNN News
WELL, THAT'S A VERY NOBLE GESTURE, DOCTOR FORSON--
ONE OTHER THING ON THIS SUBJECT, DAVID. WHILE THE CATASTROPHES CAUSED BY THE AMERICAN GOVERNMENT'S NEGLECT ONLY LEAD FURTHER WASTE AND DEPLETION OF OUR RESOURCES, I'M HAPPY TO ANNOUNCE THAT A.I.M.'S EXPANSION HAS LED TO A MAJOR BREAKTHROUGH IN RENEWABLE TECHNOLOGY--
ONE THAT PROMISES TO COMPLETELY REVOLUTIONIZE THE ENERGY ECONOMY AND MAKE FOSSIL FUELS COMPLETELY IRRELEVANT. AND THIS IS NOT THEORY-- THIS IS REAL, AND HERE TODAY!
EXIT
CLAP CLAP CLAP CLAP CLAP CLAP CLAP CLAP CLAP CLAP

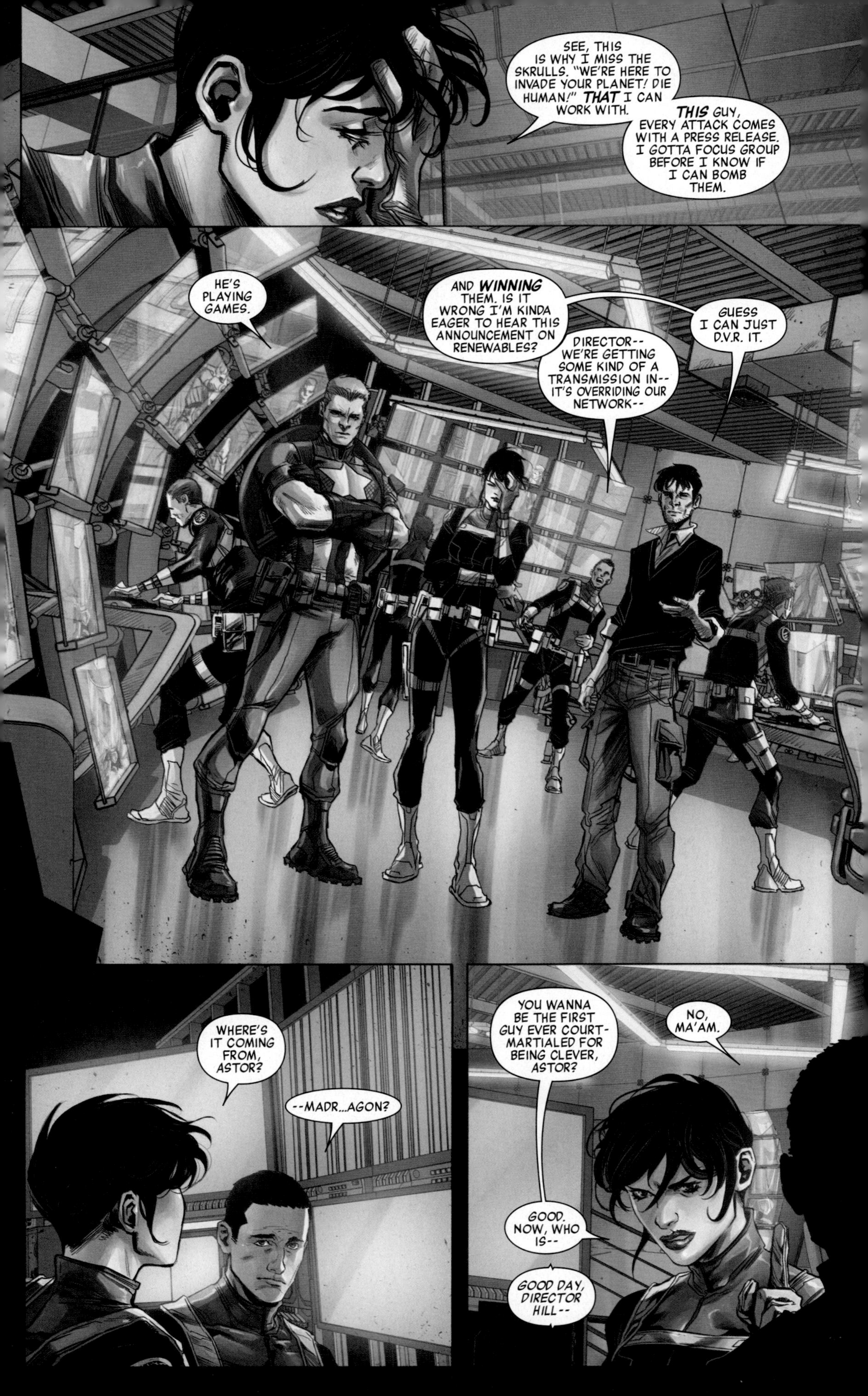
SEE, THIS IS WHY I MISS THE SKRULLS. "WE'RE HERE TO INVADE YOUR PLANET! DIE HUMAN!" THAT I CAN WORK WITH.
THIS GUY, EVERY ATTACK COMES WITH A PRESS RELEASE. I GOTTA FOCUS GROUP BEFORE I KNOW IF I CAN BOMB THEM.
HE'S PLAYING GAMES.
AND WINNING THEM. IS IT WRONG I'M KINDA EAGER TO HEAR THIS ANNOUNCEMENT ON RENEWABLES?
GUESS I CAN JUST D.V.R. IT.
DIRECTOR-- WE'RE GETTING SOME KIND OF A TRANSMISSION IN-- IT'S OVERRIDING OUR NETWORK--
WHERE'S IT COMING FROM, ASTOR?
--MADR...AGON?
YOU WANNA BE THE FIRST GUY EVER COURT-MARTIALED FOR BEING CLEVER, ASTOR?
NO, MA'AM.
GOOD. NOW, WHO IS--
GOOD DAY, DIRECTOR HILL--

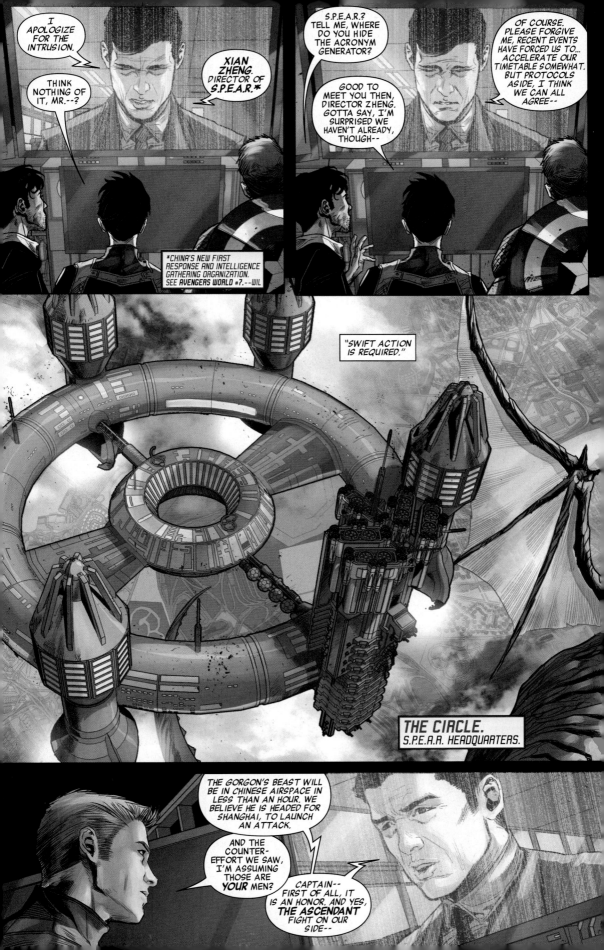

I APOLOGIZE FOR THE INTRUSION.

XIAN ZHENG. DIRECTOR OF S.P.E.A.R.*

THINK NOTHING OF IT, MR.--?

*CHINA'S NEW FIRST RESPONSE AND INTELLIGENCE GATHERING ORGANIZATION. SEE AVENGERS WORLD #7.--WIL

S.P.E.A.R.? TELL ME, WHERE DO YOU HIDE THE ACRONYM GENERATOR?

GOOD TO MEET YOU THEN, DIRECTOR ZHENG. GOTTA SAY, I'M SURPRISED WE HAVEN'T ALREADY, THOUGH--

OF COURSE. PLEASE FORGIVE ME, RECENT EVENTS HAVE FORCED US TO... ACCELERATE OUR TIMETABLE SOMEWHAT. BUT PROTOCOLS ASIDE, I THINK WE CAN ALL AGREE--

"SWIFT ACTION IS REQUIRED."

THE CIRCLE.
S.P.E.A.R. HEADQUARTERS.

THE GORGON'S BEAST WILL BE IN CHINESE AIRSPACE IN LESS THAN AN HOUR. WE BELIEVE HE IS HEADED FOR SHANGHAI, TO LAUNCH AN ATTACK.

AND THE COUNTER-EFFORT WE SAW, I'M ASSUMING THOSE ARE YOUR MEN?

CAPTAIN-- FIRST OF ALL, IT IS AN HONOR. AND YES, THE ASCENDANT FIGHT ON OUR SIDE--

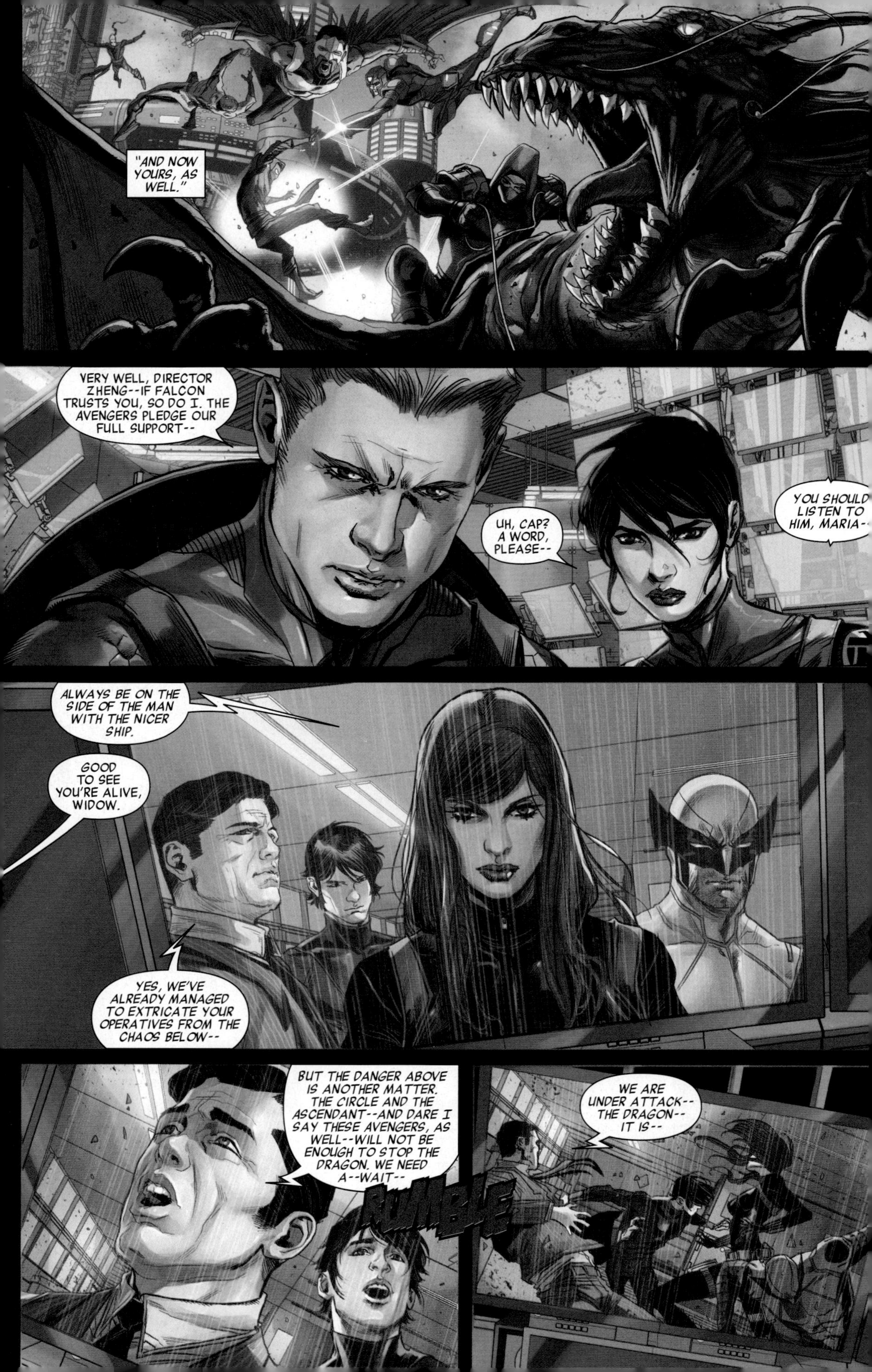
"AND NOW YOURS, AS WELL."
VERY WELL, DIRECTOR ZHENG--IF FALCON TRUSTS YOU, SO DO I. THE AVENGERS PLEDGE OUR FULL SUPPORT--
UH, CAP? A WORD, PLEASE--
YOU SHOULD LISTEN TO HIM, MARIA--
ALWAYS BE ON THE SIDE OF THE MAN WITH THE NICER SHIP.
GOOD TO SEE YOU'RE ALIVE, WIDOW.
YES, WE'VE ALREADY MANAGED TO EXTRICATE YOUR OPERATIVES FROM THE CHAOS BELOW--
BUT THE DANGER ABOVE IS ANOTHER MATTER. THE CIRCLE AND THE ASCENDANT--AND DARE I SAY THESE AVENGERS, AS WELL--WILL NOT BE ENOUGH TO STOP THE DRAGON. WE NEED A--WAIT--
RUMBLE
WE ARE UNDER ATTACK-- THE DRAGON-- IT IS--

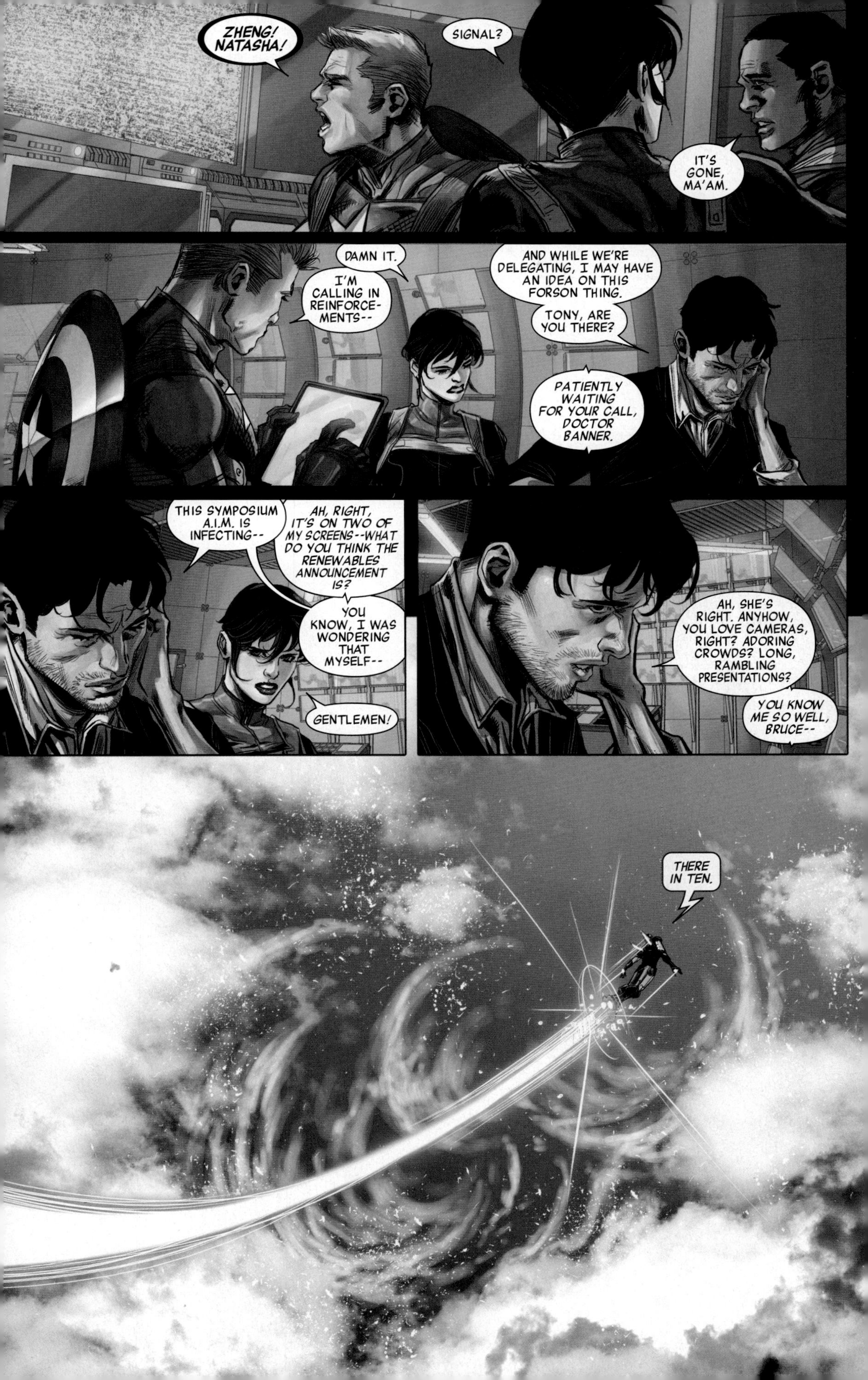
ZHENG! NATASHA!
SIGNAL?
IT'S GONE, MA'AM.
DAMN IT.
I'M CALLING IN REINFORCE-MENTS--
AND WHILE WE'RE DELEGATING, I MAY HAVE AN IDEA ON THIS FORSON THING.
TONY, ARE YOU THERE?
PATIENTLY WAITING FOR YOUR CALL, DOCTOR BANNER.
THIS SYMPOSIUM A.I.M. IS INFECTING--
AH, RIGHT, IT'S ON TWO OF MY SCREENS--WHAT DO YOU THINK THE RENEWABLES ANNOUNCEMENT IS?
YOU KNOW, I WAS WONDERING THAT MYSELF--
GENTLEMEN!
AH, SHE'S RIGHT. ANYHOW, YOU LOVE CAMERAS, RIGHT? ADORING CROWDS? LONG, RAMBLING PRESENTATIONS?
YOU KNOW ME SO WELL, BRUCE--
THERE IN TEN.

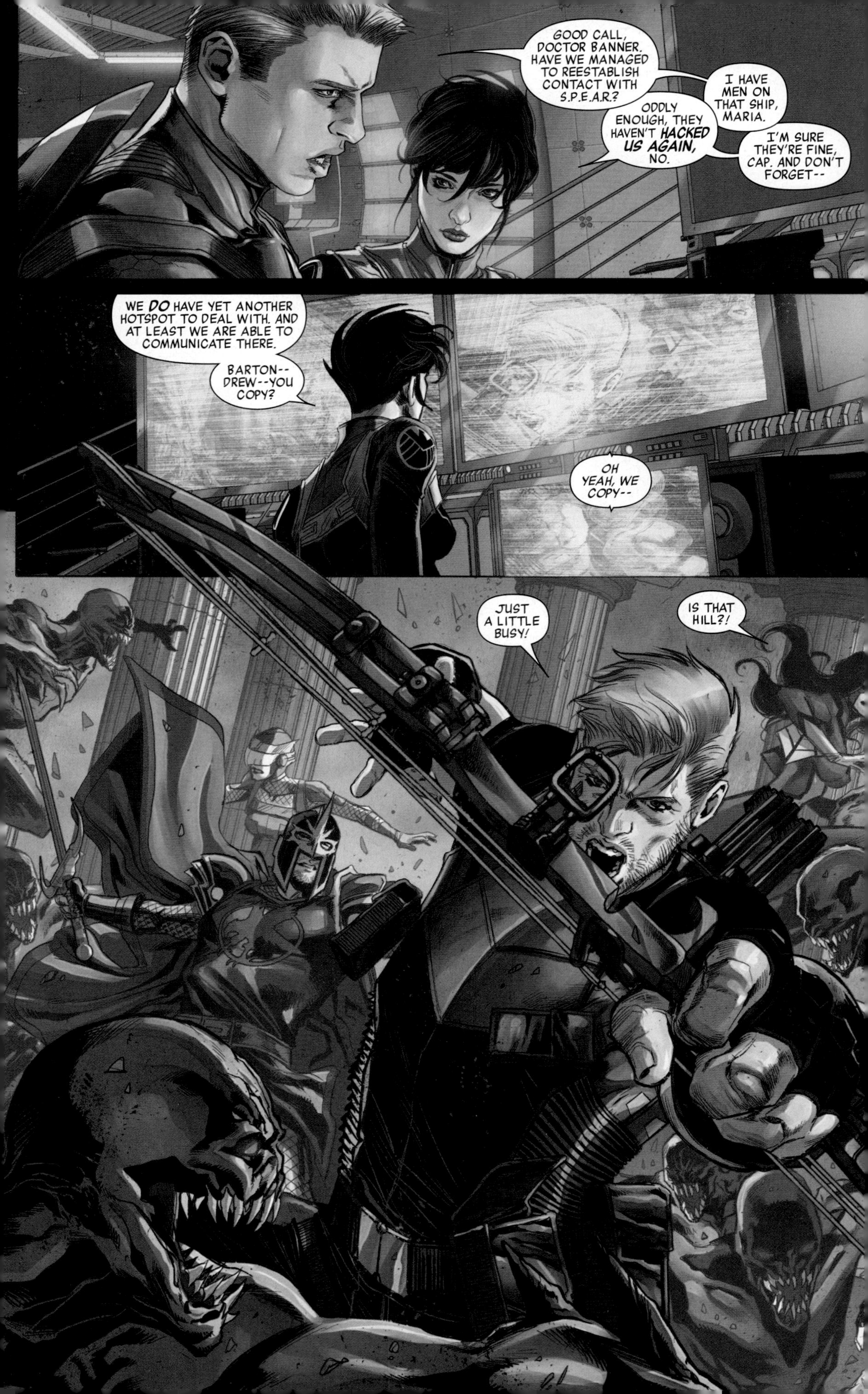
GOOD CALL, DOCTOR BANNER. HAVE WE MANAGED TO REESTABLISH CONTACT WITH S.P.E.A.R.?
I HAVE MEN ON THAT SHIP, MARIA.
ODDLY ENOUGH, THEY HAVEN'T HACKED US AGAIN, NO.
I'M SURE THEY'RE FINE, CAP. AND DON'T FORGET--
WE DO HAVE YET ANOTHER HOTSPOT TO DEAL WITH. AND AT LEAST WE ARE ABLE TO COMMUNICATE THERE.
BARTON--DREW--YOU COPY?
OH YEAH, WE COPY--
JUST A LITTLE BUSY!
IS THAT HILL?!

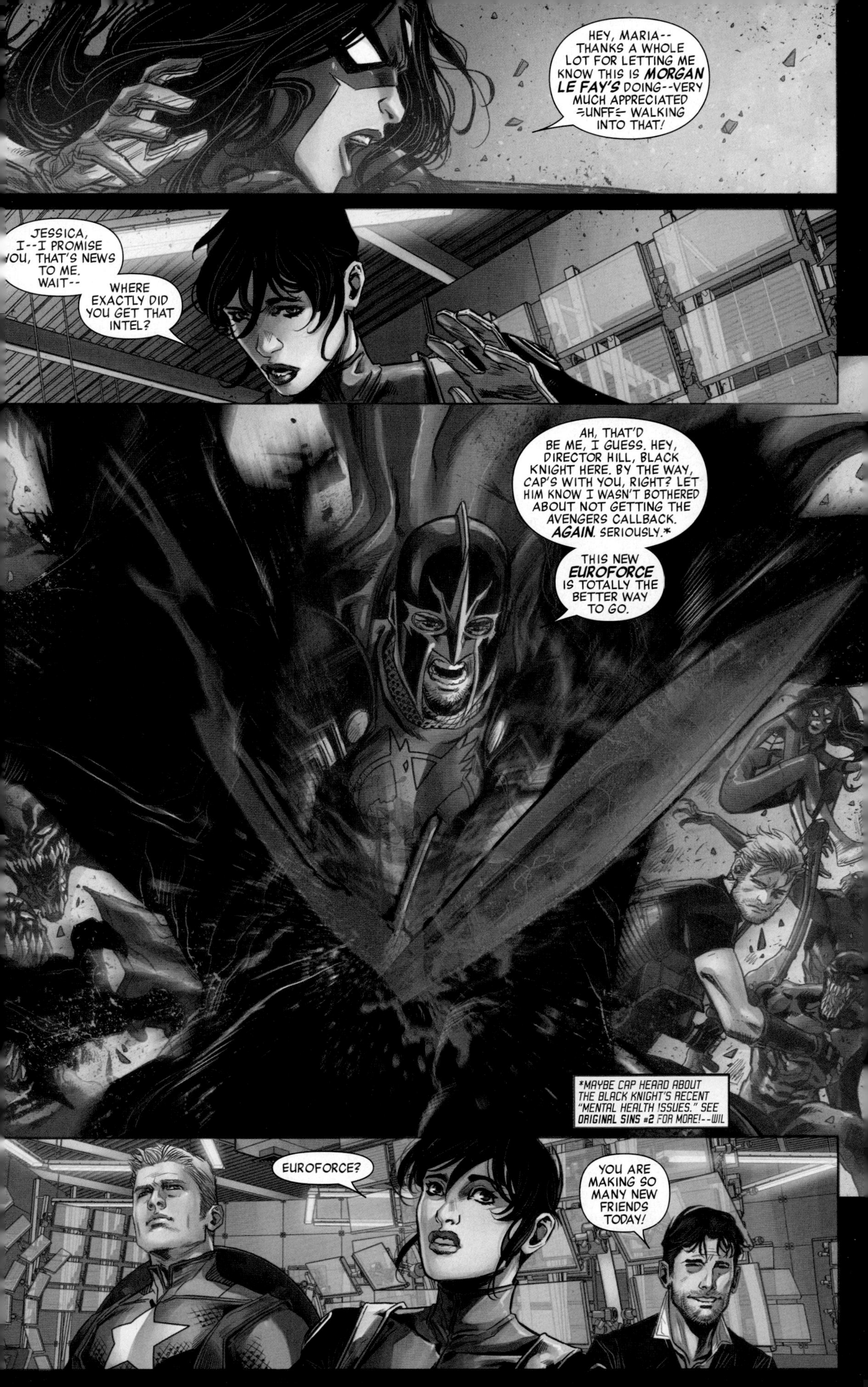
HEY, MARIA-- THANKS A WHOLE LOT FOR LETTING ME KNOW THIS IS MORGAN LE FAY'S DOING--VERY MUCH APPRECIATED =UNFF= WALKING INTO THAT!
JESSICA, I--I PROMISE YOU, THAT'S NEWS TO ME. WAIT--
WHERE EXACTLY DID YOU GET THAT INTEL?
AH, THAT'D BE ME, I GUESS. HEY, DIRECTOR HILL, BLACK KNIGHT HERE. BY THE WAY, CAP'S WITH YOU, RIGHT? LET HIM KNOW I WASN'T BOTHERED ABOUT NOT GETTING THE AVENGERS CALLBACK. AGAIN. SERIOUSLY.*
THIS NEW EUROFORCE IS TOTALLY THE BETTER WAY TO GO.
*MAYBE CAP HEARD ABOUT THE BLACK KNIGHT'S RECENT "MENTAL HEALTH ISSUES." SEE ORIGINAL SINS #2 FOR MORE!--WIL
EUROFORCE?
YOU ARE MAKING SO MANY NEW FRIENDS TODAY!

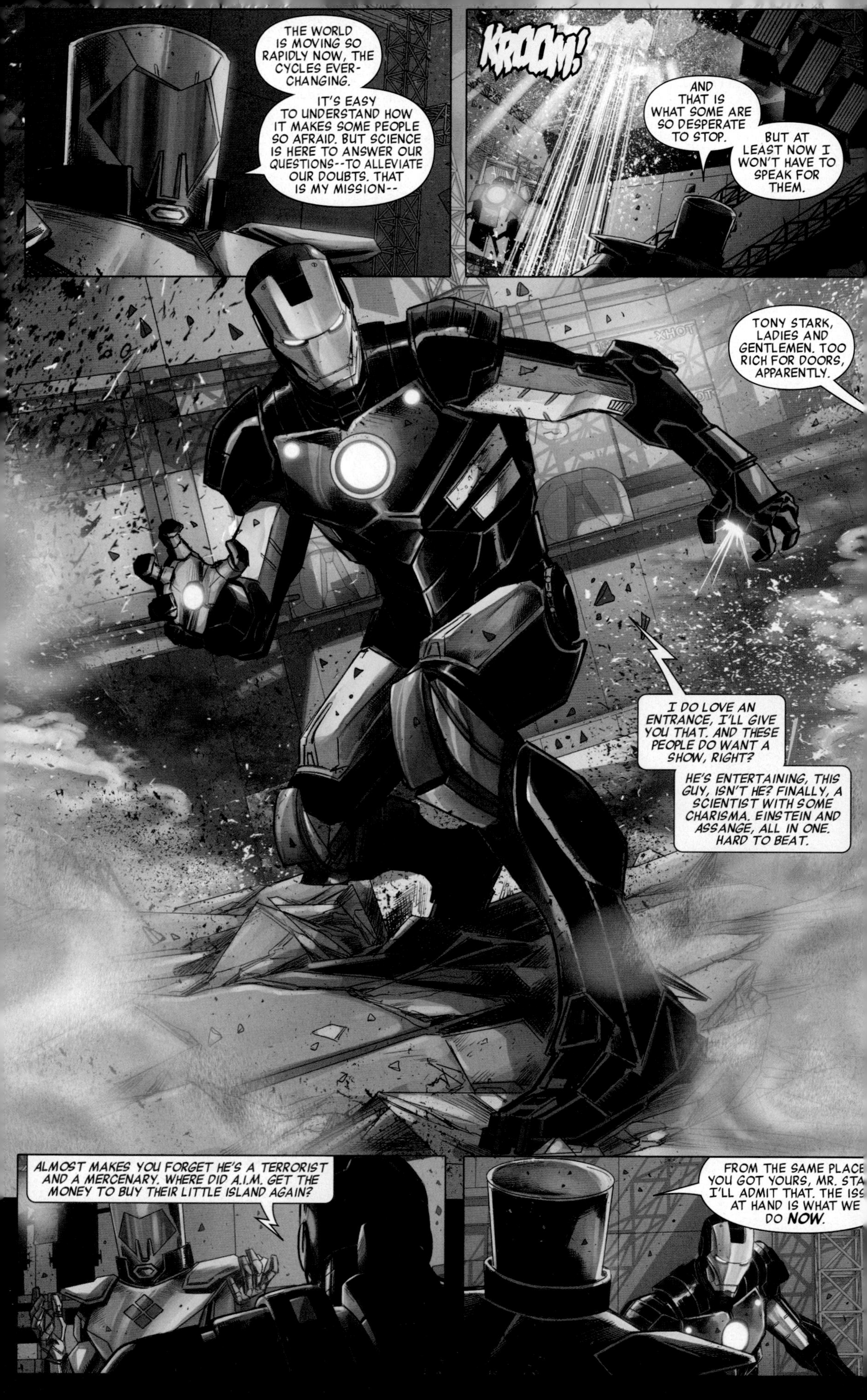
THE WORLD IS MOVING SO RAPIDLY NOW, THE CYCLES EVER-CHANGING.
IT'S EASY TO UNDERSTAND HOW IT MAKES SOME PEOPLE SO AFRAID. BUT SCIENCE IS HERE TO ANSWER OUR QUESTIONS--TO ALLEVIATE OUR DOUBTS. THAT IS MY MISSION--
KROOM!
AND THAT IS WHAT SOME ARE SO DESPERATE TO STOP.
BUT AT LEAST NOW I WON'T HAVE TO SPEAK FOR THEM.
TONY STARK, LADIES AND GENTLEMEN. TOO RICH FOR DOORS, APPARENTLY.
I DO LOVE AN ENTRANCE, I'LL GIVE YOU THAT. AND THESE PEOPLE DO WANT A SHOW, RIGHT?
HE'S ENTERTAINING, THIS GUY, ISN'T HE? FINALLY, A SCIENTIST WITH SOME CHARISMA. EINSTEIN AND ASSANGE, ALL IN ONE. HARD TO BEAT.
ALMOST MAKES YOU FORGET HE'S A TERRORIST AND A MERCENARY. WHERE DID A.I.M. GET THE MONEY TO BUY THEIR LITTLE ISLAND AGAIN?
FROM THE SAME PLACE YOU GOT YOURS, MR. STA I'LL ADMIT THAT. THE ISS AT HAND IS WHAT WE DO *NOW*.

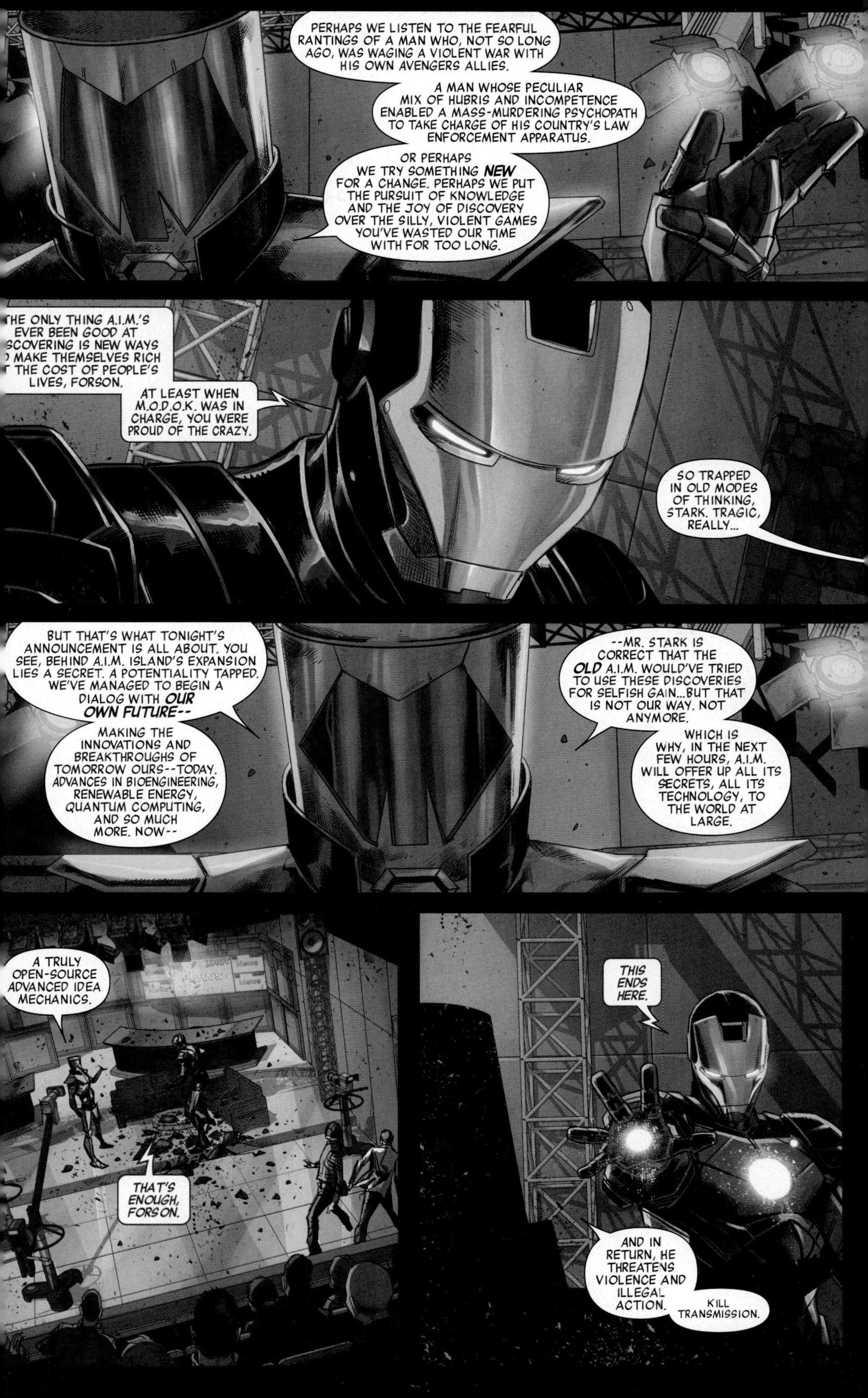
PERHAPS WE LISTEN TO THE FEARFUL RANTINGS OF A MAN WHO, NOT SO LONG AGO, WAS WAGING A VIOLENT WAR WITH HIS OWN AVENGERS ALLIES.
A MAN WHOSE PECULIAR MIX OF HUBRIS AND INCOMPETENCE ENABLED A MASS-MURDERING PSYCHOPATH TO TAKE CHARGE OF HIS COUNTRY'S LAW ENFORCEMENT APPARATUS.
OR PERHAPS WE TRY SOMETHING NEW FOR A CHANGE. PERHAPS WE PUT THE PURSUIT OF KNOWLEDGE AND THE JOY OF DISCOVERY OVER THE SILLY, VIOLENT GAMES YOU'VE WASTED OUR TIME WITH FOR TOO LONG.
THE ONLY THING A.I.M.'S EVER BEEN GOOD AT SCOVERING IS NEW WAYS) MAKE THEMSELVES RICH T THE COST OF PEOPLE'S LIVES, FORSON.
AT LEAST WHEN M.O.D.O.K. WAS IN CHARGE, YOU WERE PROUD OF THE CRAZY.
SO TRAPPED IN OLD MODES OF THINKING, STARK. TRAGIC, REALLY...
BUT THAT'S WHAT TONIGHT'S ANNOUNCEMENT IS ALL ABOUT. YOU SEE, BEHIND A.I.M. ISLAND'S EXPANSION LIES A SECRET. A POTENTIALITY TAPPED. WE'VE MANAGED TO BEGIN A DIALOG WITH OUR OWN FUTURE--
MAKING THE INNOVATIONS AND BREAKTHROUGHS OF TOMORROW OURS--TODAY. ADVANCES IN BIOENGINEERING, RENEWABLE ENERGY, QUANTUM COMPUTING, AND SO MUCH MORE. NOW--
--MR. STARK IS CORRECT THAT THE OLD A.I.M. WOULD'VE TRIED TO USE THESE DISCOVERIES FOR SELFISH GAIN...BUT THAT IS NOT OUR WAY. NOT ANYMORE.
WHICH IS WHY, IN THE NEXT FEW HOURS, A.I.M. WILL OFFER UP ALL ITS SECRETS, ALL ITS TECHNOLOGY, TO THE WORLD AT LARGE.
A TRULY OPEN-SOURCE ADVANCED IDEA MECHANICS.
THAT'S ENOUGH, FORSON.
THIS ENDS HERE.
AND IN RETURN, HE THREATENS VIOLENCE AND ILLEGAL ACTION.
KILL TRANSMISSION.

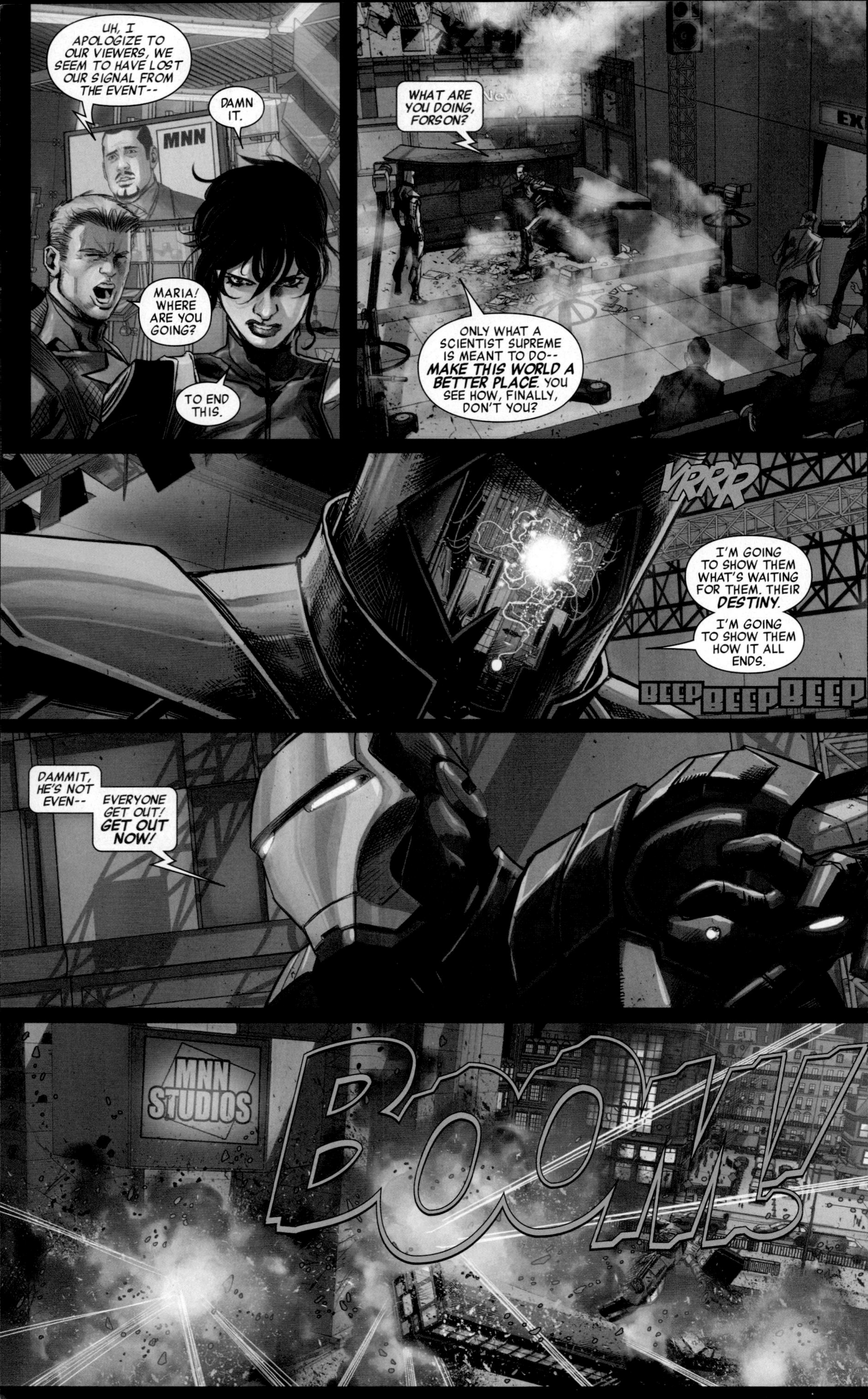
UH, I APOLOGIZE TO OUR VIEWERS, WE SEEM TO HAVE LOST OUR SIGNAL FROM THE EVENT--
DAMN IT.
MNN
MARIA! WHERE ARE YOU GOING?
TO END THIS.
WHAT ARE YOU DOING, FORSON?
ONLY WHAT A SCIENTIST SUPREME IS MEANT TO DO-- **MAKE THIS WORLD A BETTER PLACE.** YOU SEE HOW, FINALLY, DON'T YOU?
VRRR
I'M GOING TO SHOW THEM WHAT'S WAITING FOR THEM. THEIR ***DESTINY***.
I'M GOING TO SHOW THEM HOW IT ALL ENDS.
BEEP BEEP BEEP
DAMMIT, HE'S NOT EVEN--
EVERYONE GET OUT! **GET OUT NOW!**
MNN STUDIOS
BOOM!

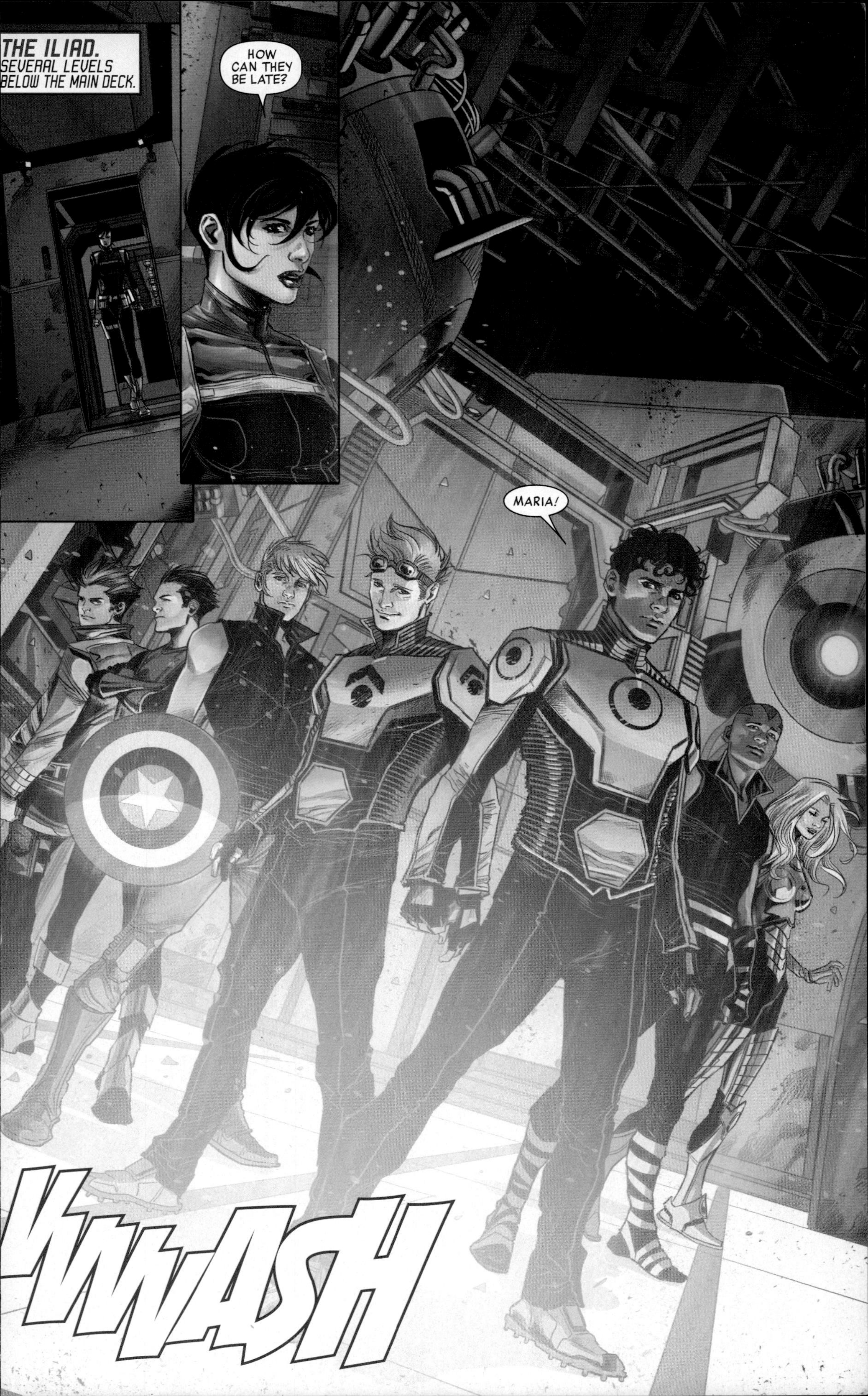
THE ILIAD. SEVERAL LEVELS BELOW THE MAIN DECK.
HOW CAN THEY BE LATE?
MARIA!
VVVVASH

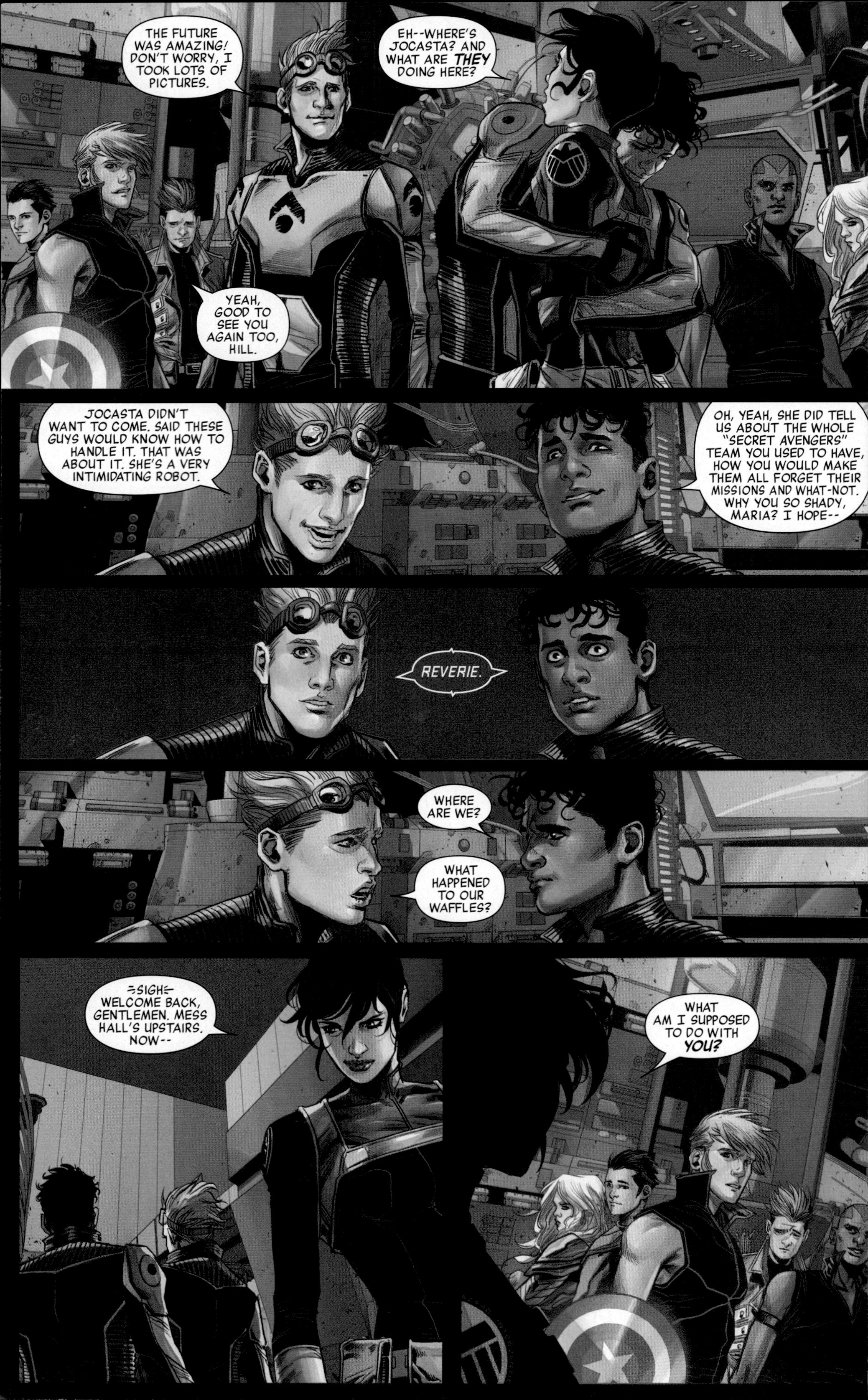
THE FUTURE WAS AMAZING! DON'T WORRY, I TOOK LOTS OF PICTURES.
EH--WHERE'S JOCASTA? AND WHAT ARE THEY DOING HERE?
YEAH, GOOD TO SEE YOU AGAIN TOO, HILL.
JOCASTA DIDN'T WANT TO COME. SAID THESE GUYS WOULD KNOW HOW TO HANDLE IT. THAT WAS ABOUT IT. SHE'S A VERY INTIMIDATING ROBOT.
OH, YEAH, SHE DID TELL US ABOUT THE WHOLE "SECRET AVENGERS" TEAM YOU USED TO HAVE, HOW YOU WOULD MAKE THEM ALL FORGET THEIR MISSIONS AND WHAT-NOT. WHY YOU SO SHADY, MARIA? I HOPE--
REVERIE.
WHERE ARE WE?
WHAT HAPPENED TO OUR WAFFLES?
=SIGH= WELCOME BACK, GENTLEMEN. MESS HALL'S UPSTAIRS. NOW--
WHAT AM I SUPPOSED TO DO WITH YOU?

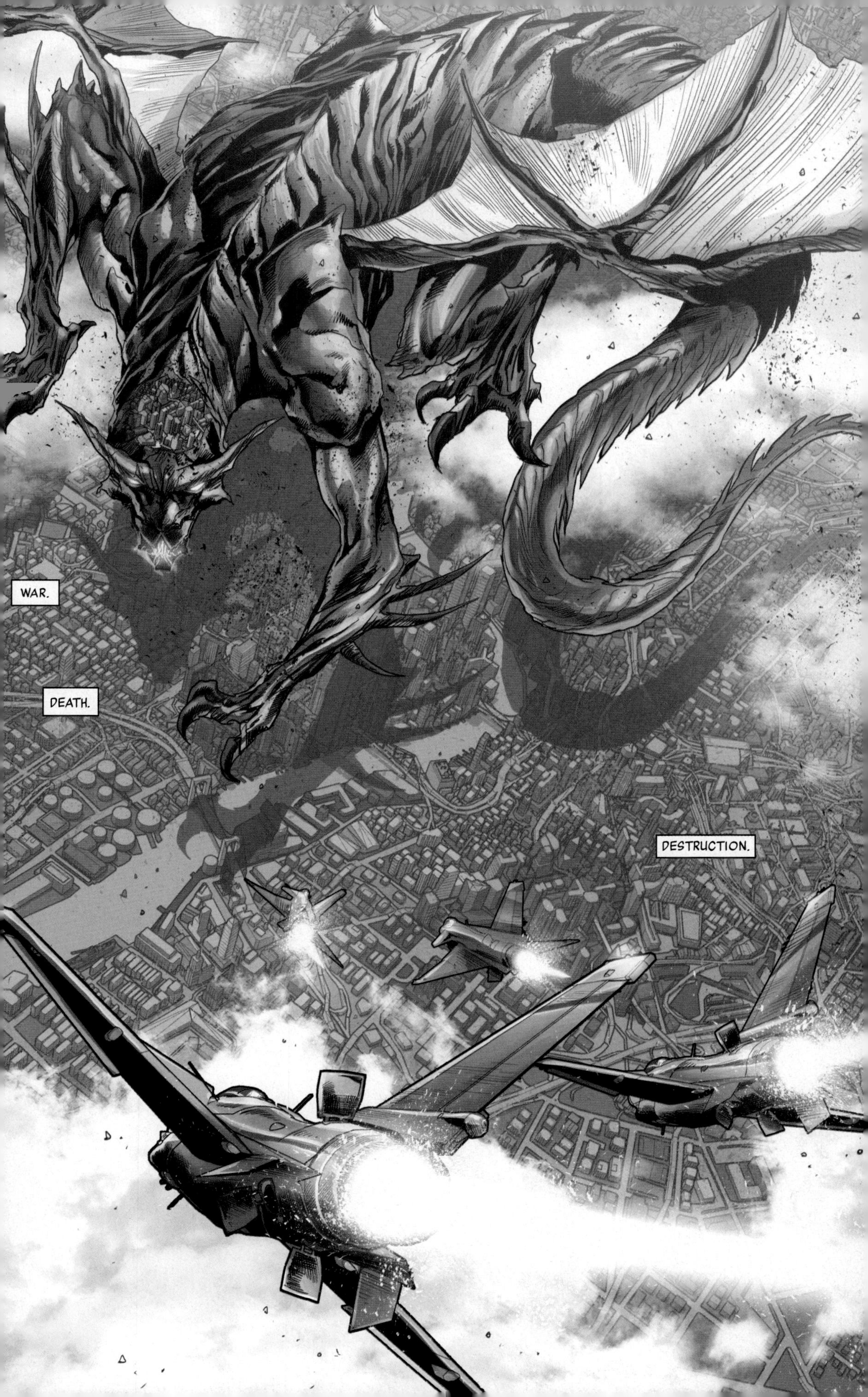
WAR.
DEATH.
DESTRUCTION.

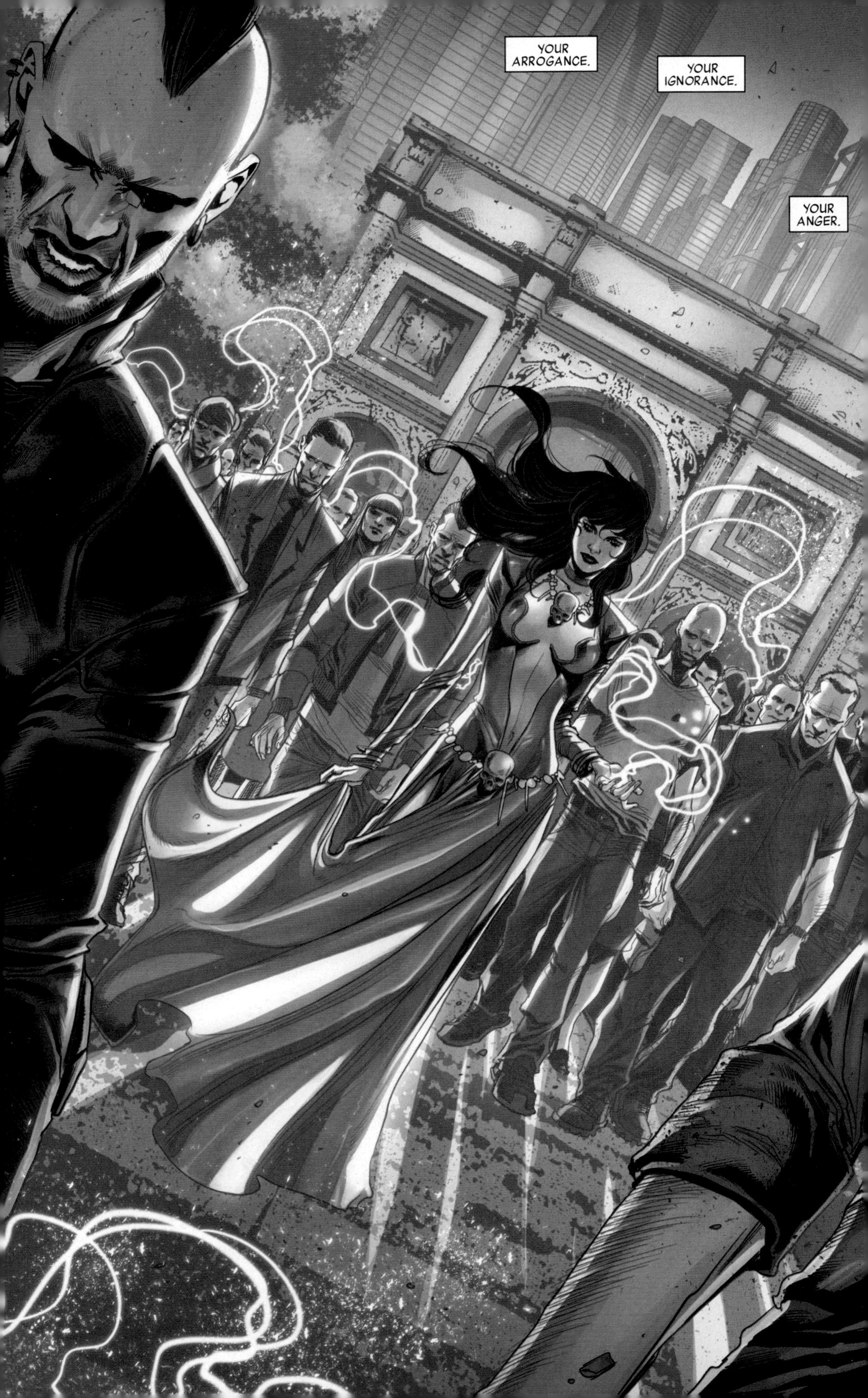
YOUR ARROGANCE.
YOUR IGNORANCE.
YOUR ANGER.

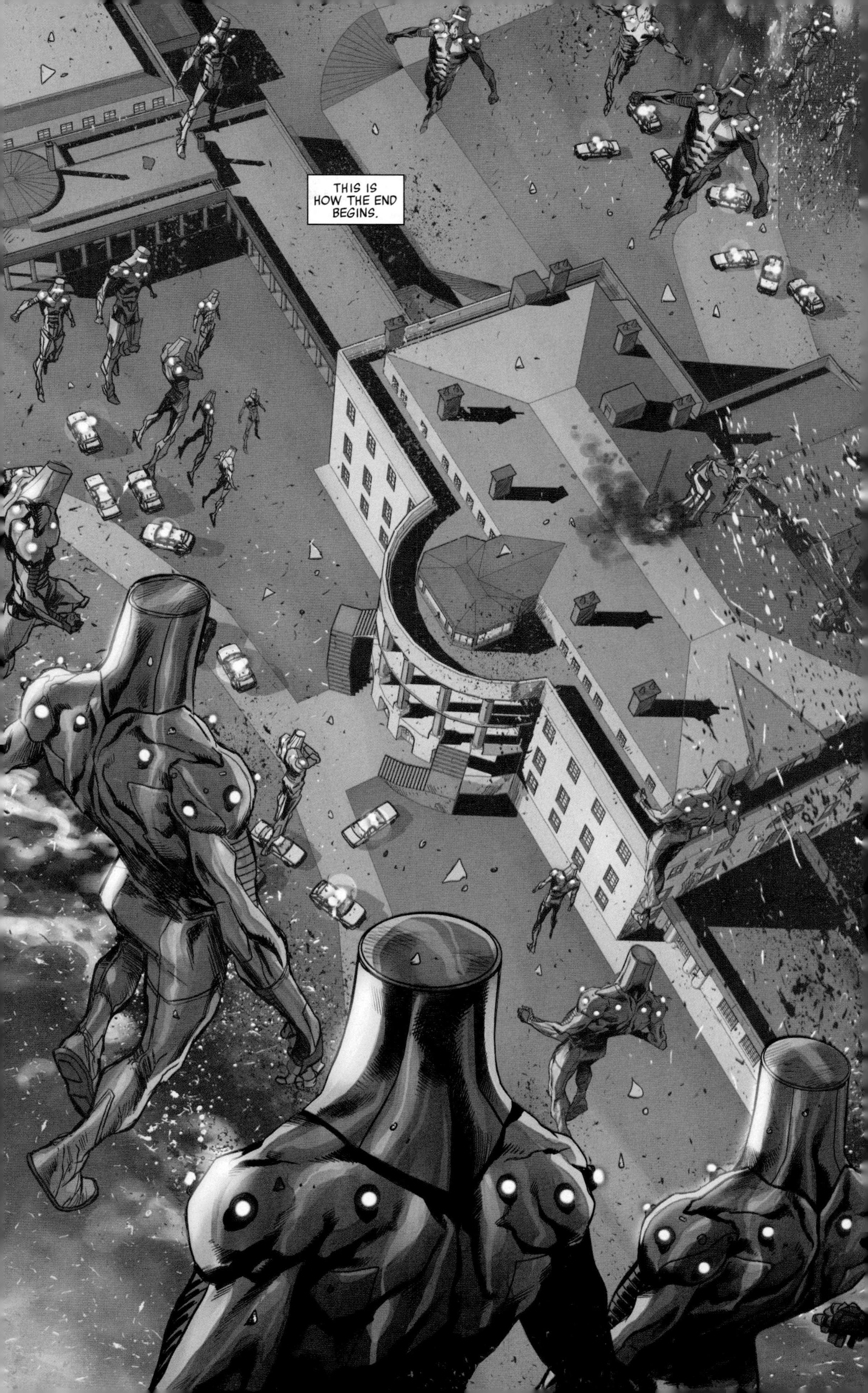
THIS IS HOW THE END BEGINS.

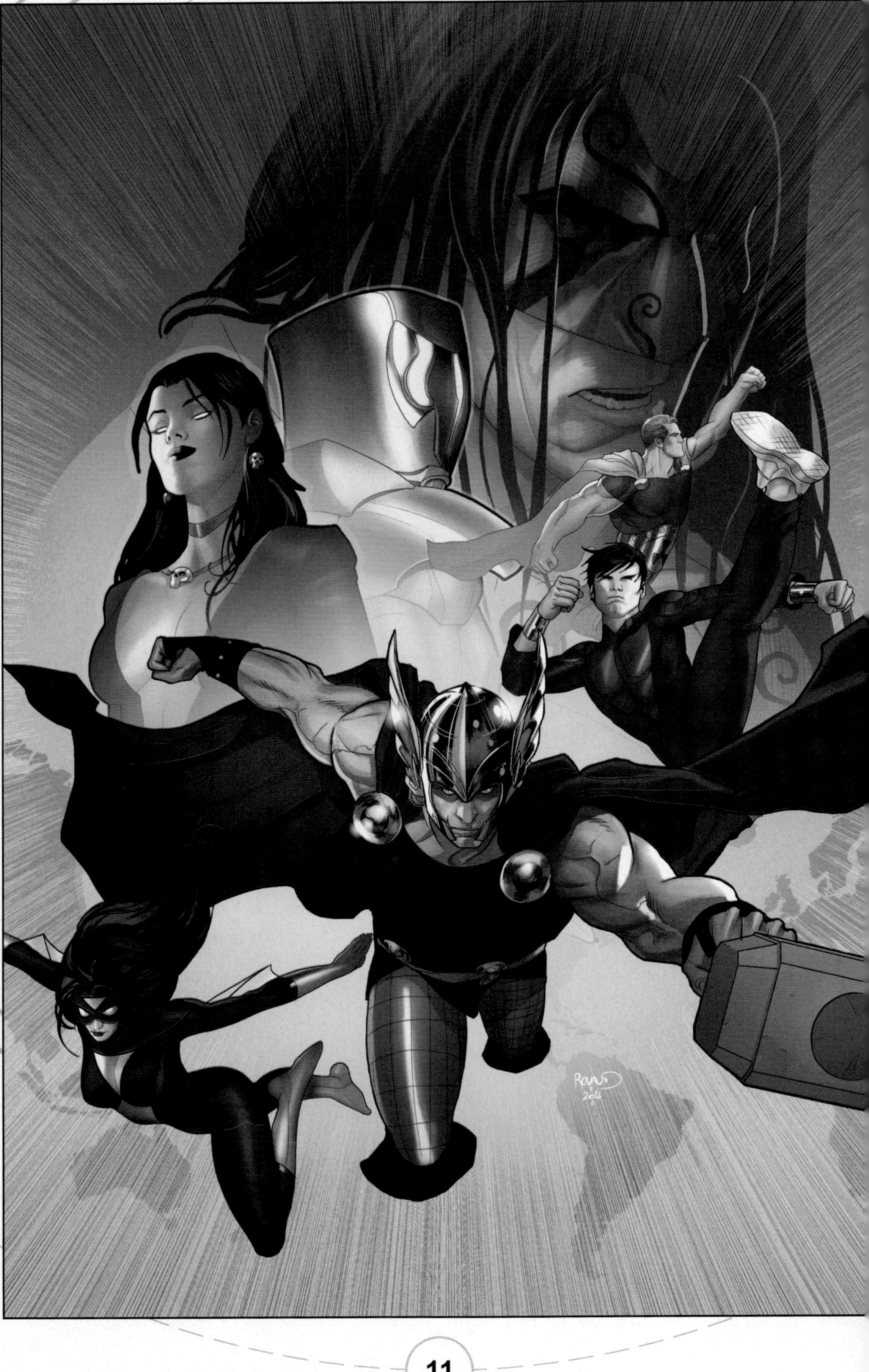

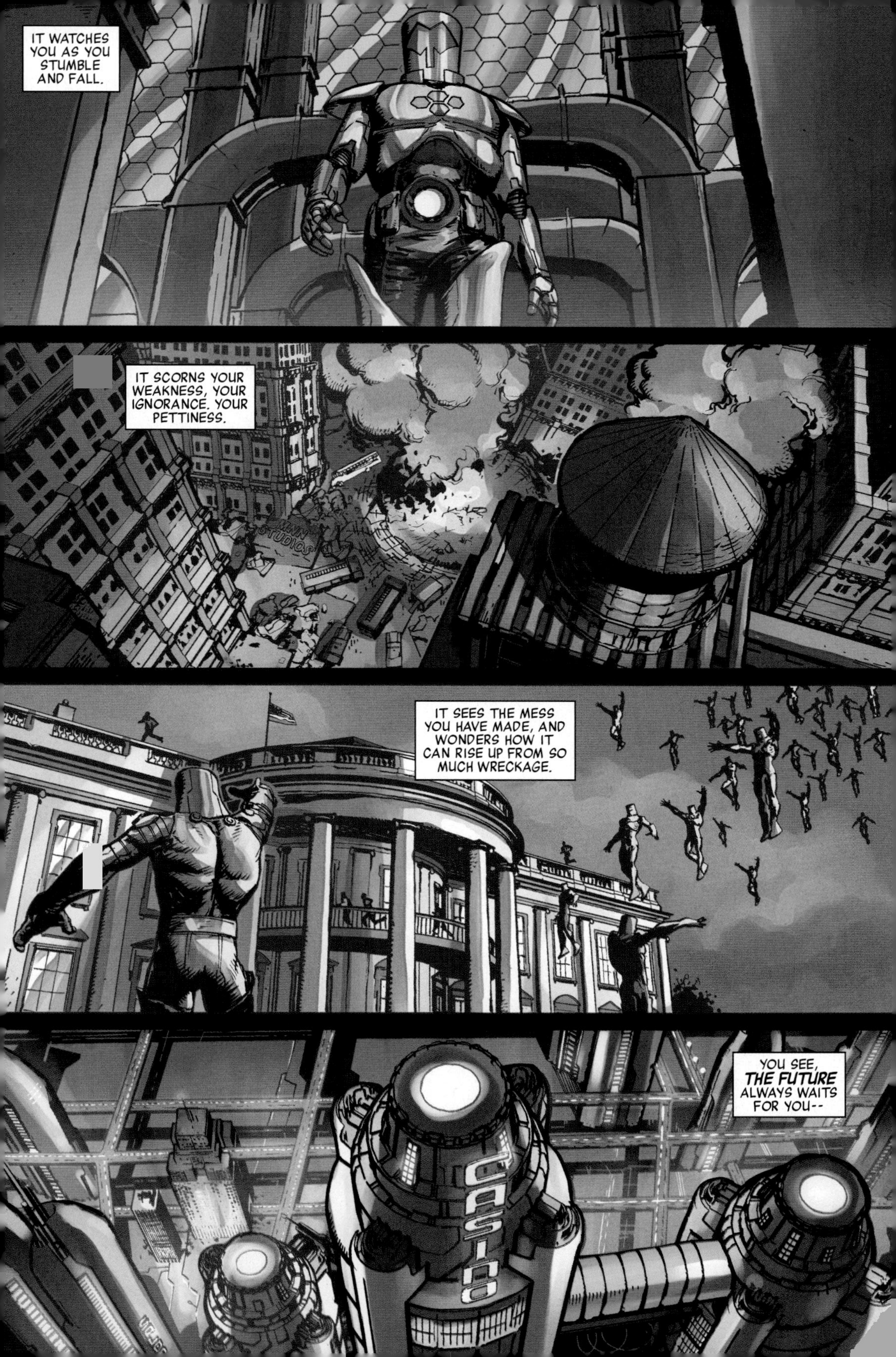
IT WATCHES YOU AS YOU STUMBLE AND FALL.
IT SCORNS YOUR WEAKNESS, YOUR IGNORANCE. YOUR PETTINESS.
IT SEES THE MESS YOU HAVE MADE, AND WONDERS HOW IT CAN RISE UP FROM SO MUCH WRECKAGE.
YOU SEE, THE FUTURE ALWAYS WAITS FOR YOU--
CASINO

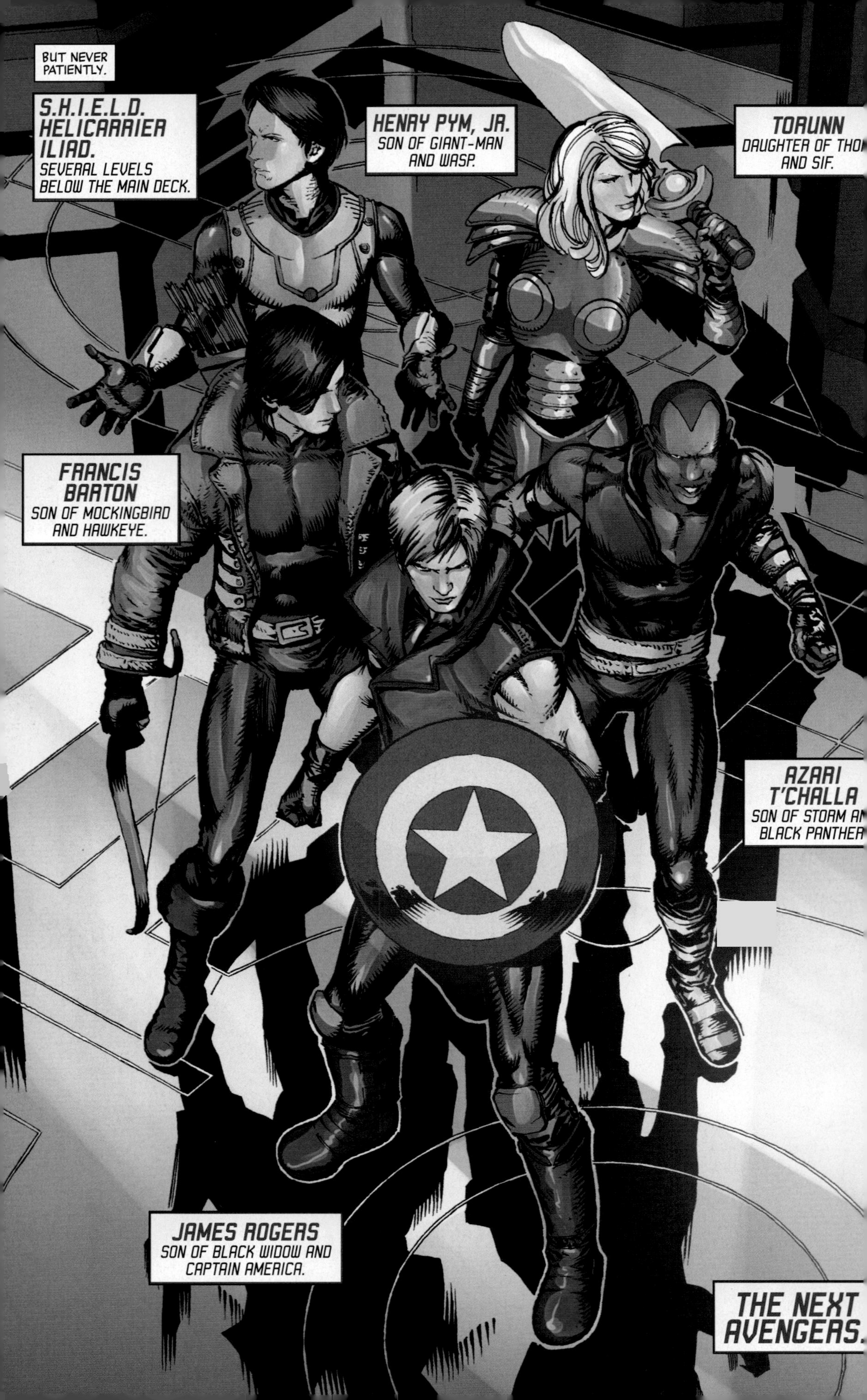

BUT NEVER PATIENTLY.
S.H.I.E.L.D. HELICARRIER ILIAD. SEVERAL LEVELS BELOW THE MAIN DECK.
HENRY PYM, JR. SON OF GIANT-MAN AND WASP.
TORUNN DAUGHTER OF THO AND SIF.
FRANCIS BARTON SON OF MOCKINGBIRD AND HAWKEYE.
AZARI T'CHALLA SON OF STORM A BLACK PANTHER
JAMES ROGERS SON OF BLACK WIDOW AND CAPTAIN AMERICA.
THE NEXT AVENGERS.

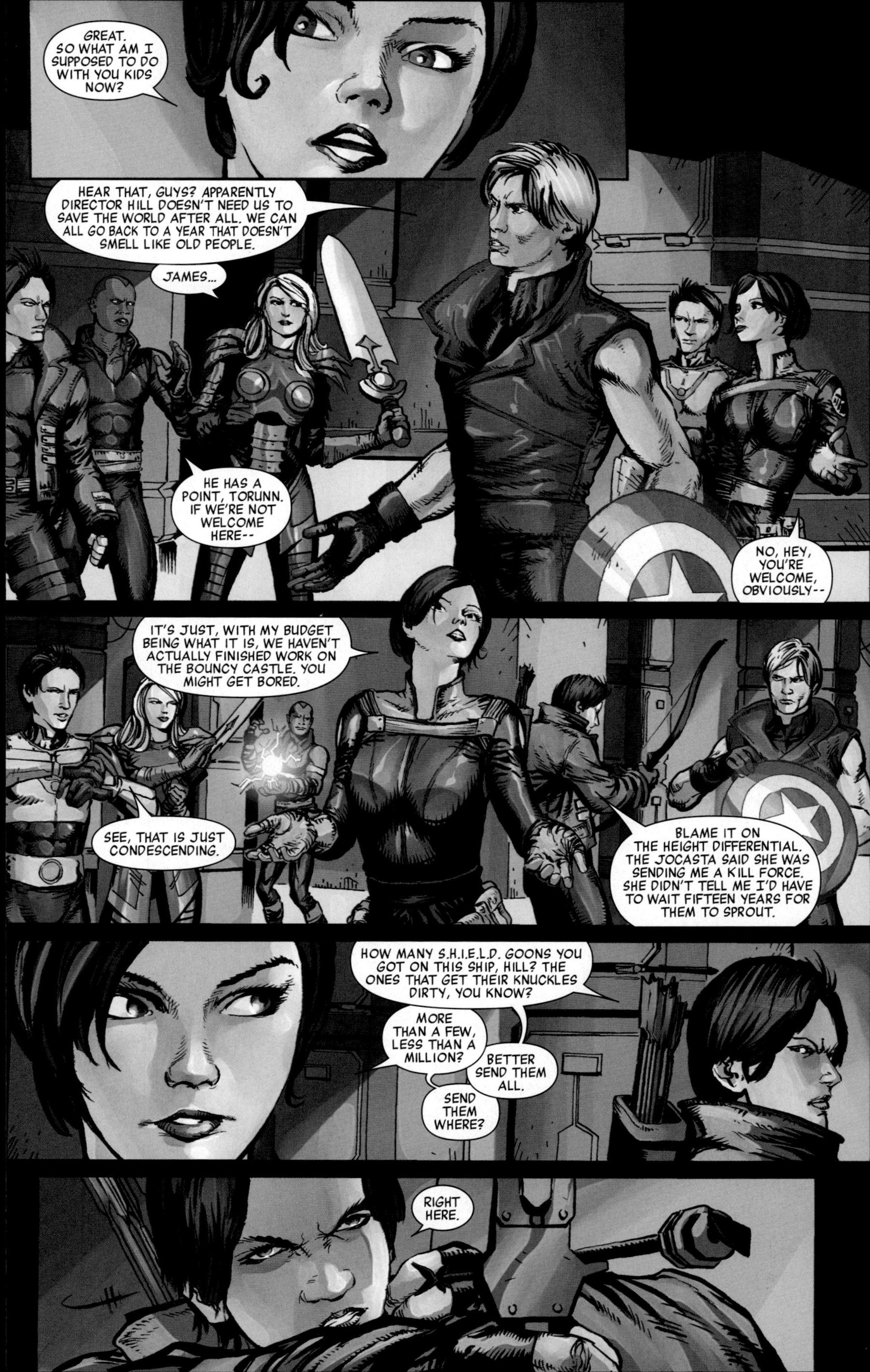
GREAT. SO WHAT AM I SUPPOSED TO DO WITH YOU KIDS NOW?
HEAR THAT, GUYS? APPARENTLY DIRECTOR HILL DOESN'T NEED US TO SAVE THE WORLD AFTER ALL. WE CAN ALL GO BACK TO A YEAR THAT DOESN'T SMELL LIKE OLD PEOPLE.
JAMES...
HE HAS A POINT, TORUNN. IF WE'RE NOT WELCOME HERE--
NO, HEY, YOU'RE WELCOME, OBVIOUSLY--
IT'S JUST, WITH MY BUDGET BEING WHAT IT IS, WE HAVEN'T ACTUALLY FINISHED WORK ON THE BOUNCY CASTLE. YOU MIGHT GET BORED.
SEE, THAT IS JUST CONDESCENDING.
BLAME IT ON THE HEIGHT DIFFERENTIAL. THE JOCASTA SAID SHE WAS SENDING ME A KILL FORCE. SHE DIDN'T TELL ME I'D HAVE TO WAIT FIFTEEN YEARS FOR THEM TO SPROUT.
HOW MANY S.H.I.E.L.D. GOONS YOU GOT ON THIS SHIP, HILL? THE ONES THAT GET THEIR KNUCKLES DIRTY, YOU KNOW?
MORE THAN A FEW, LESS THAN A MILLION?
BETTER SEND THEM ALL.
SEND THEM WHERE?
RIGHT HERE.

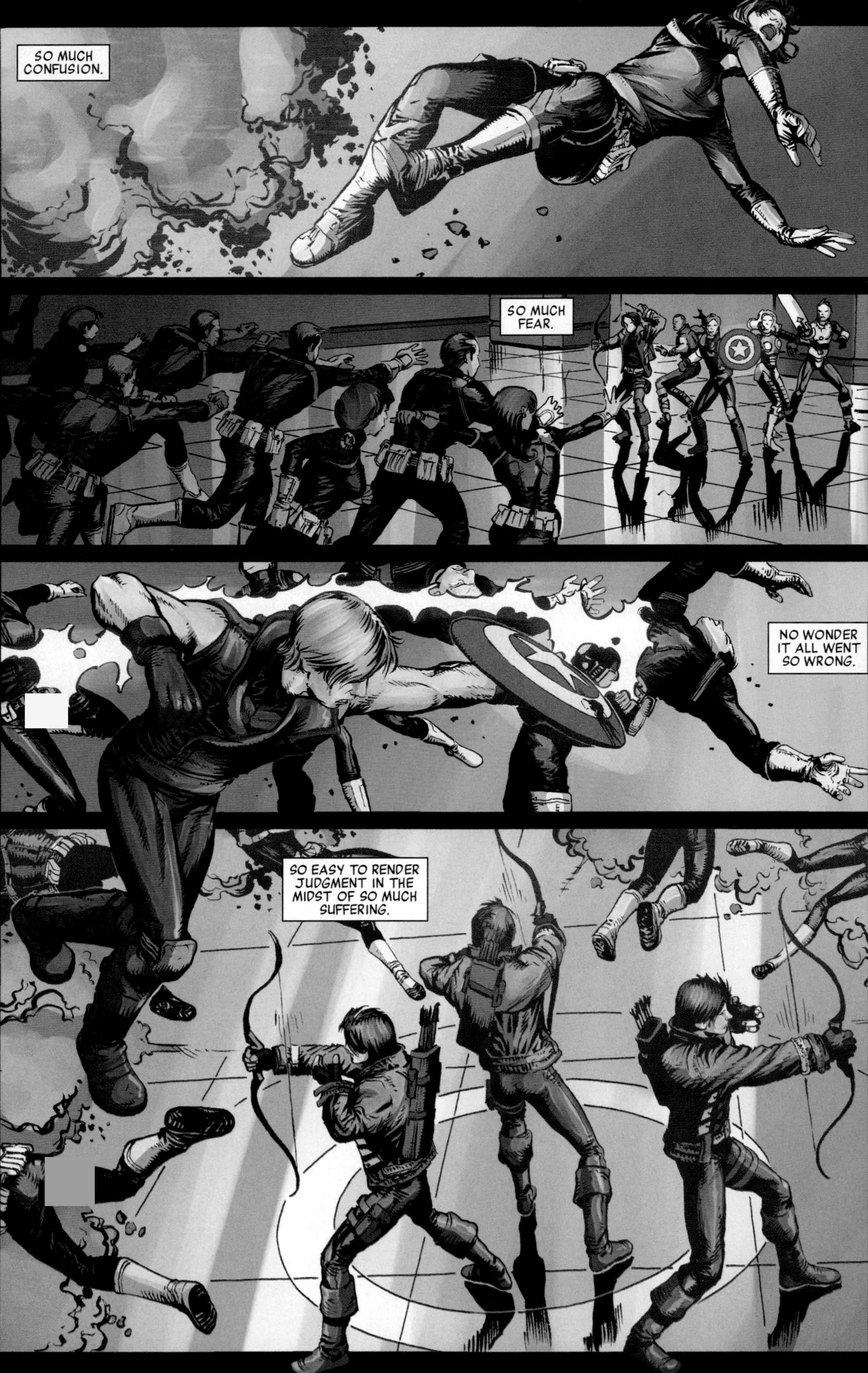
SO MUCH CONFUSION.
SO MUCH FEAR.
NO WONDER IT ALL WENT SO WRONG.
SO EASY TO RENDER JUDGMENT IN THE MIDST OF SO MUCH SUFFERING.

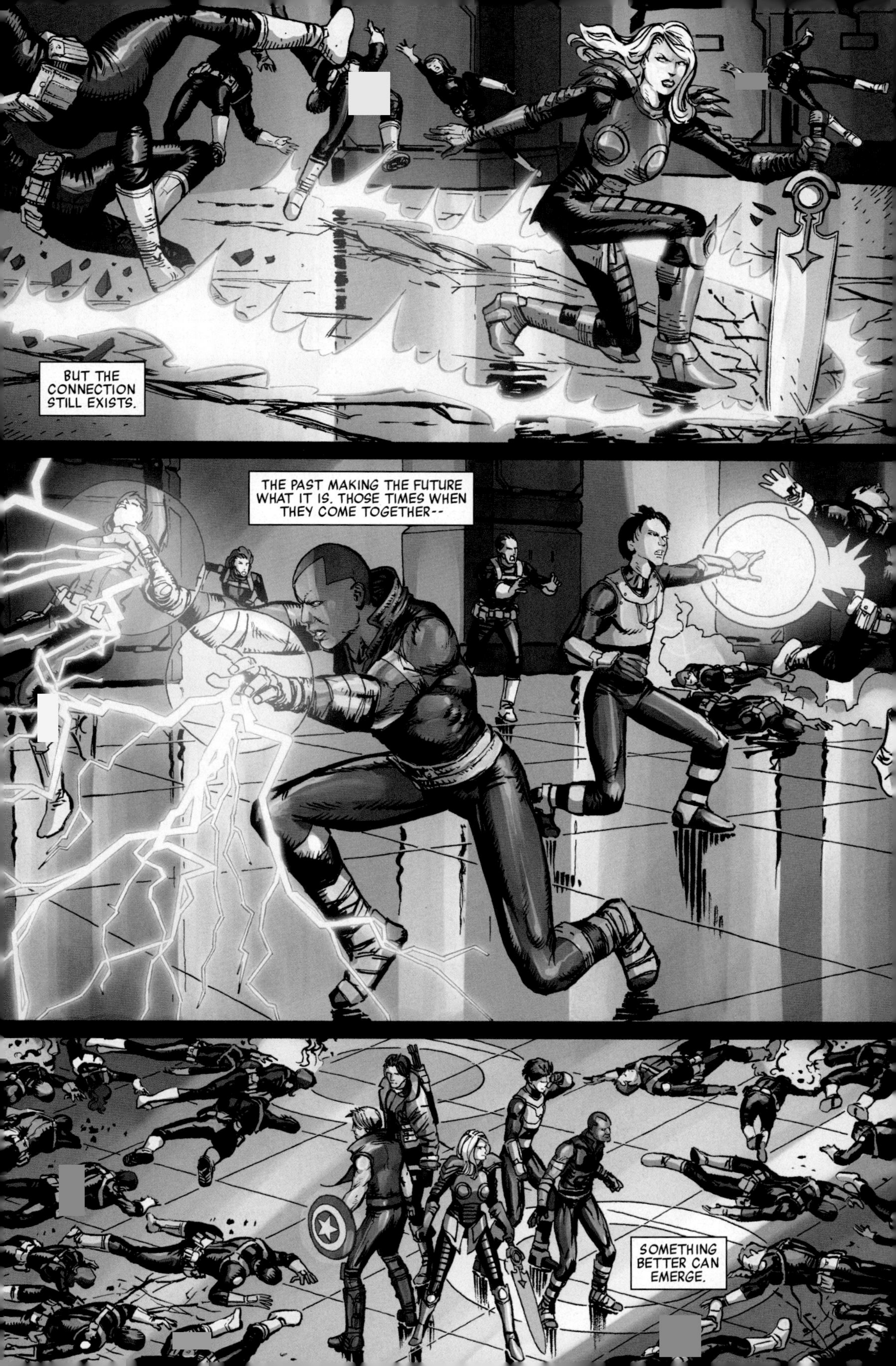
BUT THE CONNECTION STILL EXISTS.
THE PAST MAKING THE FUTURE WHAT IT IS. THOSE TIMES WHEN THEY COME TOGETHER--
SOMETHING BETTER CAN EMERGE.

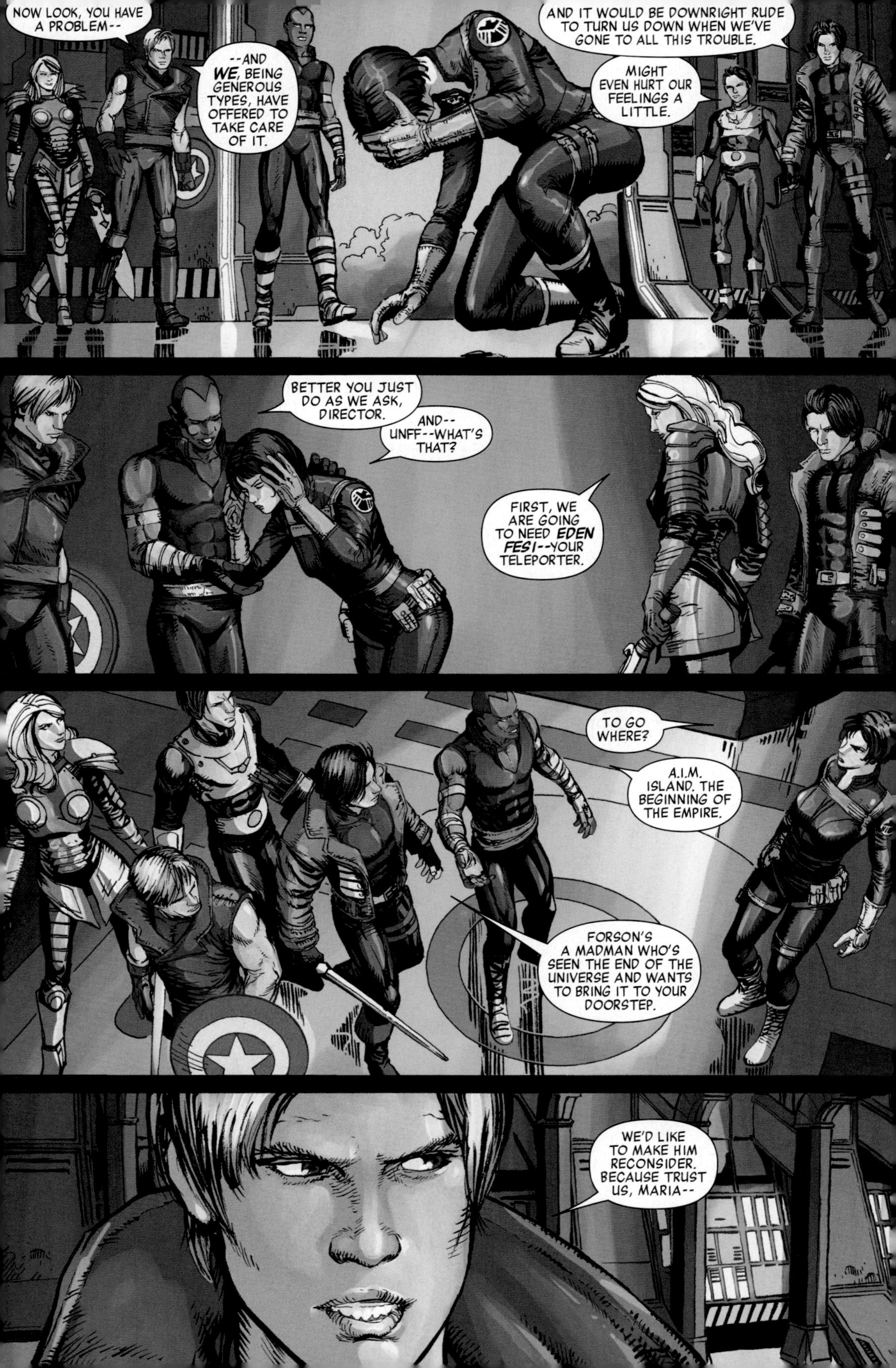
NOW LOOK, YOU HAVE A PROBLEM--
--AND WE, BEING GENEROUS TYPES, HAVE OFFERED TO TAKE CARE OF IT.
AND IT WOULD BE DOWNRIGHT RUDE TO TURN US DOWN WHEN WE'VE GONE TO ALL THIS TROUBLE.
MIGHT EVEN HURT OUR FEELINGS A LITTLE.
BETTER YOU JUST DO AS WE ASK, DIRECTOR.
AND--UNFF--WHAT'S THAT?
FIRST, WE ARE GOING TO NEED EDEN FESI--YOUR TELEPORTER.
TO GO WHERE?
A.I.M. ISLAND. THE BEGINNING OF THE EMPIRE.
FORSON'S A MADMAN WHO'S SEEN THE END OF THE UNIVERSE AND WANTS TO BRING IT TO YOUR DOORSTEP.
WE'D LIKE TO MAKE HIM RECONSIDER. BECAUSE TRUST US, MARIA--

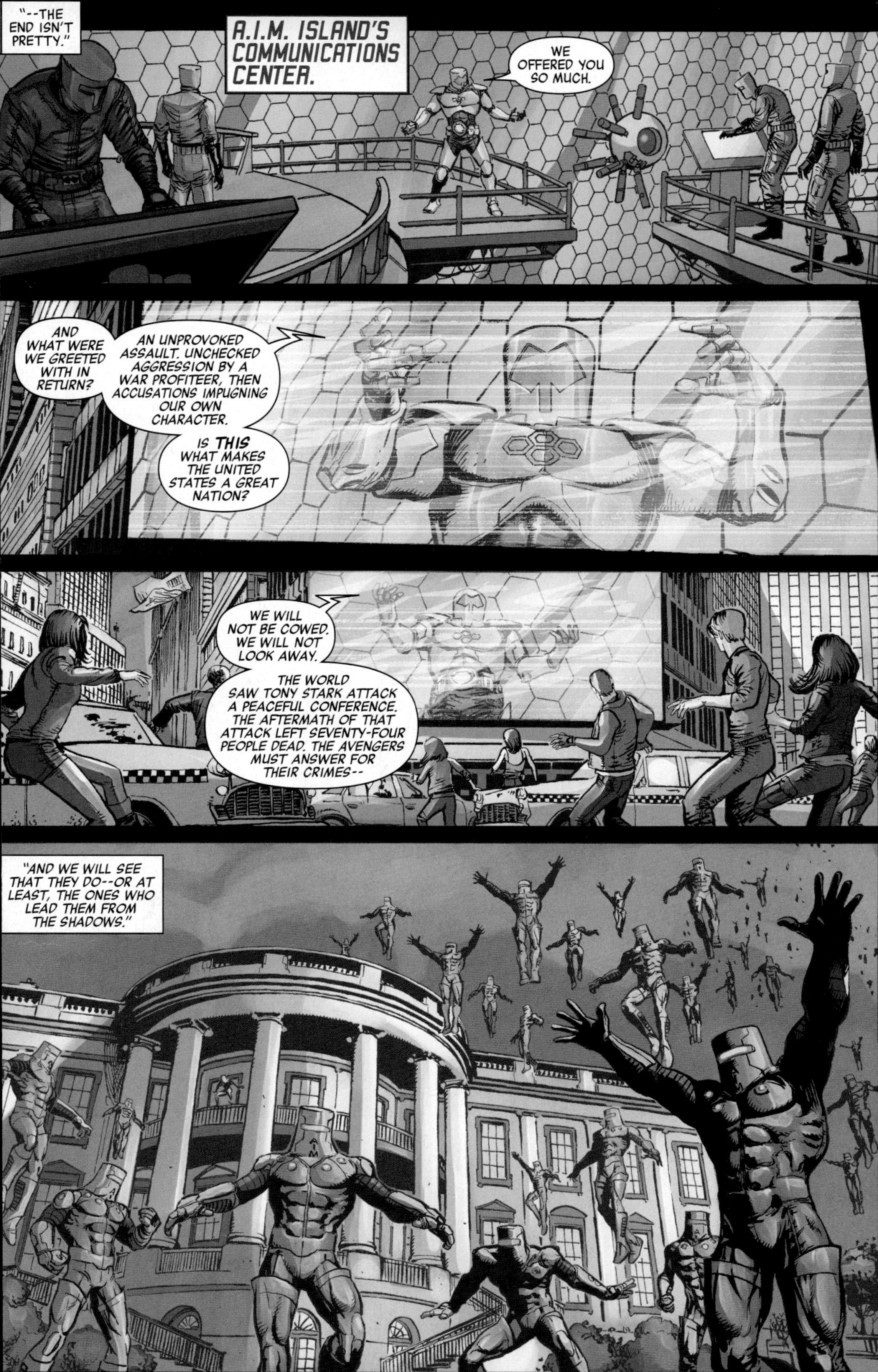
"--THE END ISN'T PRETTY."
A.I.M. ISLAND'S COMMUNICATIONS CENTER.
WE OFFERED YOU SO MUCH.
AND WHAT WERE WE GREETED WITH IN RETURN?
AN UNPROVOKED ASSAULT. UNCHECKED AGGRESSION BY A WAR PROFITEER, THEN ACCUSATIONS IMPUGNING OUR OWN CHARACTER.
IS THIS WHAT MAKES THE UNITED STATES A GREAT NATION?
WE WILL NOT BE COWED. WE WILL NOT LOOK AWAY.
THE WORLD SAW TONY STARK ATTACK A PEACEFUL CONFERENCE. THE AFTERMATH OF THAT ATTACK LEFT SEVENTY-FOUR PEOPLE DEAD. THE AVENGERS MUST ANSWER FOR THEIR CRIMES--
"AND WE WILL SEE THAT THEY DO--OR AT LEAST, THE ONES WHO LEAD THEM FROM THE SHADOWS."

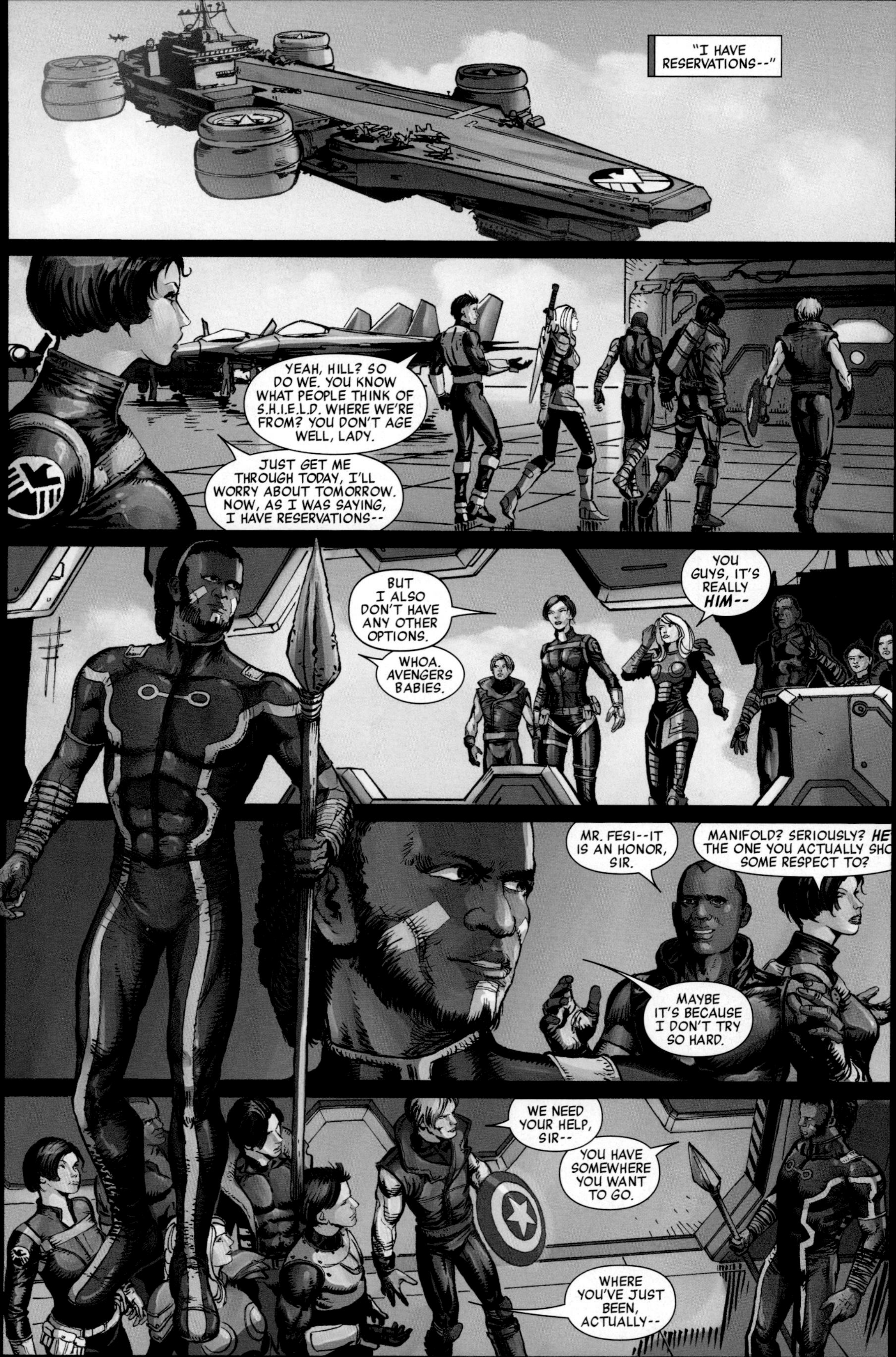
"I HAVE RESERVATIONS--"
YEAH, HILL? SO DO WE. YOU KNOW WHAT PEOPLE THINK OF S.H.I.E.L.D. WHERE WE'RE FROM? YOU DON'T AGE WELL, LADY.
JUST GET ME THROUGH TODAY, I'LL WORRY ABOUT TOMORROW. NOW, AS I WAS SAYING, I HAVE RESERVATIONS--
BUT I ALSO DON'T HAVE ANY OTHER OPTIONS.
WHOA. AVENGERS BABIES.
YOU GUYS, IT'S REALLY HIM--
MR. FESI--IT IS AN HONOR, SIR.
MANIFOLD? SERIOUSLY? HE THE ONE YOU ACTUALLY SHO SOME RESPECT TO?
MAYBE IT'S BECAUSE I DON'T TRY SO HARD.
WE NEED YOUR HELP, SIR--
YOU HAVE SOMEWHERE YOU WANT TO GO.
WHERE YOU'VE JUST BEEN, ACTUALLY--

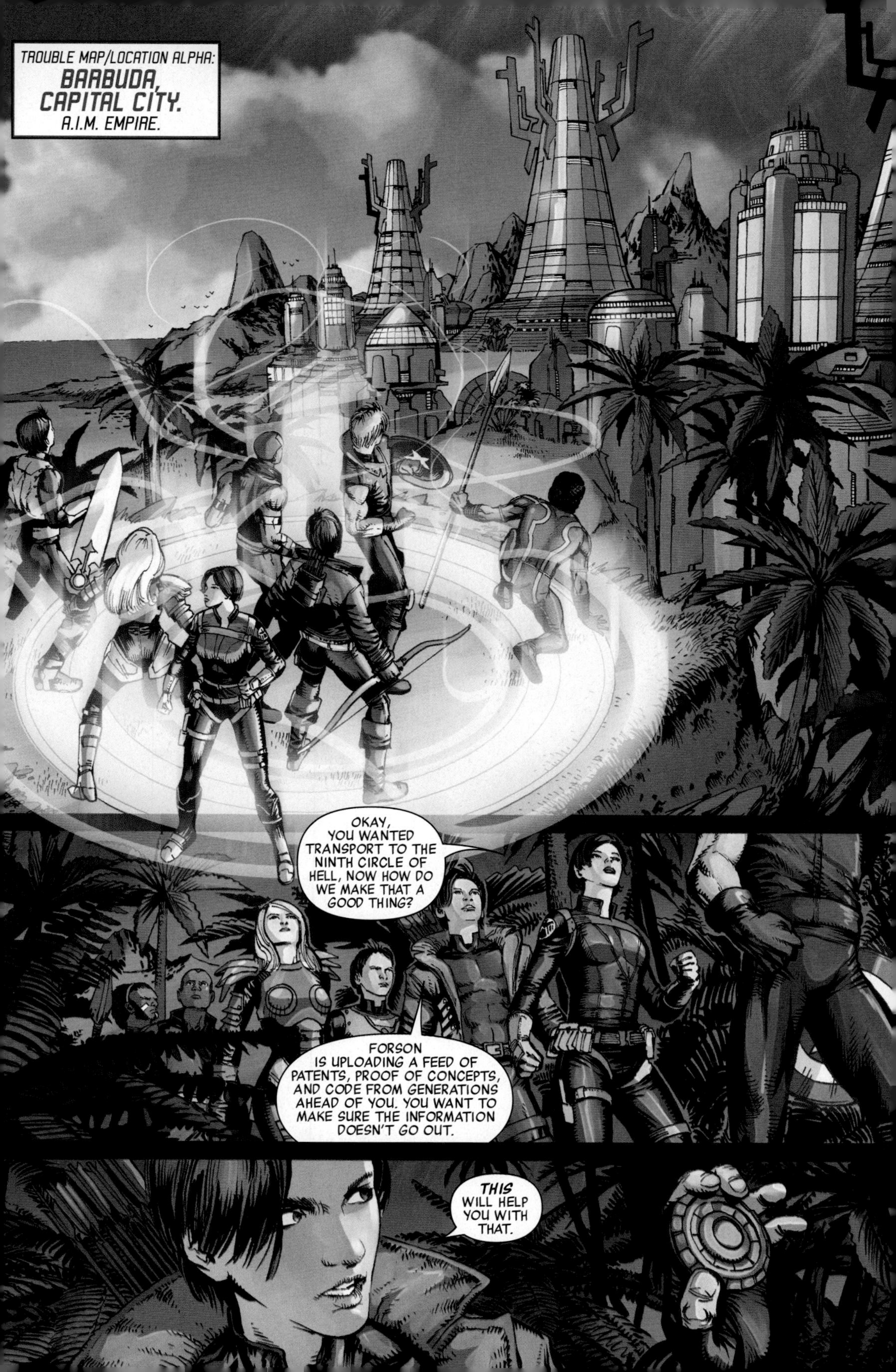
TROUBLE MAP/LOCATION ALPHA:
BARBUDA, CAPITAL CITY.
A.I.M. EMPIRE.
OKAY, YOU WANTED TRANSPORT TO THE NINTH CIRCLE OF HELL, NOW HOW DO WE MAKE THAT A GOOD THING?
FORSON IS UPLOADING A FEED OF PATENTS, PROOF OF CONCEPTS, AND CODE FROM GENERATIONS AHEAD OF YOU. YOU WANT TO MAKE SURE THE INFORMATION DOESN'T GO OUT.
THIS WILL HELP YOU WITH THAT.

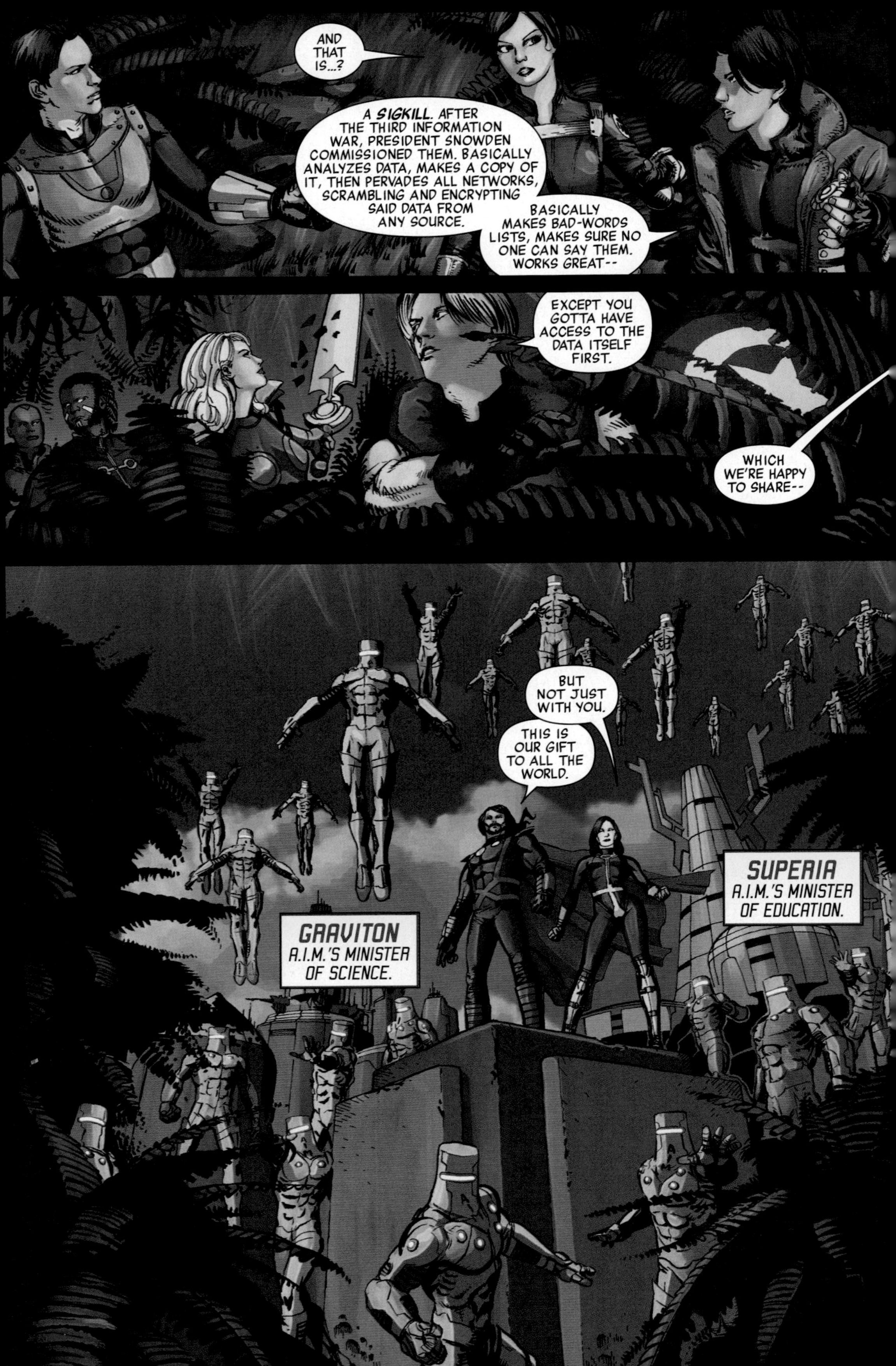
AND THAT IS...?
A SIGKILL. AFTER THE THIRD INFORMATION WAR, PRESIDENT SNOWDEN COMMISSIONED THEM. BASICALLY ANALYZES DATA, MAKES A COPY OF IT, THEN PERVADES ALL NETWORKS, SCRAMBLING AND ENCRYPTING SAID DATA FROM ANY SOURCE.
BASICALLY MAKES BAD-WORDS LISTS, MAKES SURE NO ONE CAN SAY THEM. WORKS GREAT--
EXCEPT YOU GOTTA HAVE ACCESS TO THE DATA ITSELF FIRST.
WHICH WE'RE HAPPY TO SHARE--
BUT NOT JUST WITH YOU.
THIS IS OUR GIFT TO ALL THE WORLD.
GRAVITON
A.I.M.'S MINISTER OF SCIENCE.
SUPERIA
A.I.M.'S MINISTER OF EDUCATION.

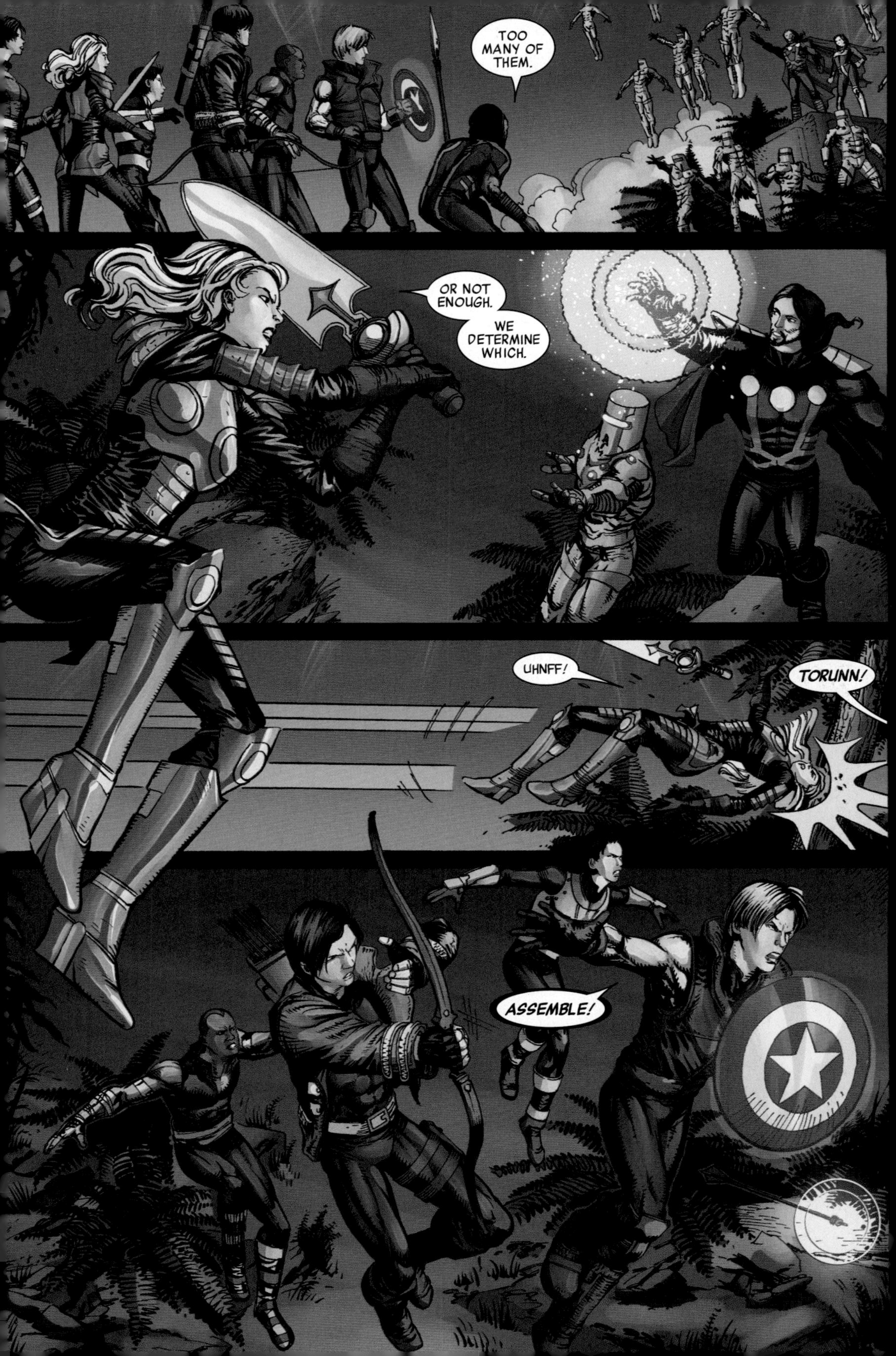
TOO MANY OF THEM.
OR NOT ENOUGH.
WE DETERMINE WHICH.
UHNFF!
TORUNN!
ASSEMBLE!

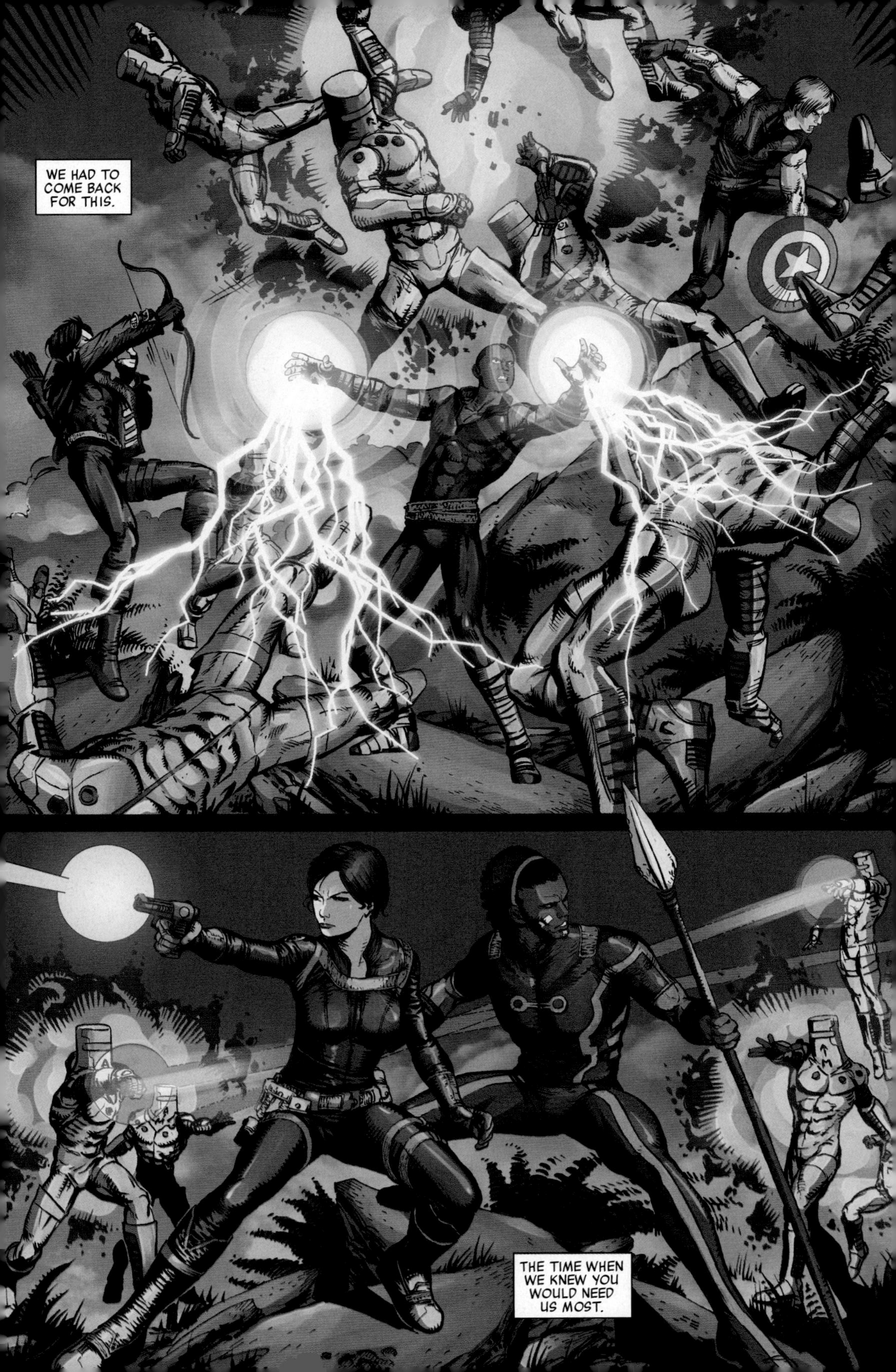
WE HAD TO COME BACK FOR THIS.
THE TIME WHEN WE KNEW YOU WOULD NEED US MOST.

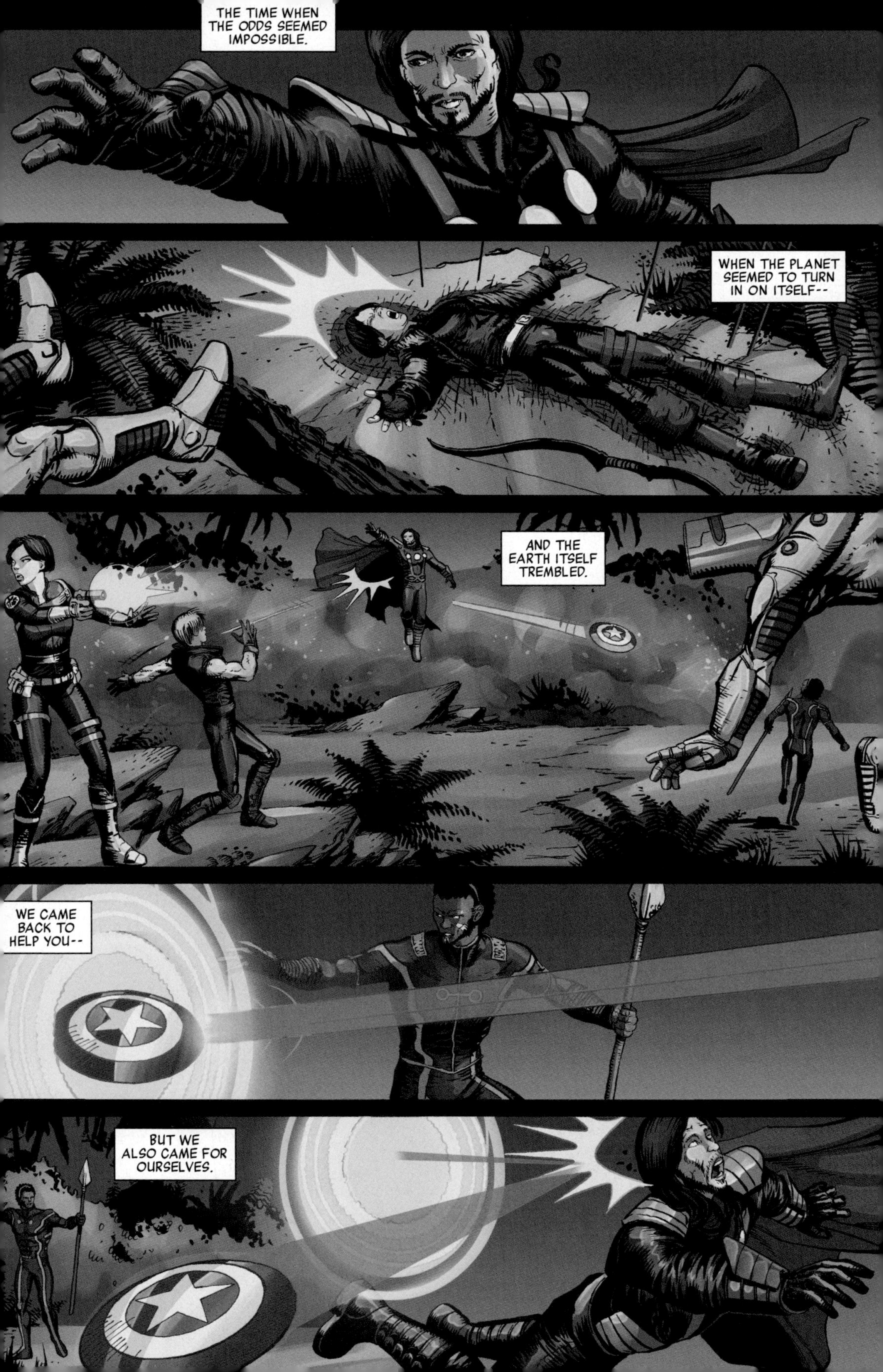
THE TIME WHEN THE ODDS SEEMED IMPOSSIBLE.
WHEN THE PLANET SEEMED TO TURN IN ON ITSELF--
AND THE EARTH ITSELF TREMBLED.
WE CAME BACK TO HELP YOU--
BUT WE ALSO CAME FOR OURSELVES.

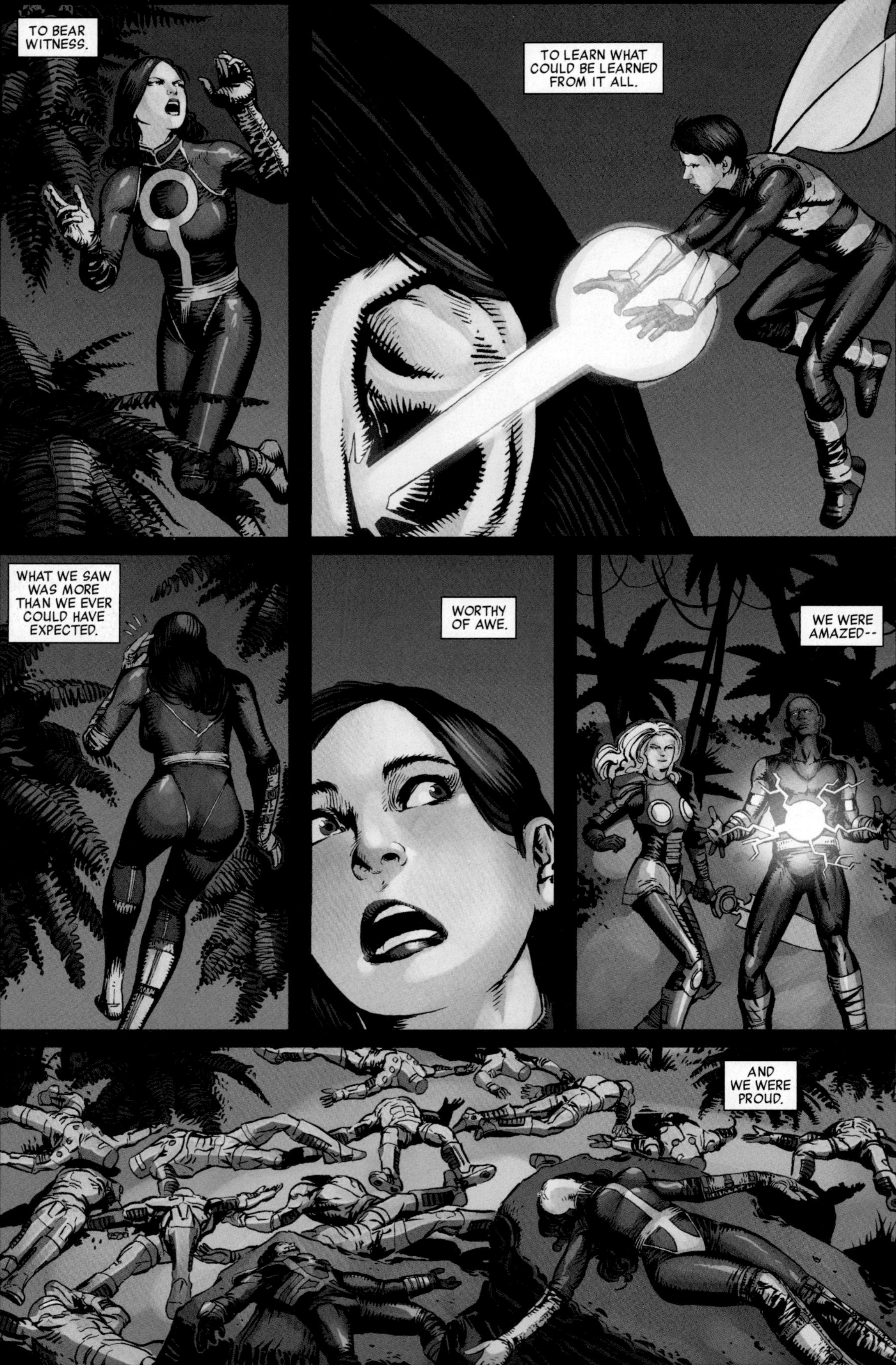
TO BEAR WITNESS.
TO LEARN WHAT COULD BE LEARNED FROM IT ALL.
WHAT WE SAW WAS MORE THAN WE EVER COULD HAVE EXPECTED.
WORTHY OF AWE.
WE WERE AMAZED--
AND WE WERE PROUD.

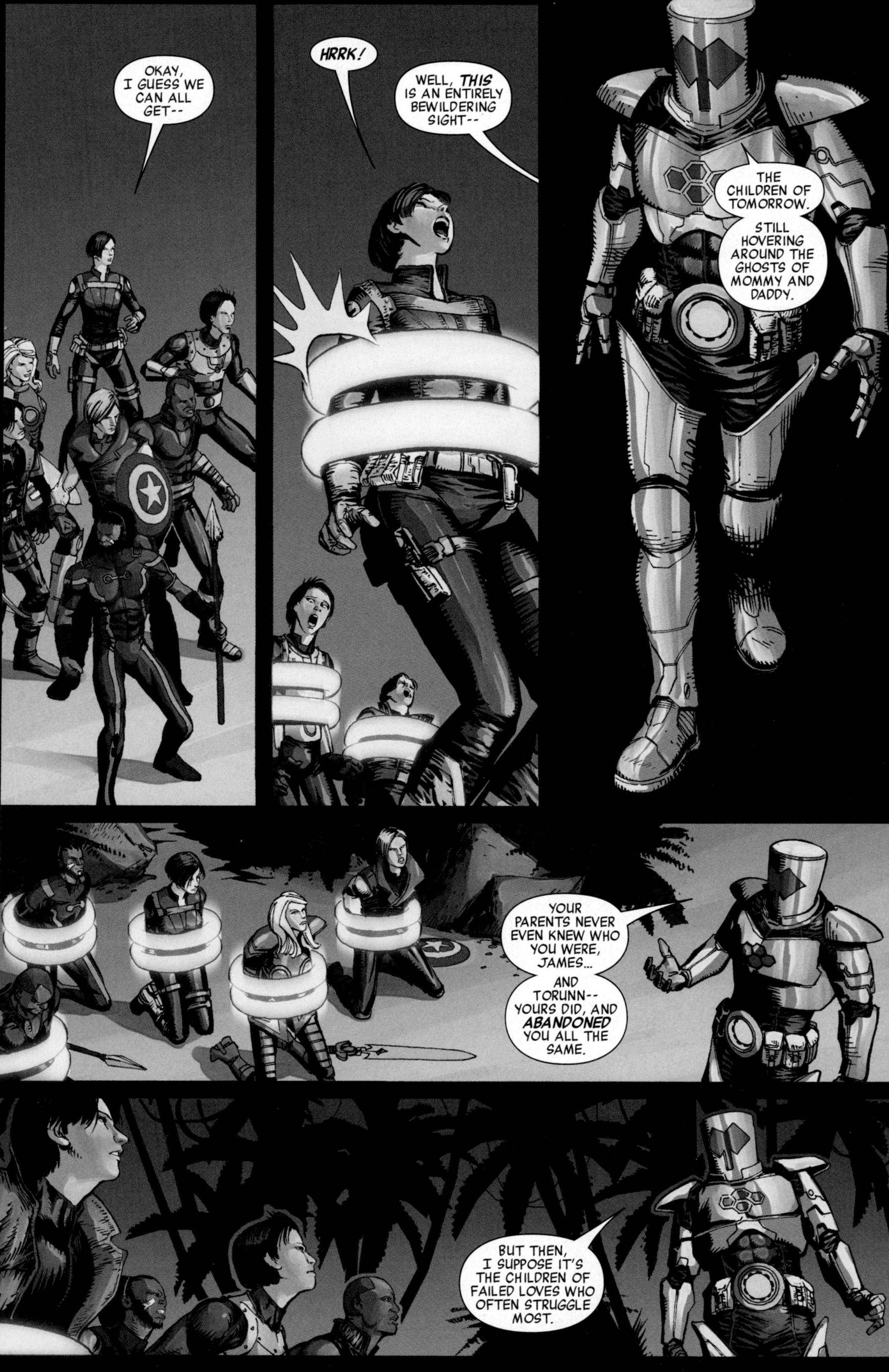
OKAY, I GUESS WE CAN ALL GET--
HRRK!
WELL, THIS IS AN ENTIRELY BEWILDERING SIGHT--
THE CHILDREN OF TOMORROW.
STILL HOVERING AROUND THE GHOSTS OF MOMMY AND DADDY.
YOUR PARENTS NEVER EVEN KNEW WHO YOU WERE, JAMES...
AND TORUNN-- YOURS DID, AND ABANDONED YOU ALL THE SAME.
BUT THEN, I SUPPOSE IT'S THE CHILDREN OF FAILED LOVES WHO OFTEN STRUGGLE MOST.

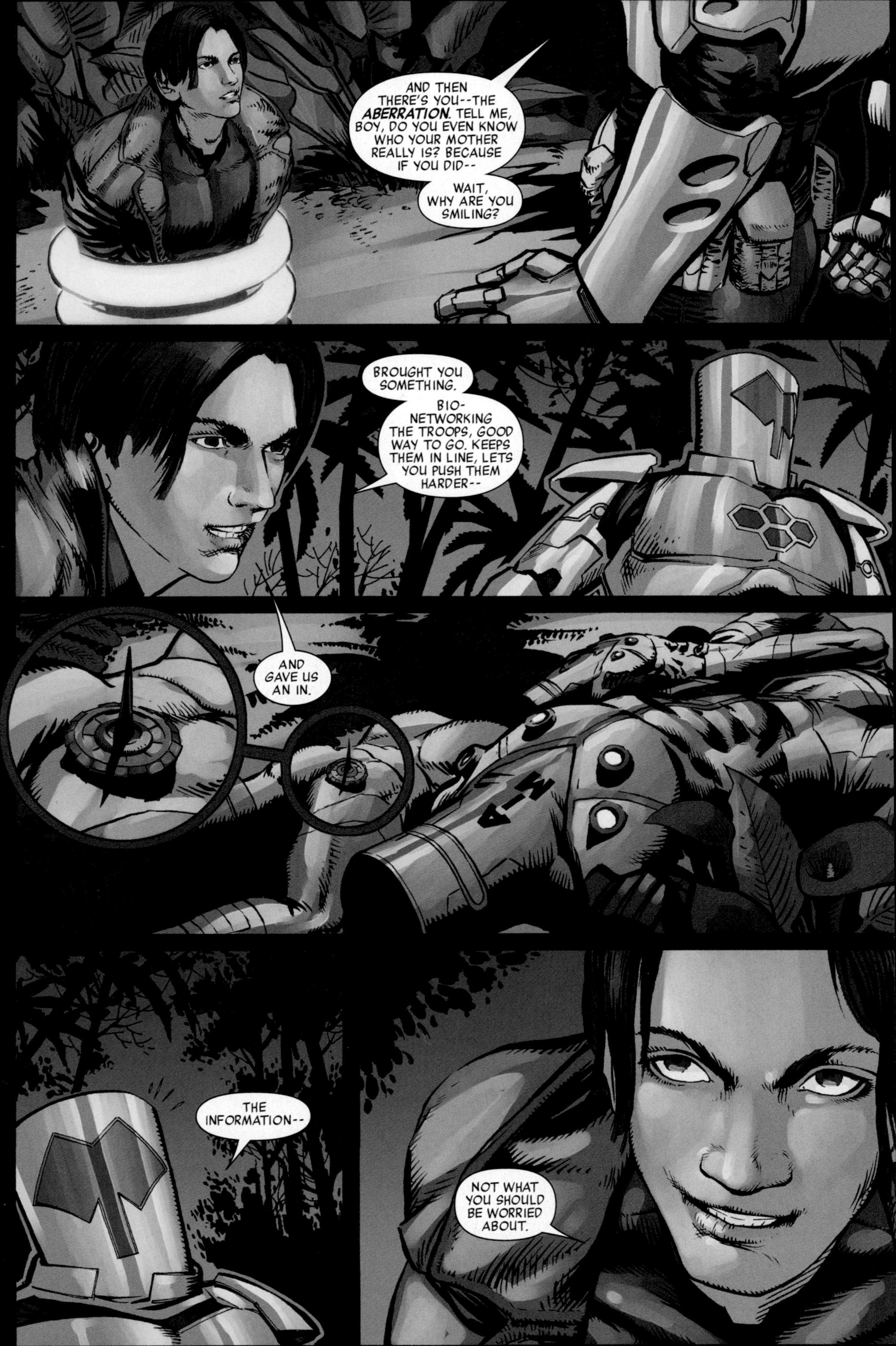
AND THEN THERE'S YOU--THE ABERRATION. TELL ME, BOY, DO YOU EVEN KNOW WHO YOUR MOTHER REALLY IS? BECAUSE IF YOU DID--
WAIT, WHY ARE YOU SMILING?
BROUGHT YOU SOMETHING.
BIO-NETWORKING THE TROOPS, GOOD WAY TO GO. KEEPS THEM IN LINE, LETS YOU PUSH THEM HARDER--
AND GAVE US AN IN.
M-A
THE INFORMATION--
NOT WHAT YOU SHOULD BE WORRIED ABOUT.

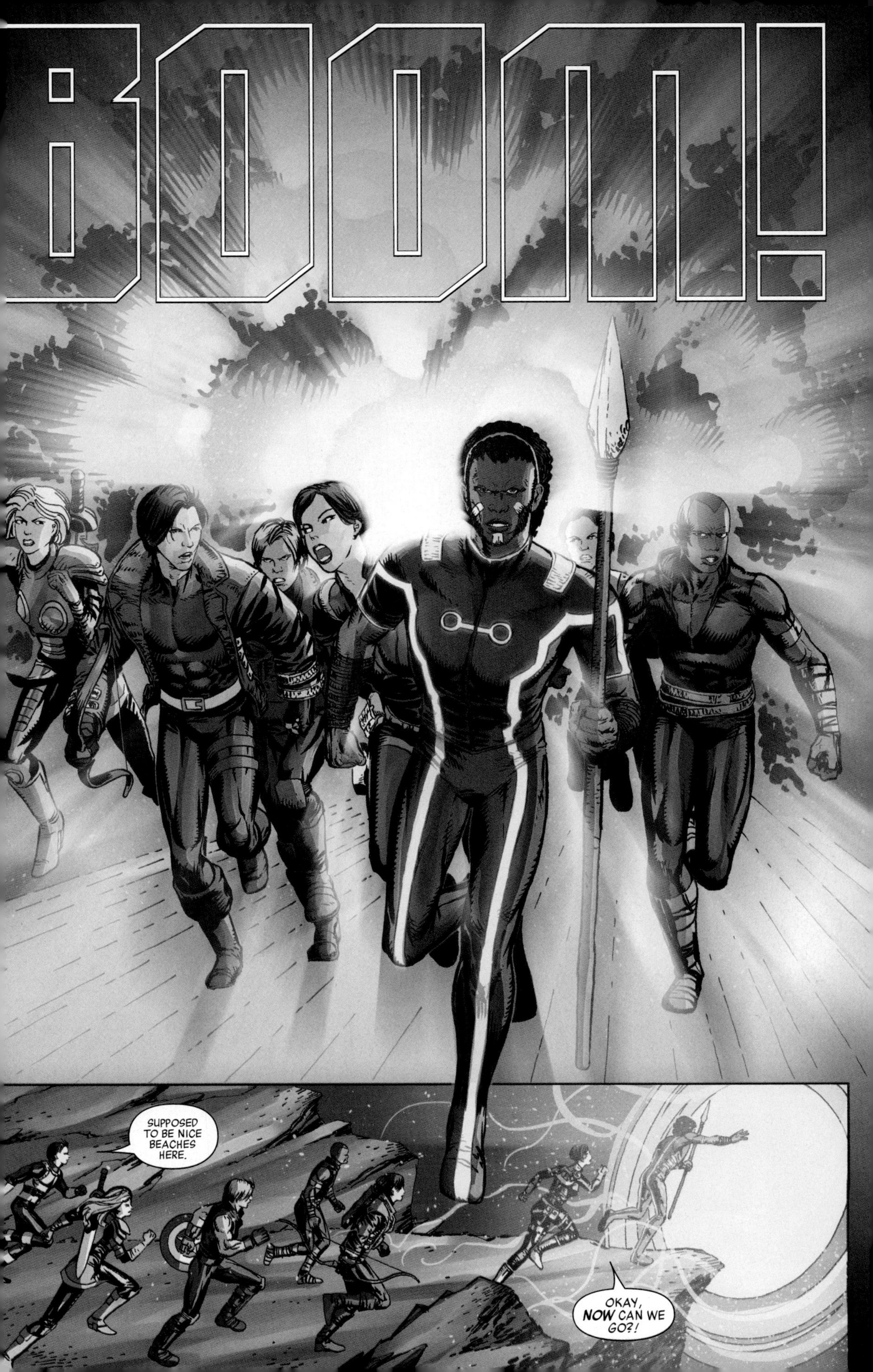
BOOM!
SUPPOSED TO BE NICE BEACHES HERE.
OKAY, NOW CAN WE GO?!

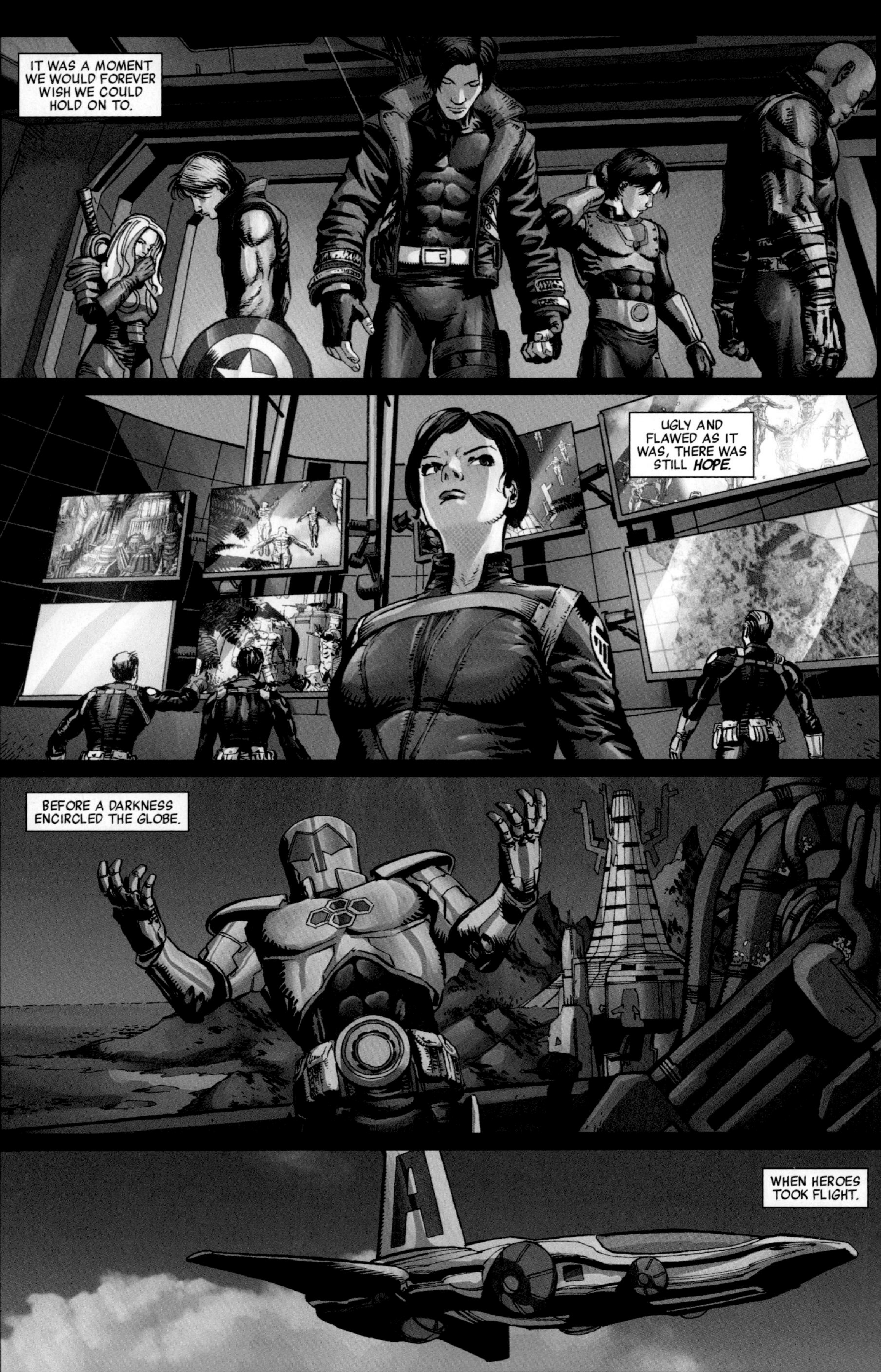
IT WAS A MOMENT WE WOULD FOREVER WISH WE COULD HOLD ON TO.
UGLY AND FLAWED AS IT WAS, THERE WAS STILL HOPE.
BEFORE A DARKNESS ENCIRCLED THE GLOBE.
WHEN HEROES TOOK FLIGHT.

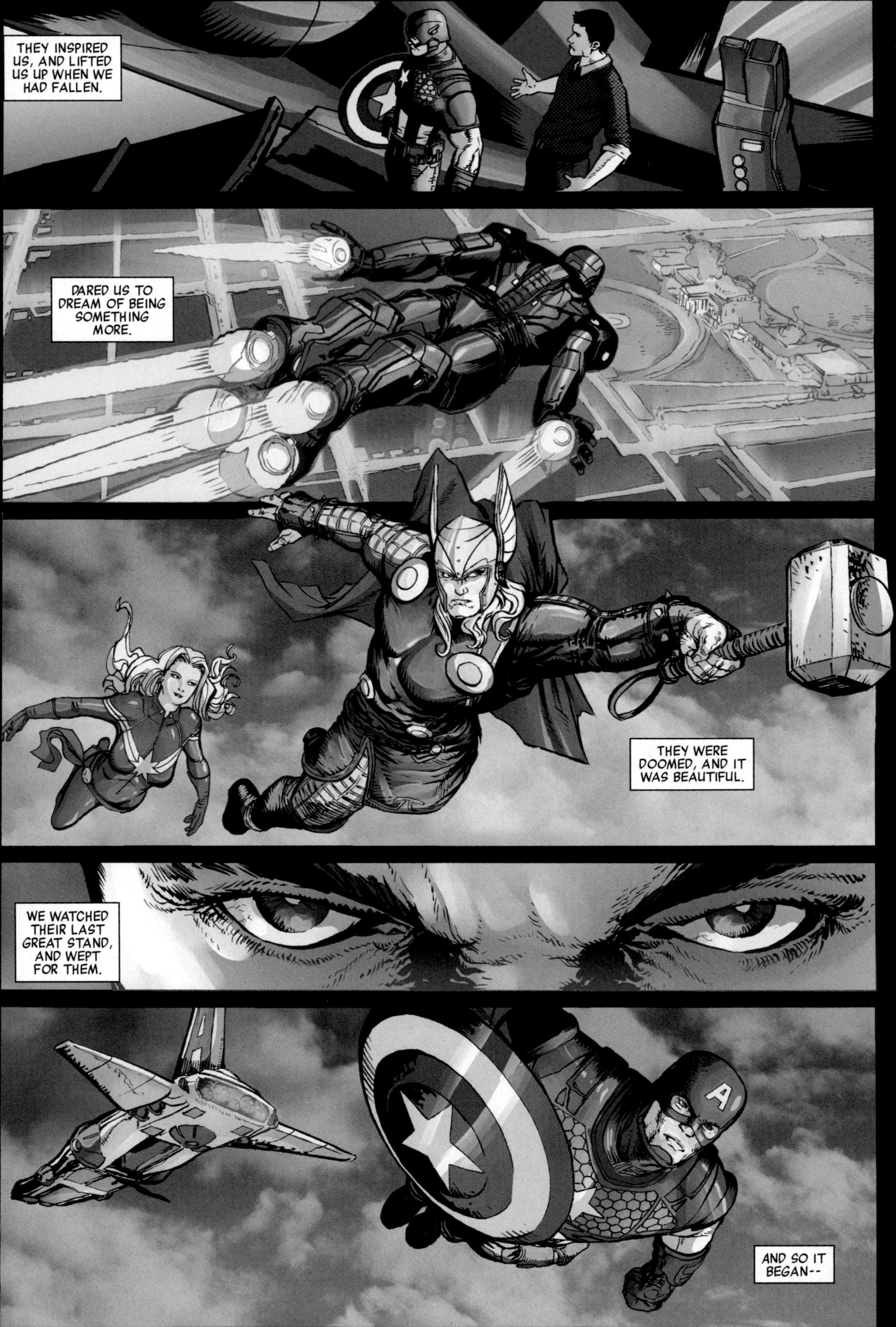
THEY INSPIRED US, AND LIFTED US UP WHEN WE HAD FALLEN.
DARED US TO DREAM OF BEING SOMETHING MORE.
THEY WERE DOOMED, AND IT WAS BEAUTIFUL.
WE WATCHED THEIR LAST GREAT STAND, AND WEPT FOR THEM.
AND SO IT BEGAN--

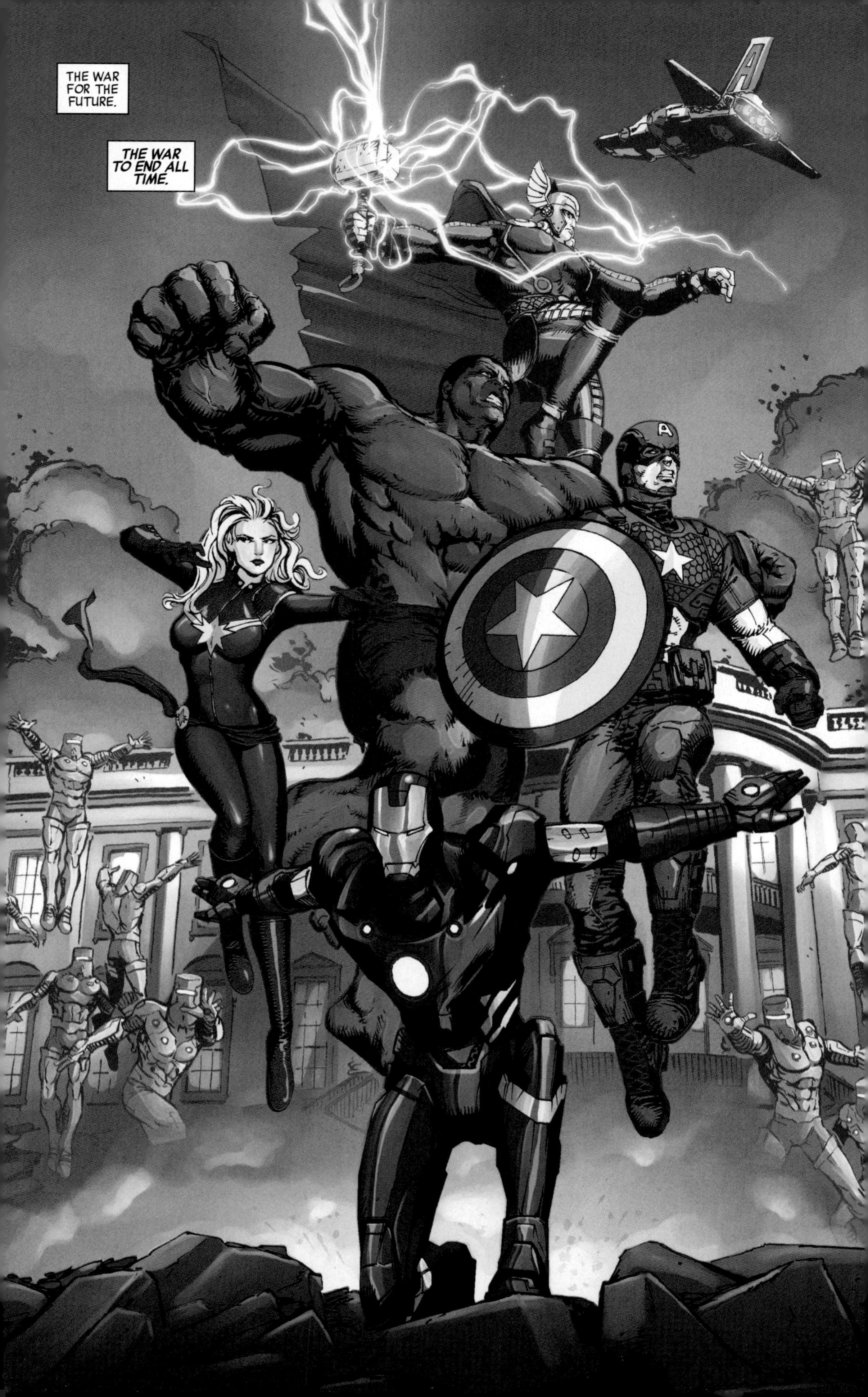
THE WAR FOR THE FUTURE.
THE WAR TO END ALL TIME.

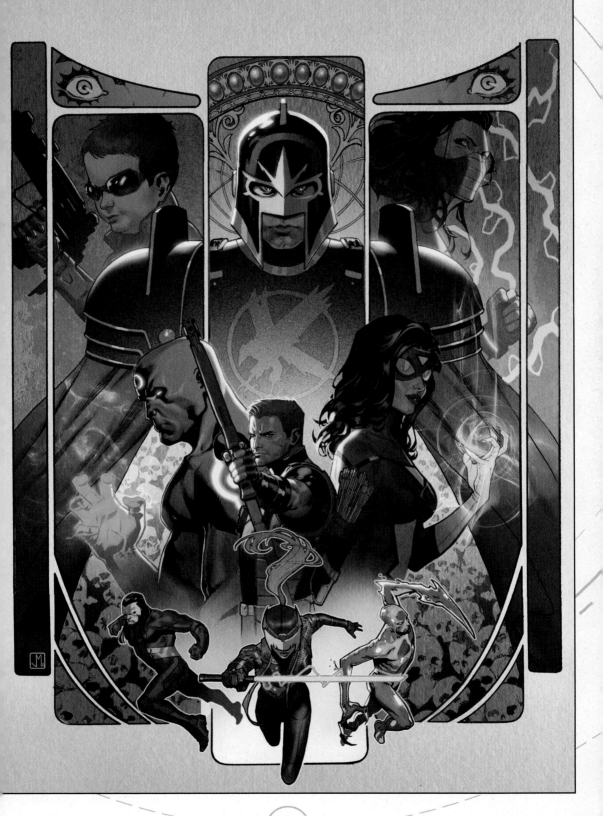

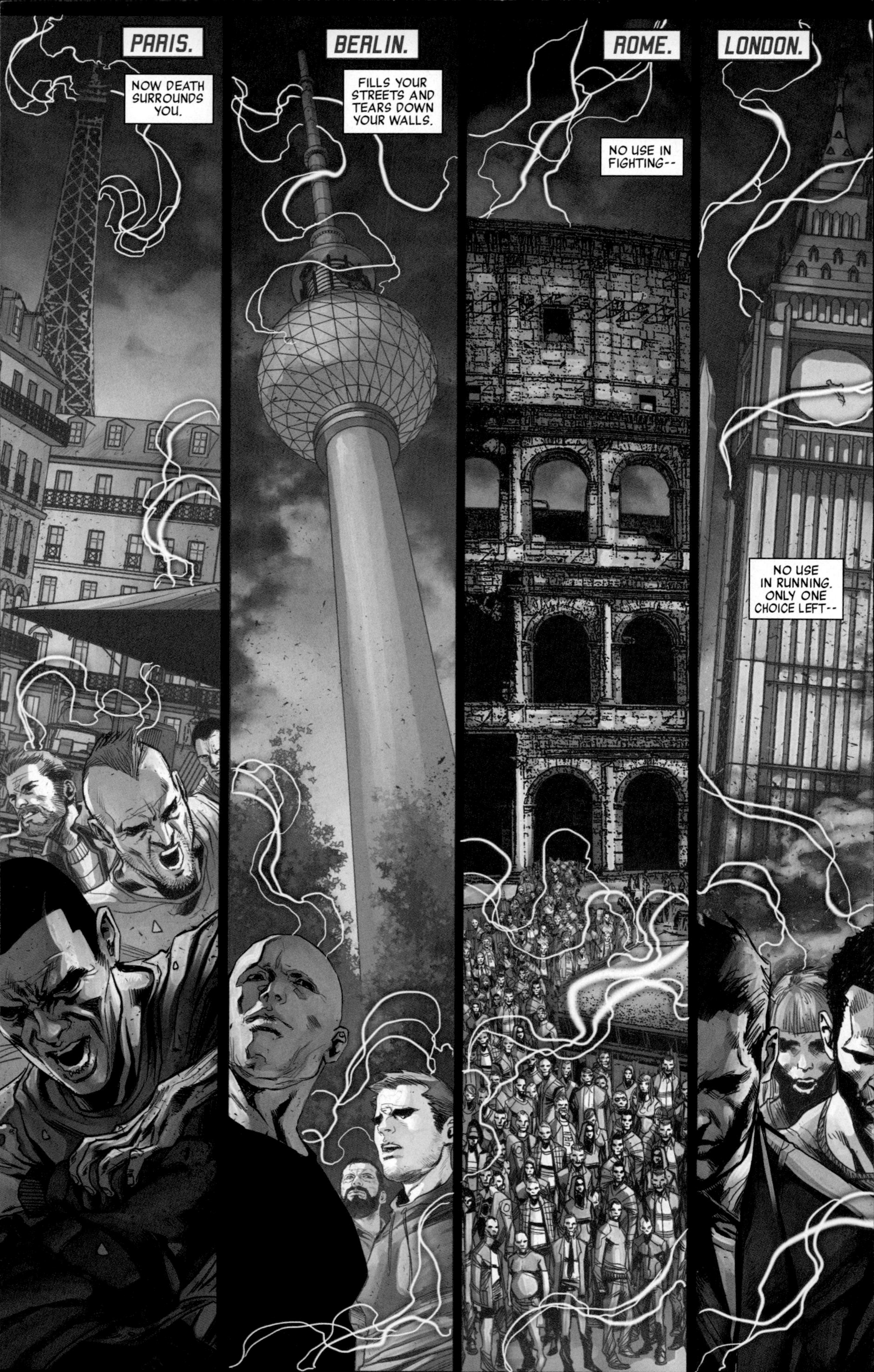
PARIS.
NOW DEATH SURROUNDS YOU.
BERLIN.
FILLS YOUR STREETS AND TEARS DOWN YOUR WALLS.
ROME.
NO USE IN FIGHTING--
LONDON.
NO USE IN RUNNING. ONLY ONE CHOICE LEFT--

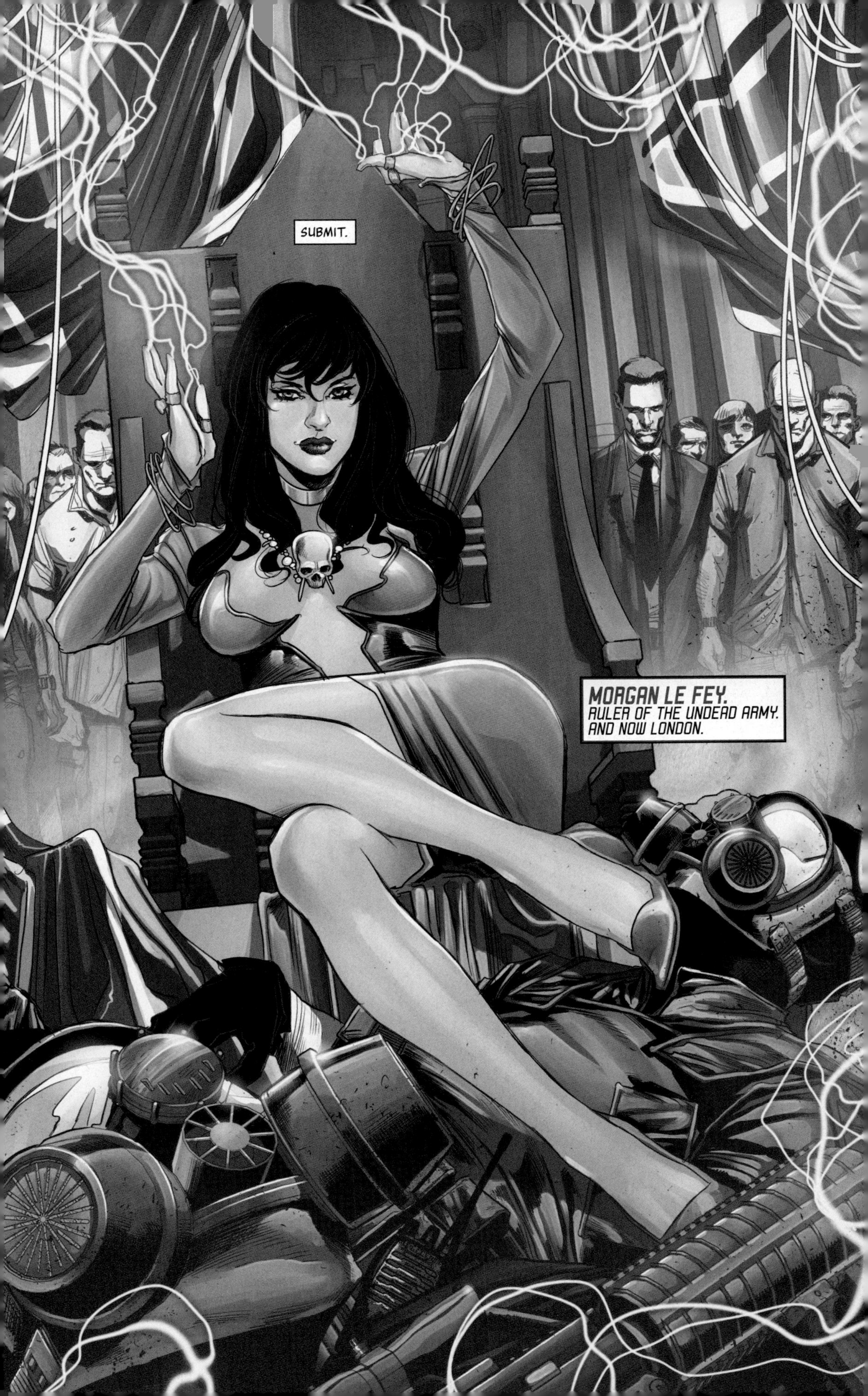
SUBMIT.
MORGAN LE FEY.
RULER OF THE UNDEAD ARMY.
AND NOW LONDON.

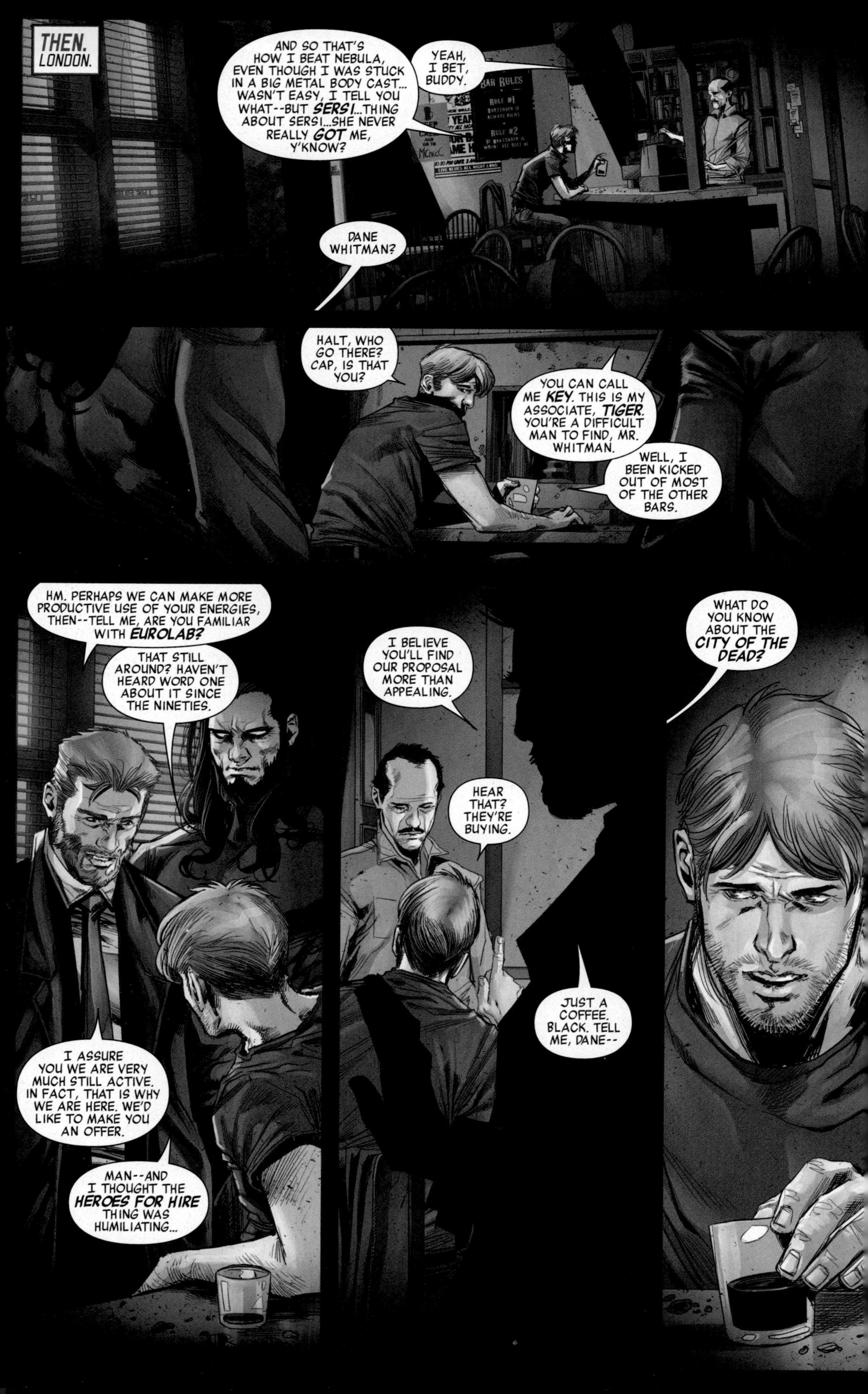
THEN. LONDON.
AND SO THAT'S HOW I BEAT NEBULA, EVEN THOUGH I WAS STUCK IN A BIG METAL BODY CAST... WASN'T EASY, I TELL YOU WHAT--BUT SERSI...THING ABOUT SERSI...SHE NEVER REALLY GOT ME, Y'KNOW?
YEAH, I BET, BUDDY.
BAR RULES
RULE #1
RULE #2
DANE WHITMAN?
HALT, WHO GO THERE? CAP, IS THAT YOU?
YOU CAN CALL ME KEY. THIS IS MY ASSOCIATE, TIGER. YOU'RE A DIFFICULT MAN TO FIND, MR. WHITMAN.
WELL, I BEEN KICKED OUT OF MOST OF THE OTHER BARS.
HM. PERHAPS WE CAN MAKE MORE PRODUCTIVE USE OF YOUR ENERGIES, THEN--TELL ME, ARE YOU FAMILIAR WITH EUROLAB?
THAT STILL AROUND? HAVEN'T HEARD WORD ONE ABOUT IT SINCE THE NINETIES.
I ASSURE YOU WE ARE VERY MUCH STILL ACTIVE. IN FACT, THAT IS WHY WE ARE HERE. WE'D LIKE TO MAKE YOU AN OFFER.
MAN--AND I THOUGHT THE HEROES FOR HIRE THING WAS HUMILIATING...
I BELIEVE YOU'LL FIND OUR PROPOSAL MORE THAN APPEALING.
HEAR THAT? THEY'RE BUYING.
JUST A COFFEE. BLACK. TELL ME, DANE--
WHAT DO YOU KNOW ABOUT THE CITY OF THE DEAD?

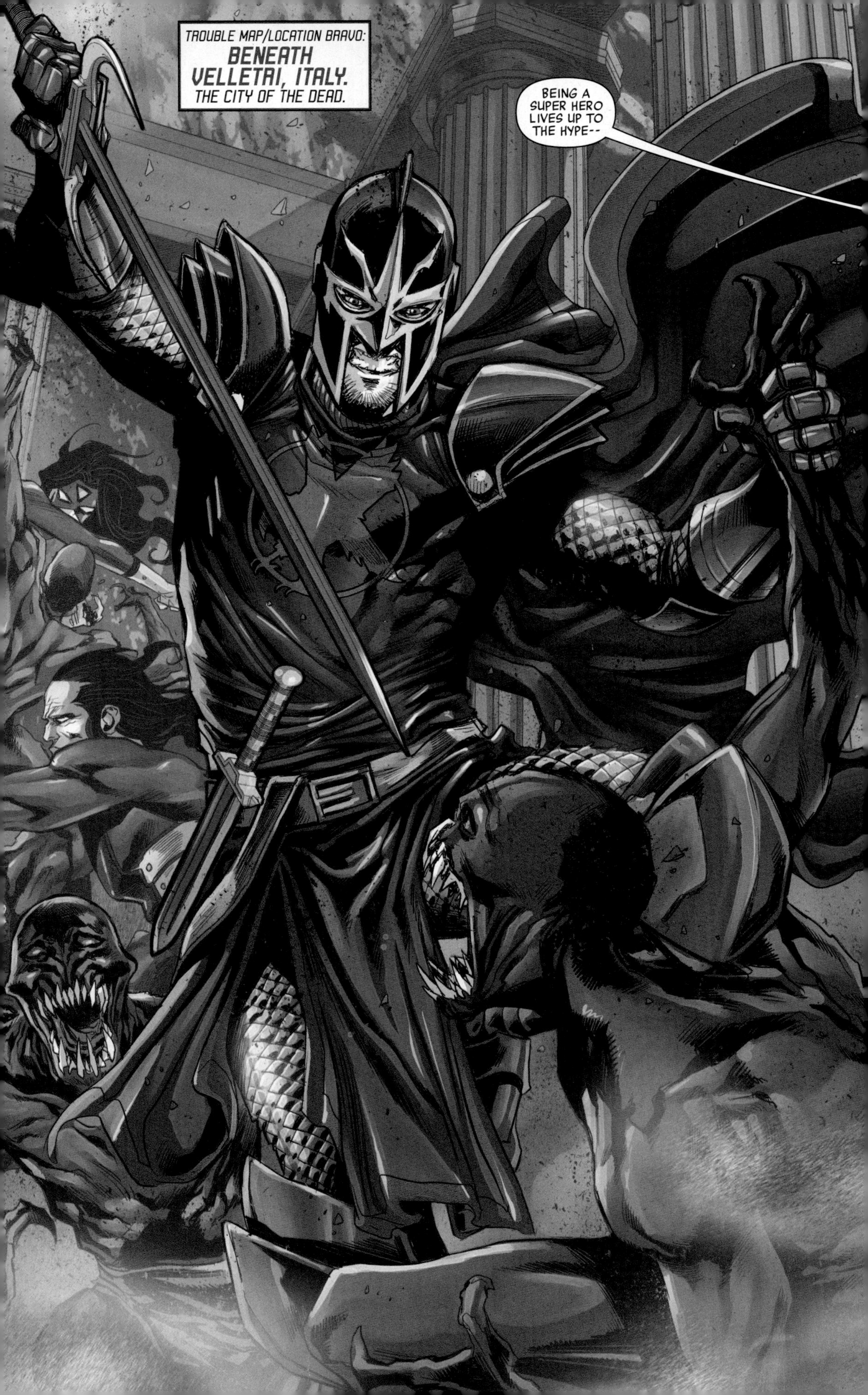
TROUBLE MAP/LOCATION BRAVO:
BENEATH VELLETRI, ITALY.
THE CITY OF THE DEAD.
BEING A SUPER HERO LIVES UP TO THE HYPE--

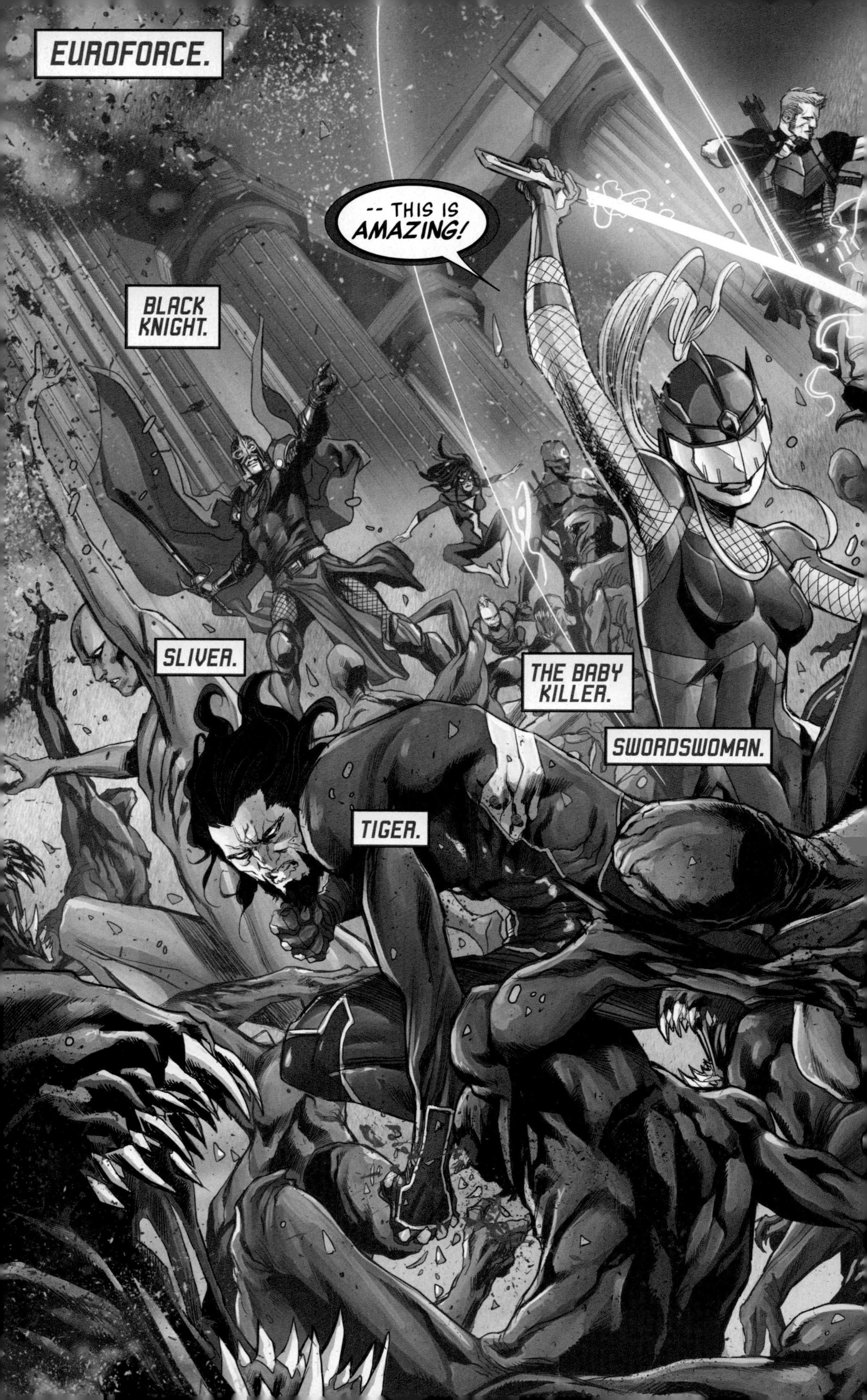
EUROFORCE.
-- THIS IS AMAZING!
BLACK KNIGHT.
SLIVER.
THE BABY KILLER.
SWORDSWOMAN.
TIGER.

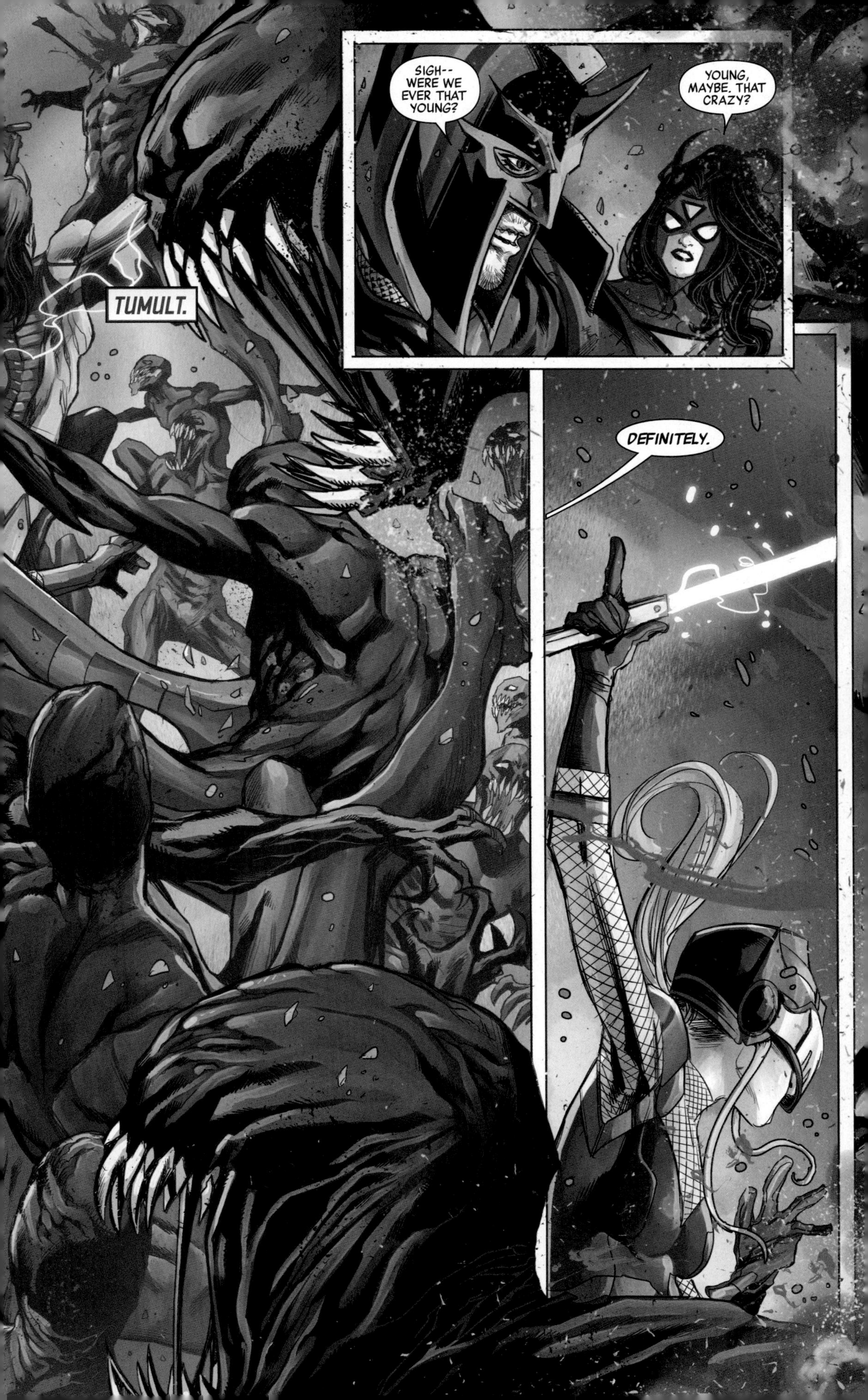
TUMULT.
SIGH-- WERE WE EVER THAT YOUNG?
YOUNG, MAYBE. THAT CRAZY?
DEFINITELY.

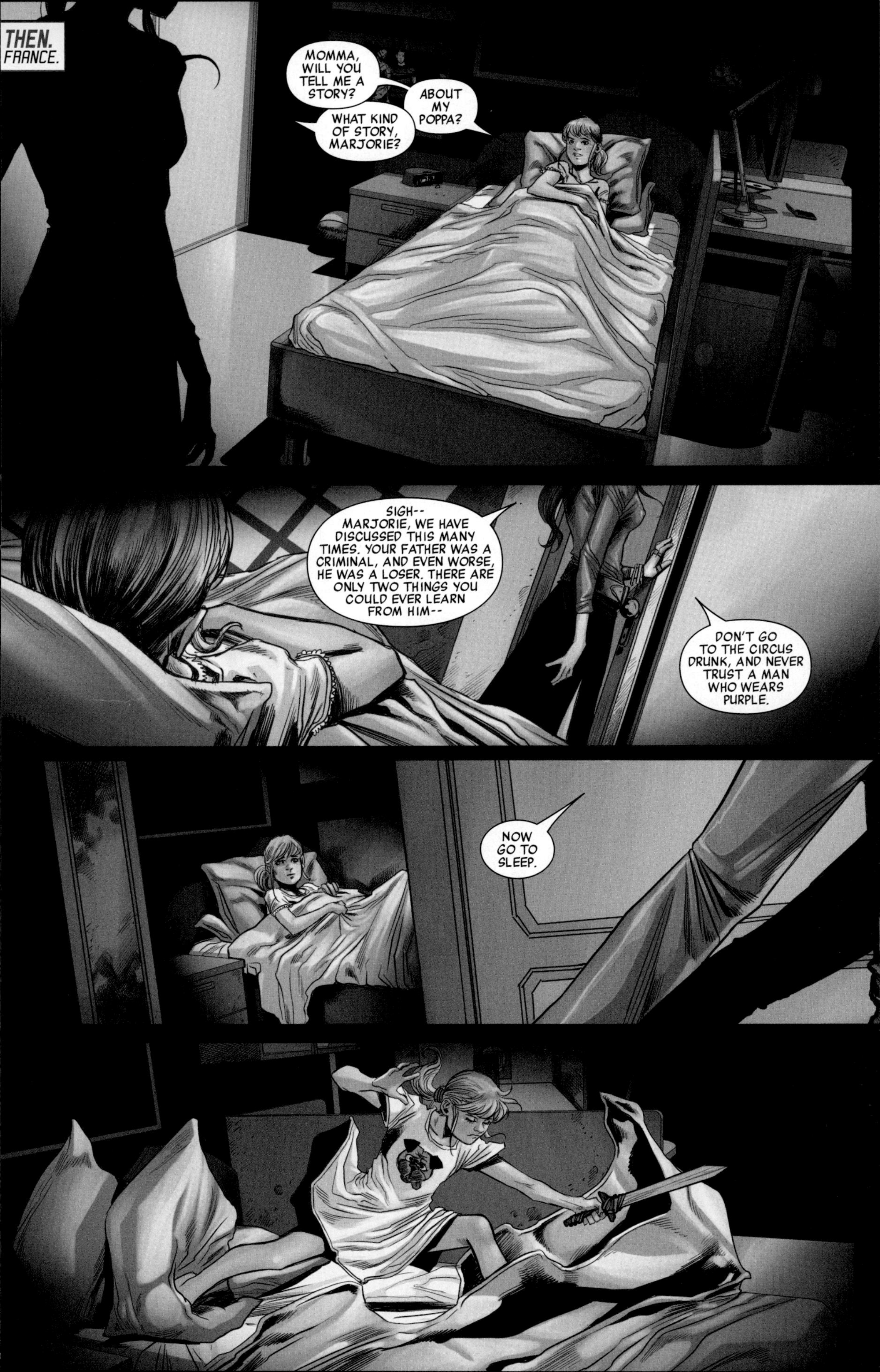
THEN.
FRANCE.
MOMMA, WILL YOU TELL ME A STORY?
WHAT KIND OF STORY, MARJORIE?
ABOUT MY POPPA?
SIGH-- MARJORIE, WE HAVE DISCUSSED THIS MANY TIMES. YOUR FATHER WAS A CRIMINAL, AND EVEN WORSE, HE WAS A LOSER. THERE ARE ONLY TWO THINGS YOU COULD EVER LEARN FROM HIM--
DON'T GO TO THE CIRCUS DRUNK, AND NEVER TRUST A MAN WHO WEARS PURPLE.
NOW GO TO SLEEP.

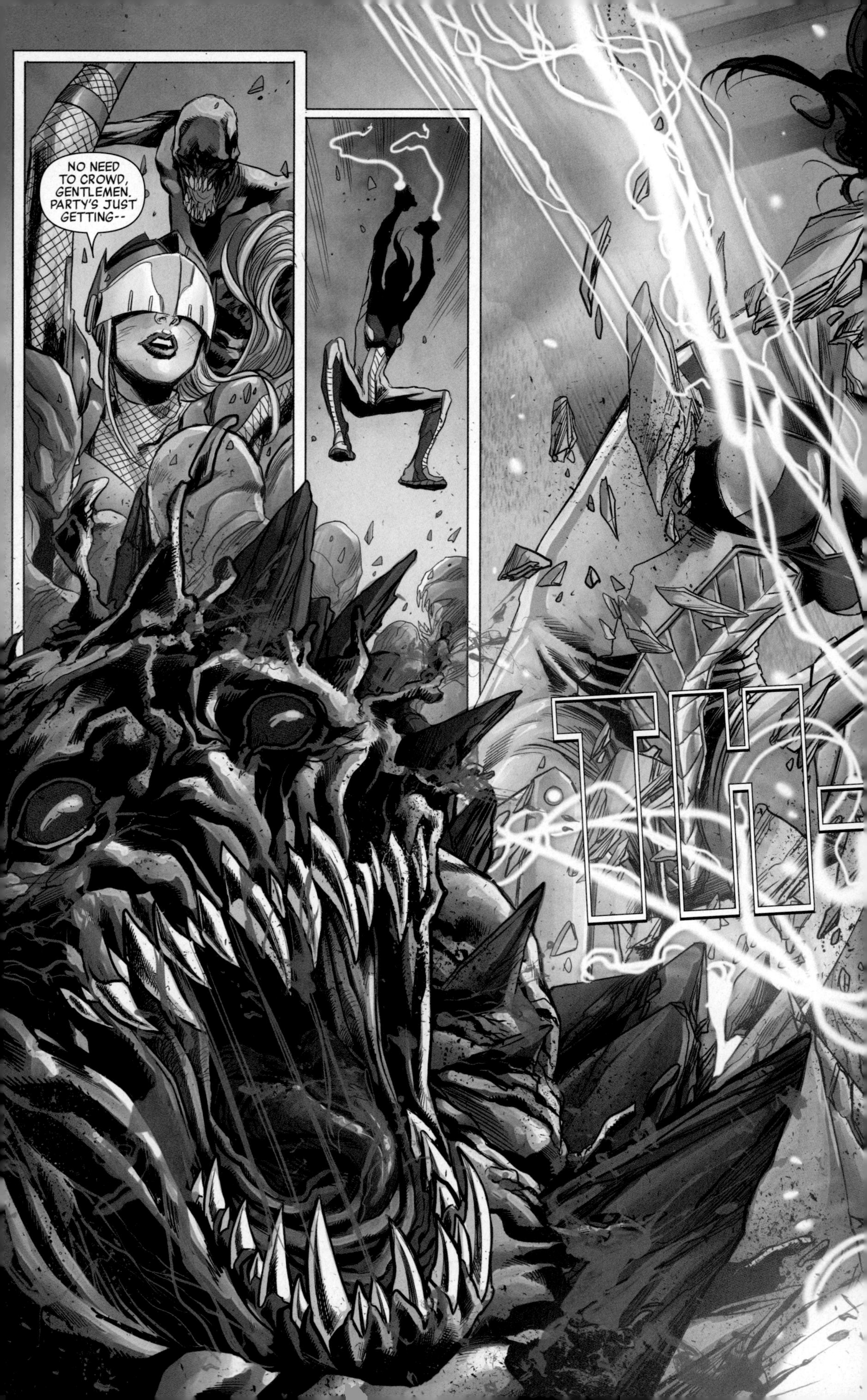
NO NEED TO CROWD, GENTLEMEN. PARTY'S JUST GETTING--
THK-

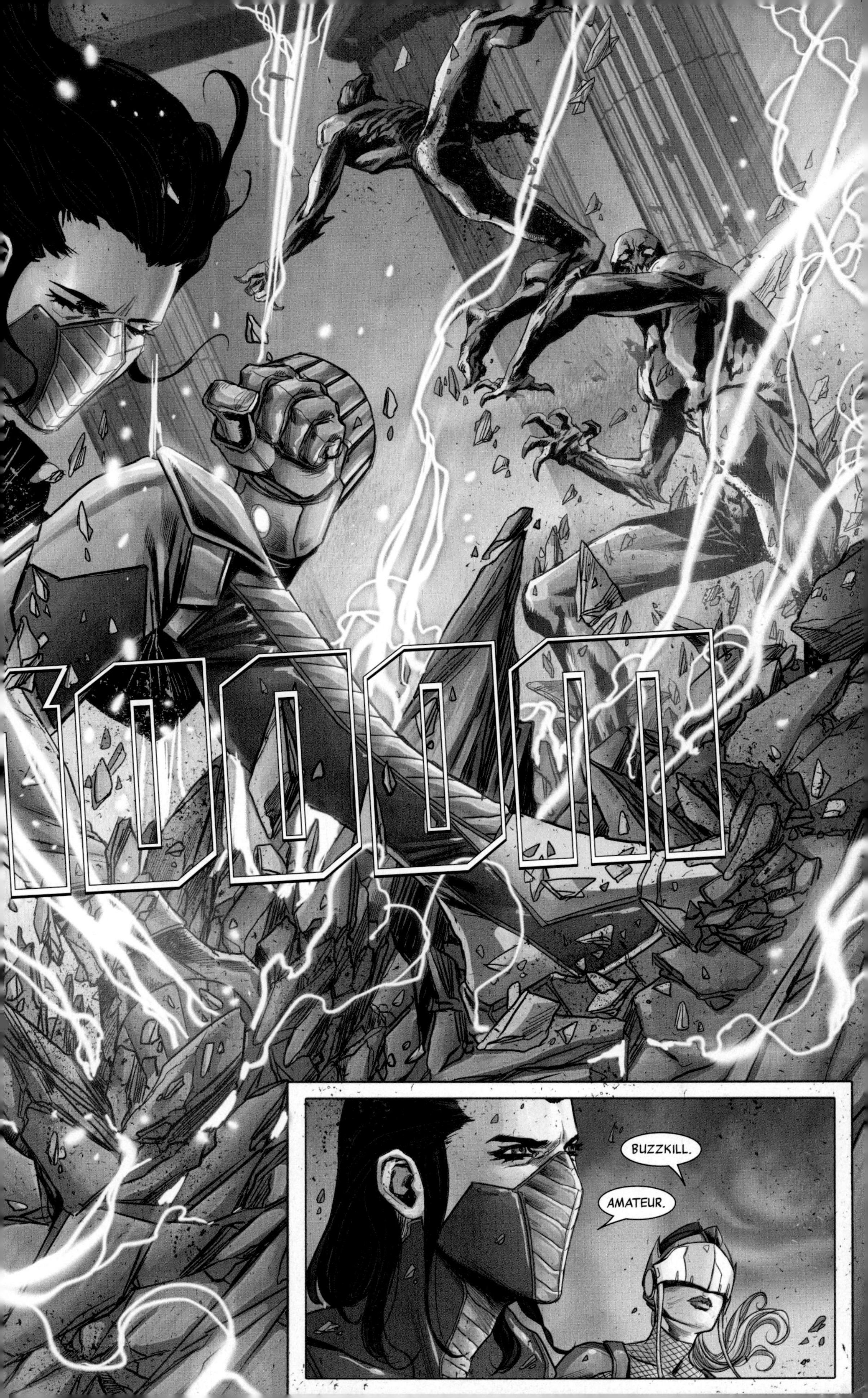

THOOOM
BUZZKILL.
AMATEUR.

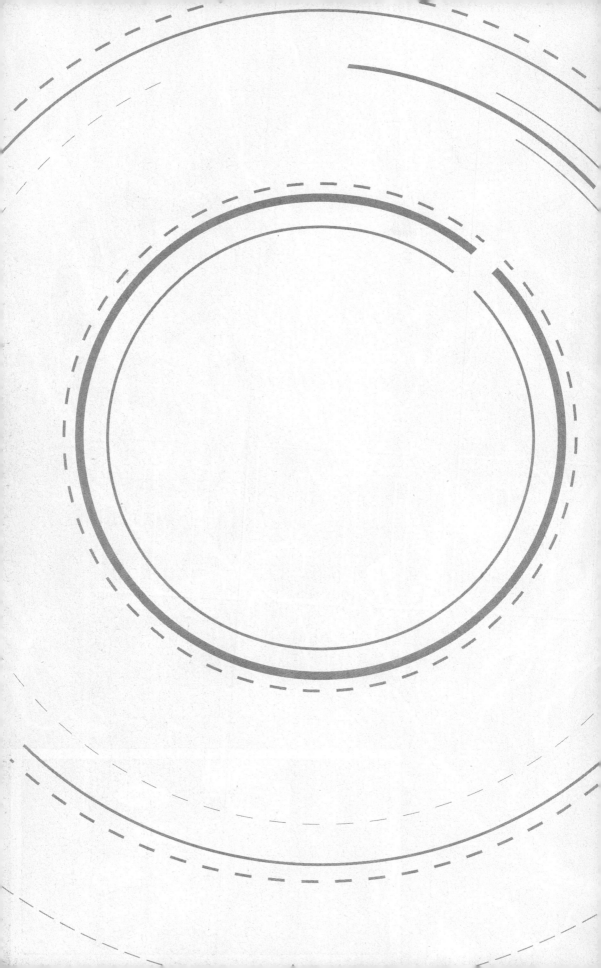

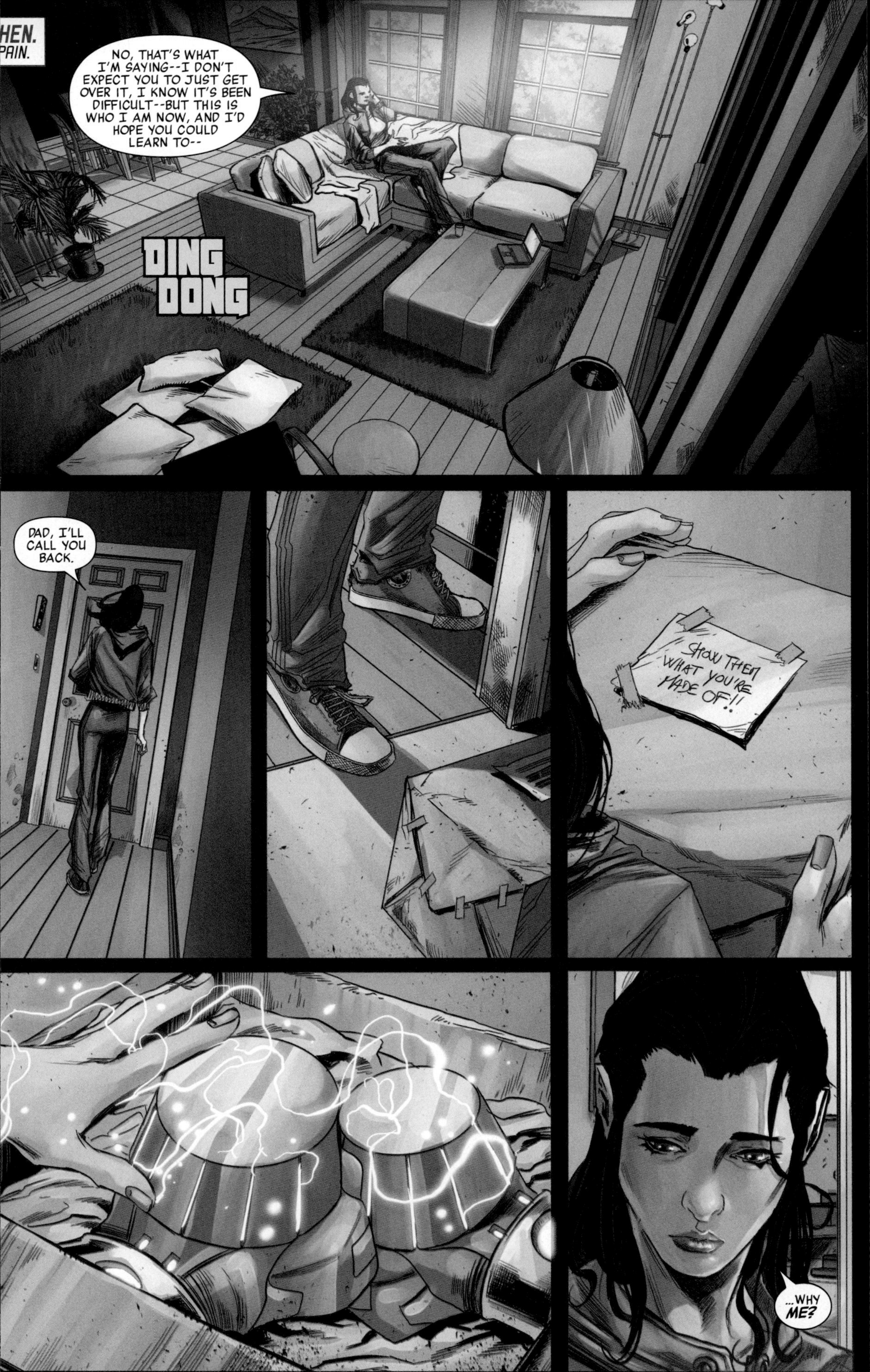
HEN.
PAIN.
NO, THAT'S WHAT I'M SAYING--I DON'T EXPECT YOU TO JUST GET OVER IT, I KNOW IT'S BEEN DIFFICULT--BUT THIS IS WHO I AM NOW, AND I'D HOPE YOU COULD LEARN TO--
DING DONG
DAD, I'LL CALL YOU BACK.
SHOW THEM WHAT YOU'RE MADE OF!!
...WHY ME?

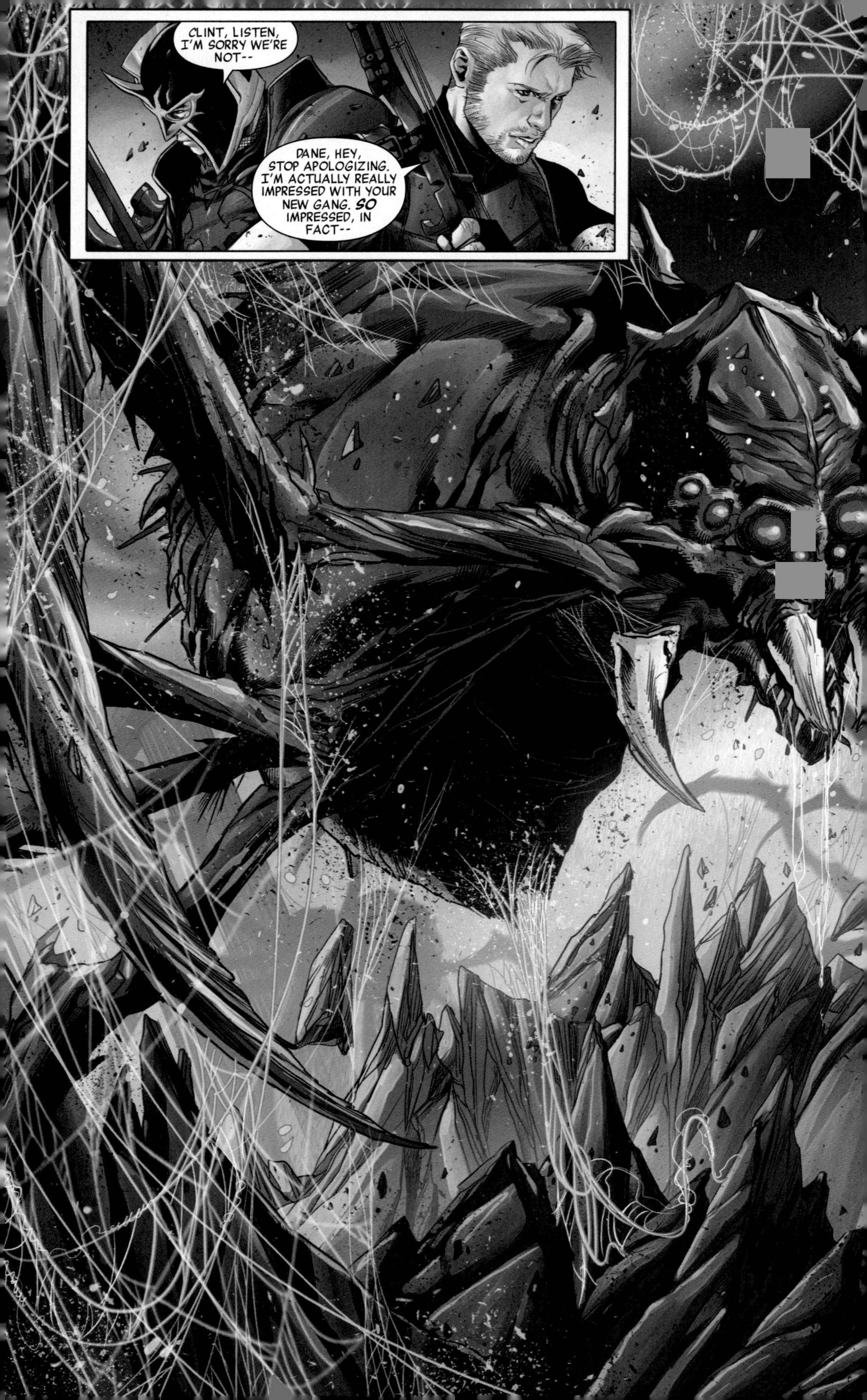
CLINT, LISTEN, I'M SORRY WE'RE NOT--
DANE, HEY, STOP APOLOGIZING. I'M ACTUALLY REALLY IMPRESSED WITH YOUR NEW GANG. **SO** IMPRESSED, IN FACT--

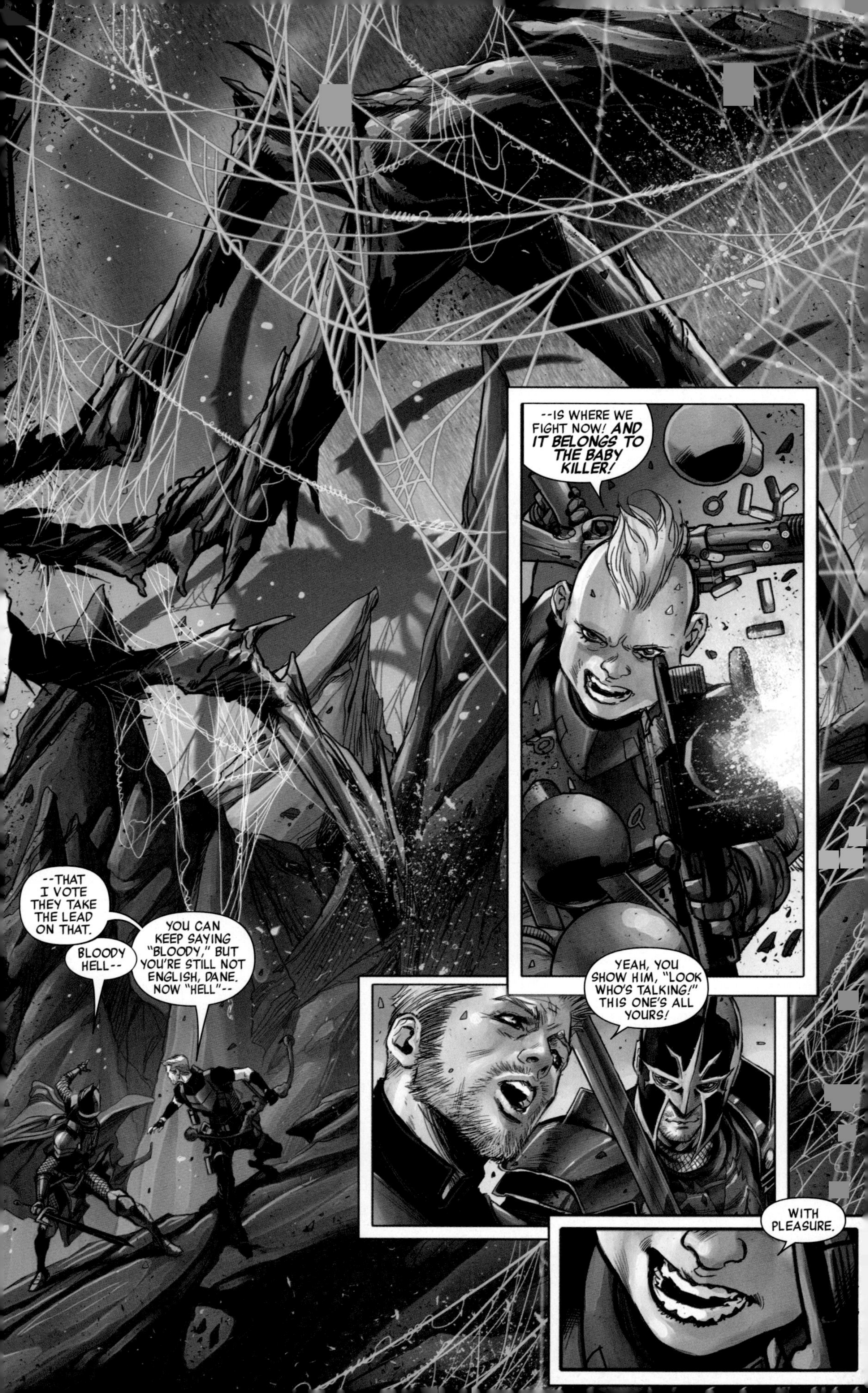

--THAT I VOTE THEY TAKE THE LEAD ON THAT.
BLOODY HELL--
YOU CAN KEEP SAYING "BLOODY," BUT YOU'RE STILL NOT ENGLISH, DANE. NOW "HELL"--
--IS WHERE WE FIGHT NOW! AND IT BELONGS TO THE BABY KILLER!
YEAH, YOU SHOW HIM, "LOOK WHO'S TALKING!" THIS ONE'S ALL YOURS!
WITH PLEASURE.

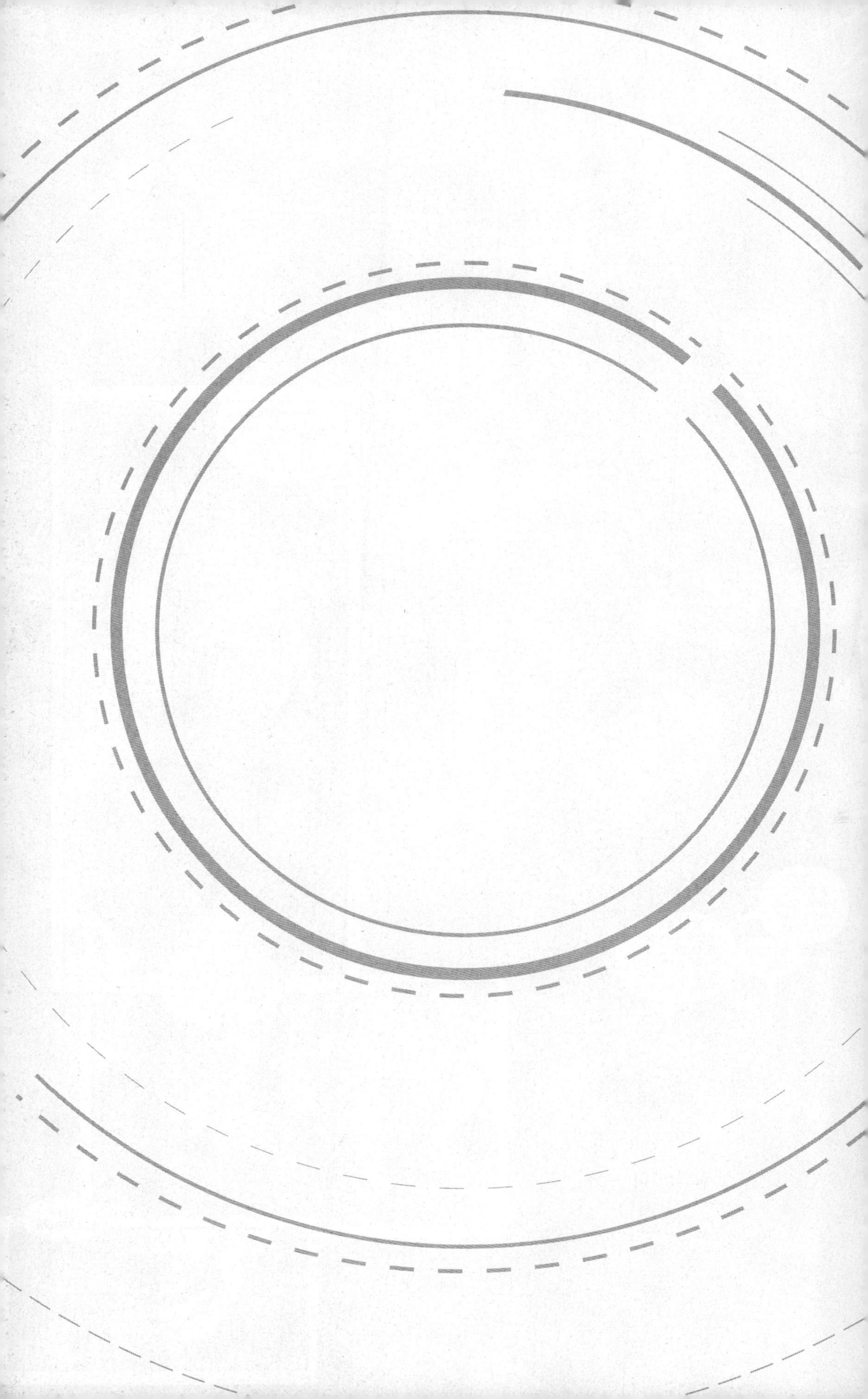

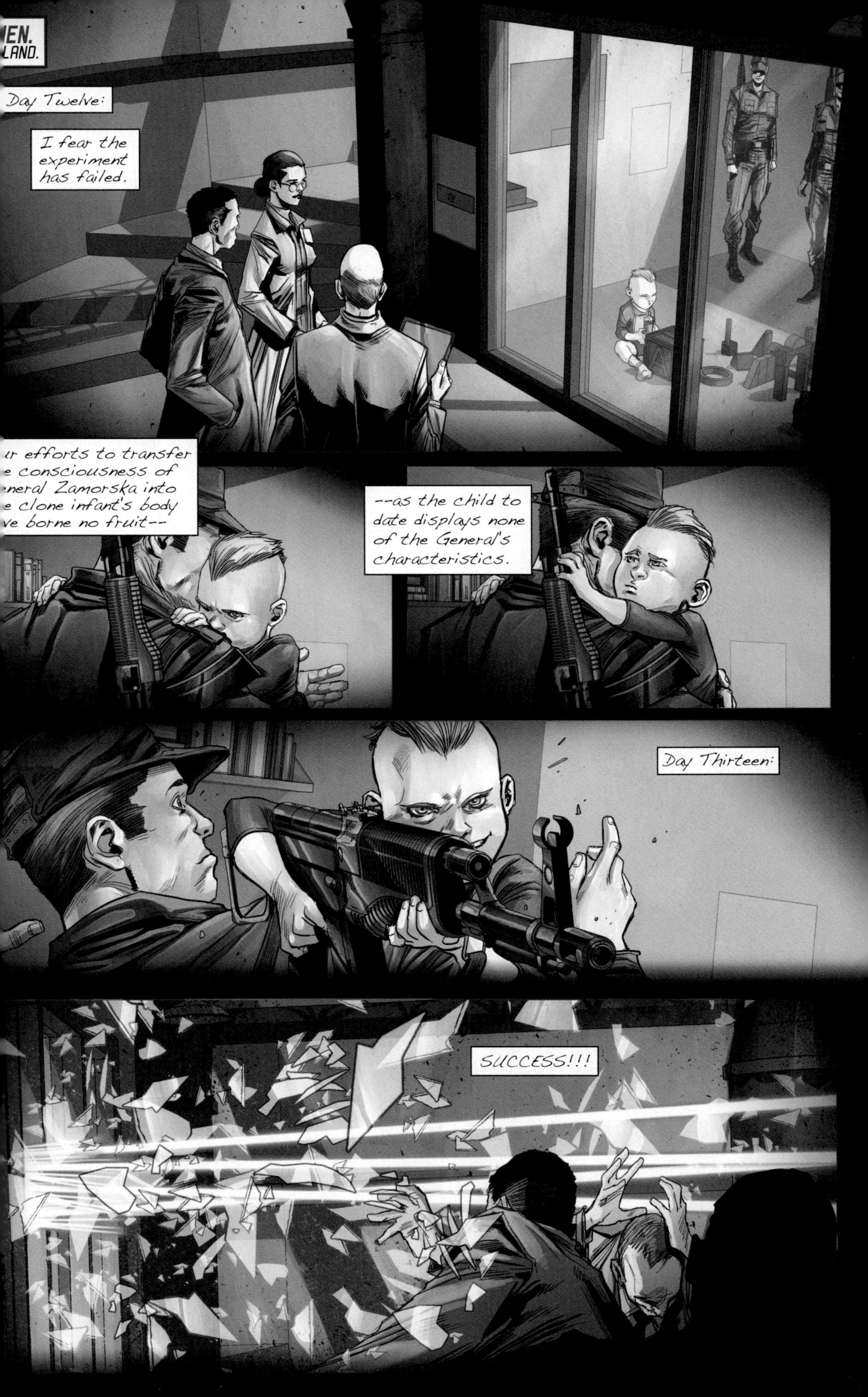
EN.
LAND.
Day Twelve:
I fear the experiment has failed.
ur efforts to transfer e consciousness of eneral Zamorska into e clone infant's body ve borne no fruit--
--as the child to date displays none of the General's characteristics.
Day Thirteen:
SUCCESS!!!

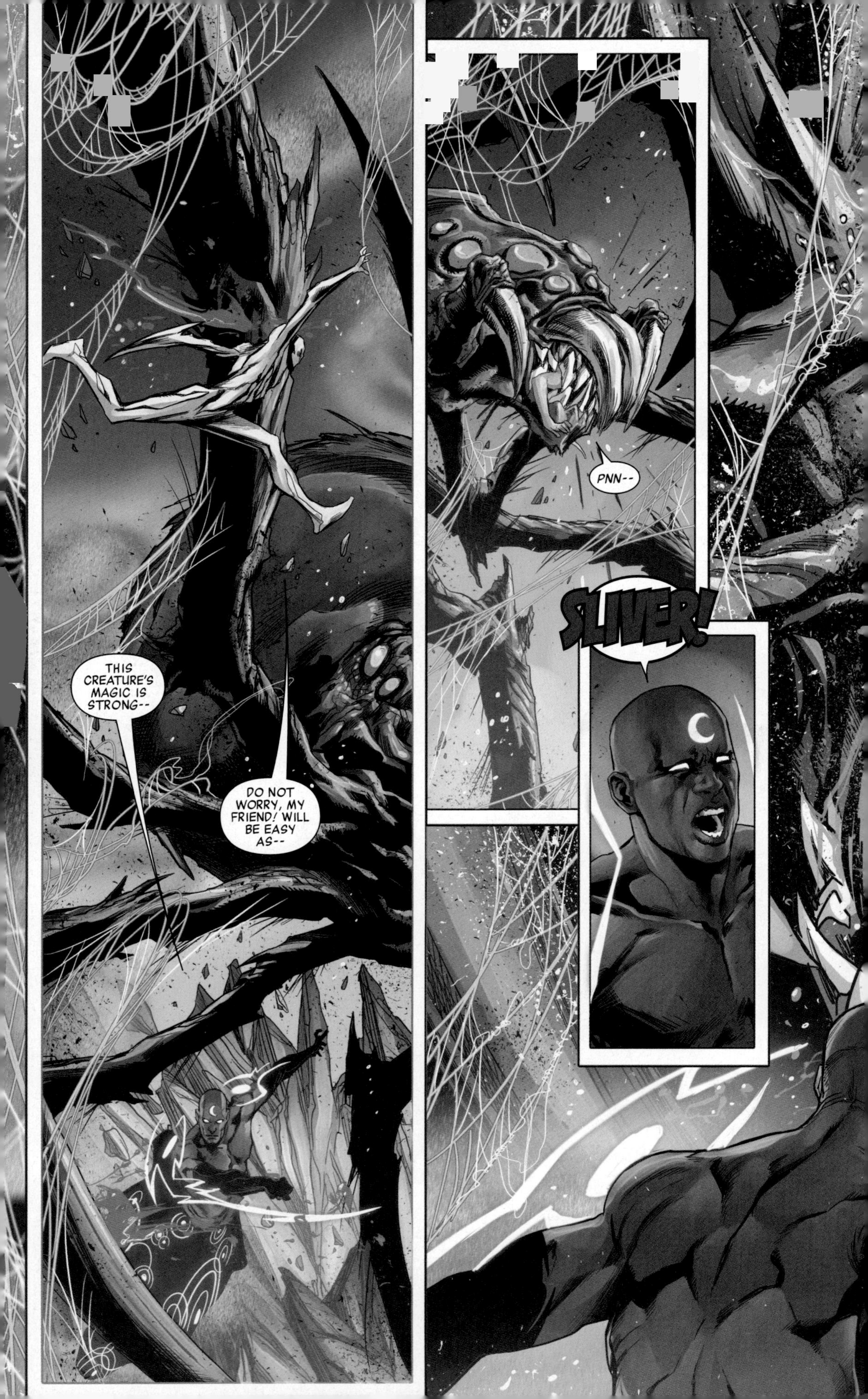
THIS CREATURE'S MAGIC IS STRONG--
DO NOT WORRY, MY FRIEND! WILL BE EASY AS--
PNN--
SLIVER!

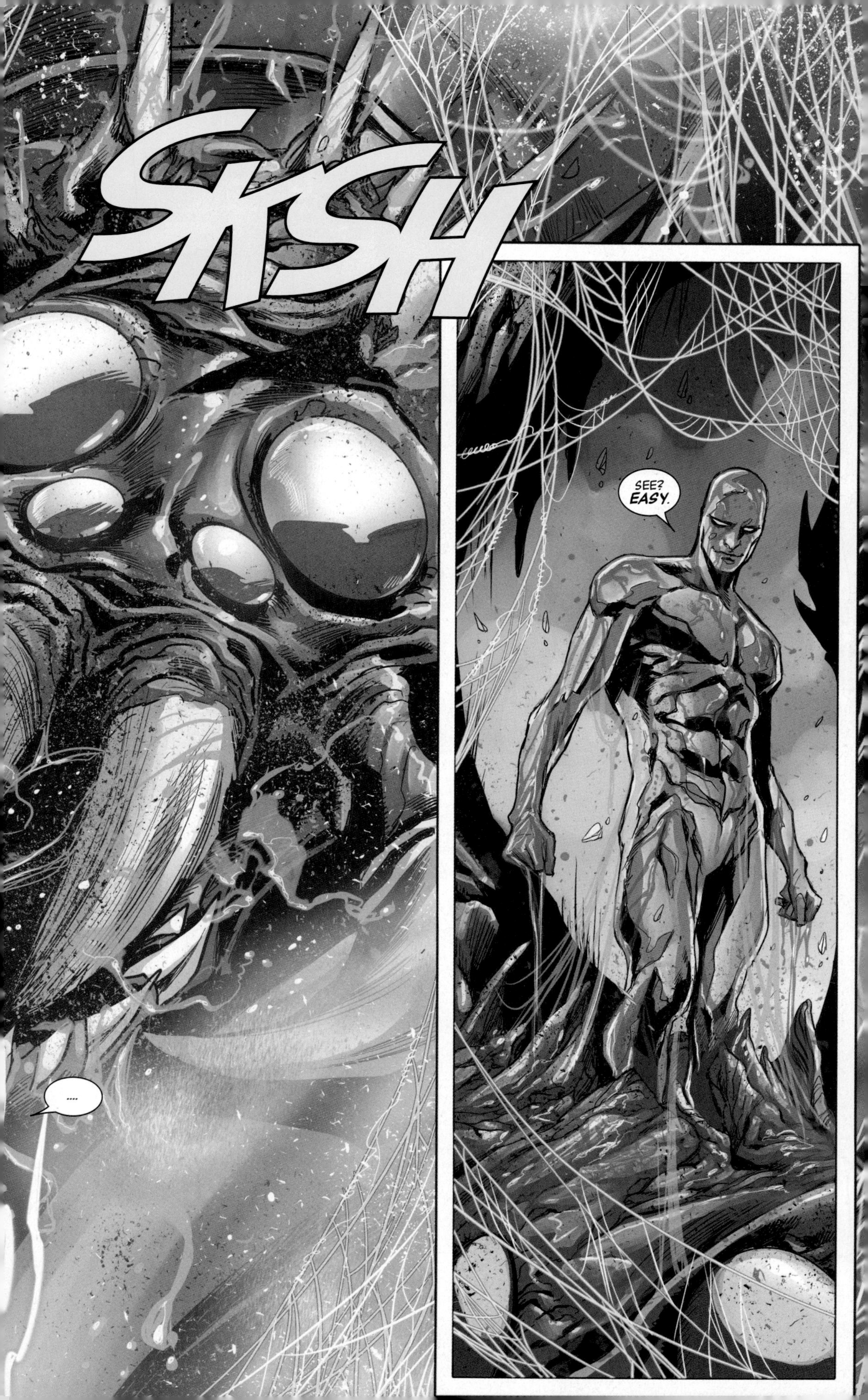
SKSH
SEE? EASY.
....

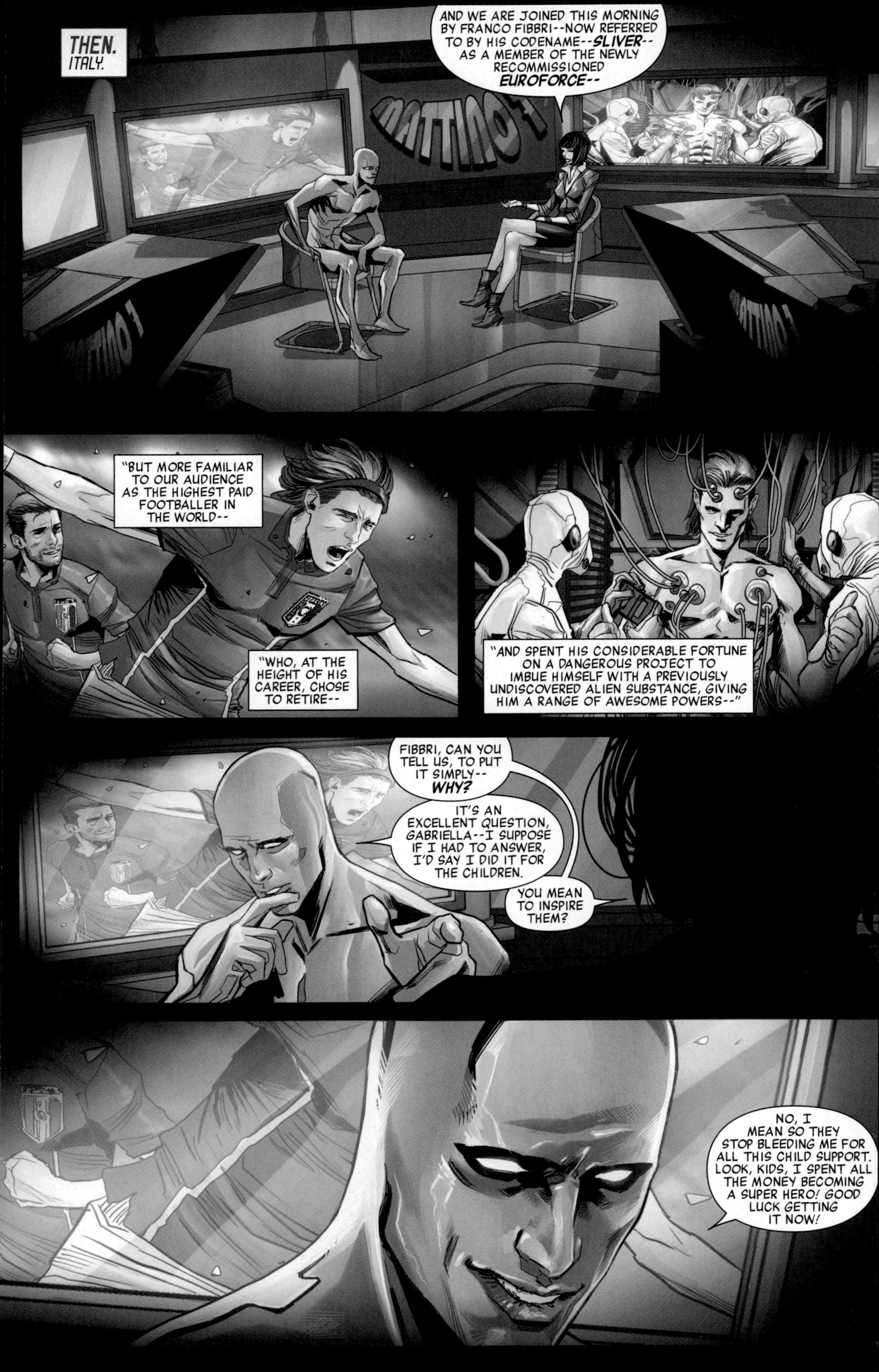
THEN. ITALY.
AND WE ARE JOINED THIS MORNING BY FRANCO FIBBRI--NOW REFERRED TO BY HIS CODENAME--SLIVER--AS A MEMBER OF THE NEWLY RECOMMISSIONED EUROFORCE--
"BUT MORE FAMILIAR TO OUR AUDIENCE AS THE HIGHEST PAID FOOTBALLER IN THE WORLD--
"WHO, AT THE HEIGHT OF HIS CAREER, CHOSE TO RETIRE--
"AND SPENT HIS CONSIDERABLE FORTUNE ON A DANGEROUS PROJECT TO IMBUE HIMSELF WITH A PREVIOUSLY UNDISCOVERED ALIEN SUBSTANCE, GIVING HIM A RANGE OF AWESOME POWERS--"
FIBBRI, CAN YOU TELL US, TO PUT IT SIMPLY--WHY?
IT'S AN EXCELLENT QUESTION, GABRIELLA--I SUPPOSE IF I HAD TO ANSWER, I'D SAY I DID IT FOR THE CHILDREN.
YOU MEAN TO INSPIRE THEM?
NO, I MEAN SO THEY STOP BLEEDING ME FOR ALL THIS CHILD SUPPORT. LOOK, KIDS, I SPENT ALL THE MONEY BECOMING A SUPER HERO! GOOD LUCK GETTING IT NOW!

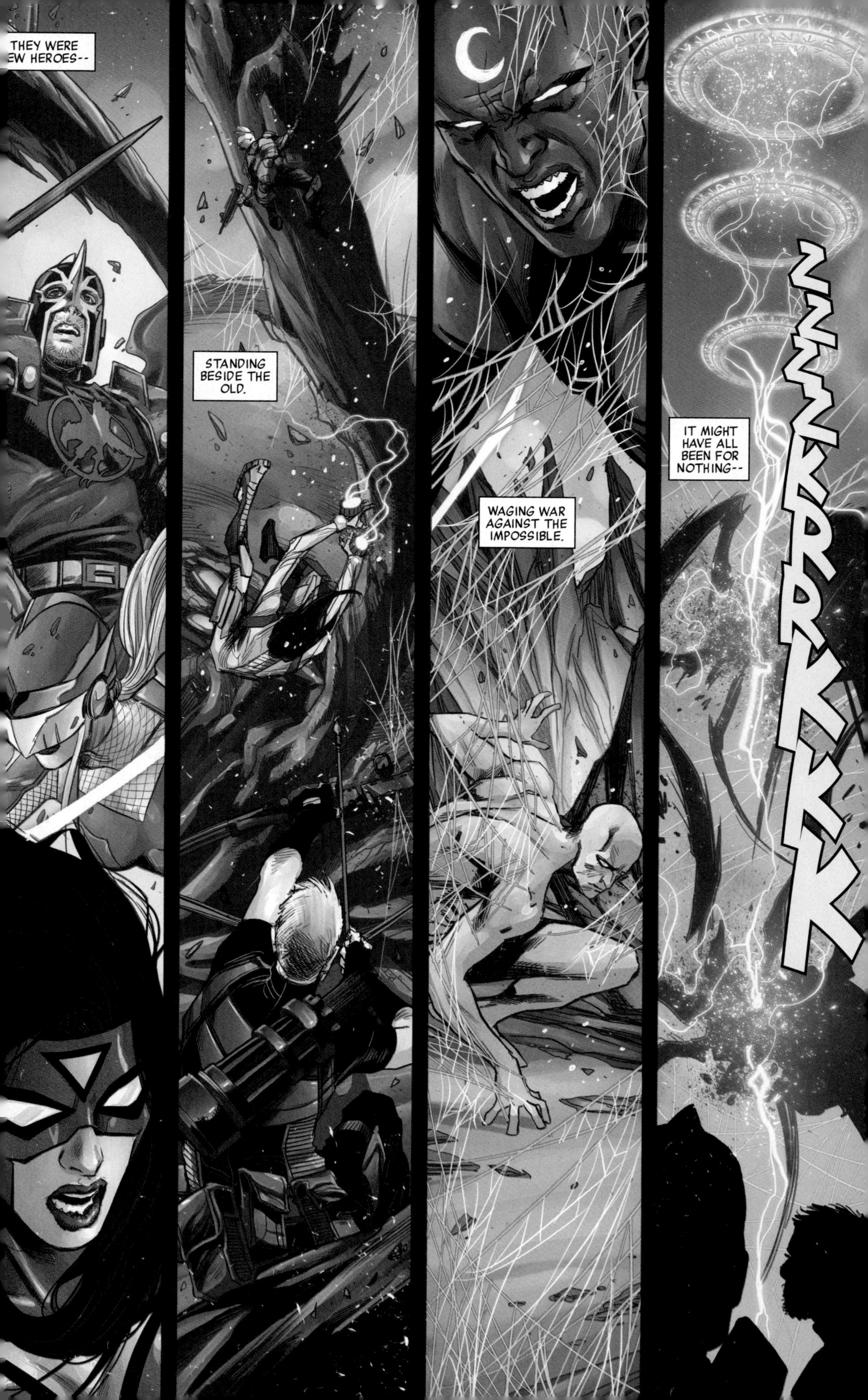
THEY WERE
EW HEROES--
STANDING BESIDE THE OLD.
WAGING WAR AGAINST THE IMPOSSIBLE.
IT MIGHT HAVE ALL BEEN FOR NOTHING--
ZZZKRRKKKK

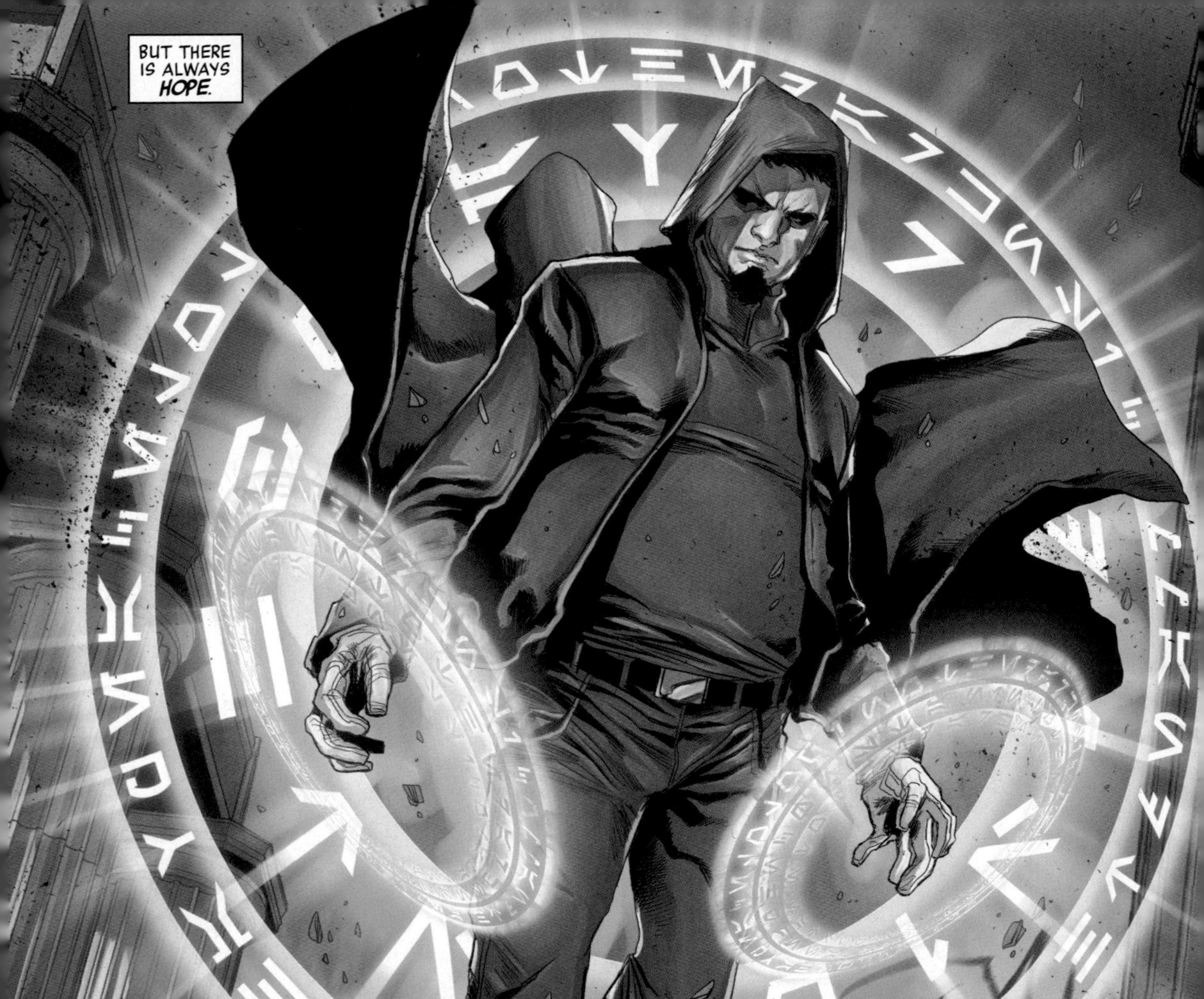
BUT THERE IS ALWAYS HOPE.
SEBASTIAN DRUID. NEW EXPERT OF THE OCCULT.

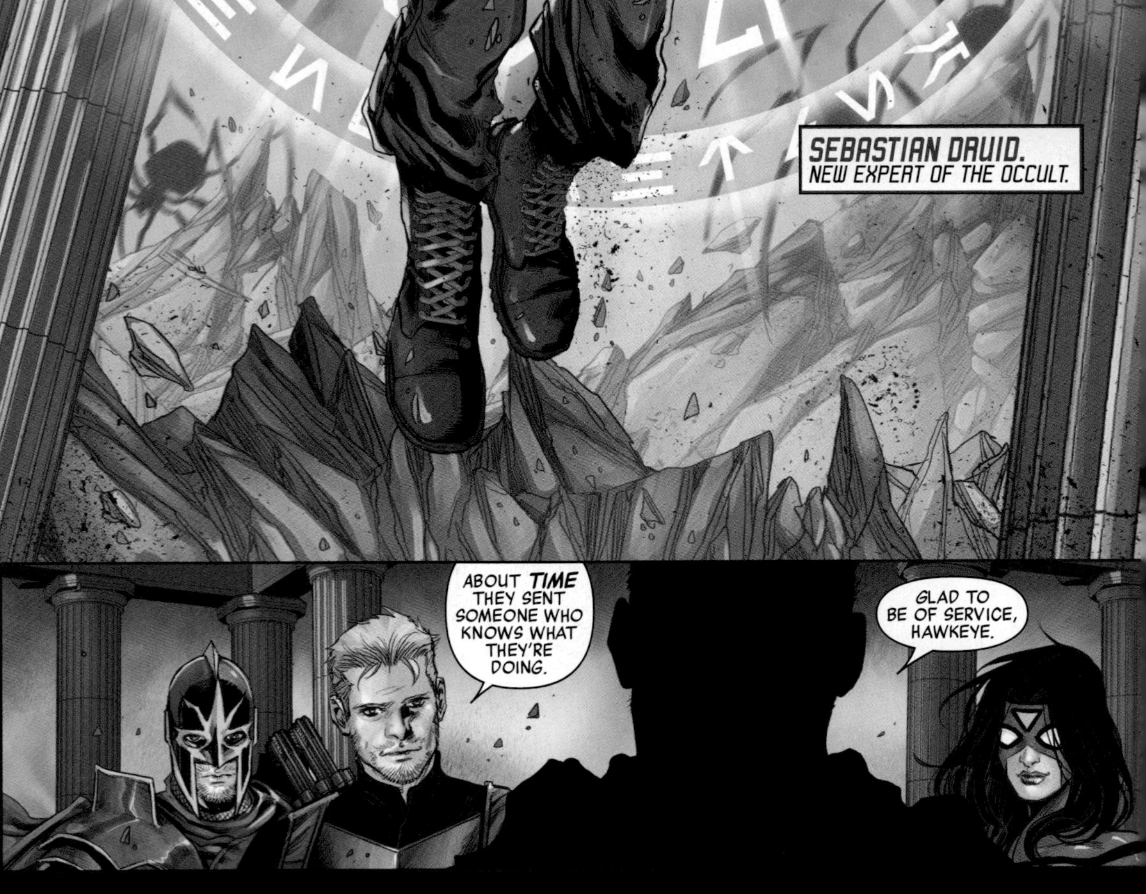
ABOUT TIME THEY SENT SOMEONE WHO KNOWS WHAT THEY'RE DOING.
GLAD TO BE OF SERVICE, HAWKEYE.

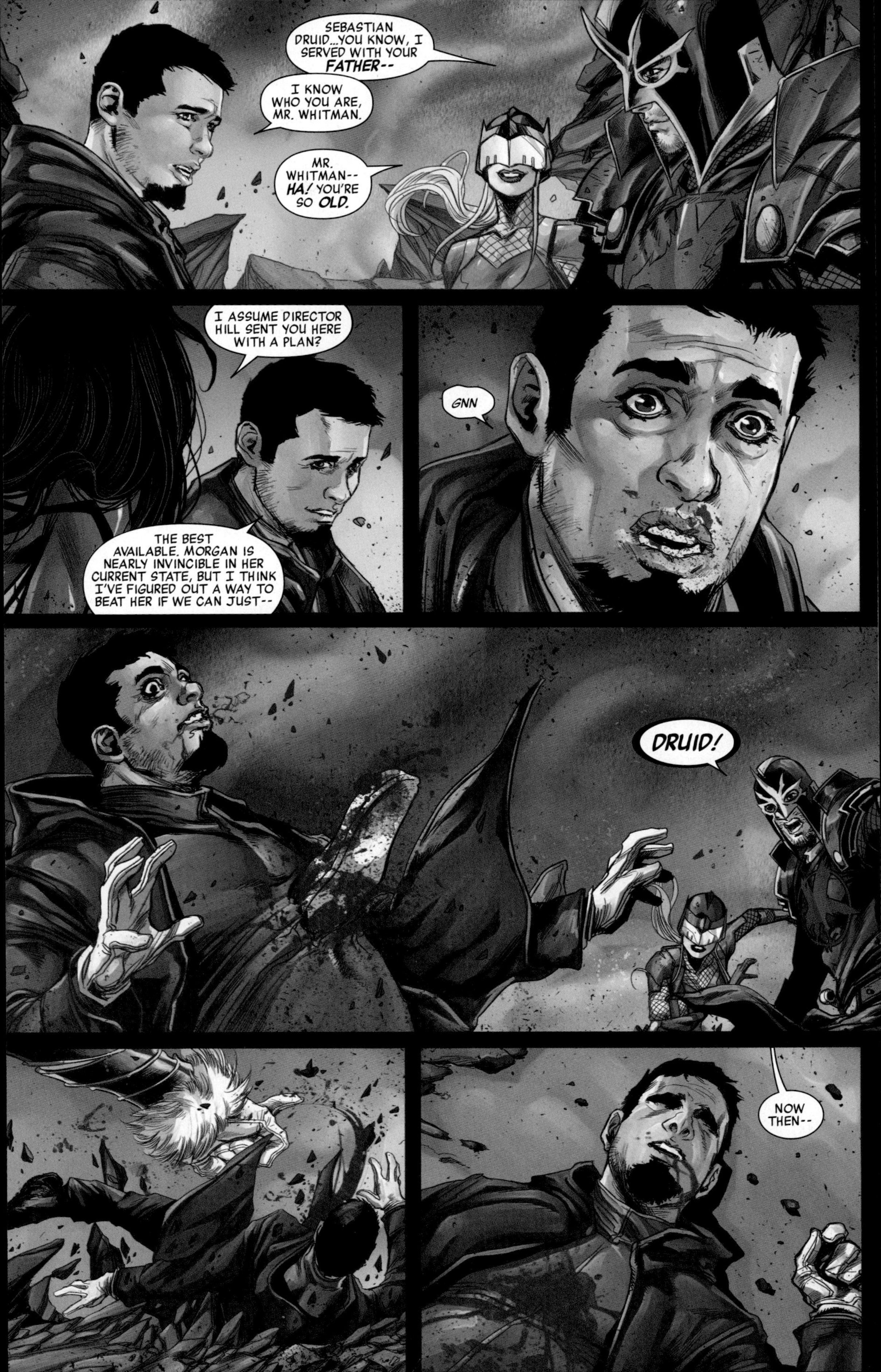
SEBASTIAN DRUID...YOU KNOW, I SERVED WITH YOUR FATHER--
I KNOW WHO YOU ARE, MR. WHITMAN.
MR. WHITMAN-- HA! YOU'RE SO OLD.
I ASSUME DIRECTOR HILL SENT YOU HERE WITH A PLAN?
THE BEST AVAILABLE. MORGAN IS NEARLY INVINCIBLE IN HER CURRENT STATE, BUT I THINK I'VE FIGURED OUT A WAY TO BEAT HER IF WE CAN JUST--
GNN
DRUID!
NOW THEN--

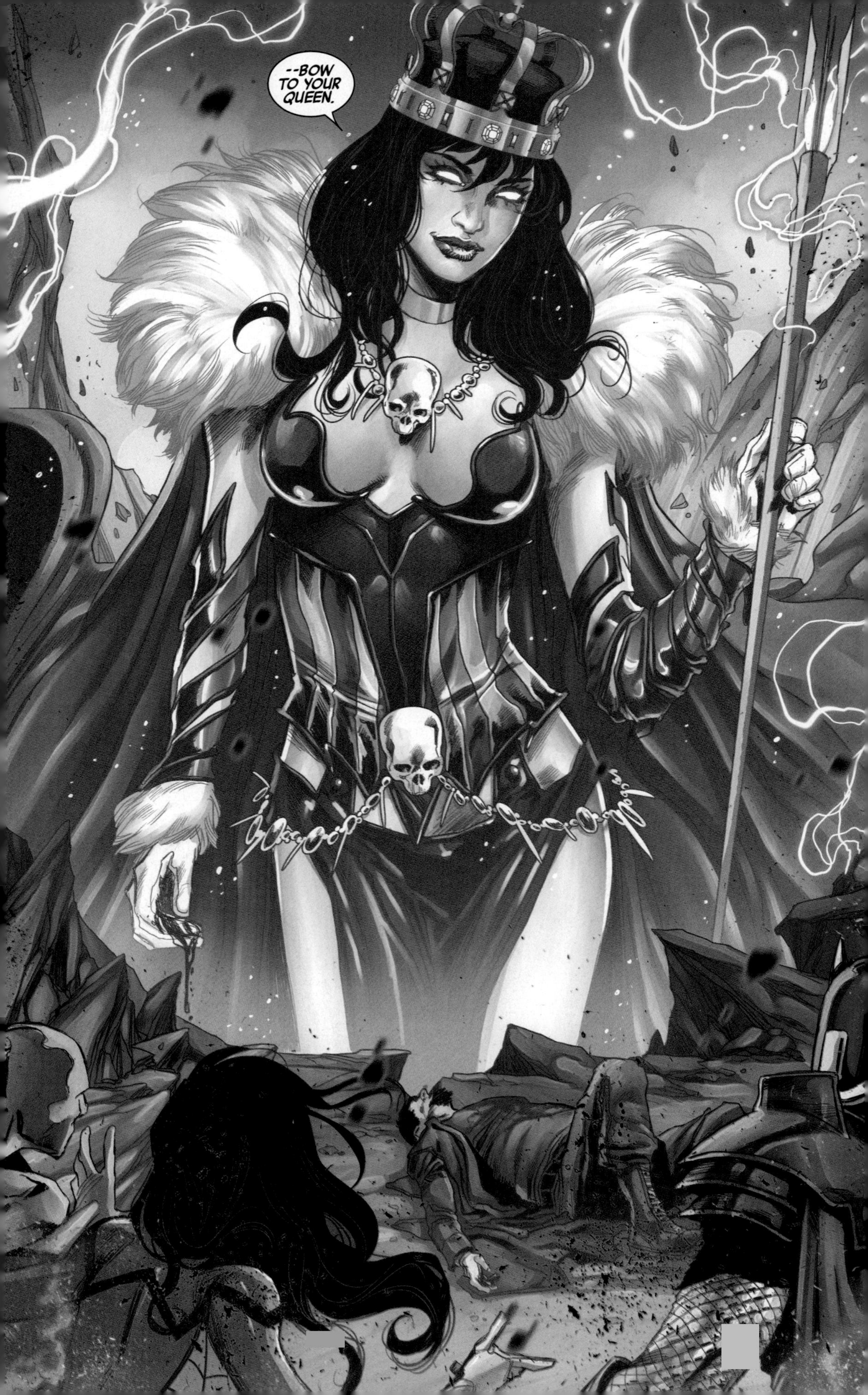
--BOW TO YOUR QUEEN.

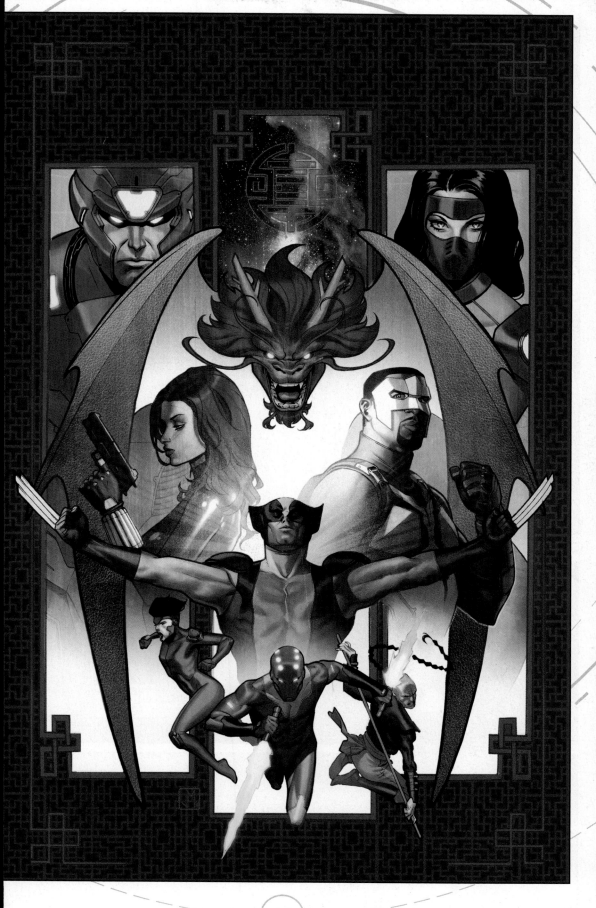

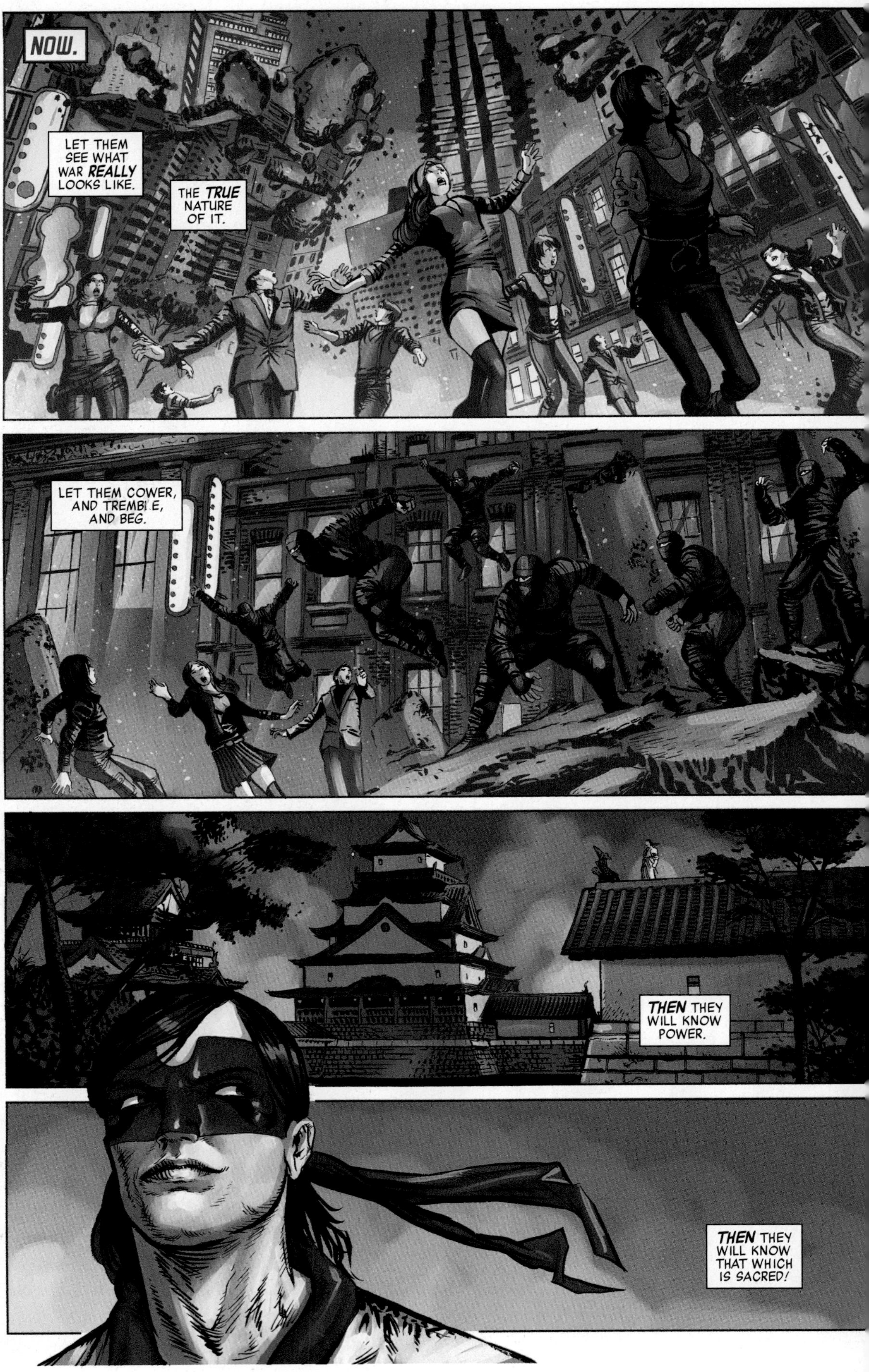
NOW.
LET THEM SEE WHAT WAR REALLY LOOKS LIKE.
THE TRUE NATURE OF IT.
LET THEM COWER, AND TREMBLE, AND BEG.
THEN THEY WILL KNOW POWER.
THEN THEY WILL KNOW THAT WHICH IS SACRED!

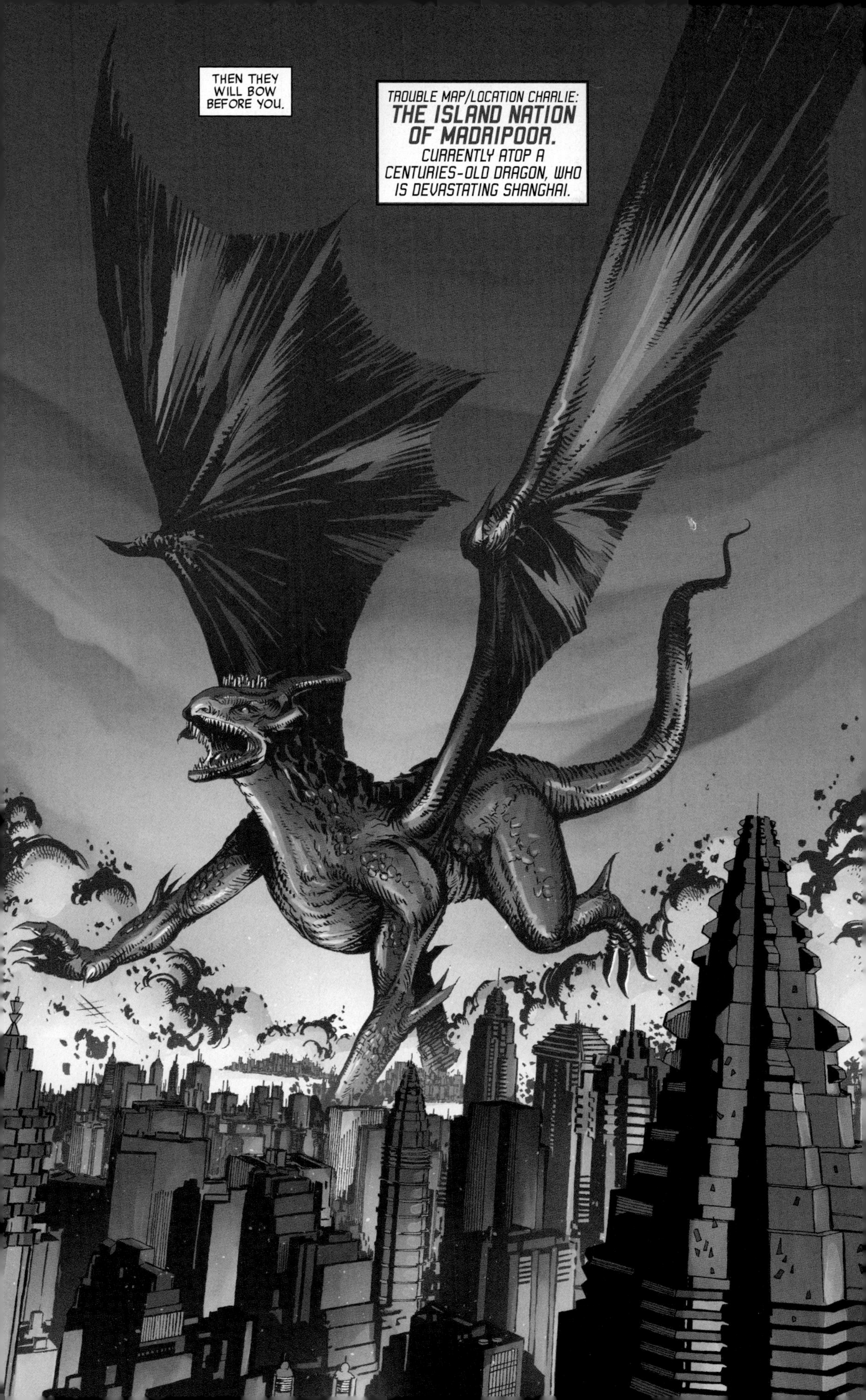
THEN THEY WILL BOW BEFORE YOU.
TROUBLE MAP/LOCATION CHARLIE: THE ISLAND NATION OF MADRIPOOR. CURRENTLY ATOP A CENTURIES-OLD DRAGON, WHO IS DEVASTATING SHANGHAI.

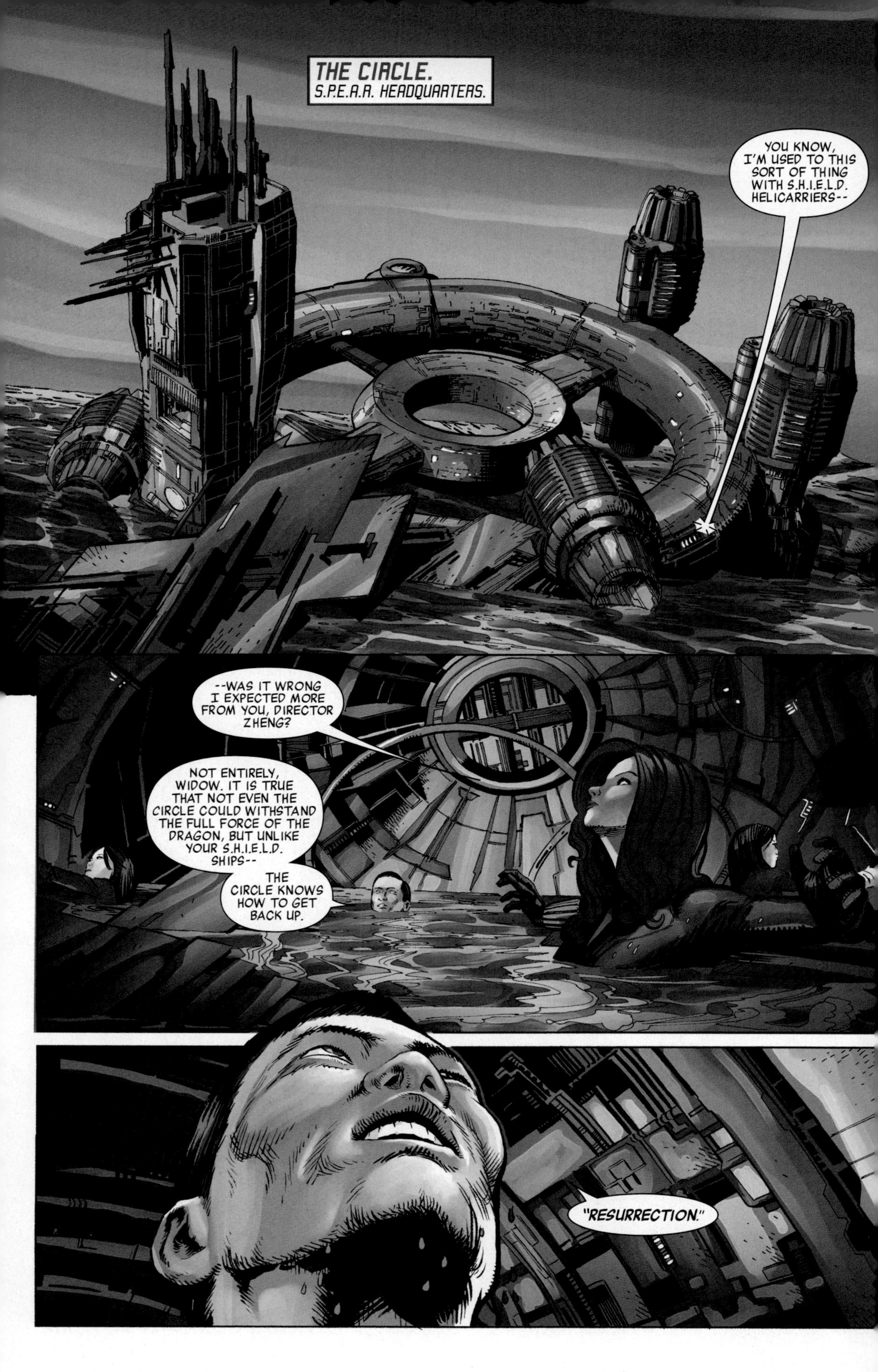
THE CIRCLE.
S.P.E.A.R. HEADQUARTERS.
YOU KNOW, I'M USED TO THIS SORT OF THING WITH S.H.I.E.L.D. HELICARRIERS--
--WAS IT WRONG I EXPECTED MORE FROM YOU, DIRECTOR ZHENG?
NOT ENTIRELY, WIDOW. IT IS TRUE THAT NOT EVEN THE CIRCLE COULD WITHSTAND THE FULL FORCE OF THE DRAGON, BUT UNLIKE YOUR S.H.I.E.L.D. SHIPS--
THE CIRCLE KNOWS HOW TO GET BACK UP.
"RESURRECTION."

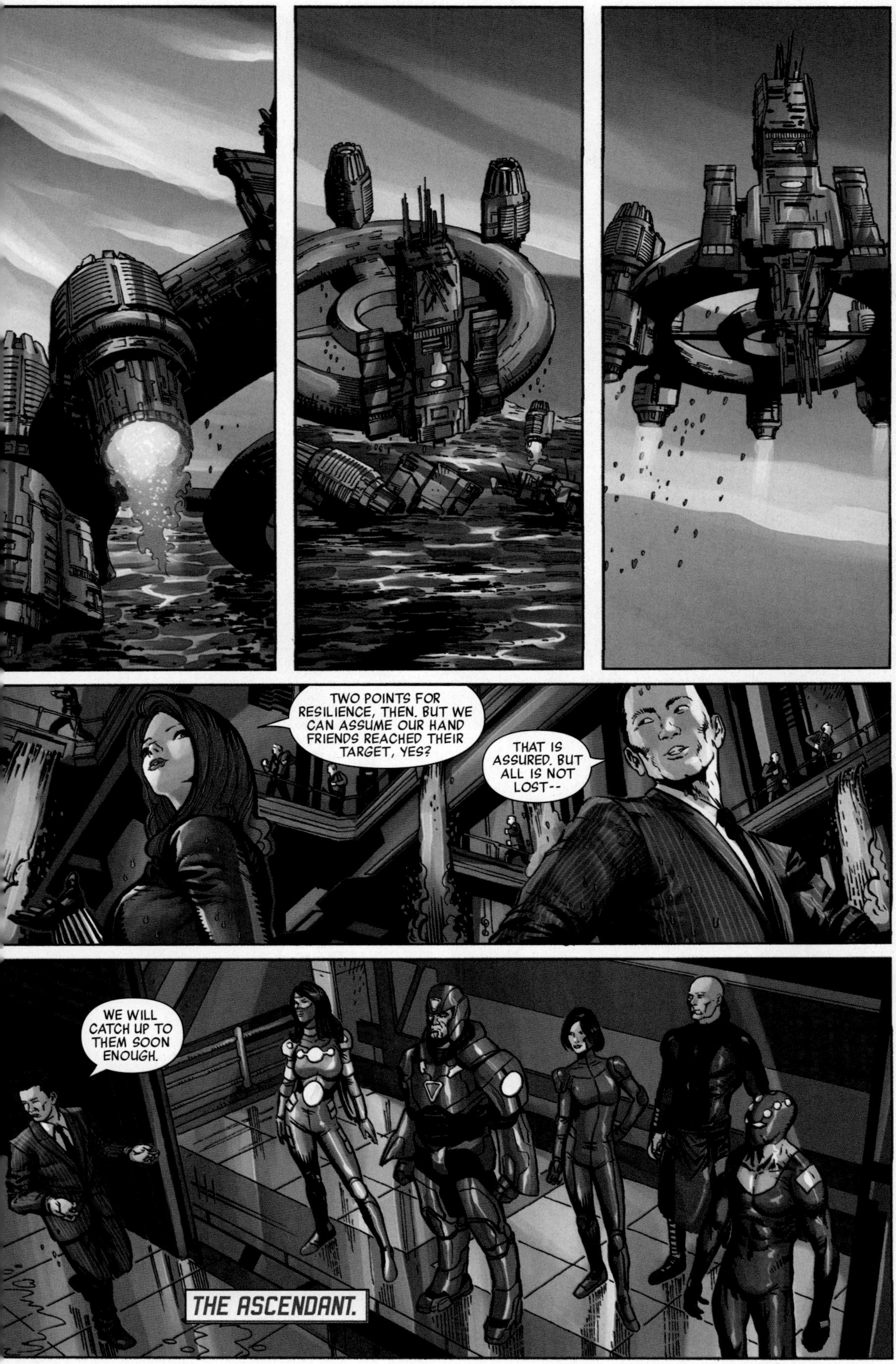

TWO POINTS FOR RESILIENCE, THEN. BUT WE CAN ASSUME OUR HAND FRIENDS REACHED THEIR TARGET, YES?
THAT IS ASSURED. BUT ALL IS NOT LOST--
WE WILL CATCH UP TO THEM SOON ENOUGH.
THE ASCENDANT.

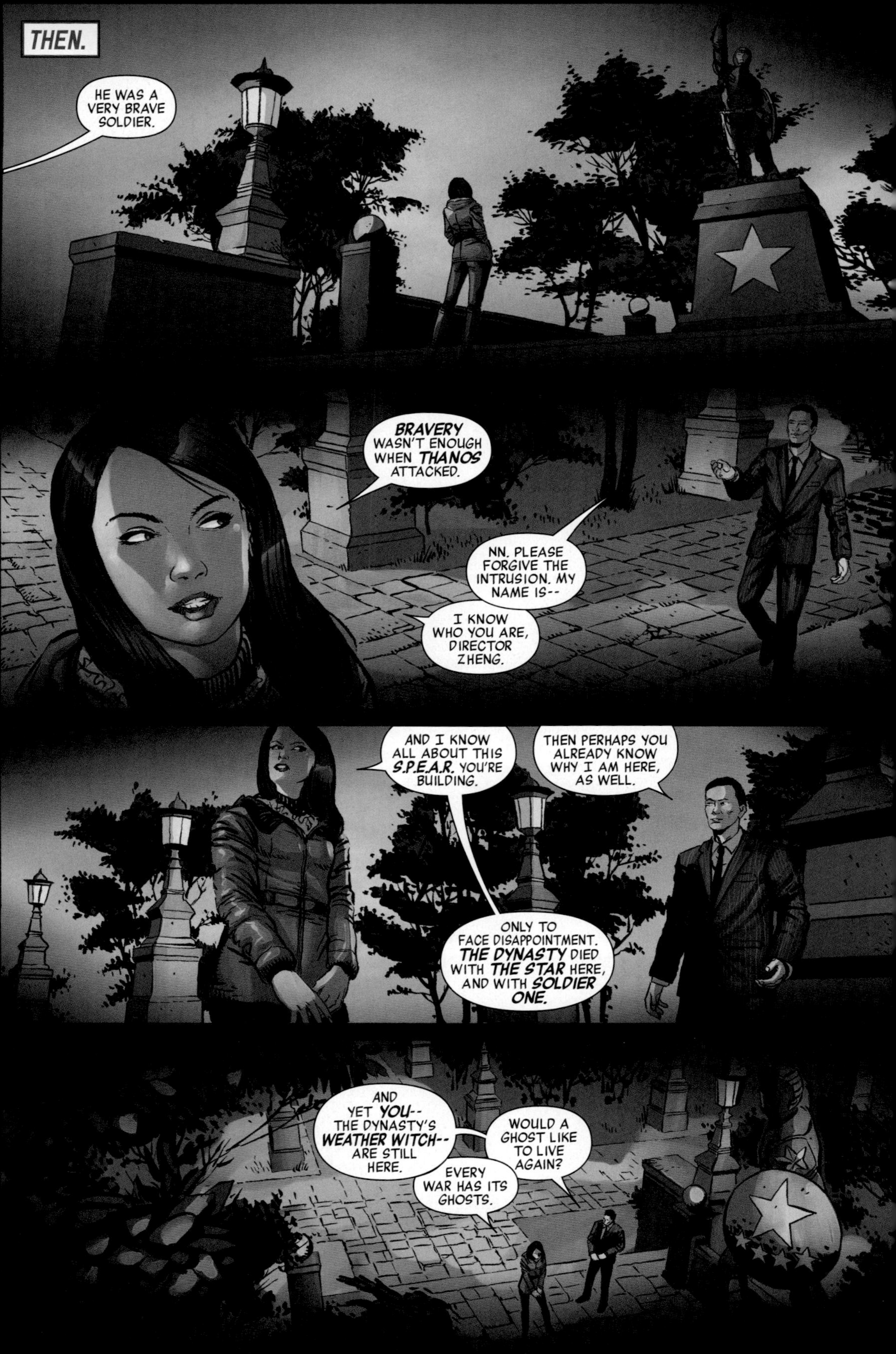
THEN.
HE WAS A VERY BRAVE SOLDIER.
BRAVERY WASN'T ENOUGH WHEN THANOS ATTACKED.
NN. PLEASE FORGIVE THE INTRUSION. MY NAME IS--
I KNOW WHO YOU ARE, DIRECTOR ZHENG.
AND I KNOW ALL ABOUT THIS S.P.E.A.R. YOU'RE BUILDING.
THEN PERHAPS YOU ALREADY KNOW WHY I AM HERE, AS WELL.
ONLY TO FACE DISAPPOINTMENT. THE DYNASTY DIED WITH THE STAR HERE, AND WITH SOLDIER ONE.
AND YET YOU-- THE DYNASTY'S WEATHER WITCH-- ARE STILL HERE.
EVERY WAR HAS ITS GHOSTS.
WOULD A GHOST LIKE TO LIVE AGAIN?

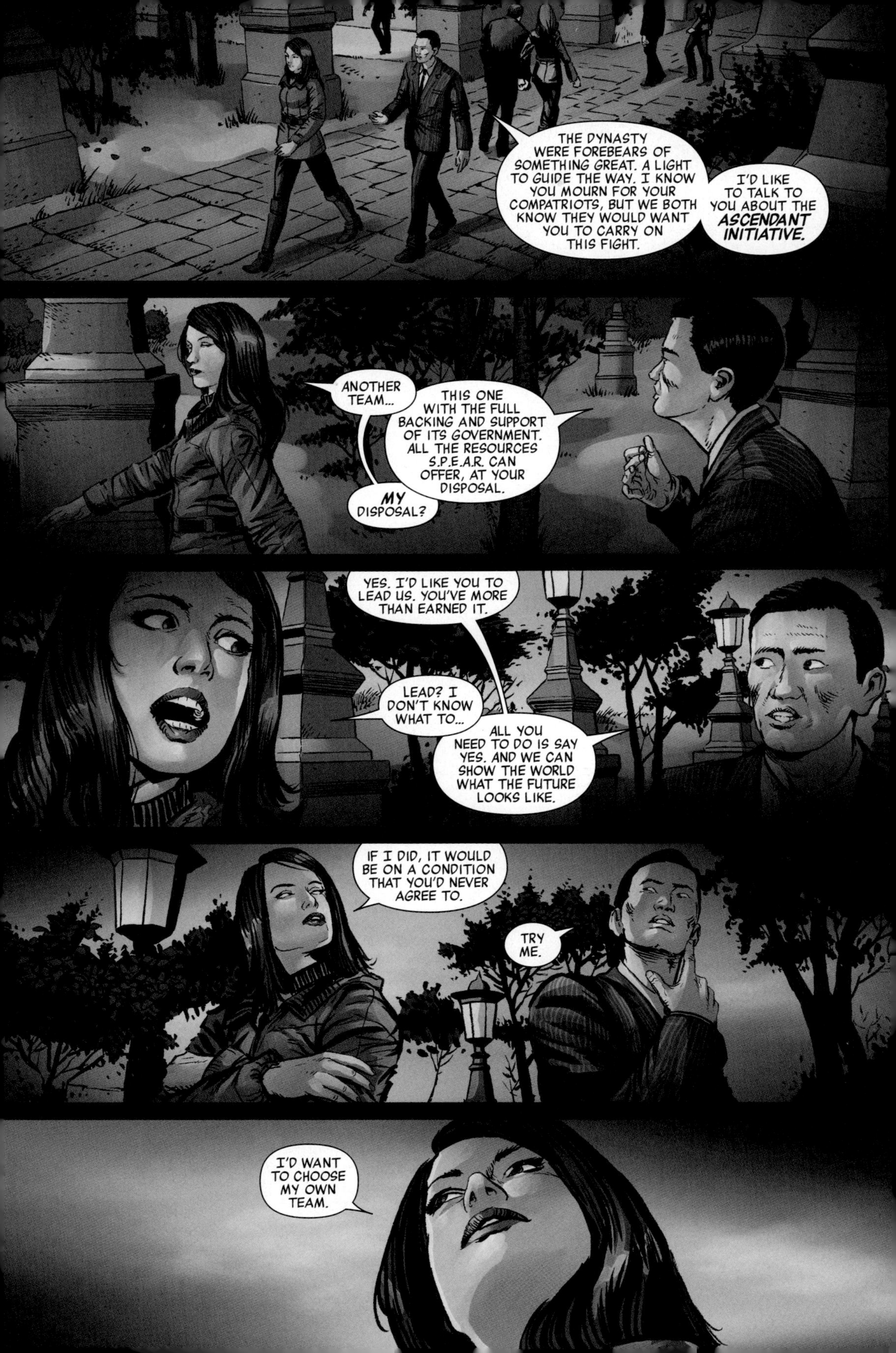
THE DYNASTY WERE FOREBEARS OF SOMETHING GREAT. A LIGHT TO GUIDE THE WAY. I KNOW YOU MOURN FOR YOUR COMPATRIOTS, BUT WE BOTH KNOW THEY WOULD WANT YOU TO CARRY ON THIS FIGHT.
I'D LIKE TO TALK TO YOU ABOUT THE ***ASCENDANT INITIATIVE.***
ANOTHER TEAM...
THIS ONE WITH THE FULL BACKING AND SUPPORT OF ITS GOVERNMENT. ALL THE RESOURCES S.P.E.A.R. CAN OFFER, AT YOUR DISPOSAL.
MY DISPOSAL?
YES. I'D LIKE YOU TO LEAD US. YOU'VE MORE THAN EARNED IT.
LEAD? I DON'T KNOW WHAT TO...
ALL YOU NEED TO DO IS SAY YES. AND WE CAN SHOW THE WORLD WHAT THE FUTURE LOOKS LIKE.
IF I DID, IT WOULD BE ON A CONDITION THAT YOU'D NEVER AGREE TO.
TRY ME.
I'D WANT TO CHOOSE MY OWN TEAM.

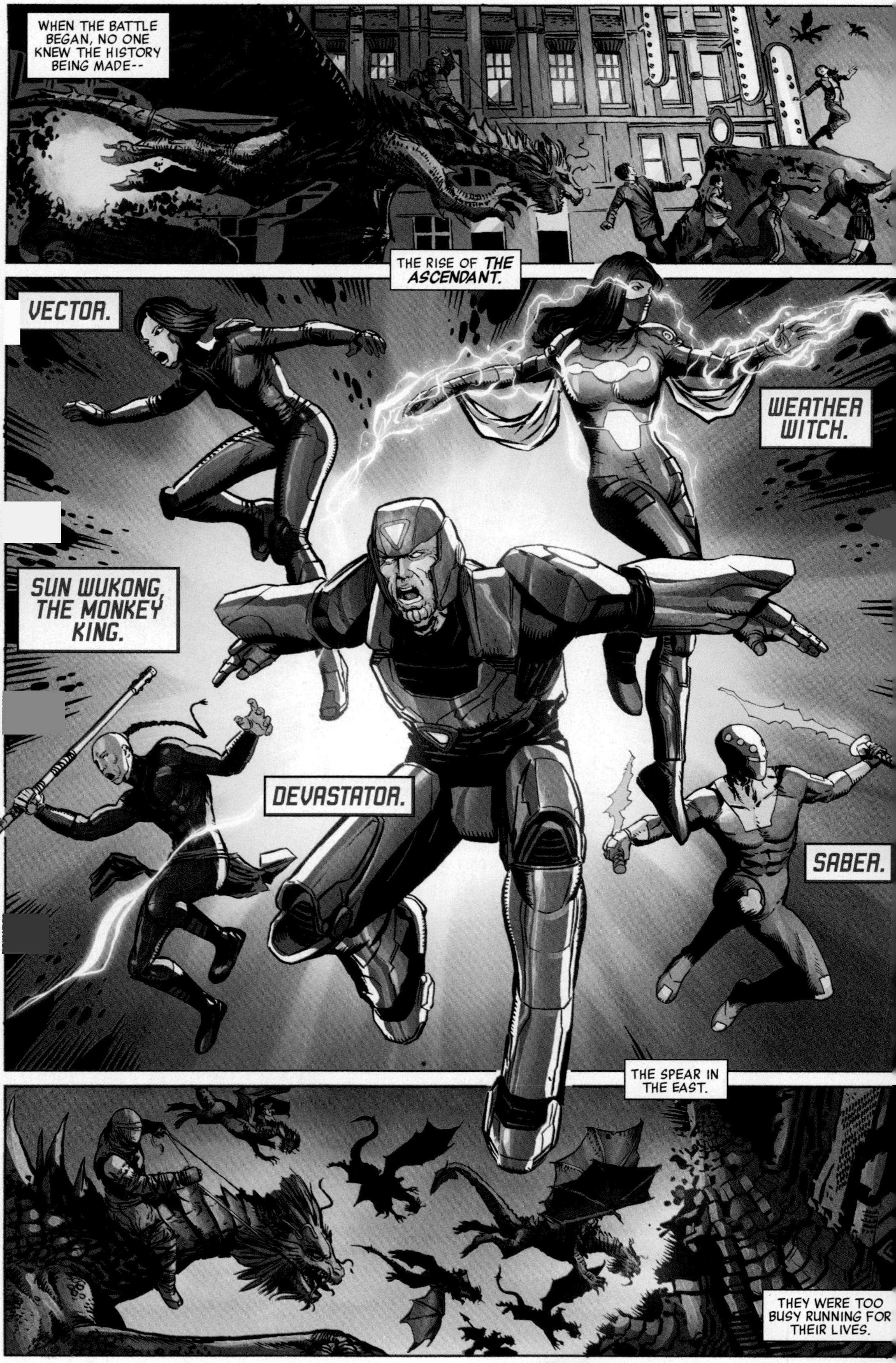
WHEN THE BATTLE BEGAN, NO ONE KNEW THE HISTORY BEING MADE--
THE RISE OF THE ASCENDANT.
VECTOR.
WEATHER WITCH.
SUN WUKONG, THE MONKEY KING.
DEVASTATOR.
SABER.
THE SPEAR IN THE EAST.
THEY WERE TOO BUSY RUNNING FOR THEIR LIVES.

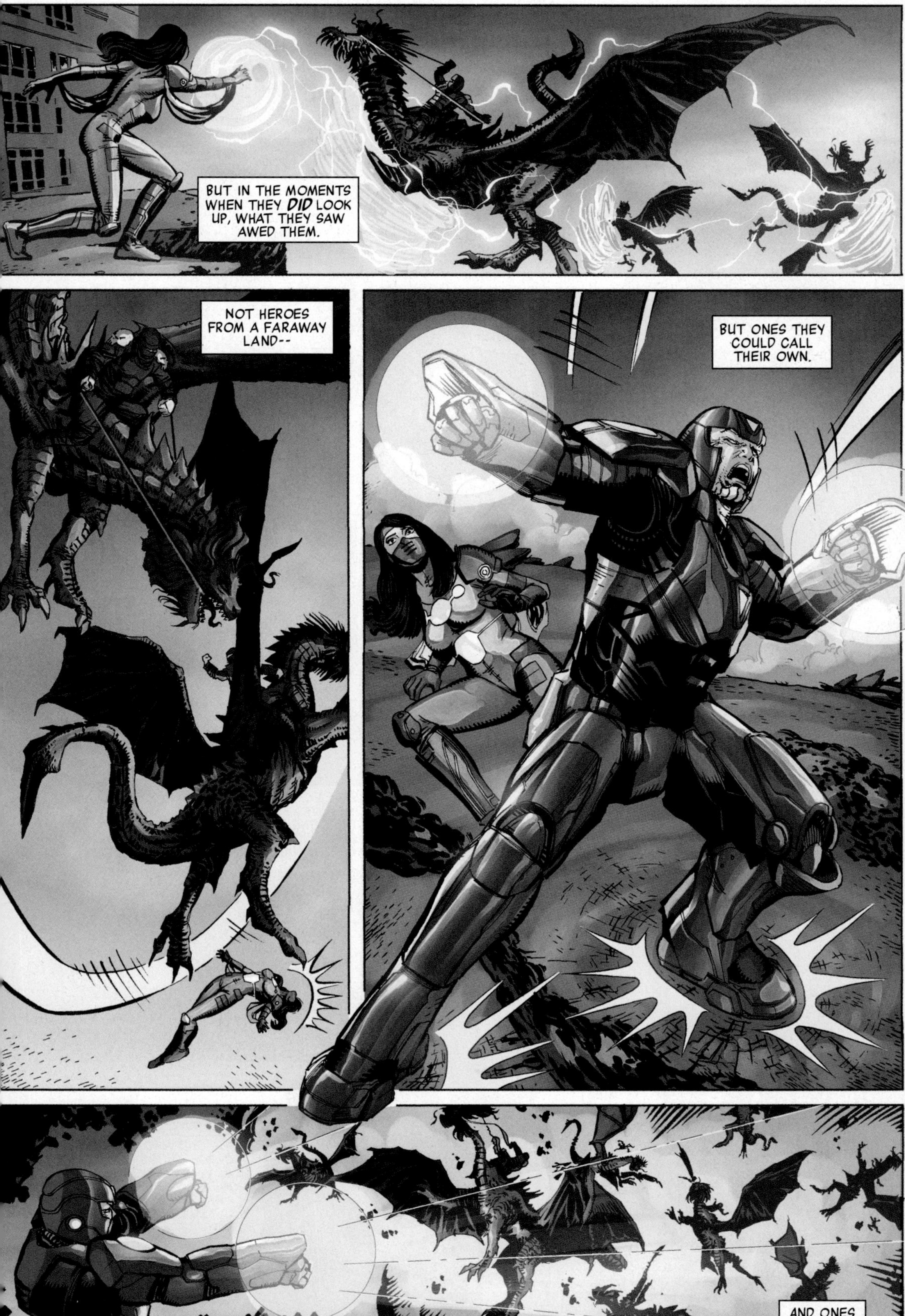
BUT IN THE MOMENTS WHEN THEY DID LOOK UP, WHAT THEY SAW AWED THEM.
NOT HEROES FROM A FARAWAY LAND--
BUT ONES THEY COULD CALL THEIR OWN.
AND ONES WHO WERE WORTHY.

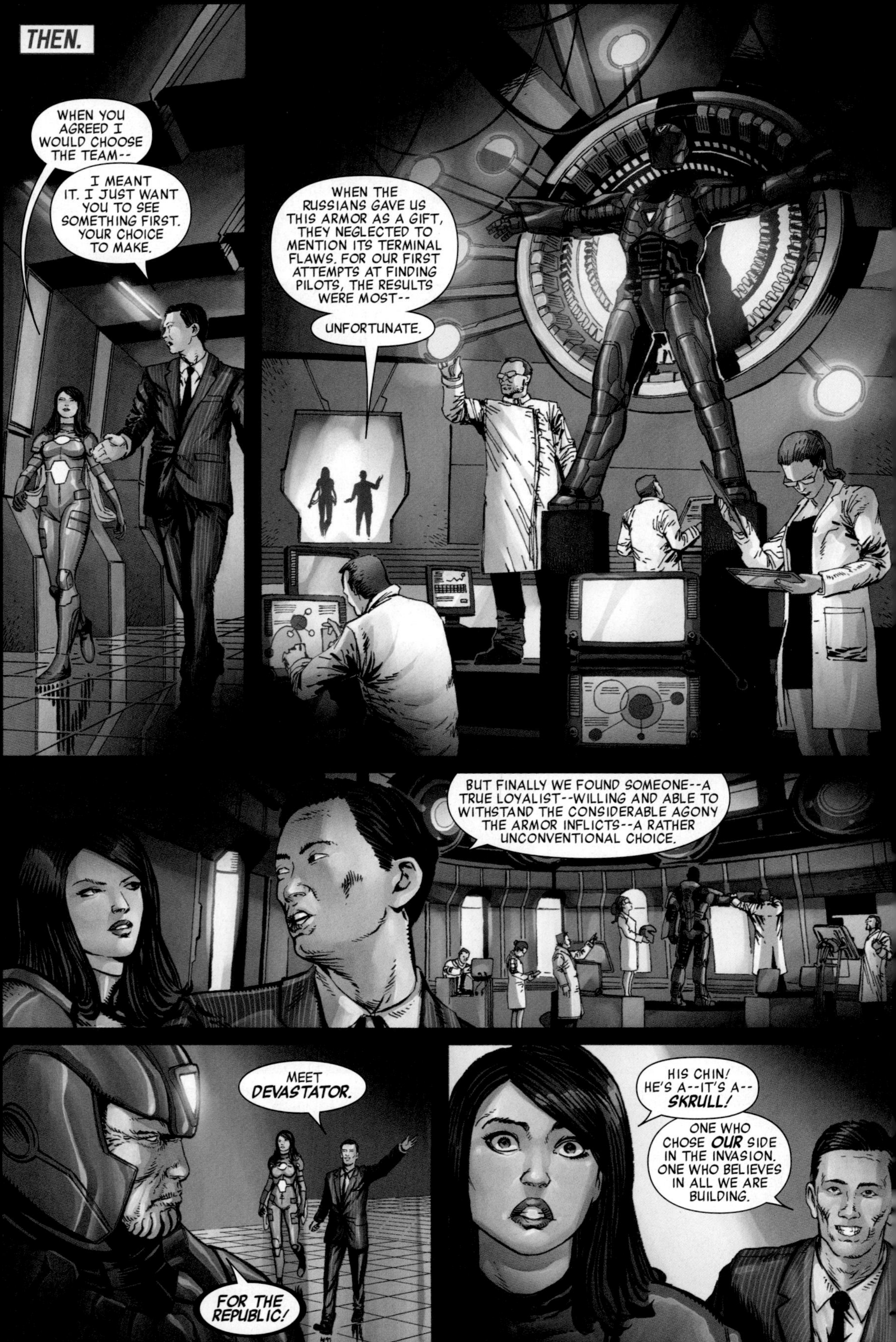
THEN.
WHEN YOU AGREED I WOULD CHOOSE THE TEAM--
I MEANT IT. I JUST WANT YOU TO SEE SOMETHING FIRST. YOUR CHOICE TO MAKE.
WHEN THE RUSSIANS GAVE US THIS ARMOR AS A GIFT, THEY NEGLECTED TO MENTION ITS TERMINAL FLAWS. FOR OUR FIRST ATTEMPTS AT FINDING PILOTS, THE RESULTS WERE MOST--
UNFORTUNATE.
BUT FINALLY WE FOUND SOMEONE--A TRUE LOYALIST--WILLING AND ABLE TO WITHSTAND THE CONSIDERABLE AGONY THE ARMOR INFLICTS--A RATHER UNCONVENTIONAL CHOICE.
MEET DEVASTATOR.
FOR THE REPUBLIC!
HIS CHIN! HE'S A--IT'S A--SKRULL!
ONE WHO CHOSE OUR SIDE IN THE INVASION. ONE WHO BELIEVES IN ALL WE ARE BUILDING.

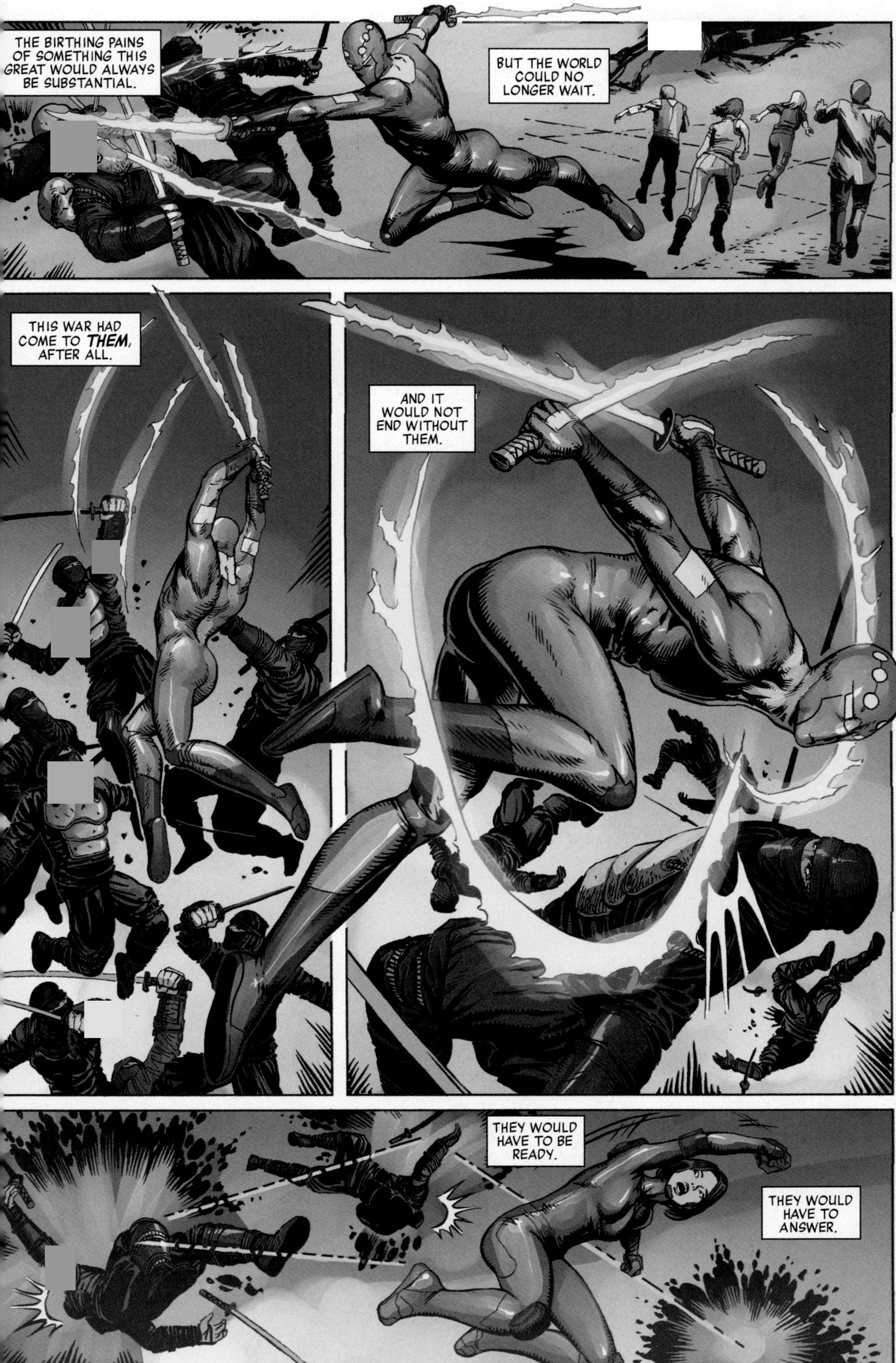
THE BIRTHING PAINS OF SOMETHING THIS GREAT WOULD ALWAYS BE SUBSTANTIAL.
BUT THE WORLD COULD NO LONGER WAIT.
THIS WAR HAD COME TO *THEM*, AFTER ALL.
AND IT WOULD NOT END WITHOUT THEM.
THEY WOULD HAVE TO BE READY.
THEY WOULD HAVE TO ANSWER.

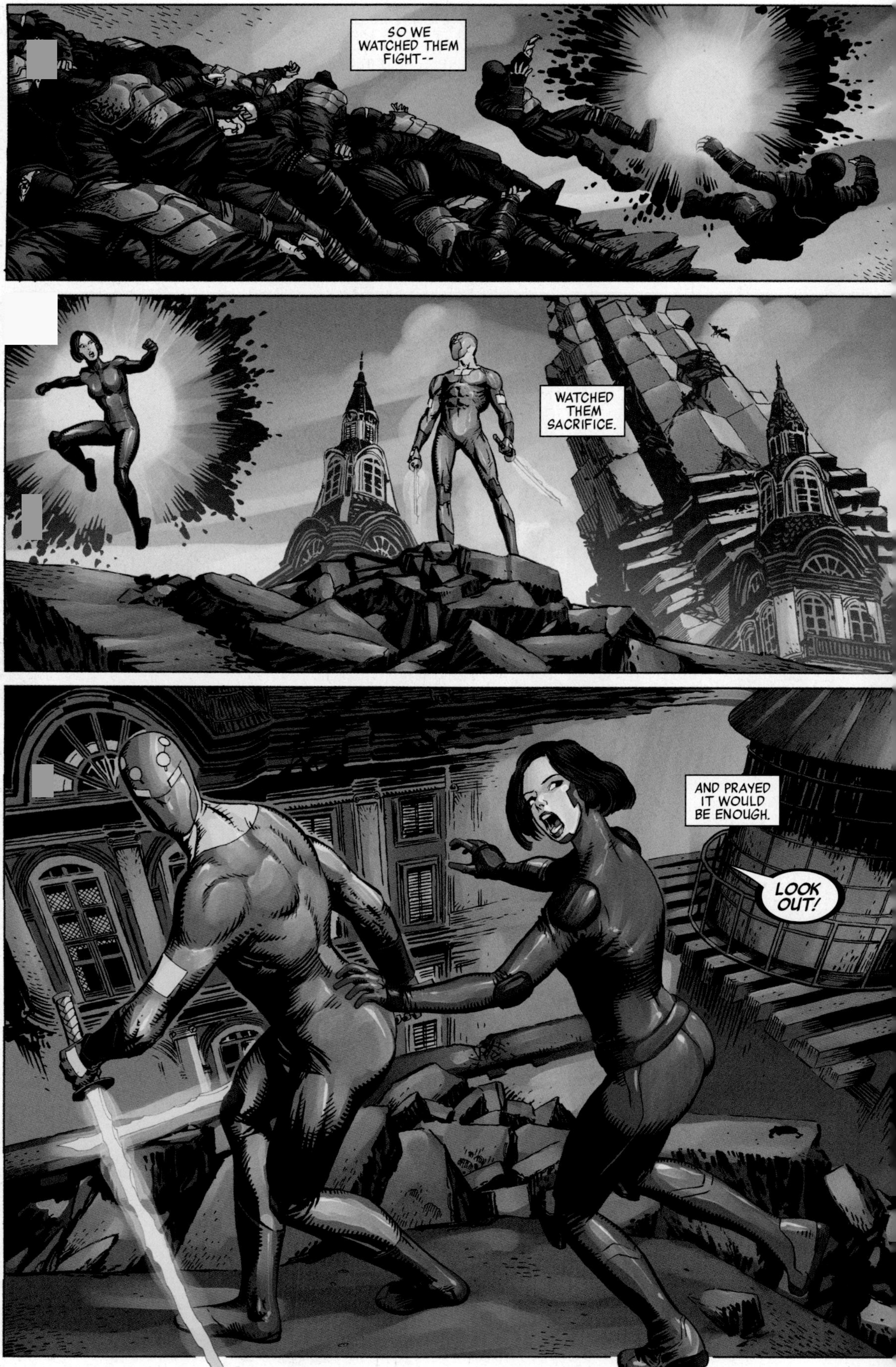
SO WE WATCHED THEM FIGHT--
WATCHED THEM SACRIFICE.
AND PRAYED IT WOULD BE ENOUGH.
LOOK OUT!

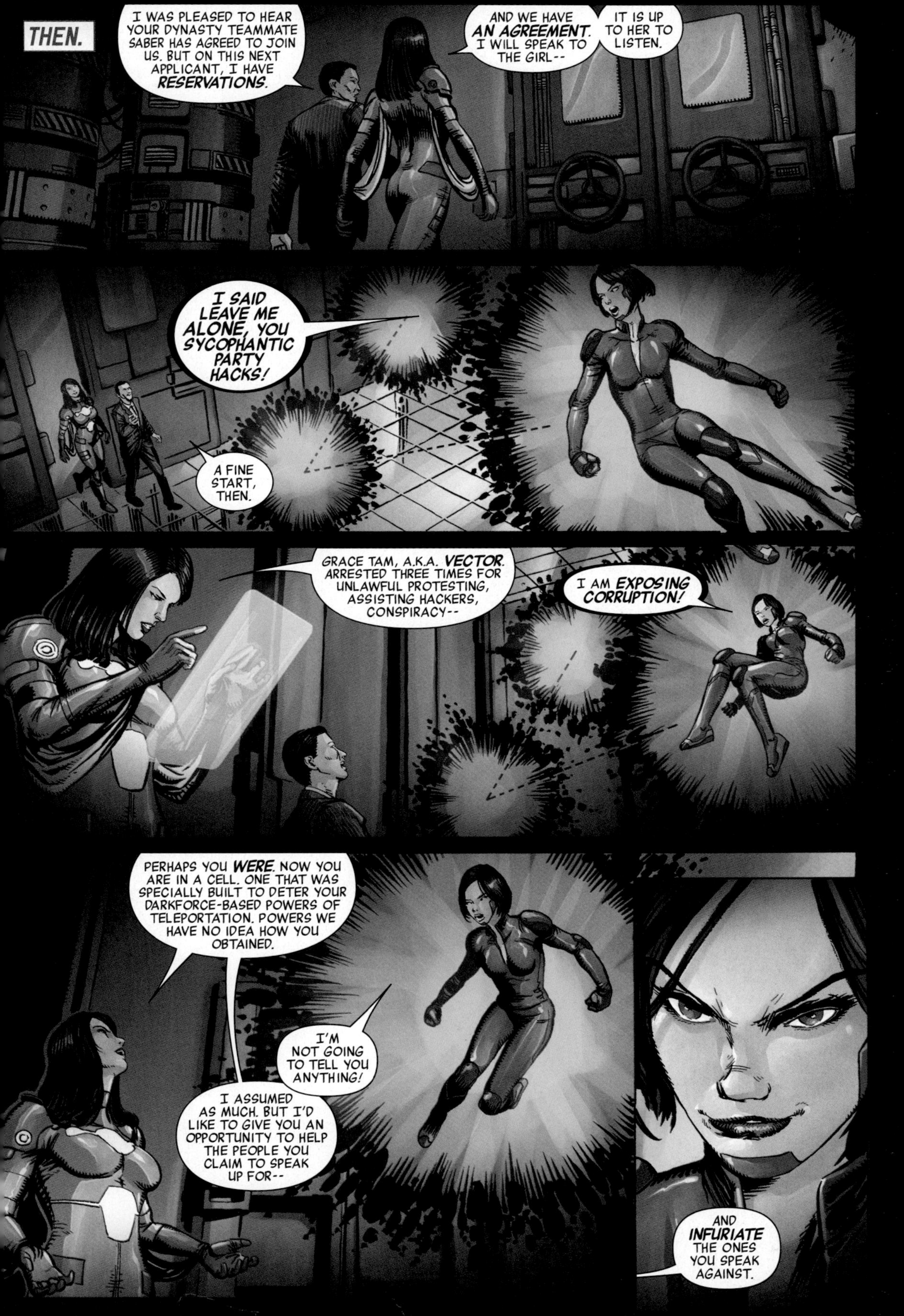
THEN.
I WAS PLEASED TO HEAR YOUR DYNASTY TEAMMATE SABER HAS AGREED TO JOIN US. BUT ON THIS NEXT APPLICANT, I HAVE RESERVATIONS.
AND WE HAVE AN AGREEMENT. I WILL SPEAK TO THE GIRL--
IT IS UP TO HER TO LISTEN.
I SAID LEAVE ME ALONE, YOU SYCOPHANTIC PARTY HACKS!
A FINE START, THEN.
GRACE TAM, A.K.A. VECTOR. ARRESTED THREE TIMES FOR UNLAWFUL PROTESTING, ASSISTING HACKERS, CONSPIRACY--
I AM EXPOSING CORRUPTION!
PERHAPS YOU WERE. NOW YOU ARE IN A CELL. ONE THAT WAS SPECIALLY BUILT TO DETER YOUR DARKFORCE-BASED POWERS OF TELEPORTATION. POWERS WE HAVE NO IDEA HOW YOU OBTAINED.
I'M NOT GOING TO TELL YOU ANYTHING!
I ASSUMED AS MUCH. BUT I'D LIKE TO GIVE YOU AN OPPORTUNITY TO HELP THE PEOPLE YOU CLAIM TO SPEAK UP FOR--
AND INFURIATE THE ONES YOU SPEAK AGAINST.

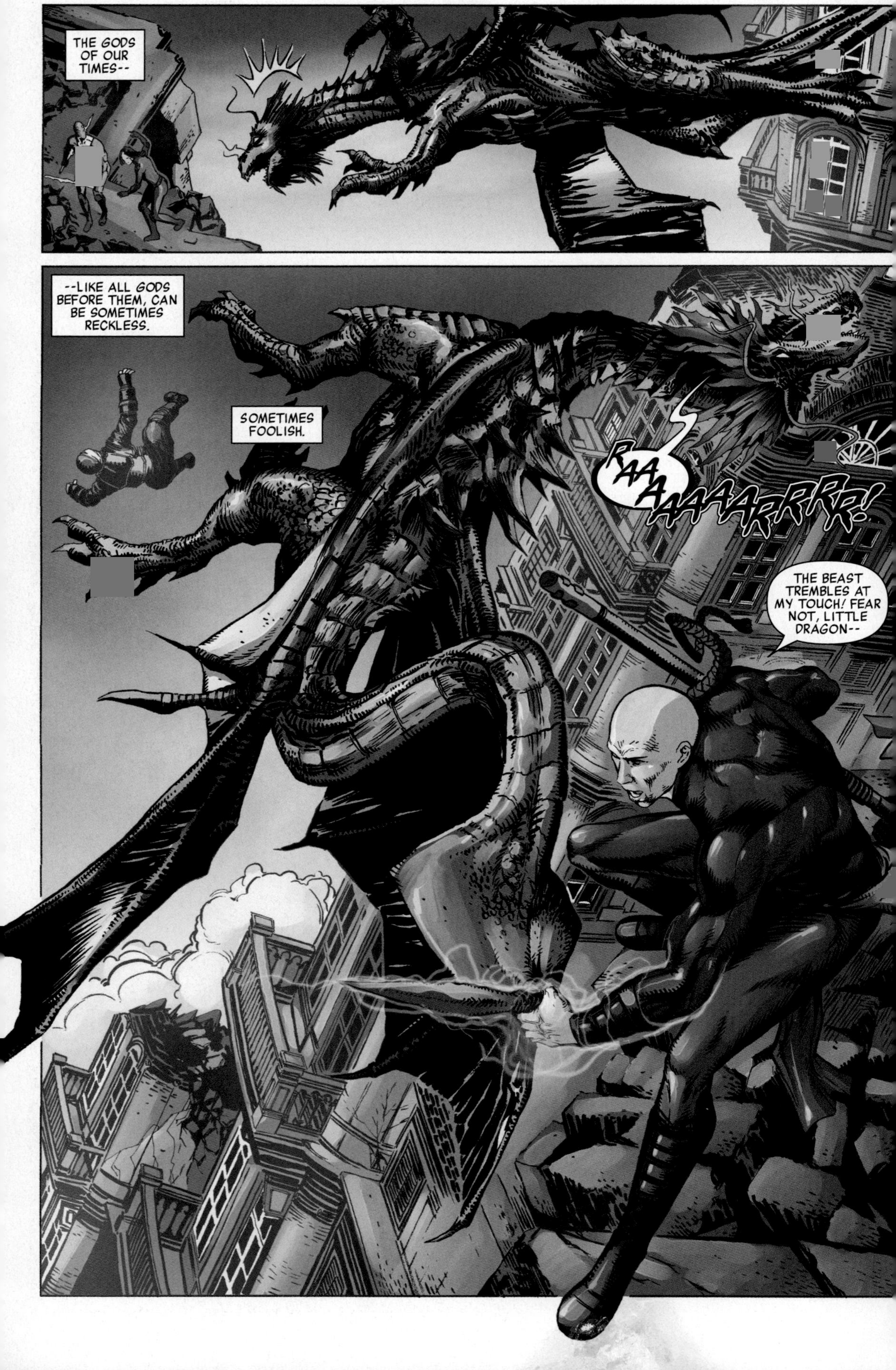
THE GODS OF OUR TIMES--
--LIKE ALL GODS BEFORE THEM, CAN BE SOMETIMES RECKLESS.
SOMETIMES FOOLISH.
RAAAAAAARRRR!
THE BEAST TREMBLES AT MY TOUCH! FEAR NOT, LITTLE DRAGON--

BUT ALSO ABLE TO AWAKEN SOMETHING INSIDE OF US.

SOMETHING *MORE*.

AND IF WHAT THEY GAVE WAS INDEED NOT ENOUGH...

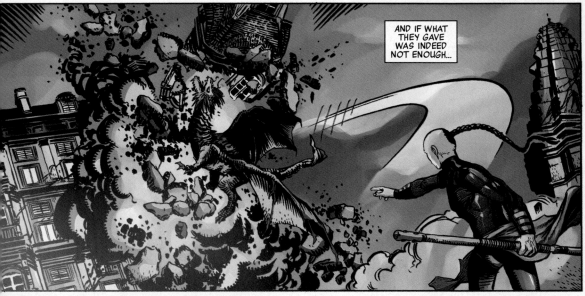

--I WILL LET NO ONE INTERRUPT YOUR SLUMBER!

...THEN *WE* WOULD BE READY TO GIVE AS WELL.

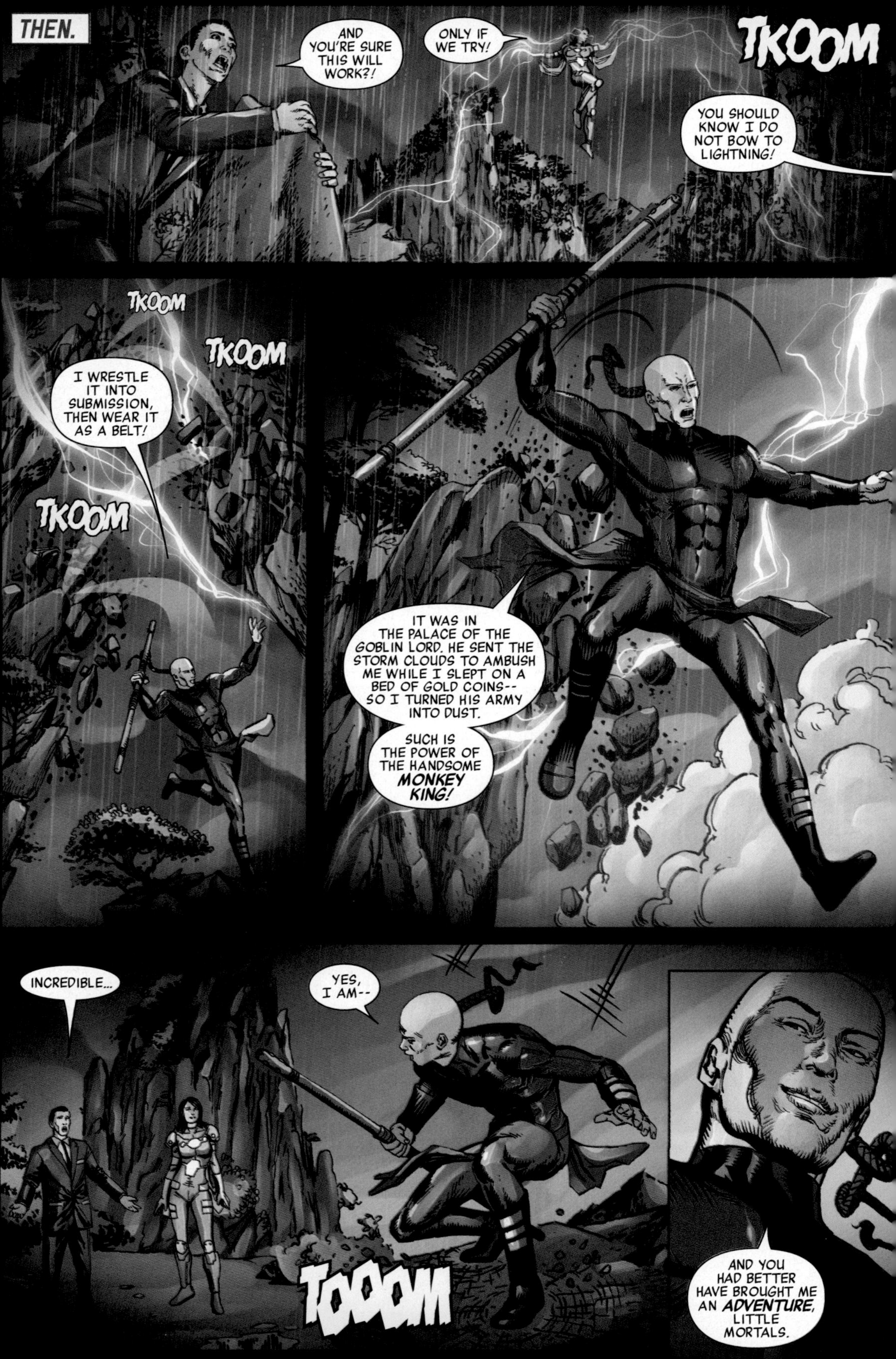
THEN.
AND YOU'RE SURE THIS WILL WORK?!
ONLY IF WE TRY!
TKOOM
YOU SHOULD KNOW I DO NOT BOW TO LIGHTNING!
TKOOM
TKOOM
I WRESTLE IT INTO SUBMISSION, THEN WEAR IT AS A BELT!
TKOOM
IT WAS IN THE PALACE OF THE GOBLIN LORD. HE SENT THE STORM CLOUDS TO AMBUSH ME WHILE I SLEPT ON A BED OF GOLD COINS-- SO I TURNED HIS ARMY INTO DUST.
SUCH IS THE POWER OF THE HANDSOME MONKEY KING!
INCREDIBLE...
YES, I AM--
TOOOM
AND YOU HAD BETTER HAVE BROUGHT ME AN ADVENTURE, LITTLE MORTALS.

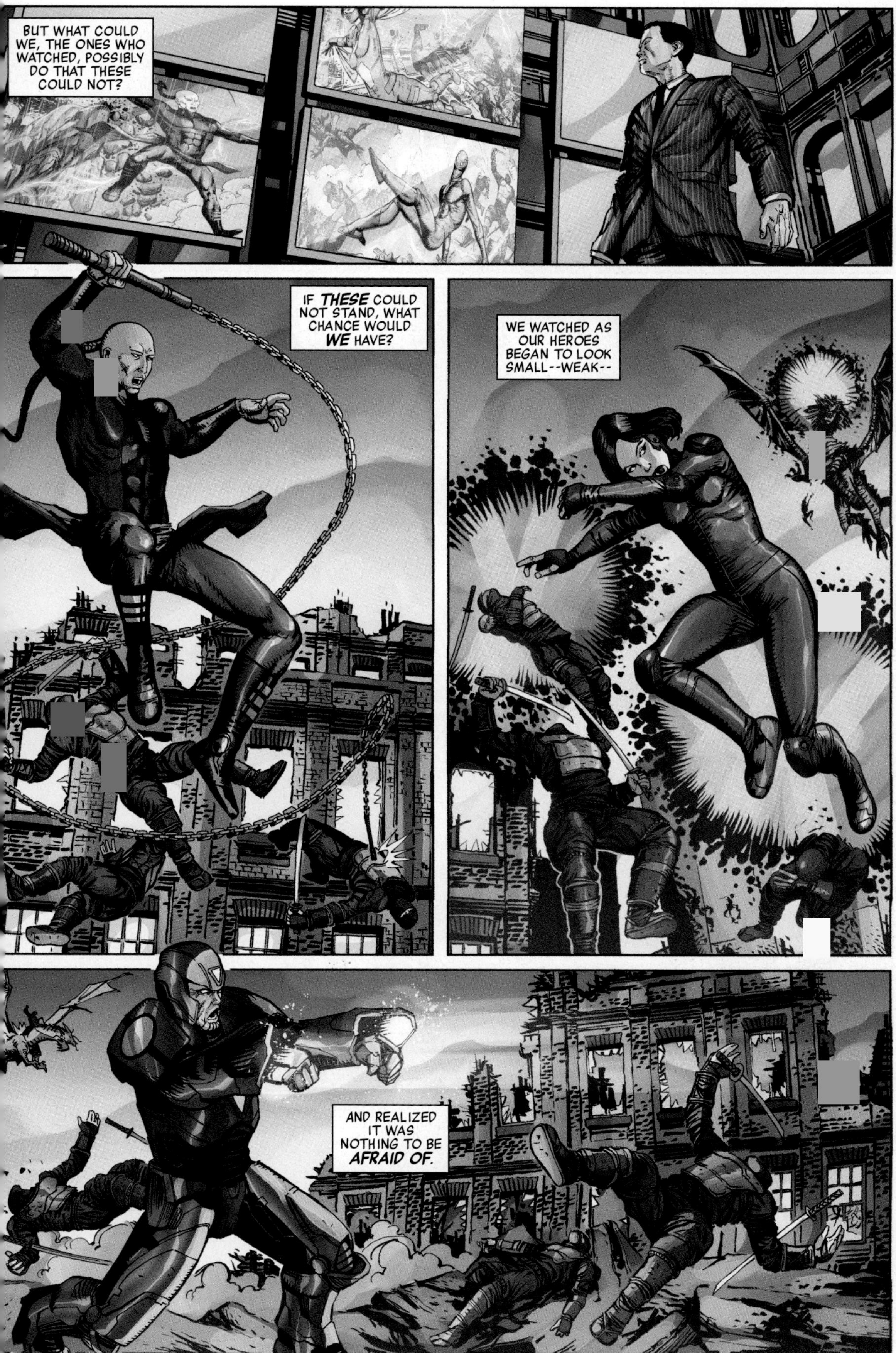
BUT WHAT COULD WE, THE ONES WHO WATCHED, POSSIBLY DO THAT THESE COULD NOT?
IF THESE COULD NOT STAND, WHAT CHANCE WOULD WE HAVE?
WE WATCHED AS OUR HEROES BEGAN TO LOOK SMALL--WEAK--
AND REALIZED IT WAS NOTHING TO BE AFRAID OF.

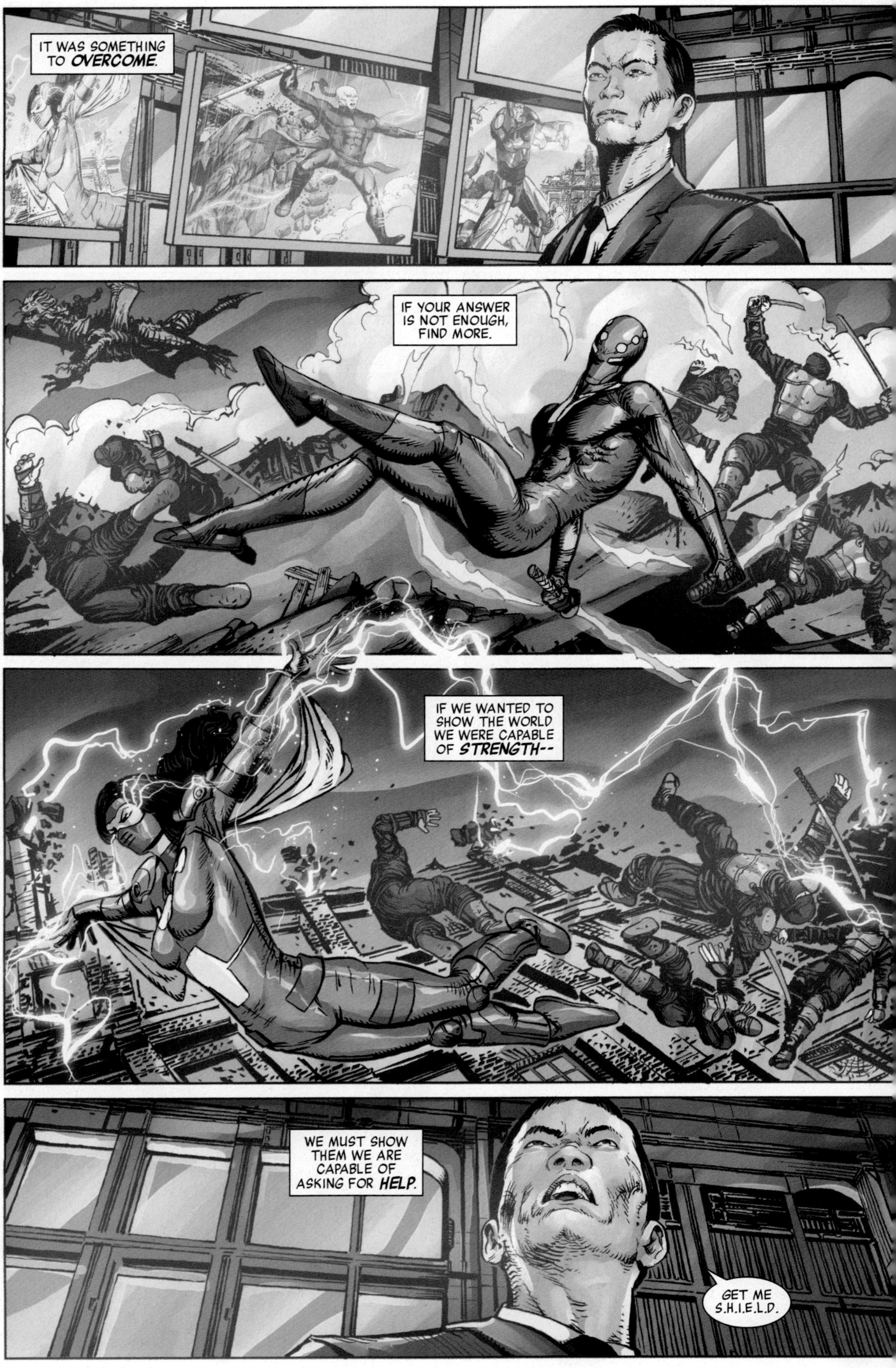
IT WAS SOMETHING TO OVERCOME.
IF YOUR ANSWER IS NOT ENOUGH, FIND MORE.
IF WE WANTED TO SHOW THE WORLD WE WERE CAPABLE OF STRENGTH--
WE MUST SHOW THEM WE ARE CAPABLE OF ASKING FOR HELP.
GET ME S.H.I.E.L.D.

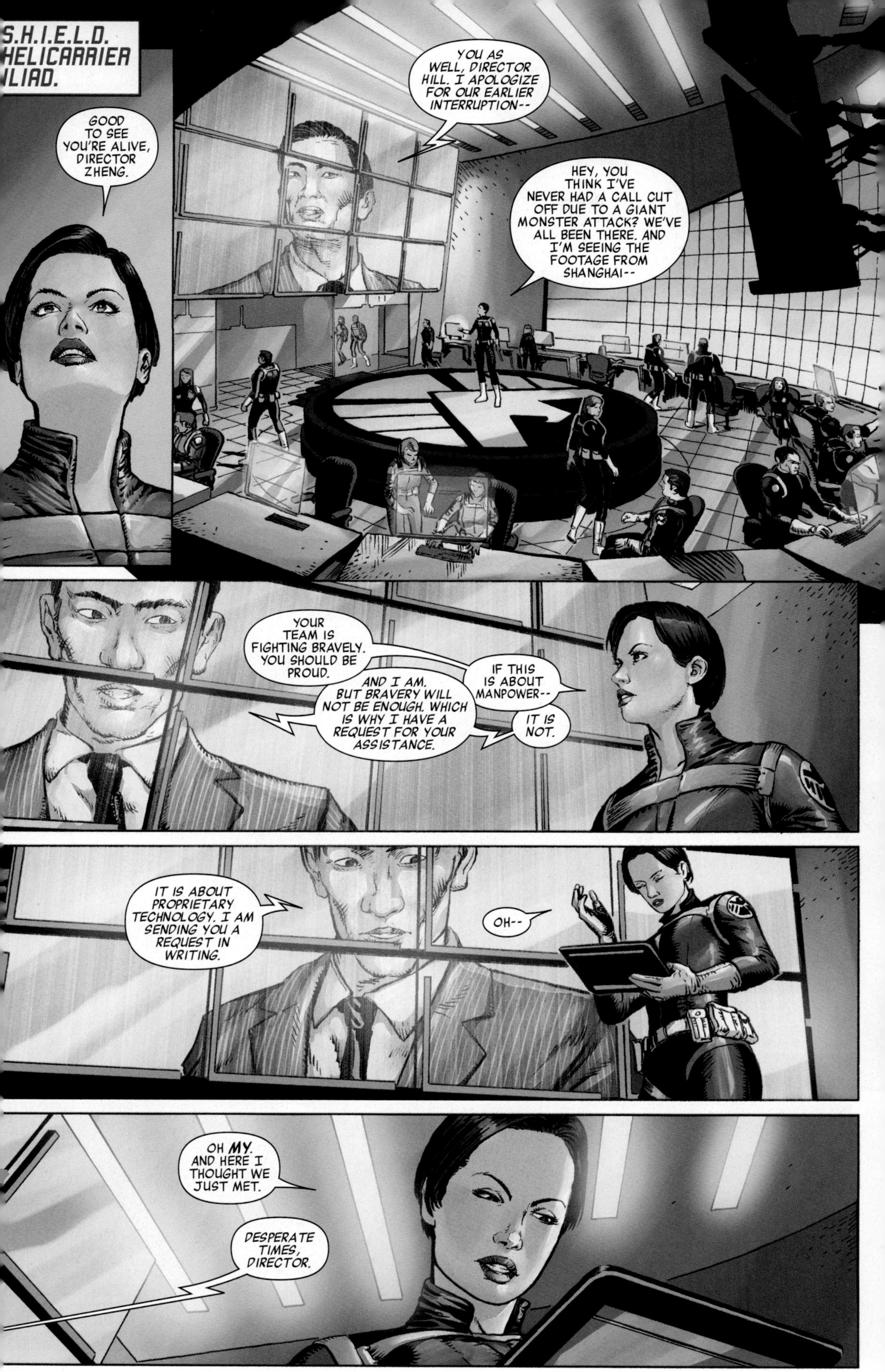
S.H.I.E.L.D. HELICARRIER ILIAD.
GOOD TO SEE YOU'RE ALIVE, DIRECTOR ZHENG.
YOU AS WELL, DIRECTOR HILL. I APOLOGIZE FOR OUR EARLIER INTERRUPTION--
HEY, YOU THINK I'VE NEVER HAD A CALL CUT OFF DUE TO A GIANT MONSTER ATTACK? WE'VE ALL BEEN THERE. AND I'M SEEING THE FOOTAGE FROM SHANGHAI--
YOUR TEAM IS FIGHTING BRAVELY. YOU SHOULD BE PROUD.
AND I AM. BUT BRAVERY WILL NOT BE ENOUGH. WHICH IS WHY I HAVE A REQUEST FOR YOUR ASSISTANCE.
IF THIS IS ABOUT MANPOWER--
IT IS NOT.
IT IS ABOUT PROPRIETARY TECHNOLOGY. I AM SENDING YOU A REQUEST IN WRITING.
OH--
OH MY. AND HERE I THOUGHT WE JUST MET.
DESPERATE TIMES, DIRECTOR.

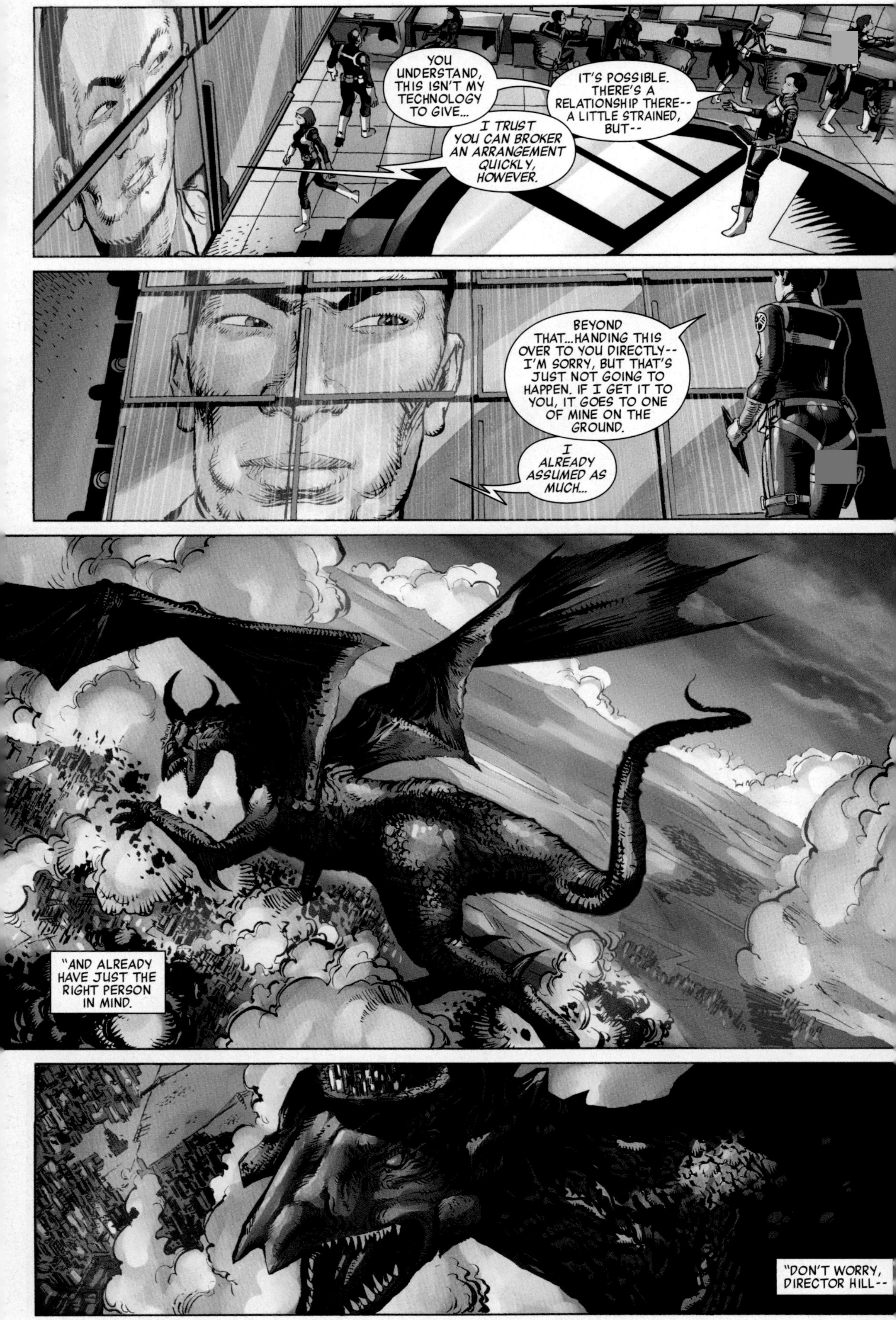
YOU UNDERSTAND, THIS ISN'T MY TECHNOLOGY TO GIVE...
IT'S POSSIBLE. THERE'S A RELATIONSHIP THERE-- A LITTLE STRAINED, BUT--
I TRUST YOU CAN BROKER AN ARRANGEMENT QUICKLY, HOWEVER.
BEYOND THAT...HANDING THIS OVER TO YOU DIRECTLY-- I'M SORRY, BUT THAT'S JUST NOT GOING TO HAPPEN. IF I GET IT TO YOU, IT GOES TO ONE OF MINE ON THE GROUND.
I ALREADY ASSUMED AS MUCH...
"AND ALREADY HAVE JUST THE RIGHT PERSON IN MIND.
"DON'T WORRY, DIRECTOR HILL--

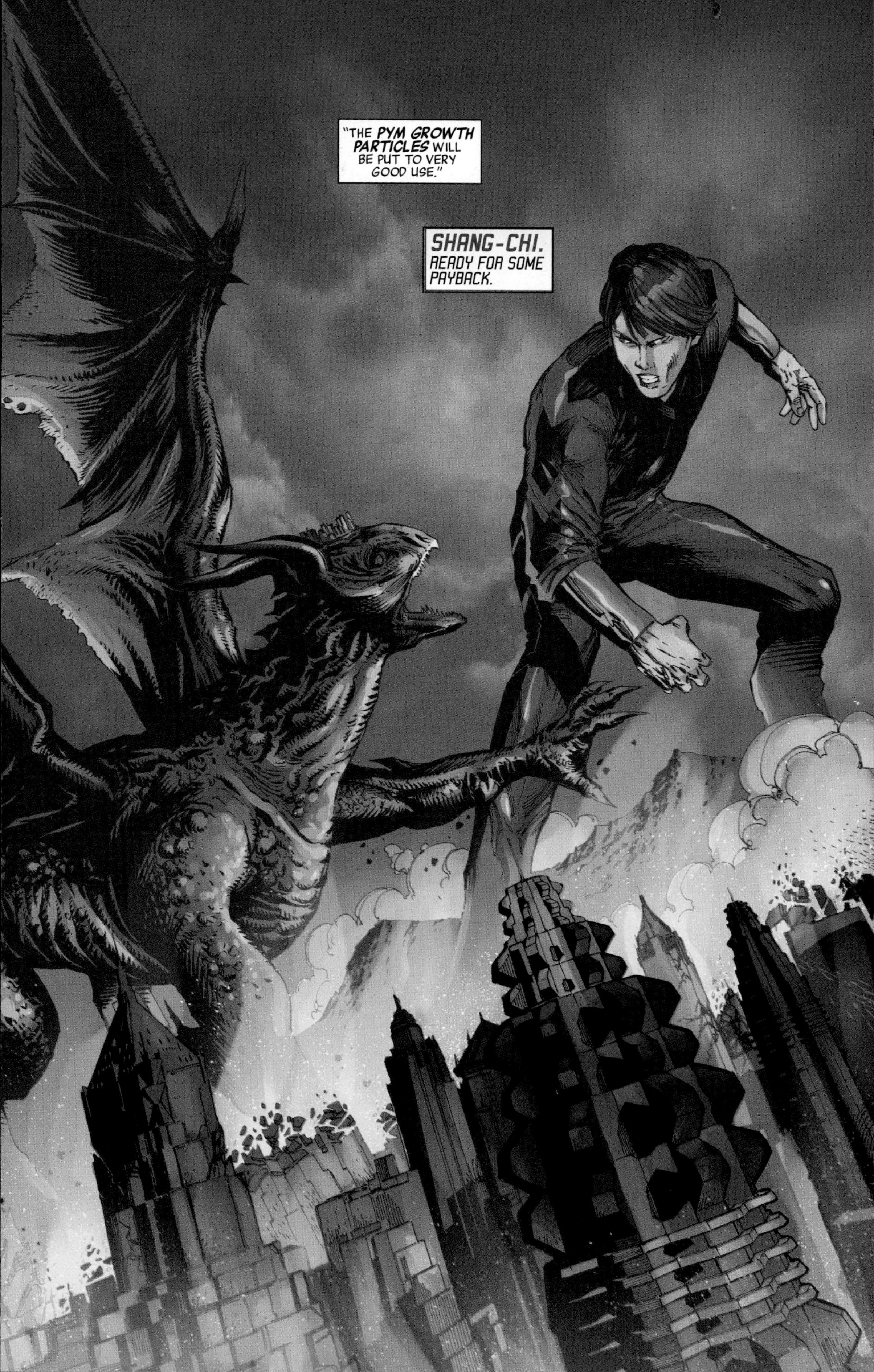
"THE PYM GROWTH PARTICLES WILL BE PUT TO VERY GOOD USE."
SHANG-CHI. READY FOR SOME PAYBACK.

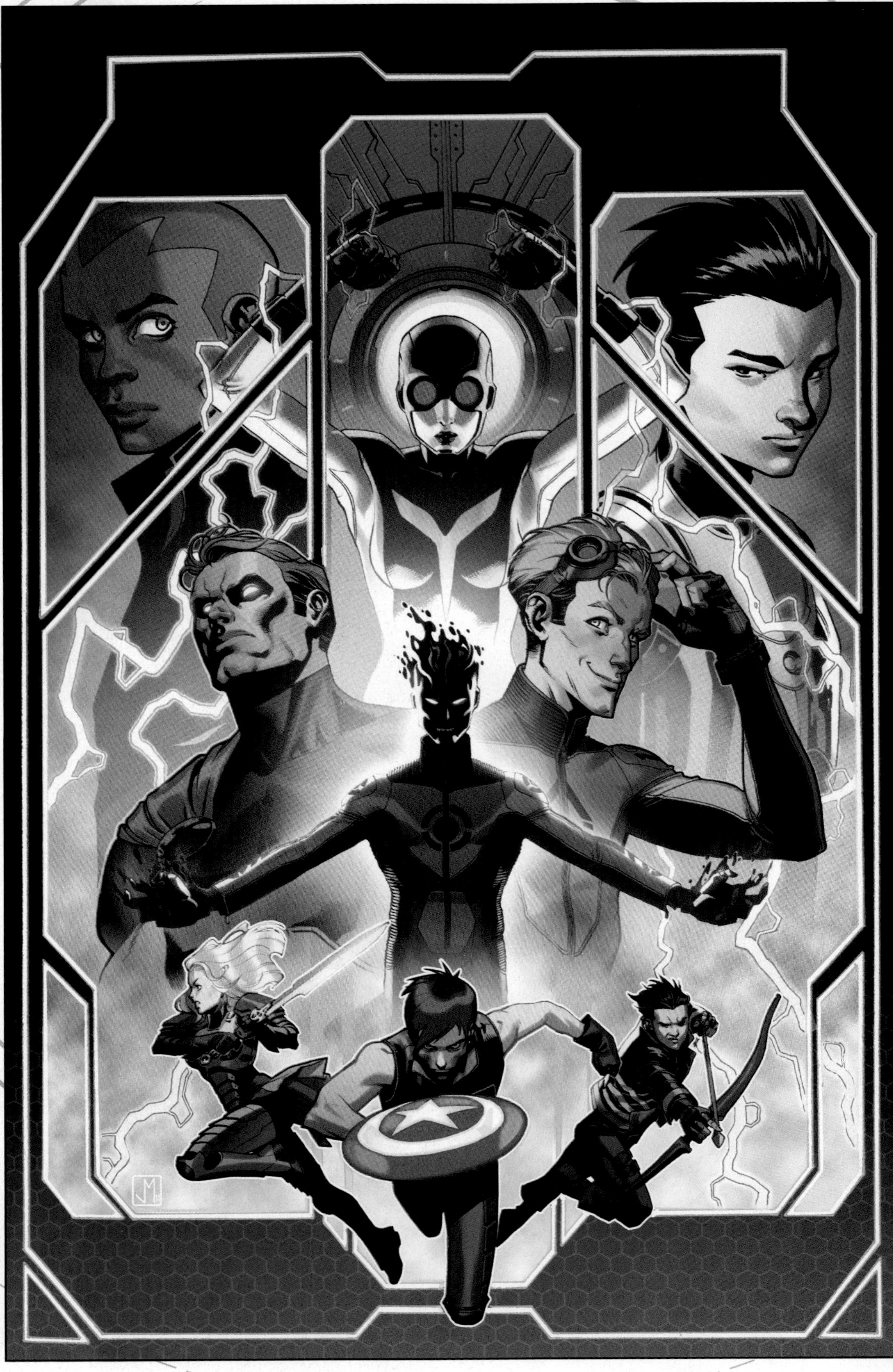

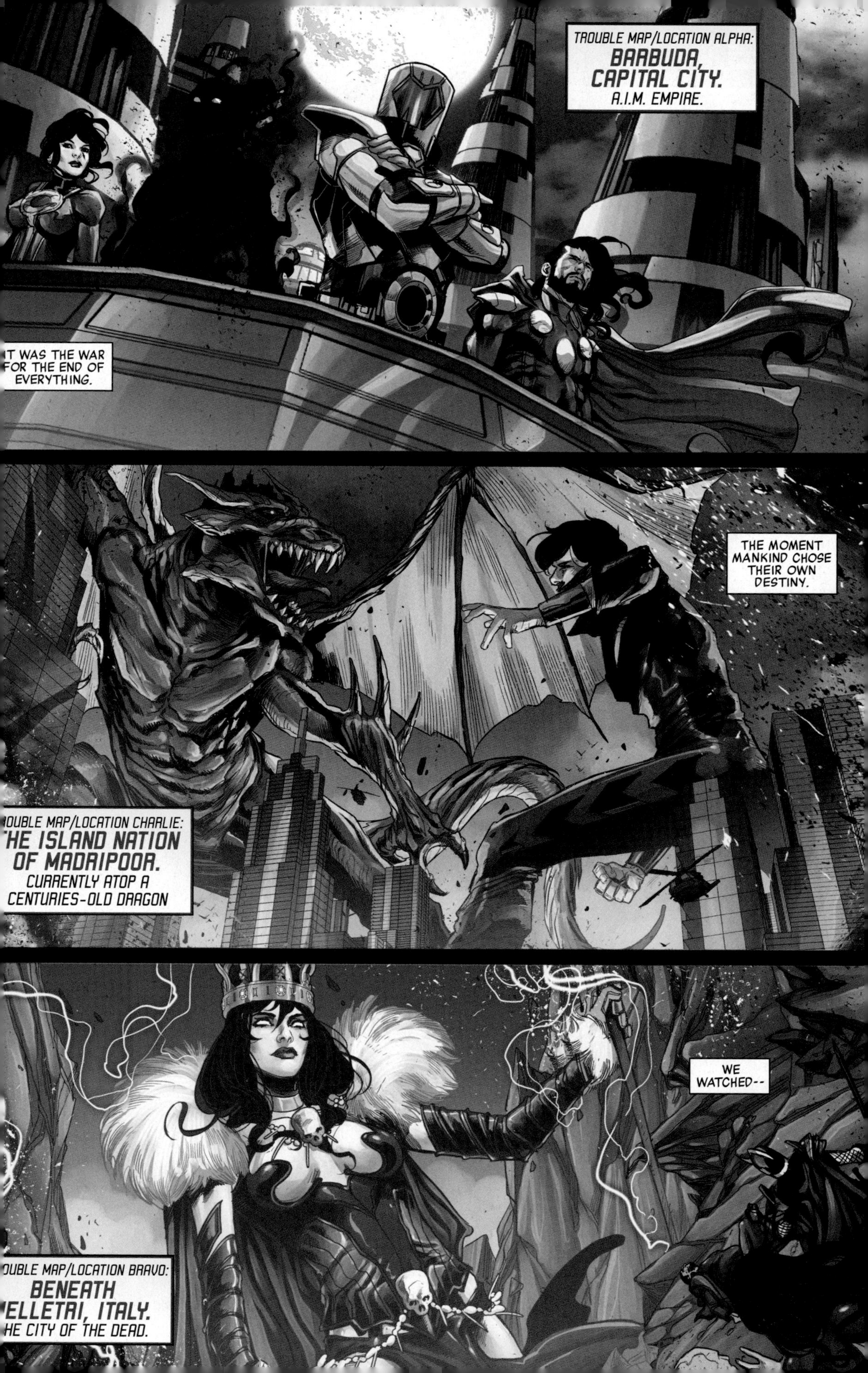
TROUBLE MAP/LOCATION ALPHA:
BARBUDA, CAPITAL CITY.
A.I.M. EMPIRE.
IT WAS THE WAR FOR THE END OF EVERYTHING.
THE MOMENT MANKIND CHOSE THEIR OWN DESTINY.
OUBLE MAP/LOCATION CHARLIE:
HE ISLAND NATION OF MADRIPOOR.
CURRENTLY ATOP A CENTURIES-OLD DRAGON
WE WATCHED--
OUBLE MAP/LOCATION BRAVO:
BENEATH ELLETRI, ITALY.
HE CITY OF THE DEAD.

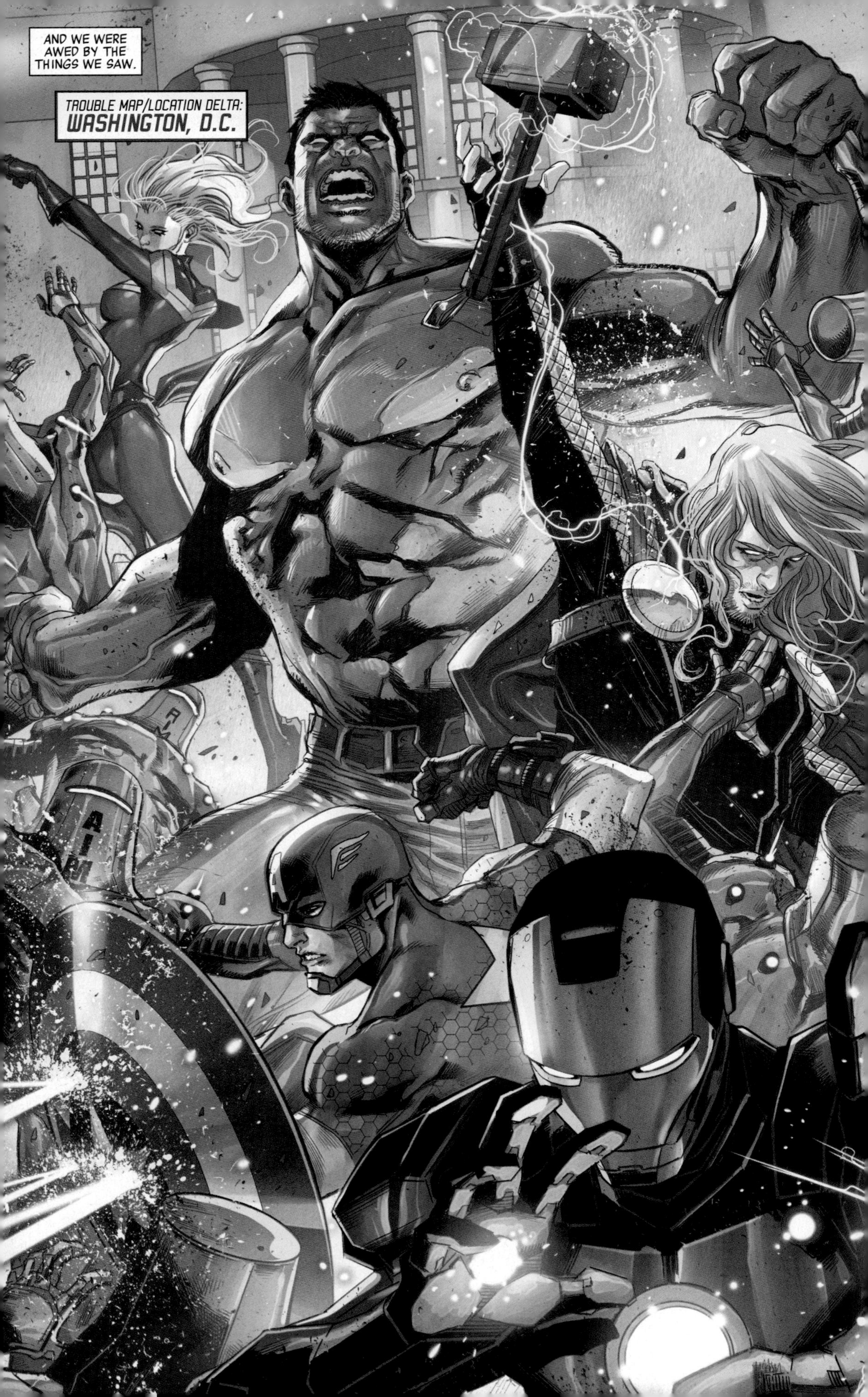
AND WE WERE AWED BY THE THINGS WE SAW.
TROUBLE MAP/LOCATION DELTA: WASHINGTON, D.C.

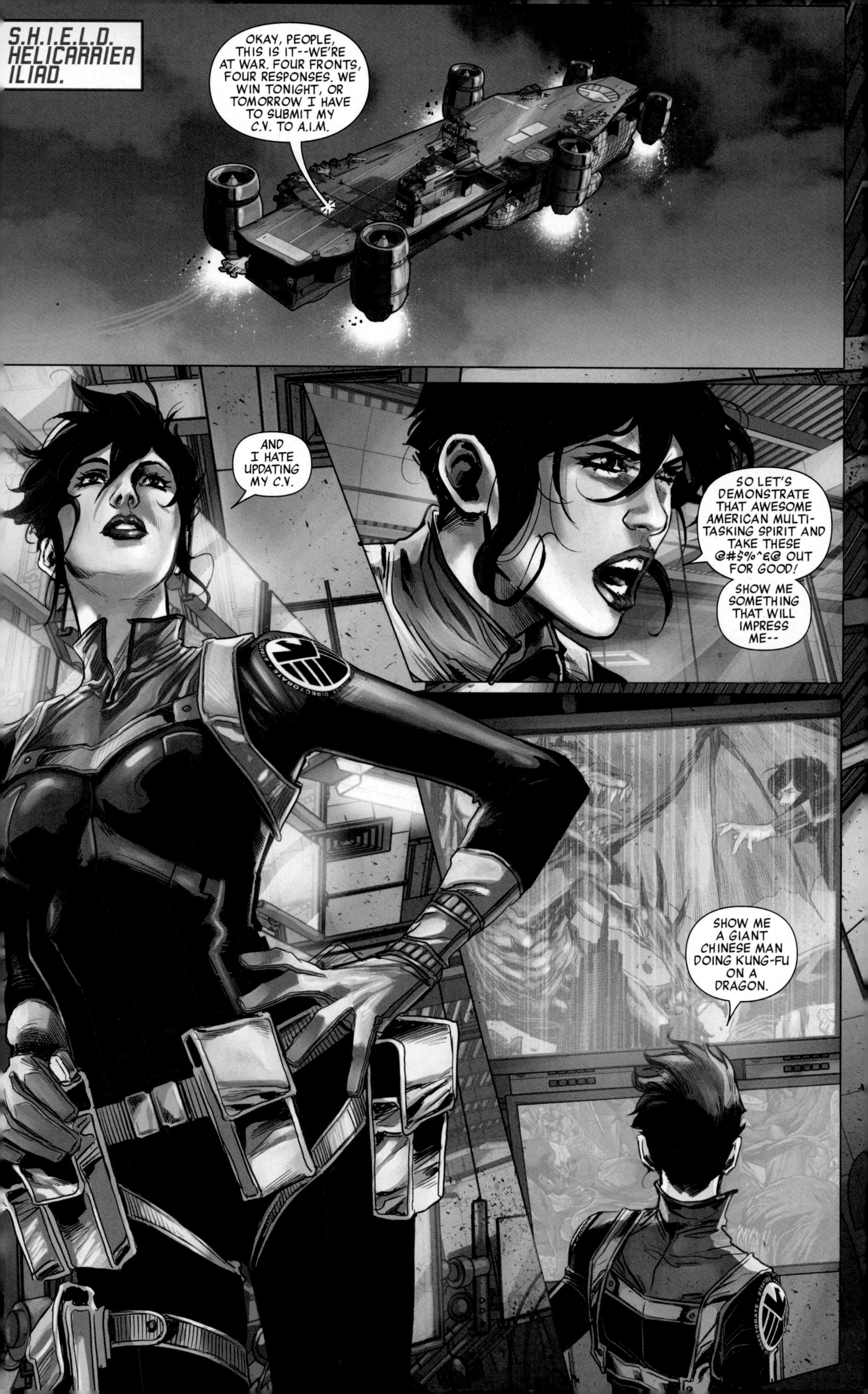
S.H.I.E.L.D. HELICARRIER ILIAD.
OKAY, PEOPLE, THIS IS IT--WE'RE AT WAR. FOUR FRONTS, FOUR RESPONSES. WE WIN TONIGHT, OR TOMORROW I HAVE TO SUBMIT MY C.V. TO A.I.M.
AND I HATE UPDATING MY C.V.
SO LET'S DEMONSTRATE THAT AWESOME AMERICAN MULTI-TASKING SPIRIT AND TAKE THESE @#$%^&@ OUT FOR GOOD!
SHOW ME SOMETHING THAT WILL IMPRESS ME--
SHOW ME A GIANT CHINESE MAN DOING KUNG-FU ON A DRAGON.

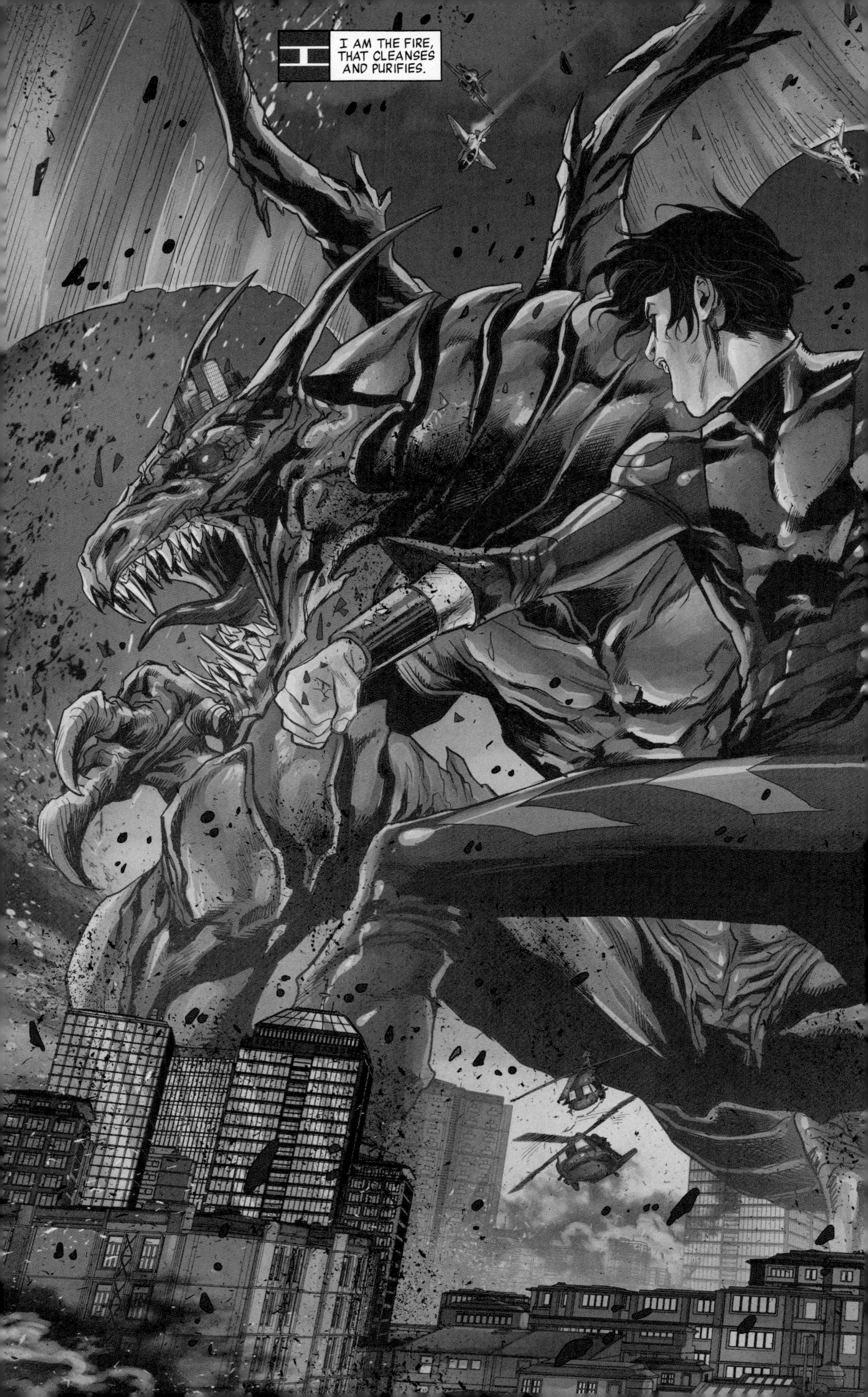
I AM THE FIRE, THAT CLEANSES AND PURIFIES.

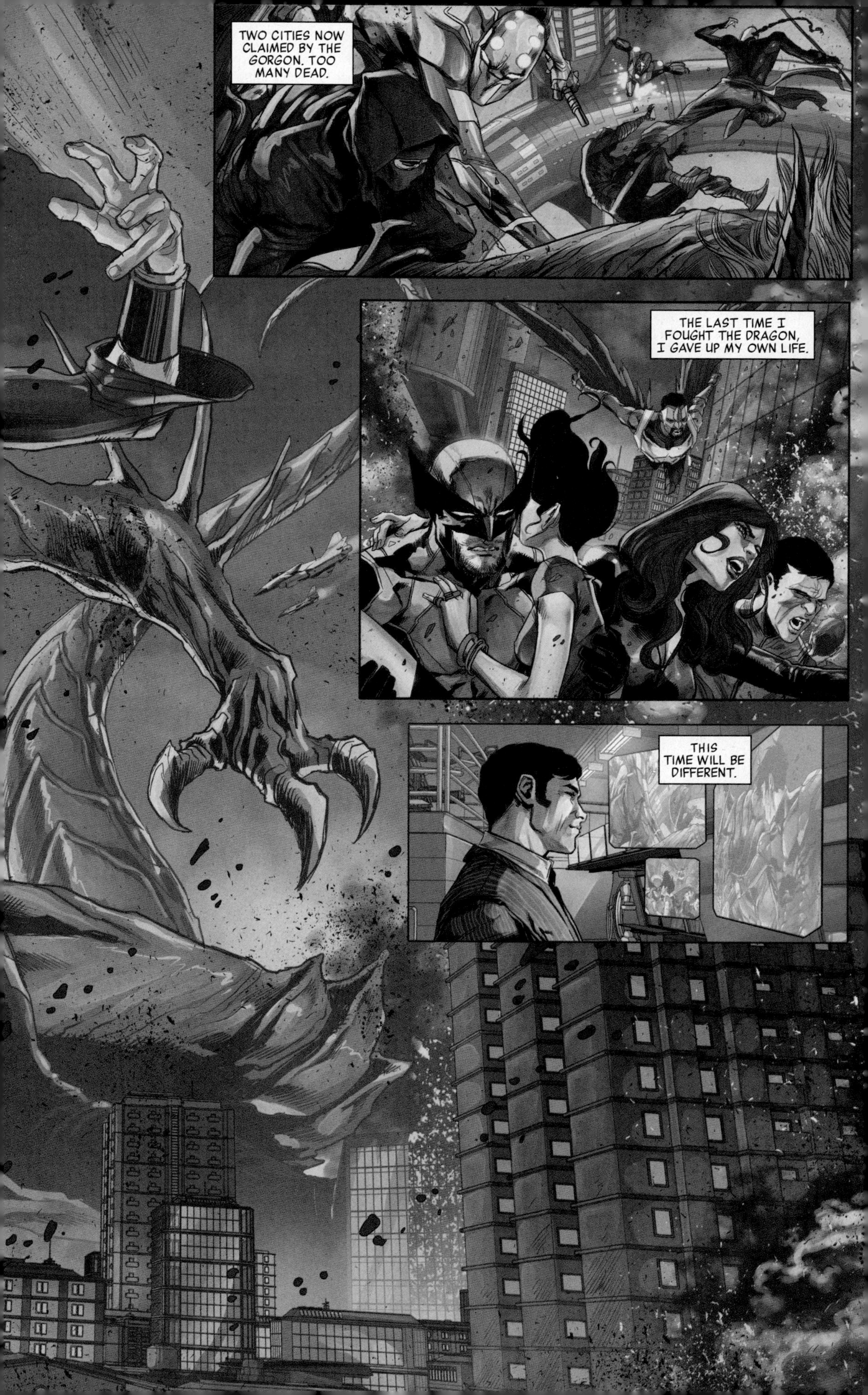
TWO CITIES NOW CLAIMED BY THE GORGON. TOO MANY DEAD.
THE LAST TIME I FOUGHT THE DRAGON, I GAVE UP MY OWN LIFE.
THIS TIME WILL BE DIFFERENT.

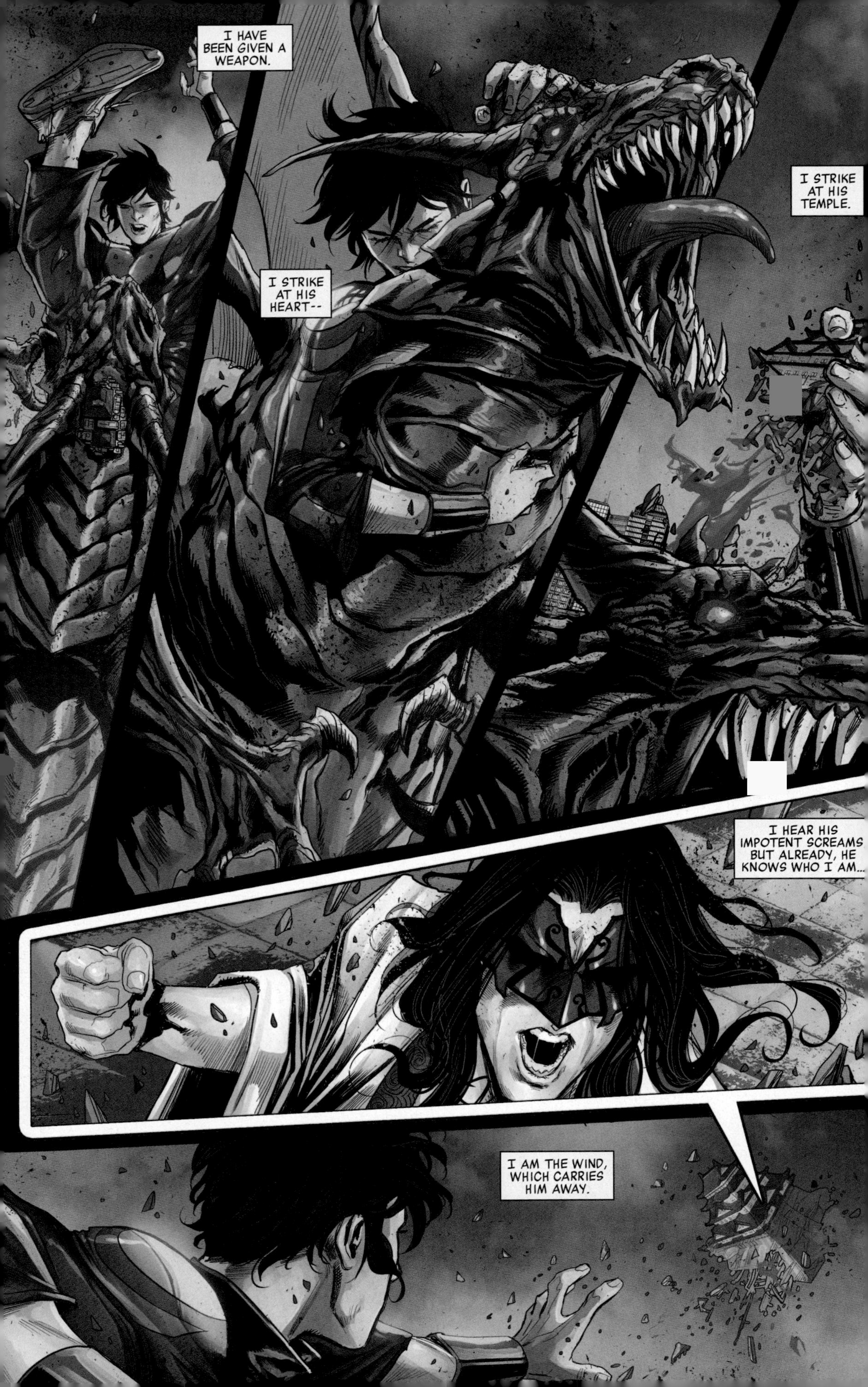
I HAVE BEEN GIVEN A WEAPON.
I STRIKE AT HIS HEART--
I STRIKE AT HIS TEMPLE.
I HEAR HIS IMPOTENT SCREAMS BUT ALREADY, HE KNOWS WHO I AM...
I AM THE WIND, WHICH CARRIES HIM AWAY.

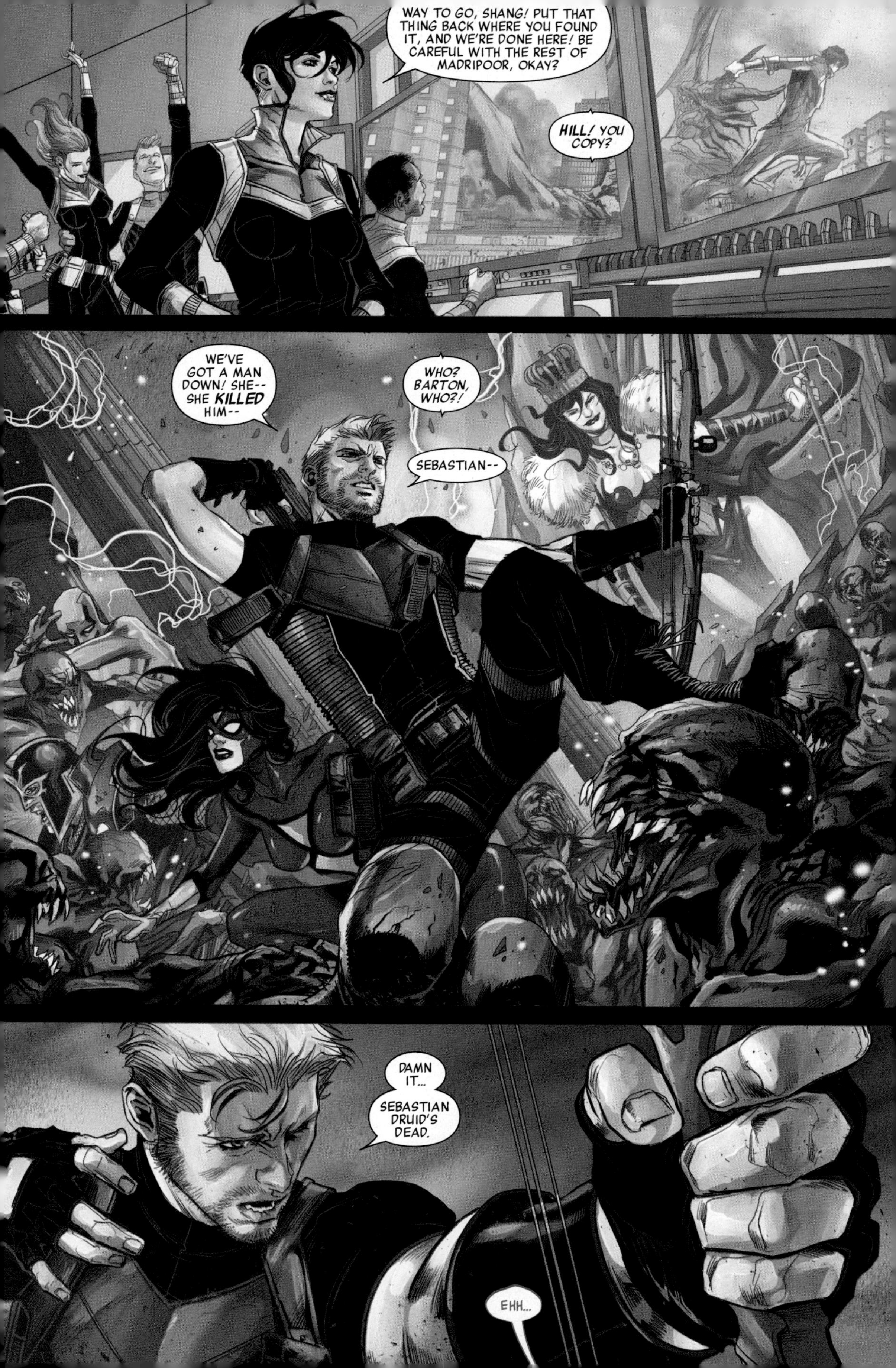
WAY TO GO, SHANG! PUT THAT THING BACK WHERE YOU FOUND IT, AND WE'RE DONE HERE! BE CAREFUL WITH THE REST OF MADRIPOOR, OKAY?
HILL! YOU COPY?
WE'VE GOT A MAN DOWN! SHE-- SHE KILLED HIM--
WHO? BARTON, WHO?!
SEBASTIAN--
DAMN IT...
SEBASTIAN DRUID'S DEAD.
EHH...

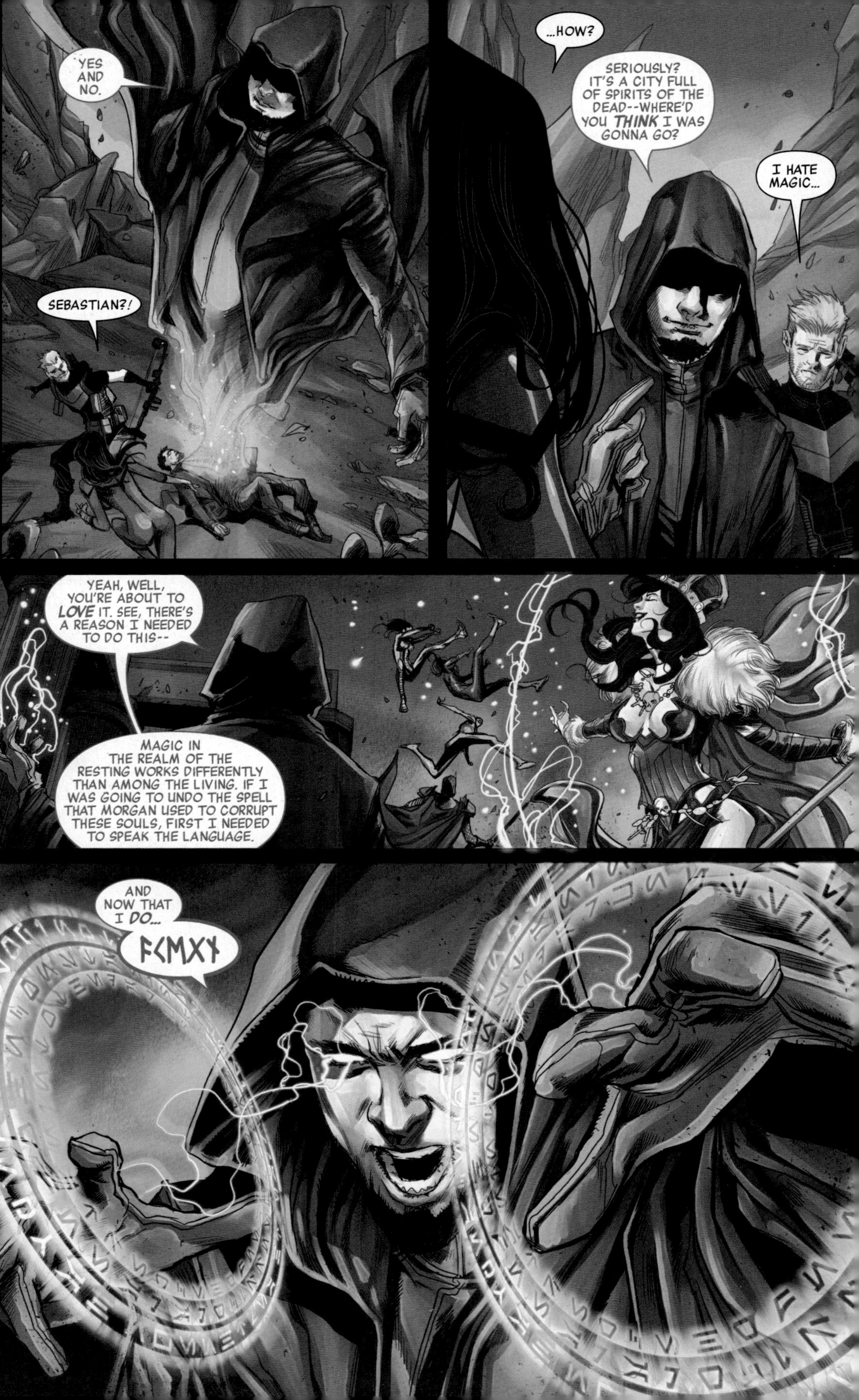
YES AND NO.
SEBASTIAN?!
...HOW?
SERIOUSLY? IT'S A CITY FULL OF SPIRITS OF THE DEAD--WHERE'D YOU THINK I WAS GONNA GO?
I HATE MAGIC...
YEAH, WELL, YOU'RE ABOUT TO LOVE IT. SEE, THERE'S A REASON I NEEDED TO DO THIS--
MAGIC IN THE REALM OF THE RESTING WORKS DIFFERENTLY THAN AMONG THE LIVING. IF I WAS GOING TO UNDO THE SPELL THAT MORGAN USED TO CORRUPT THESE SOULS, FIRST I NEEDED TO SPEAK THE LANGUAGE.
AND NOW THAT I DO...
ᚠᚲᛖᚷᛦ

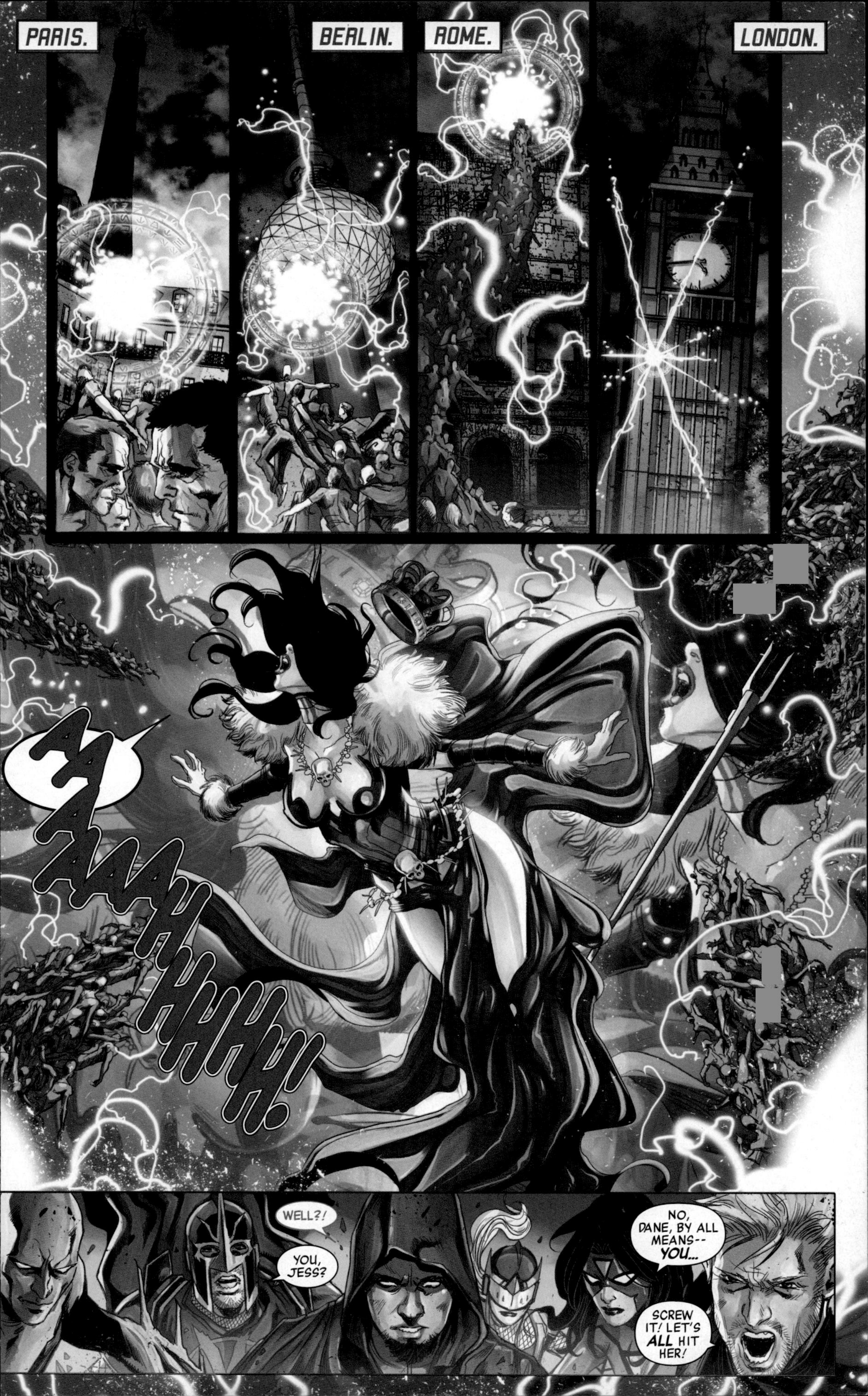

PARIS.
BERLIN.
ROME.
LONDON.
AAAAAHHHHH!
WELL?!
YOU, JESS?
NO, DANE, BY ALL MEANS-- YOU...
SCREW IT! LET'S ALL HIT HER!

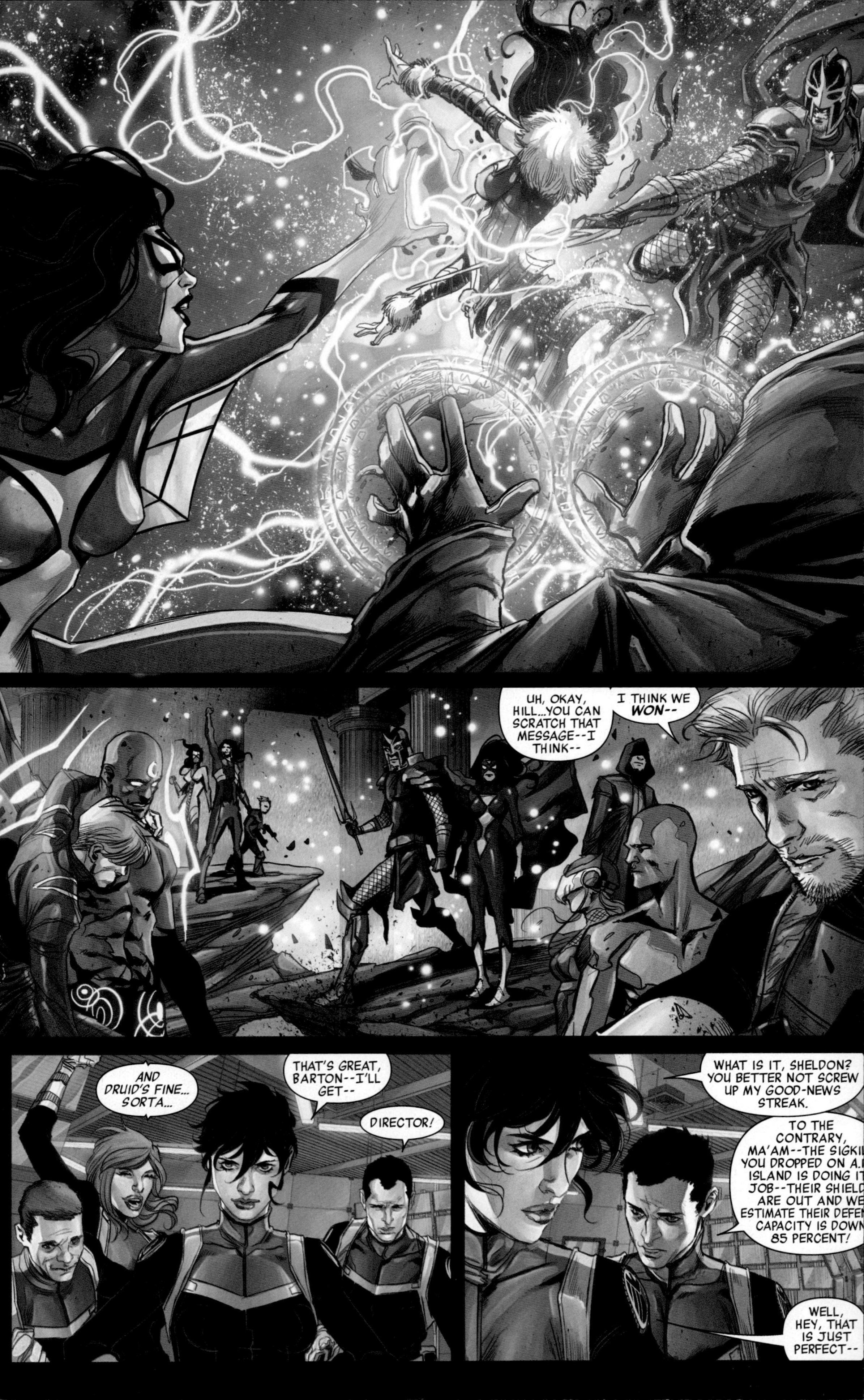
UH, OKAY, HILL...YOU CAN SCRATCH THAT MESSAGE--I THINK--
I THINK WE WON--
AND DRUID'S FINE... SORTA...
THAT'S GREAT, BARTON--I'LL GET--
DIRECTOR!
WHAT IS IT, SHELDON? YOU BETTER NOT SCREW UP MY GOOD-NEWS STREAK.
TO THE CONTRARY, MA'AM--THE SIGKI
YOU DROPPED ON A.
ISLAND IS DOING IT
JOB--THEIR SHIELD
ARE OUT AND WE
ESTIMATE THEIR DEFEN
CAPACITY IS DOWN
85 PERCENT!
WELL, HEY, THAT IS JUST PERFECT--

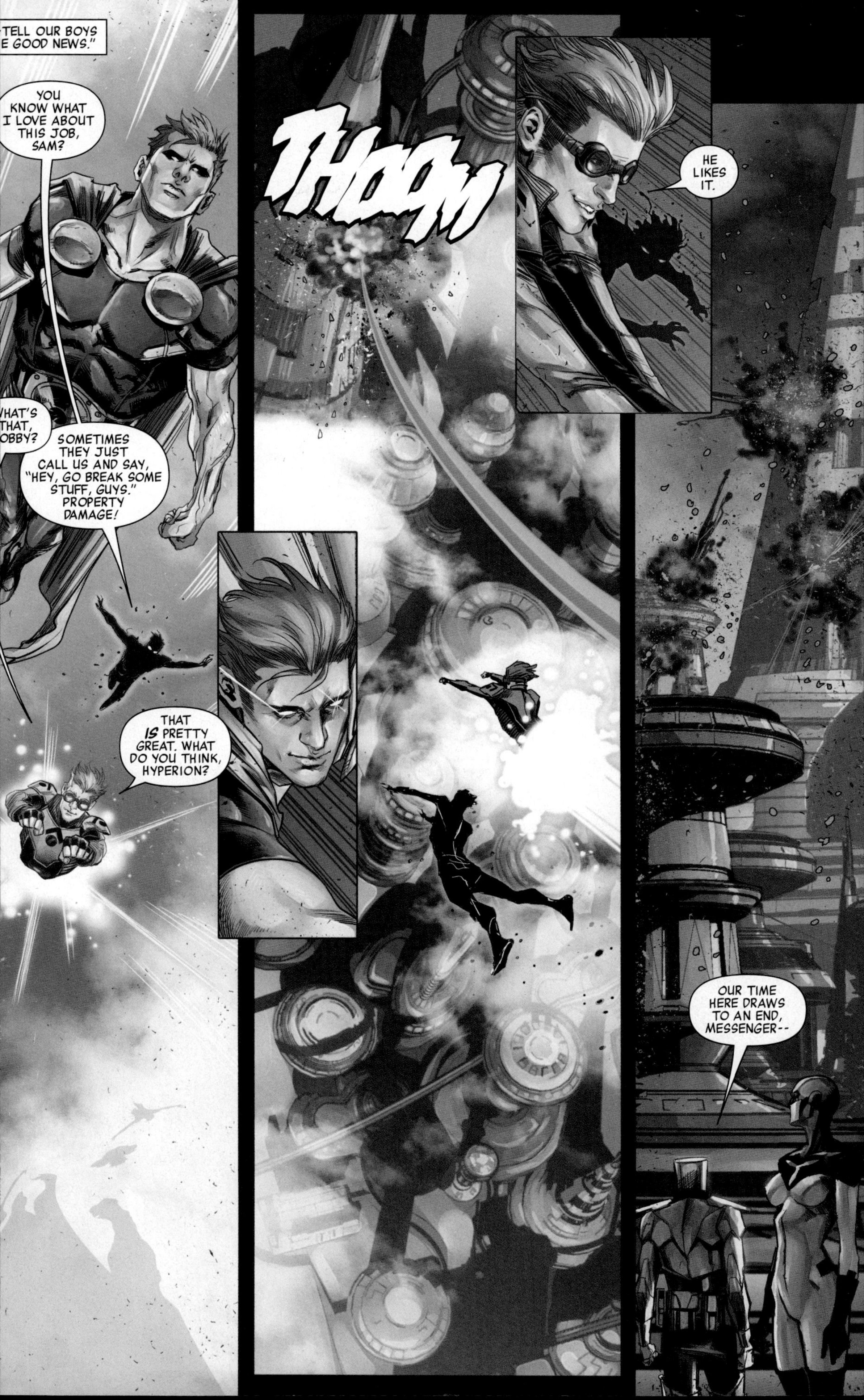
"TELL OUR BOYS THE GOOD NEWS."
YOU KNOW WHAT I LOVE ABOUT THIS JOB, SAM?
WHAT'S THAT, BOBBY?
SOMETIMES THEY JUST CALL US AND SAY, "HEY, GO BREAK SOME STUFF, GUYS." PROPERTY DAMAGE!
THAT IS PRETTY GREAT. WHAT DO YOU THINK, HYPERION?
THOOM
HE LIKES IT.
OUR TIME HERE DRAWS TO AN END, MESSENGER--

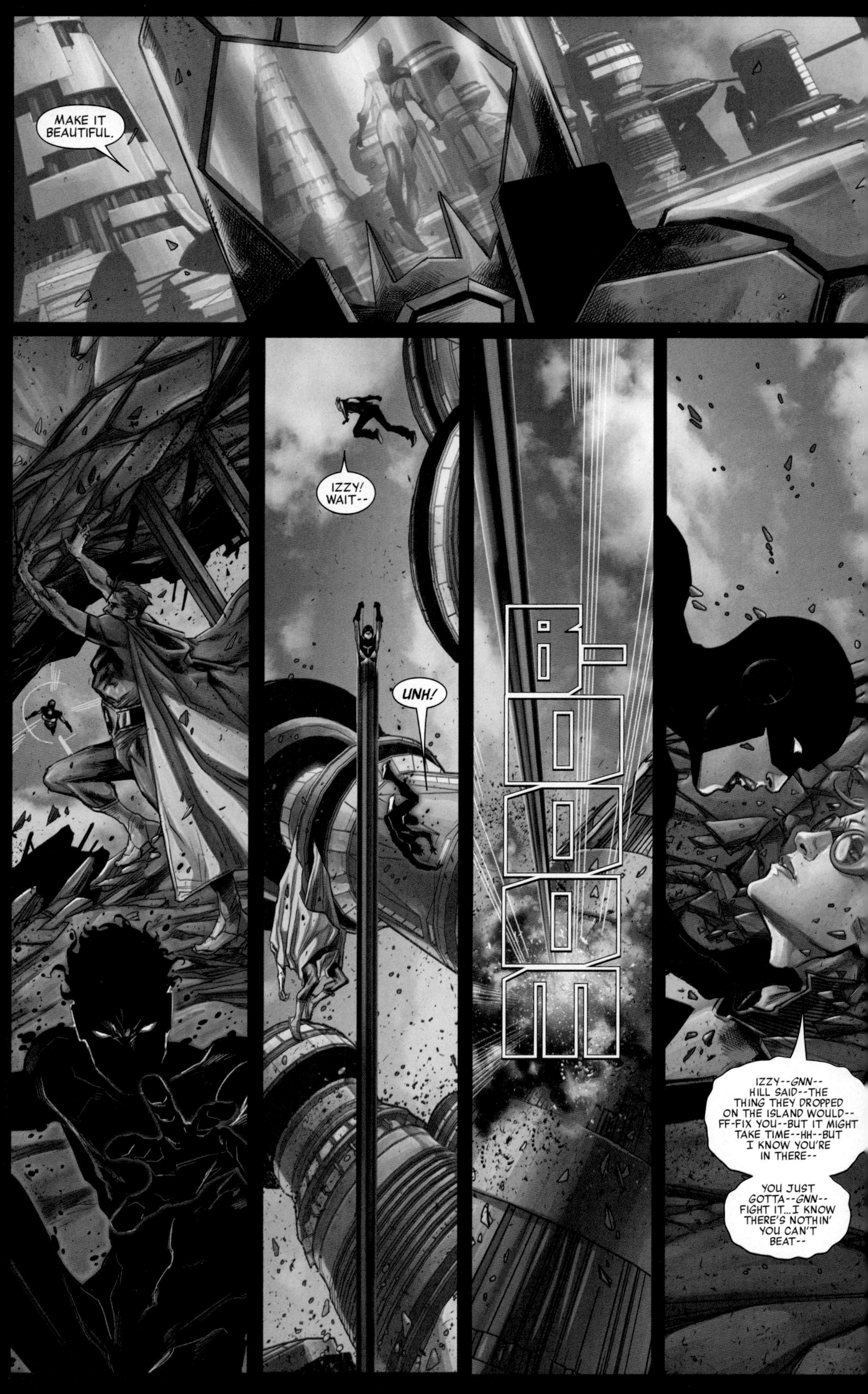
MAKE IT BEAUTIFUL.
IZZY! WAIT--
UNH!
IZZY--GNN--HILL SAID--THE THING THEY DROPPED ON THE ISLAND WOULD--FF-FIX YOU--BUT IT MIGHT TAKE TIME--HH--BUT I KNOW YOU'RE IN THERE--
YOU JUST GOTTA--GNN--FIGHT IT...I KNOW THERE'S NOTHIN' YOU CAN'T BEAT--

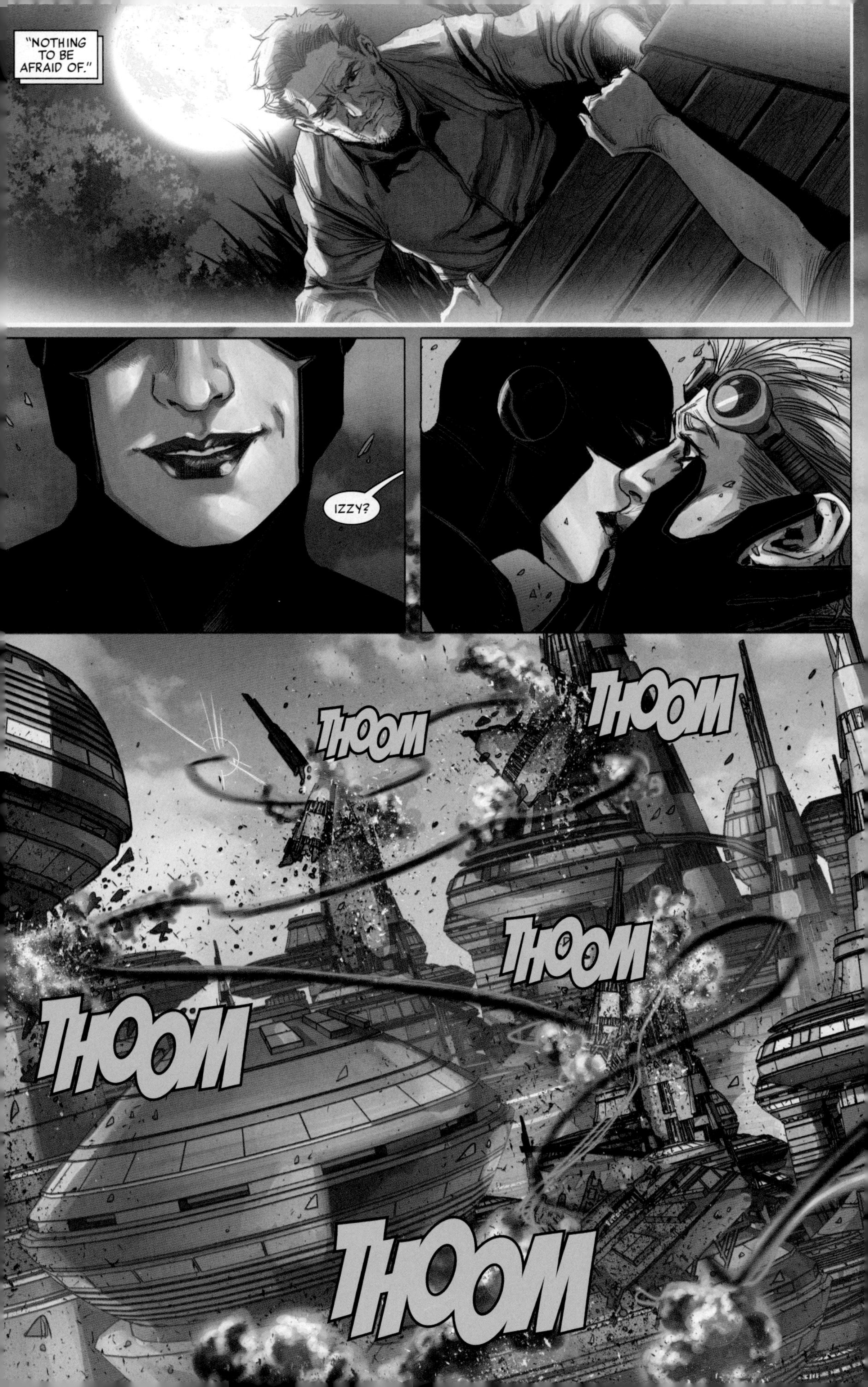
"NOTHING TO BE AFRAID OF."
IZZY?
THOOM
THOOM
THOOM
THOOM
THOOM

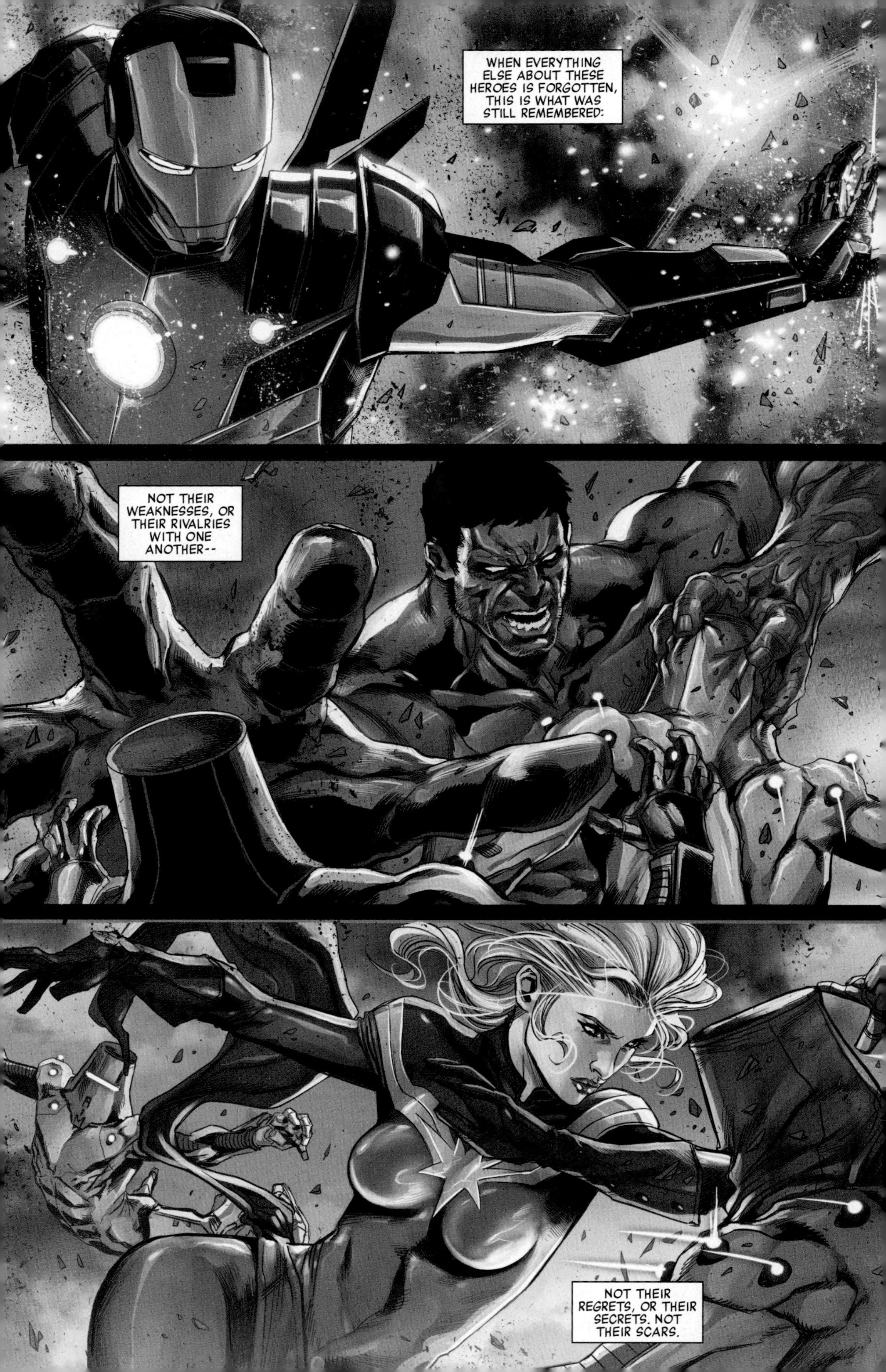
WHEN EVERYTHING ELSE ABOUT THESE HEROES IS FORGOTTEN, THIS IS WHAT WAS STILL REMEMBERED:
NOT THEIR WEAKNESSES, OR THEIR RIVALRIES WITH ONE ANOTHER--
NOT THEIR REGRETS, OR THEIR SECRETS. NOT THEIR SCARS.

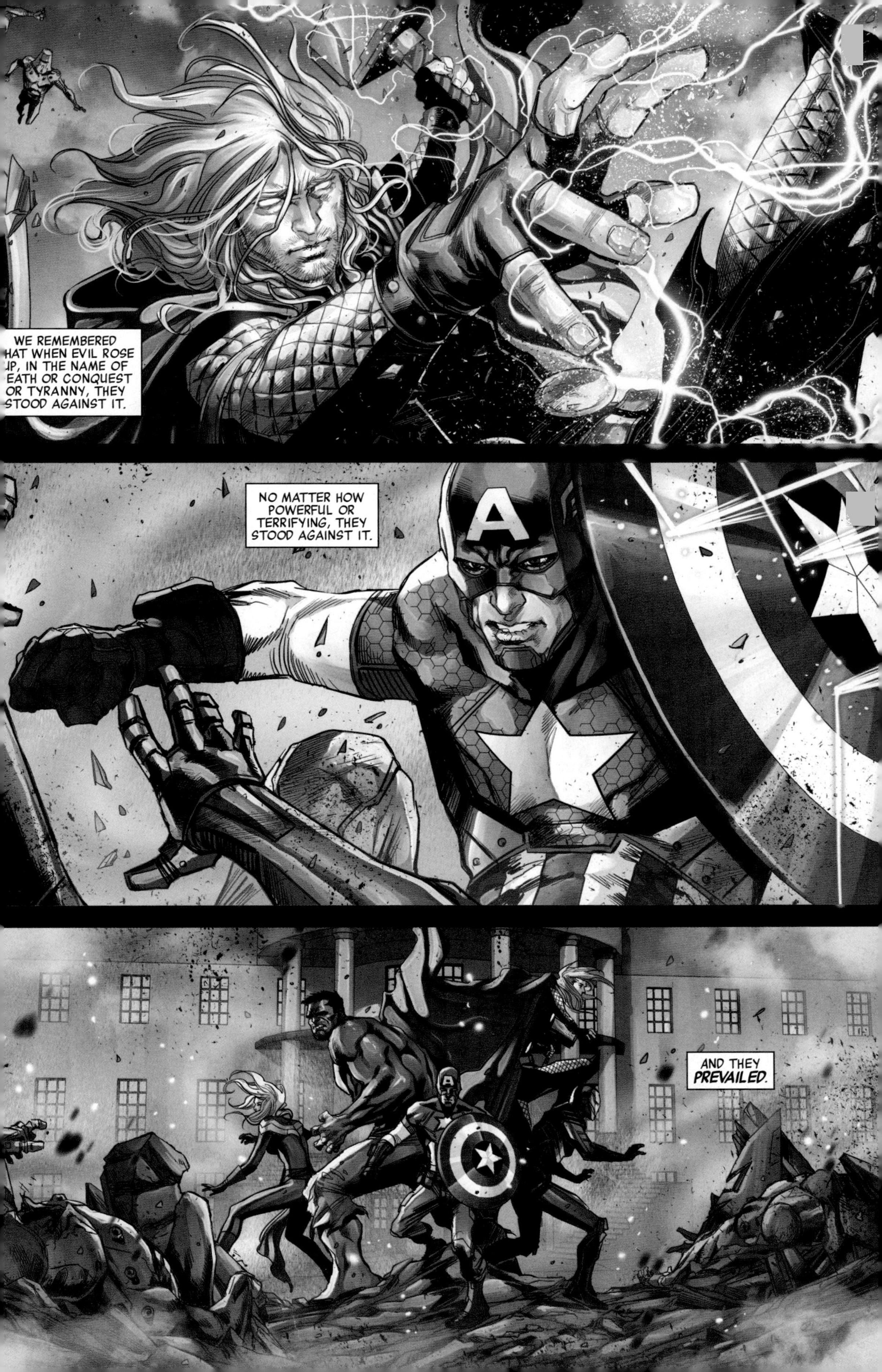
WE REMEMBERED HAT WHEN EVIL ROSE JP, IN THE NAME OF EATH OR CONQUEST OR TYRANNY, THEY STOOD AGAINST IT.
NO MATTER HOW POWERFUL OR TERRIFYING, THEY STOOD AGAINST IT.
AND THEY PREVAILED.

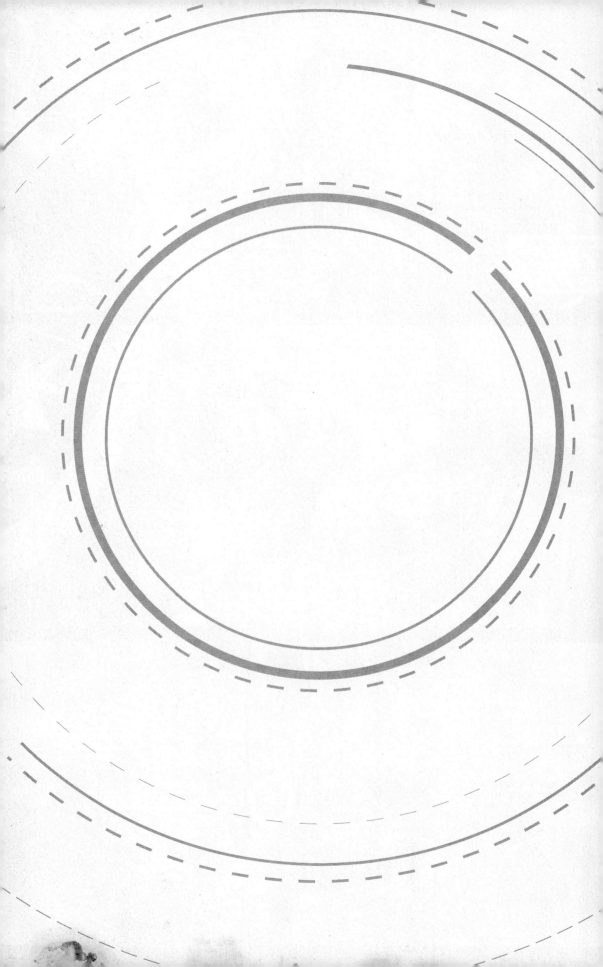

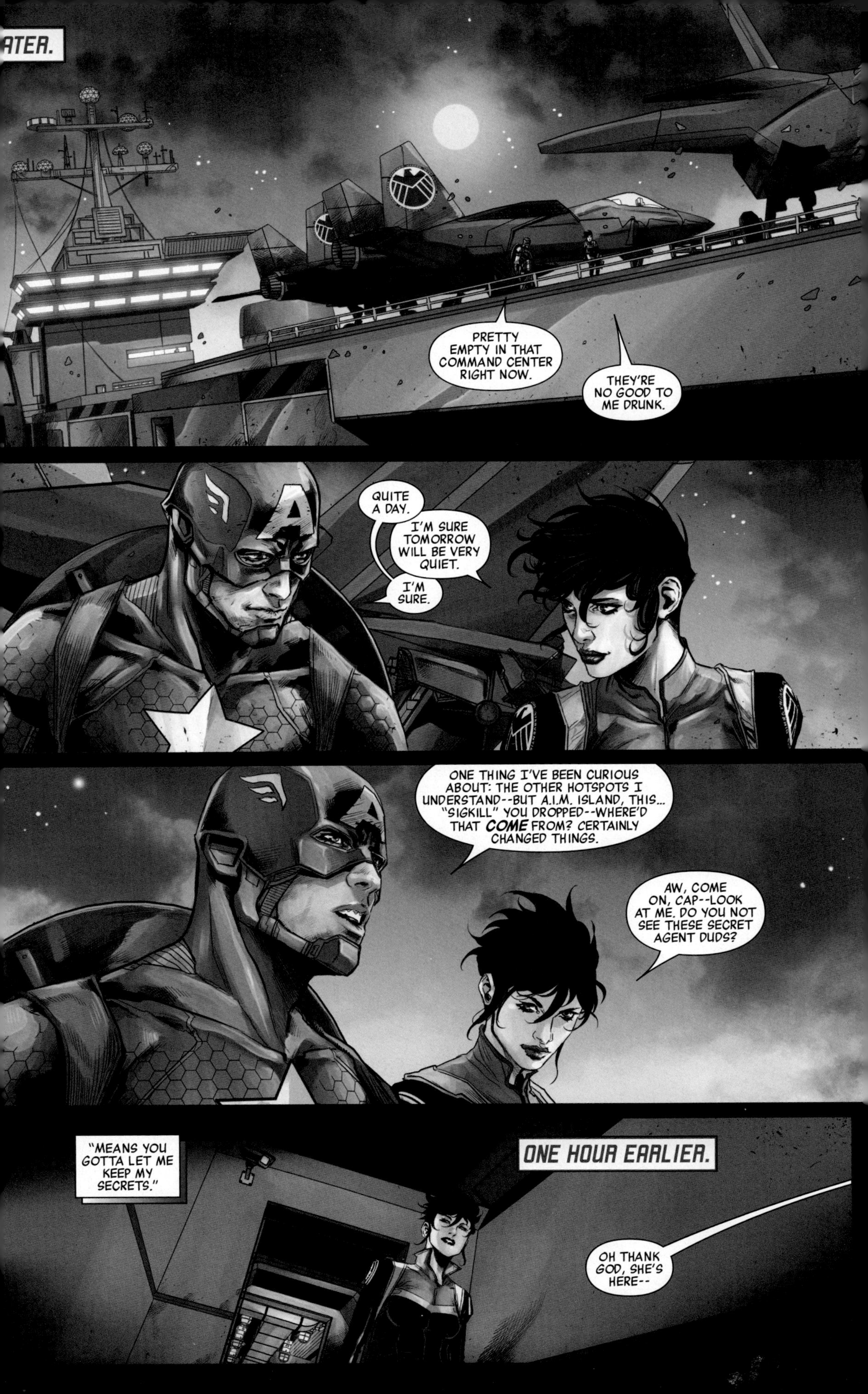
ATER.
PRETTY EMPTY IN THAT COMMAND CENTER RIGHT NOW.
THEY'RE NO GOOD TO ME DRUNK.
QUITE A DAY.
I'M SURE TOMORROW WILL BE VERY QUIET.
I'M SURE.
ONE THING I'VE BEEN CURIOUS ABOUT: THE OTHER HOTSPOTS I UNDERSTAND--BUT A.I.M. ISLAND, THIS... "SIGKILL" YOU DROPPED--WHERE'D THAT COME FROM? CERTAINLY CHANGED THINGS.
AW, COME ON, CAP--LOOK AT ME. DO YOU NOT SEE THESE SECRET AGENT DUDS?
"MEANS YOU GOTTA LET ME KEEP MY SECRETS."
ONE HOUR EARLIER.
OH THANK GOD, SHE'S HERE--

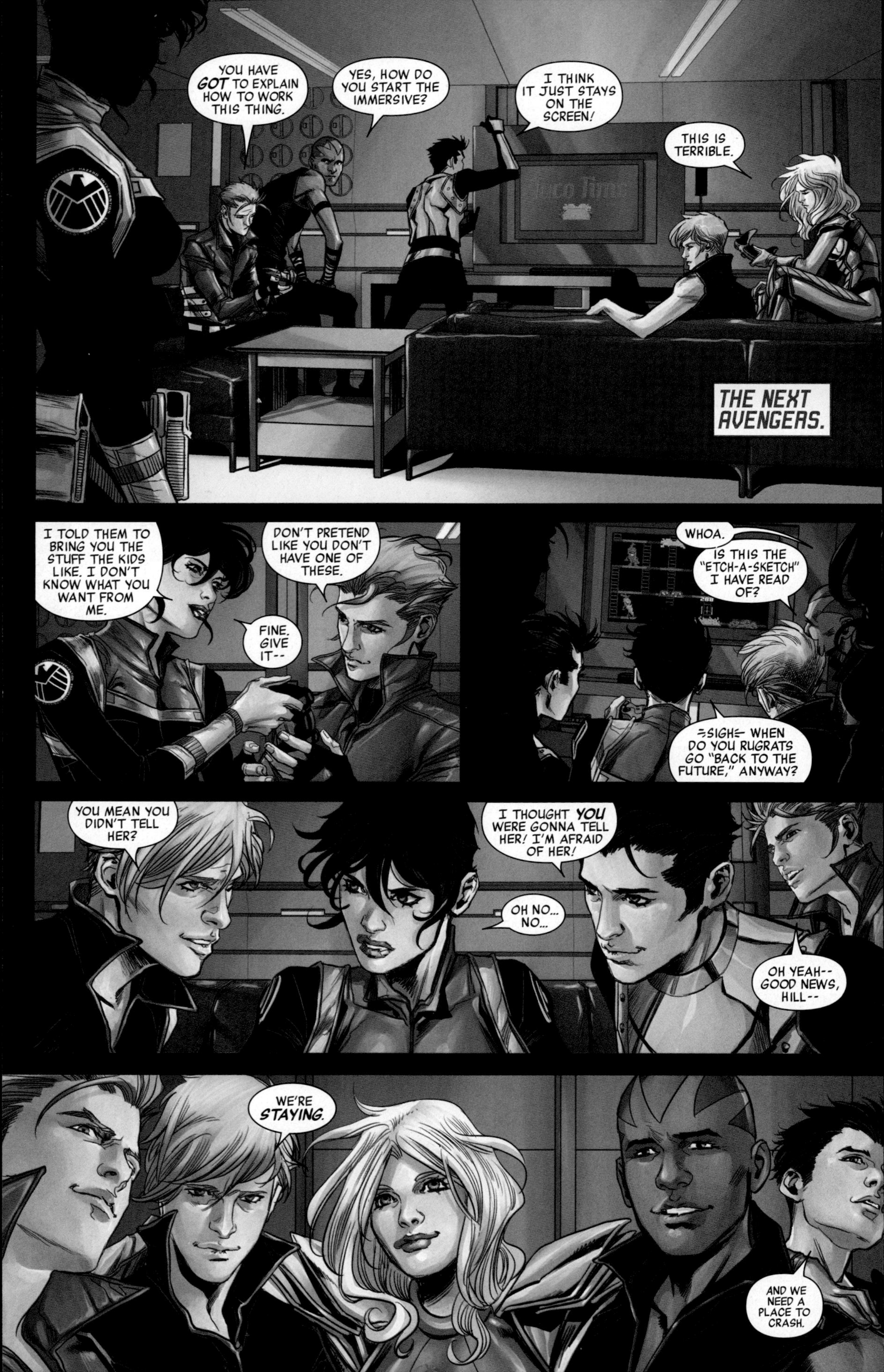

YOU HAVE GOT TO EXPLAIN HOW TO WORK THIS THING.
YES, HOW DO YOU START THE IMMERSIVE?
I THINK IT JUST STAYS ON THE SCREEN!
THIS IS TERRIBLE.
THE NEXT AVENGERS.
I TOLD THEM TO BRING YOU THE STUFF THE KIDS LIKE. I DON'T KNOW WHAT YOU WANT FROM ME.
DON'T PRETEND LIKE YOU DON'T HAVE ONE OF THESE.
FINE. GIVE IT--
WHOA.
IS THIS THE "ETCH-A-SKETCH" I HAVE READ OF?
=SIGH= WHEN DO YOU RUGRATS GO "BACK TO THE FUTURE," ANYWAY?
YOU MEAN YOU DIDN'T TELL HER?
I THOUGHT YOU WERE GONNA TELL HER! I'M AFRAID OF HER!
OH NO... NO...
OH YEAH-- GOOD NEWS, HILL--
WE'RE STAYING.
AND WE NEED A PLACE TO CRASH.

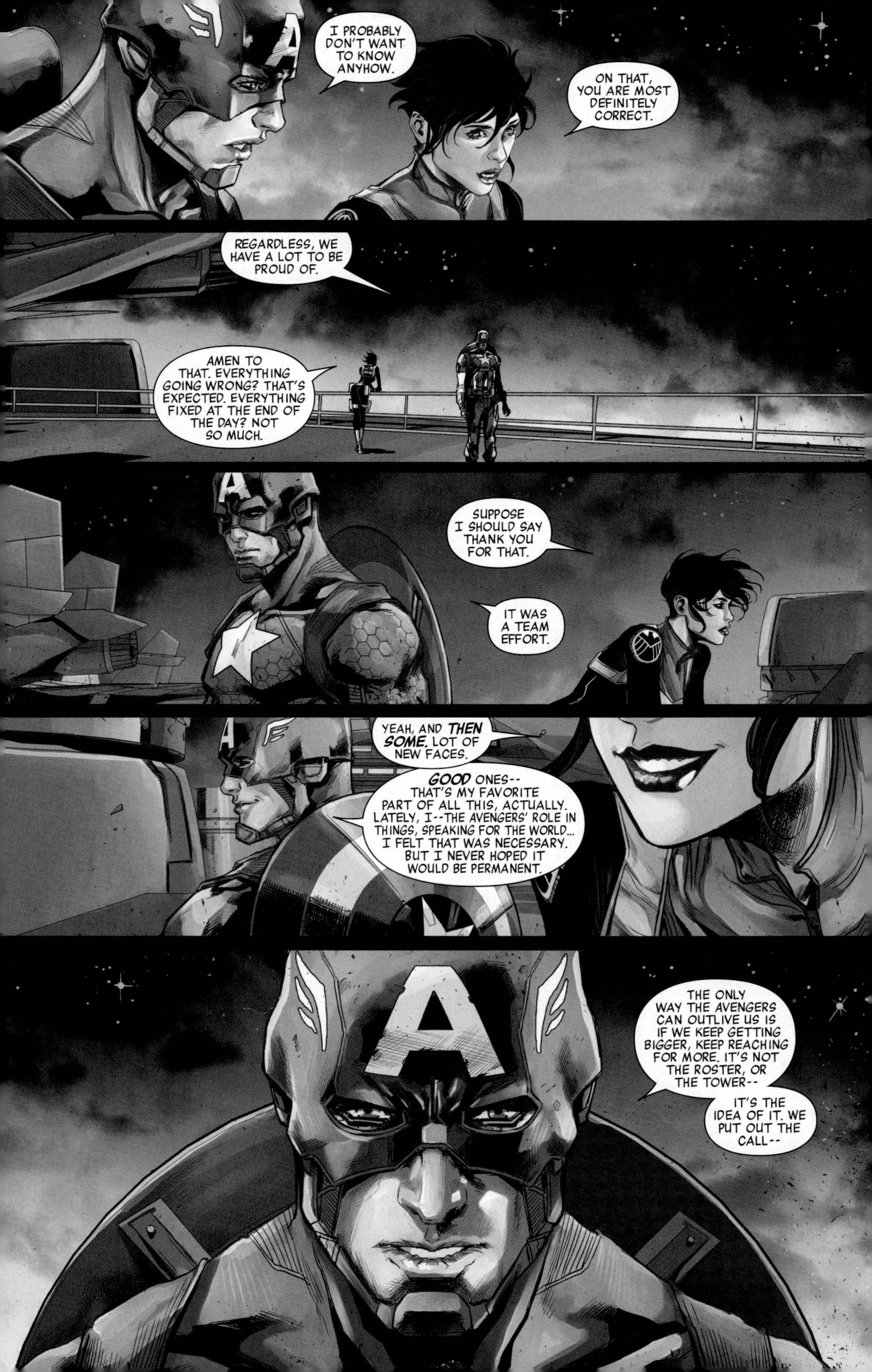
I PROBABLY DON'T WANT TO KNOW ANYHOW.
ON THAT, YOU ARE MOST DEFINITELY CORRECT.
REGARDLESS, WE HAVE A LOT TO BE PROUD OF.
AMEN TO THAT. EVERYTHING GOING WRONG? THAT'S EXPECTED. EVERYTHING FIXED AT THE END OF THE DAY? NOT SO MUCH.
SUPPOSE I SHOULD SAY THANK YOU FOR THAT.
IT WAS A TEAM EFFORT.
YEAH, AND THEN SOME. LOT OF NEW FACES.
GOOD ONES-- THAT'S MY FAVORITE PART OF ALL THIS, ACTUALLY. LATELY, I--THE AVENGERS' ROLE IN THINGS, SPEAKING FOR THE WORLD... I FELT THAT WAS NECESSARY. BUT I NEVER HOPED IT WOULD BE PERMANENT.
THE ONLY WAY THE AVENGERS CAN OUTLIVE US IS IF WE KEEP GETTING BIGGER, KEEP REACHING FOR MORE. IT'S NOT THE ROSTER, OR THE TOWER--
IT'S THE IDEA OF IT. WE PUT OUT THE CALL--

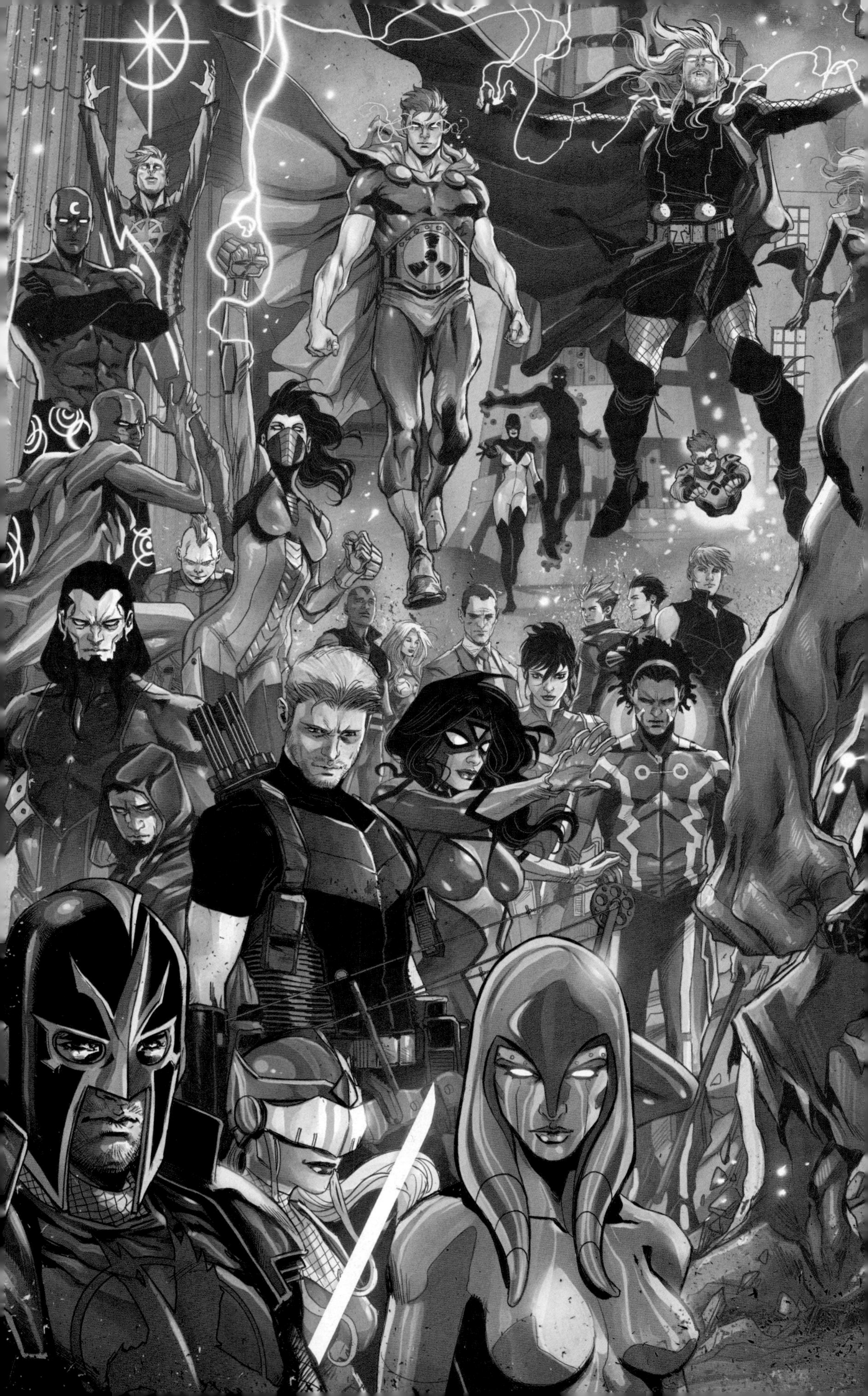

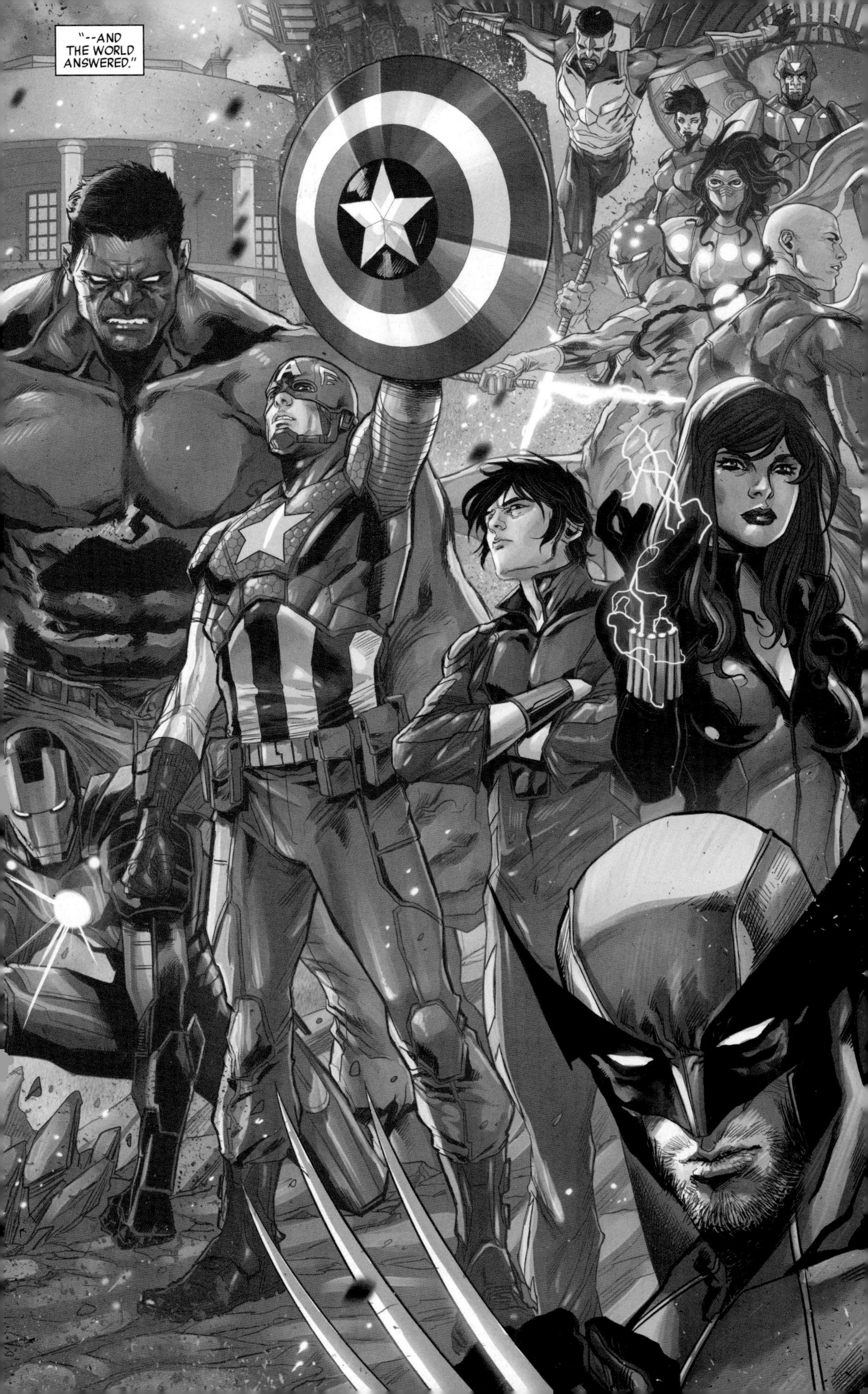
"--AND THE WORLD ANSWERED."

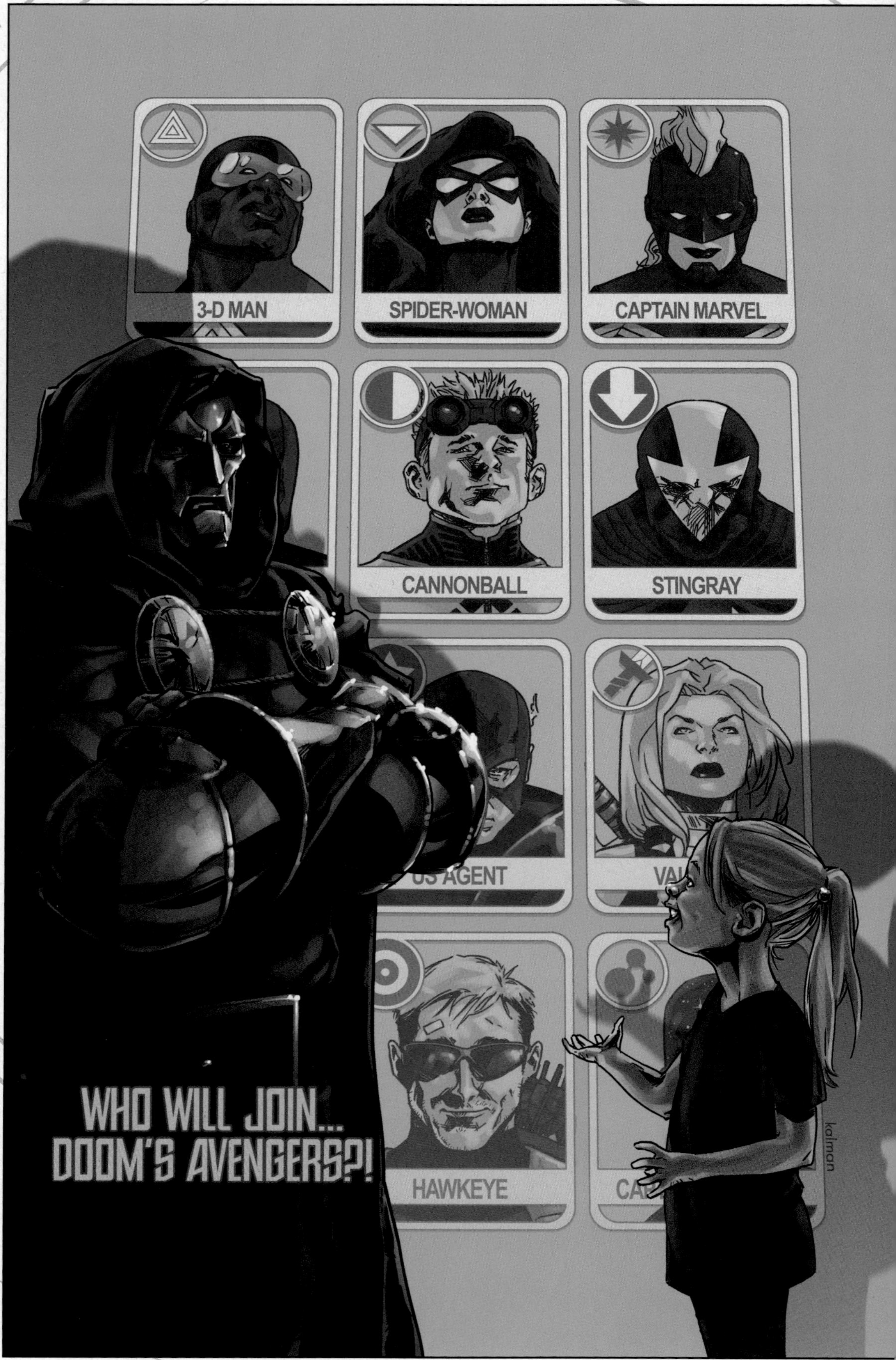
3-D MAN
SPIDER-WOMAN
CAPTAIN MARVEL
CANNONBALL
STINGRAY
US AGENT
HAWKEYE
WHO WILL JOIN...
DOOM'S AVENGERS?!

S.H.I.E.L.D. MISSION REPORT

BRUCE BANNER, STEVE ROGERS AND MARIA HILL

STEVE ROGERS (a.k.a. CAPTAIN AMERICA) and BRUCE BANNER (a.k.a. THE HULK) joined with S.H.I.E.L.D. at the request of MARIA HILL to be Avengers liaisons in creating a response team for large threats the world over. On their first day, three crises exploded around the globe. Using their combined resources, S.H.I.E.L.D. and the Avengers neutralized the threats and saved the day.

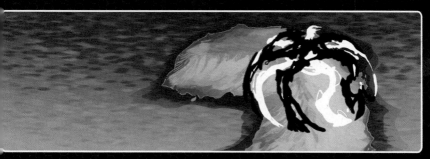

GENOSHA DURING THE INVERSION

But a new, terrible day has dawned. Steve Rogers was drained of his Super-Soldier Serum and rapidly aged into an old man. Bruce Banner is lost, replaced with a Hulk that calls himself Doc Green. On top of that, a strange event occurred on the island of Genosha, causing heroes to act like villains and villains to act like heroes. The few heroes who remained have all gone missing.

Who will protect an Avengers World that is Avengerless?

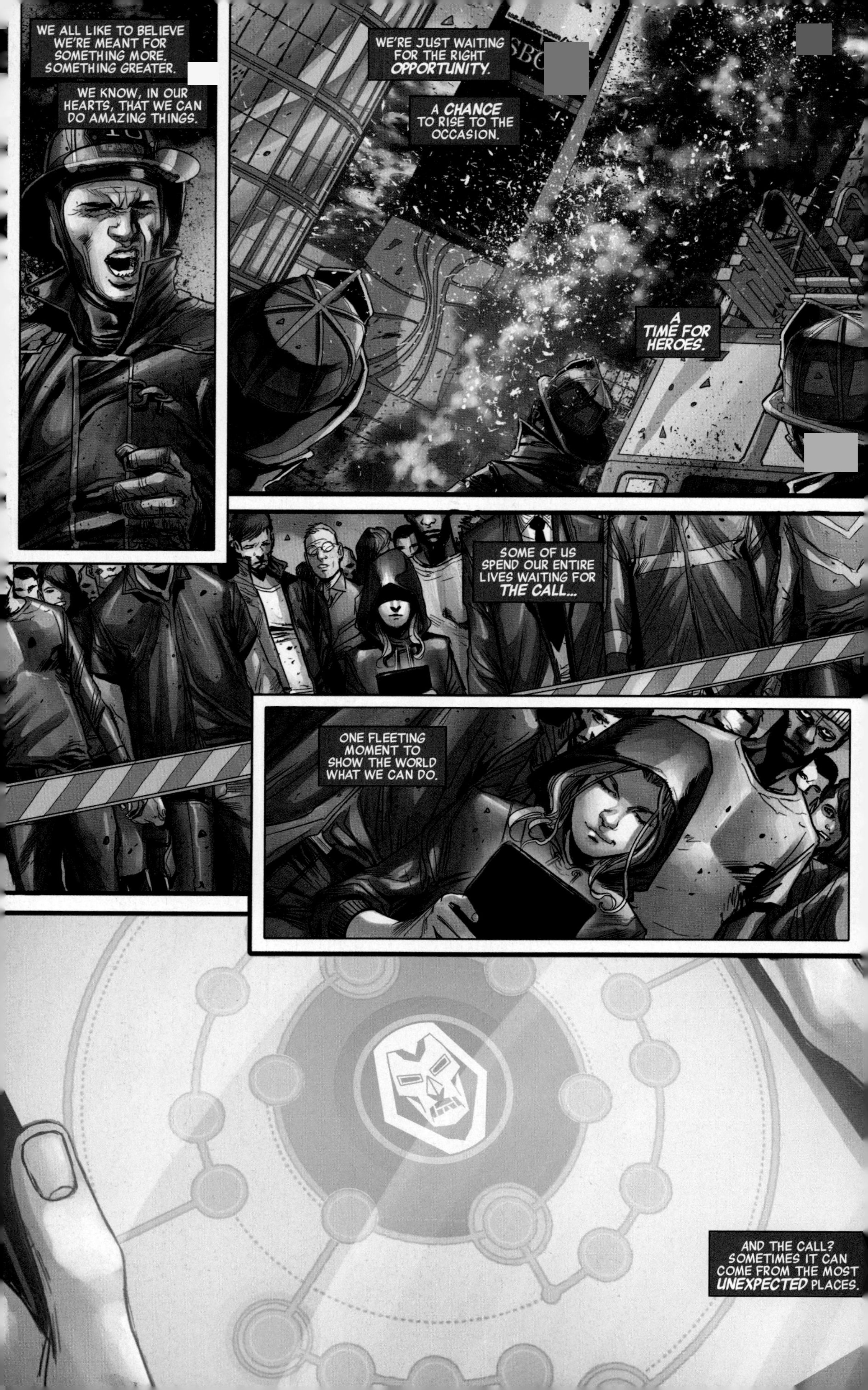

WE ALL LIKE TO BELIEVE WE'RE MEANT FOR SOMETHING MORE. SOMETHING GREATER.
WE KNOW, IN OUR HEARTS, THAT WE CAN DO AMAZING THINGS.
WE'RE JUST WAITING FOR THE RIGHT OPPORTUNITY.
A CHANCE TO RISE TO THE OCCASION.
A TIME FOR HEROES.
SOME OF US SPEND OUR ENTIRE LIVES WAITING FOR THE CALL...
ONE FLEETING MOMENT TO SHOW THE WORLD WHAT WE CAN DO.
AND THE CALL? SOMETIMES IT CAN COME FROM THE MOST UNEXPECTED PLACES.

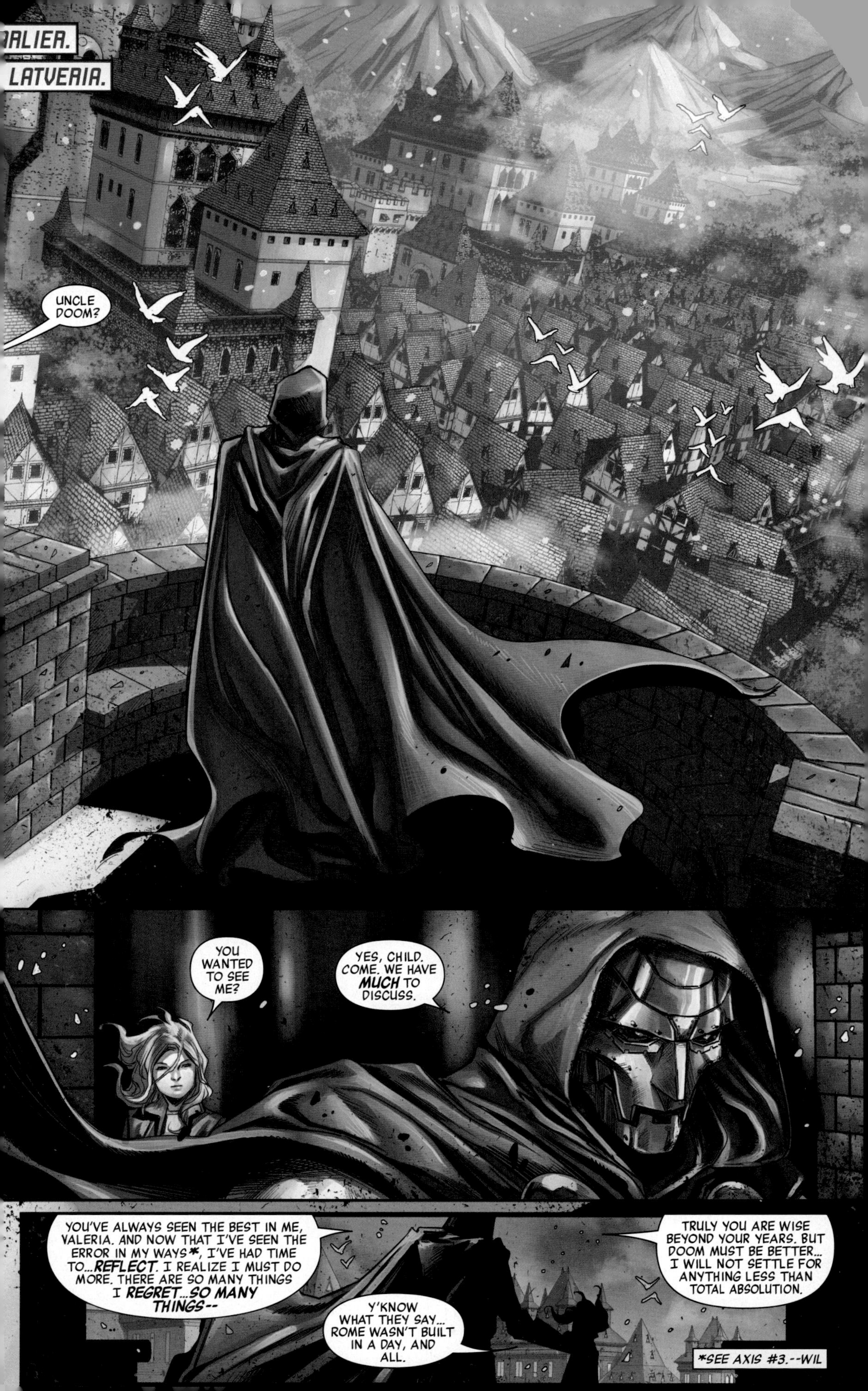

ARLIER.
LATVERIA.
UNCLE DOOM?
YOU WANTED TO SEE ME?
YES, CHILD. COME. WE HAVE MUCH TO DISCUSS.
YOU'VE ALWAYS SEEN THE BEST IN ME, VALERIA. AND NOW THAT I'VE SEEN THE ERROR IN MY WAYS*, I'VE HAD TIME TO...REFLECT. I REALIZE I MUST DO MORE. THERE ARE SO MANY THINGS I REGRET...SO MANY THINGS--
Y'KNOW WHAT THEY SAY... ROME WASN'T BUILT IN A DAY, AND ALL.
TRULY YOU ARE WISE BEYOND YOUR YEARS. BUT DOOM MUST BE BETTER... I WILL NOT SETTLE FOR ANYTHING LESS THAN TOTAL ABSOLUTION.
*SEE AXIS #3.--WIL

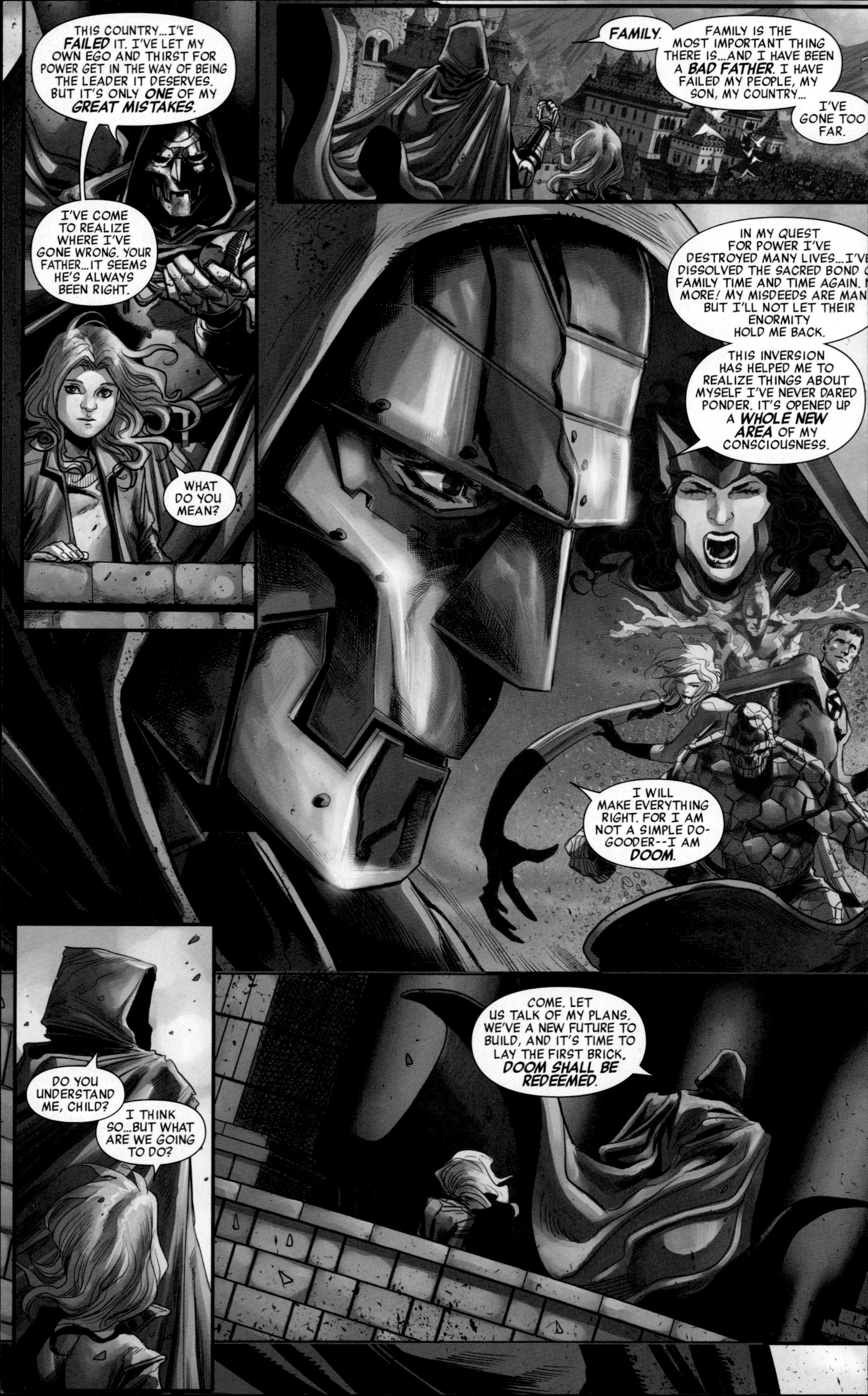
THIS COUNTRY...I'VE FAILED IT. I'VE LET MY OWN EGO AND THIRST FOR POWER GET IN THE WAY OF BEING THE LEADER IT DESERVES. BUT IT'S ONLY ONE OF MY GREAT MISTAKES.
I'VE COME TO REALIZE WHERE I'VE GONE WRONG. YOUR FATHER...IT SEEMS HE'S ALWAYS BEEN RIGHT.
WHAT DO YOU MEAN?
FAMILY.
FAMILY IS THE MOST IMPORTANT THING THERE IS...AND I HAVE BEEN A BAD FATHER. I HAVE FAILED MY PEOPLE, MY SON, MY COUNTRY...
I'VE GONE TOO FAR.
IN MY QUEST FOR POWER I'VE DESTROYED MANY LIVES...I'VE DISSOLVED THE SACRED BOND FAMILY TIME AND TIME AGAIN. MORE! MY MISDEEDS ARE MAN BUT I'LL NOT LET THEIR ENORMITY HOLD ME BACK.
THIS INVERSION HAS HELPED ME TO REALIZE THINGS ABOUT MYSELF I'VE NEVER DARED PONDER. IT'S OPENED UP A WHOLE NEW AREA OF MY CONSCIOUSNESS.
I WILL MAKE EVERYTHING RIGHT. FOR I AM NOT A SIMPLE DO-GOODER--I AM DOOM.
DO YOU UNDERSTAND ME, CHILD?
I THINK SO...BUT WHAT ARE WE GOING TO DO?
COME. LET US TALK OF MY PLANS. WE'VE A NEW FUTURE TO BUILD, AND IT'S TIME TO LAY THE FIRST BRICK. DOOM SHALL BE REDEEMED.

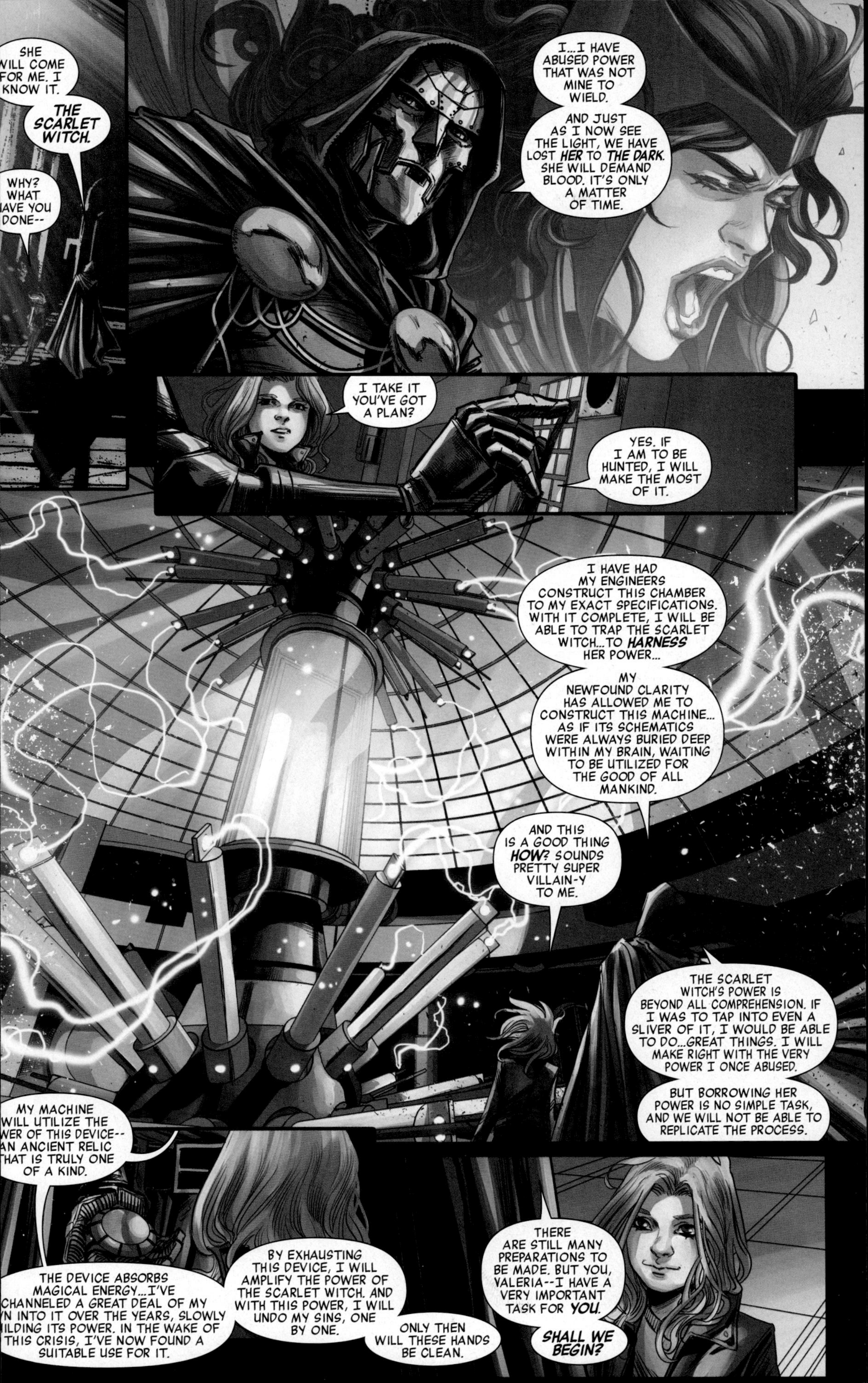

SHE WILL COME FOR ME. I KNOW IT.
THE SCARLET WITCH.
WHY? WHAT HAVE YOU DONE--
I...I HAVE ABUSED POWER THAT WAS NOT MINE TO WIELD.
AND JUST AS I NOW SEE THE LIGHT, WE HAVE LOST HER TO THE DARK. SHE WILL DEMAND BLOOD. IT'S ONLY A MATTER OF TIME.
I TAKE IT YOU'VE GOT A PLAN?
YES. IF I AM TO BE HUNTED, I WILL MAKE THE MOST OF IT.
I HAVE HAD MY ENGINEERS CONSTRUCT THIS CHAMBER TO MY EXACT SPECIFICATIONS. WITH IT COMPLETE, I WILL BE ABLE TO TRAP THE SCARLET WITCH...TO HARNESS HER POWER...
MY NEWFOUND CLARITY HAS ALLOWED ME TO CONSTRUCT THIS MACHINE... AS IF ITS SCHEMATICS WERE ALWAYS BURIED DEEP WITHIN MY BRAIN, WAITING TO BE UTILIZED FOR THE GOOD OF ALL MANKIND.
AND THIS IS A GOOD THING HOW? SOUNDS PRETTY SUPER VILLAIN-Y TO ME.
THE SCARLET WITCH'S POWER IS BEYOND ALL COMPREHENSION. IF I WAS TO TAP INTO EVEN A SLIVER OF IT, I WOULD BE ABLE TO DO...GREAT THINGS. I WILL MAKE RIGHT WITH THE VERY POWER I ONCE ABUSED.
BUT BORROWING HER POWER IS NO SIMPLE TASK, AND WE WILL NOT BE ABLE TO REPLICATE THE PROCESS.
MY MACHINE WILL UTILIZE THE WER OF THIS DEVICE-- AN ANCIENT RELIC THAT IS TRULY ONE OF A KIND.
THE DEVICE ABSORBS MAGICAL ENERGY...I'VE CHANNELED A GREAT DEAL OF MY N INTO IT OVER THE YEARS, SLOWLY ILDING ITS POWER. IN THE WAKE OF THIS CRISIS, I'VE NOW FOUND A SUITABLE USE FOR IT.
BY EXHAUSTING THIS DEVICE, I WILL AMPLIFY THE POWER OF THE SCARLET WITCH. AND WITH THIS POWER, I WILL UNDO MY SINS, ONE BY ONE.
ONLY THEN WILL THESE HANDS BE CLEAN.
THERE ARE STILL MANY PREPARATIONS TO BE MADE. BUT YOU, VALERIA--I HAVE A VERY IMPORTANT TASK FOR YOU.
SHALL WE BEGIN?

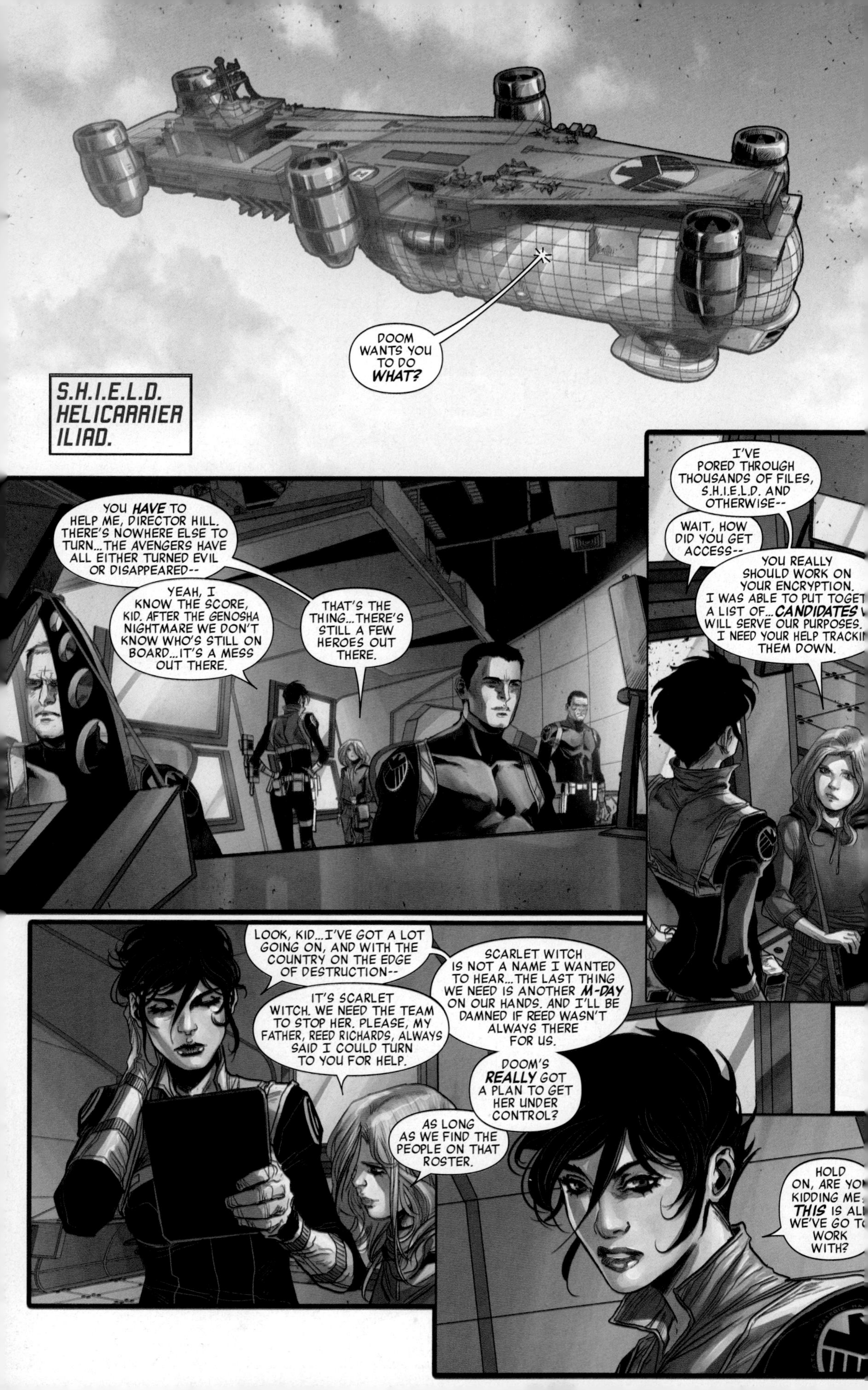

DOOM WANTS YOU TO DO WHAT?
S.H.I.E.L.D. HELICARRIER ILIAD.
YOU HAVE TO HELP ME, DIRECTOR HILL. THERE'S NOWHERE ELSE TO TURN... THE AVENGERS HAVE ALL EITHER TURNED EVIL OR DISAPPEARED--
YEAH, I KNOW THE SCORE, KID. AFTER THE GENOSHA NIGHTMARE WE DON'T KNOW WHO'S STILL ON BOARD... IT'S A MESS OUT THERE.
THAT'S THE THING... THERE'S STILL A FEW HEROES OUT THERE.
I'VE PORED THROUGH THOUSANDS OF FILES, S.H.I.E.L.D. AND OTHERWISE--
WAIT, HOW DID YOU GET ACCESS--
YOU REALLY SHOULD WORK ON YOUR ENCRYPTION. I WAS ABLE TO PUT TOGET A LIST OF... CANDIDATES WILL SERVE OUR PURPOSES. I NEED YOUR HELP TRACKI THEM DOWN.
LOOK, KID... I'VE GOT A LOT GOING ON, AND WITH THE COUNTRY ON THE EDGE OF DESTRUCTION--
IT'S SCARLET WITCH. WE NEED THE TEAM TO STOP HER. PLEASE, MY FATHER, REED RICHARDS, ALWAYS SAID I COULD TURN TO YOU FOR HELP.
SCARLET WITCH IS NOT A NAME I WANTED TO HEAR... THE LAST THING WE NEED IS ANOTHER M-DAY ON OUR HANDS. AND I'LL BE DAMNED IF REED WASN'T ALWAYS THERE FOR US.
DOOM'S REALLY GOT A PLAN TO GET HER UNDER CONTROL?
AS LONG AS WE FIND THE PEOPLE ON THAT ROSTER.
HOLD ON, ARE YO KIDDING ME. THIS IS AL WE'VE GOT TO WORK WITH?

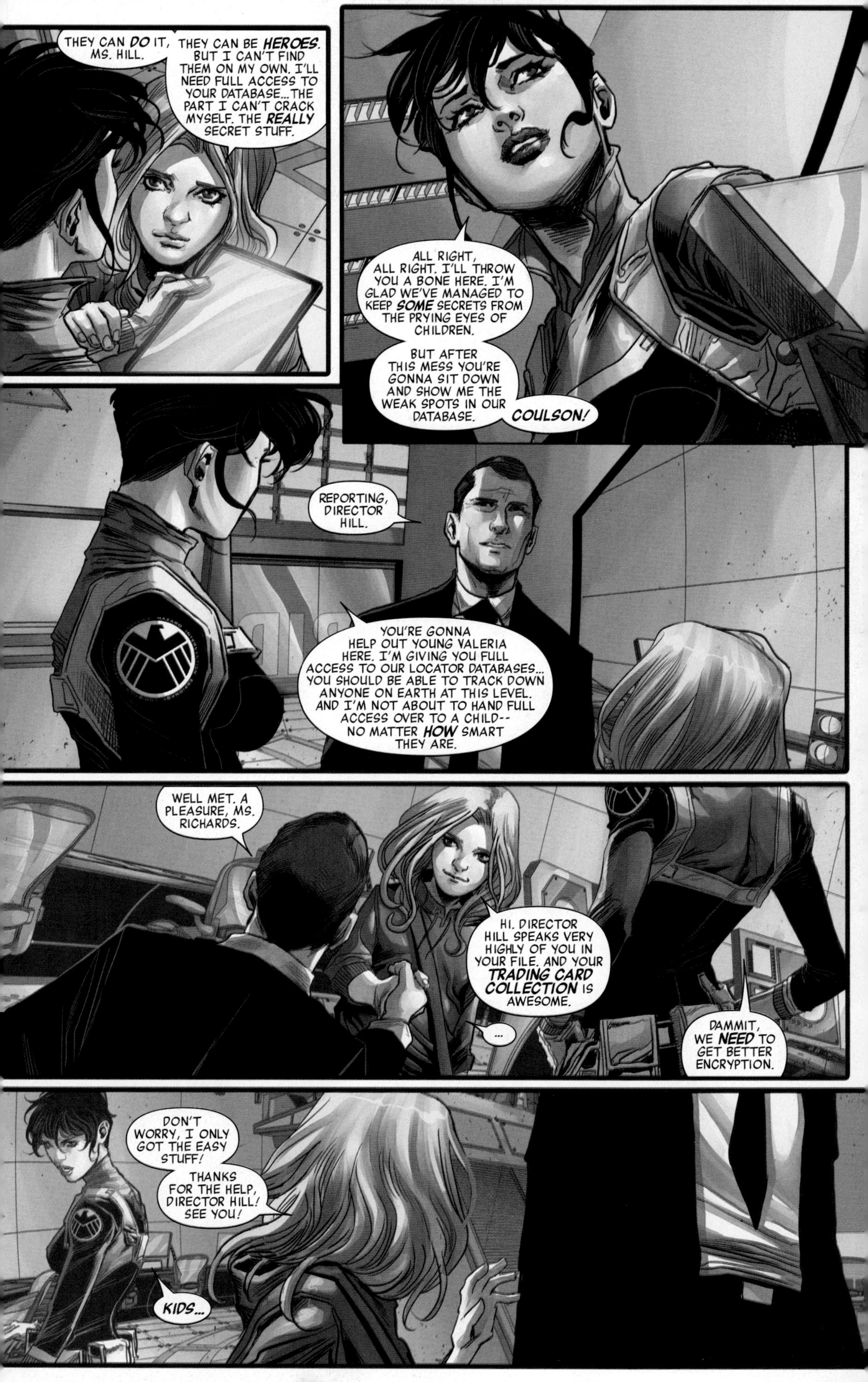
THEY CAN DO IT, MS. HILL.
THEY CAN BE HEROES. BUT I CAN'T FIND THEM ON MY OWN. I'LL NEED FULL ACCESS TO YOUR DATABASE...THE PART I CAN'T CRACK MYSELF. THE REALLY SECRET STUFF.
ALL RIGHT, ALL RIGHT. I'LL THROW YOU A BONE HERE. I'M GLAD WE'VE MANAGED TO KEEP SOME SECRETS FROM THE PRYING EYES OF CHILDREN.
BUT AFTER THIS MESS YOU'RE GONNA SIT DOWN AND SHOW ME THE WEAK SPOTS IN OUR DATABASE.
COULSON!
REPORTING, DIRECTOR HILL.
YOU'RE GONNA HELP OUT YOUNG VALERIA HERE. I'M GIVING YOU FULL ACCESS TO OUR LOCATOR DATABASES... YOU SHOULD BE ABLE TO TRACK DOWN ANYONE ON EARTH AT THIS LEVEL. AND I'M NOT ABOUT TO HAND FULL ACCESS OVER TO A CHILD-- NO MATTER HOW SMART THEY ARE.
WELL MET. A PLEASURE, MS. RICHARDS.
HI. DIRECTOR HILL SPEAKS VERY HIGHLY OF YOU IN YOUR FILE. AND YOUR TRADING CARD COLLECTION IS AWESOME.
...
DAMMIT, WE NEED TO GET BETTER ENCRYPTION.
DON'T WORRY, I ONLY GOT THE EASY STUFF!
THANKS FOR THE HELP, DIRECTOR HILL! SEE YOU!
KIDS...

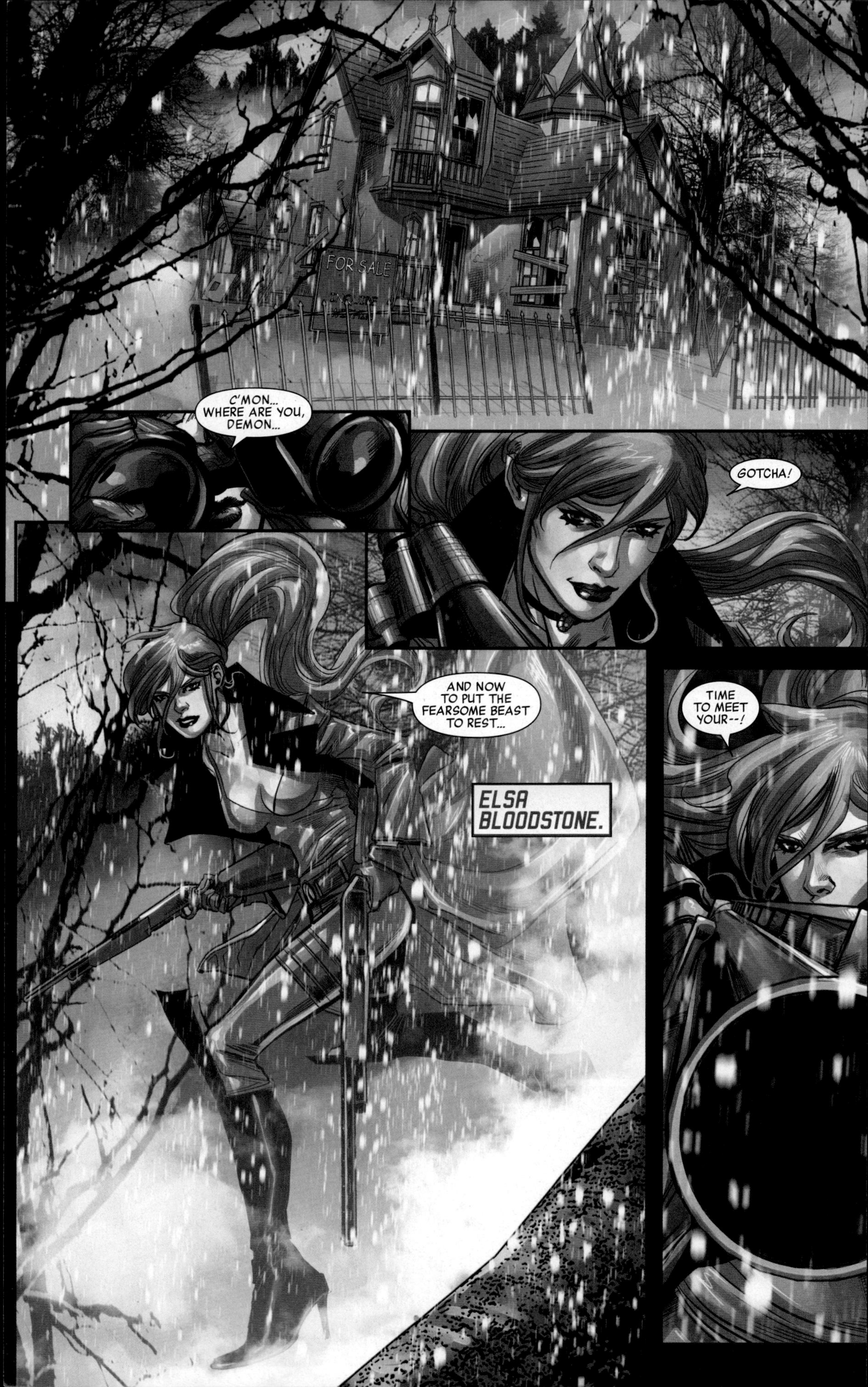
FOR SALE
C'MON... WHERE ARE YOU, DEMON...
GOTCHA!
AND NOW TO PUT THE FEARSOME BEAST TO REST...
ELSA BLOODSTONE.
TIME TO MEET YOUR--!

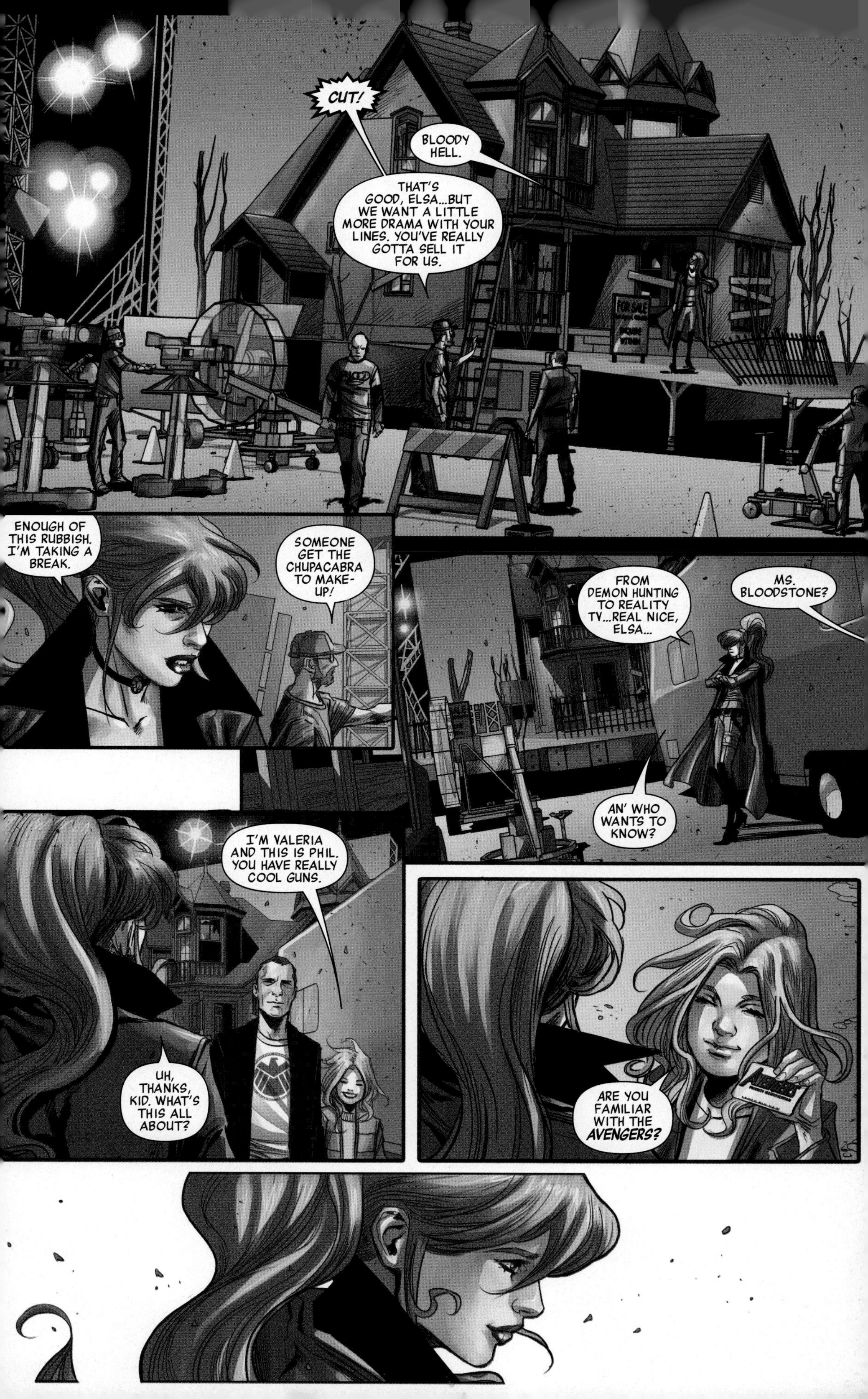
CUT!
BLOODY HELL.
THAT'S GOOD, ELSA...BUT WE WANT A LITTLE MORE DRAMA WITH YOUR LINES. YOU'VE REALLY GOTTA SELL IT FOR US.
FOR SALE
ENOUGH OF THIS RUBBISH. I'M TAKING A BREAK.
SOMEONE GET THE CHUPACABRA TO MAKE-UP!
FROM DEMON HUNTING TO REALITY TV...REAL NICE, ELSA...
MS. BLOODSTONE?
AN' WHO WANTS TO KNOW?
I'M VALERIA AND THIS IS PHIL. YOU HAVE REALLY COOL GUNS.
UH, THANKS, KID. WHAT'S THIS ALL ABOUT?
ARE YOU FAMILIAR WITH THE AVENGERS?

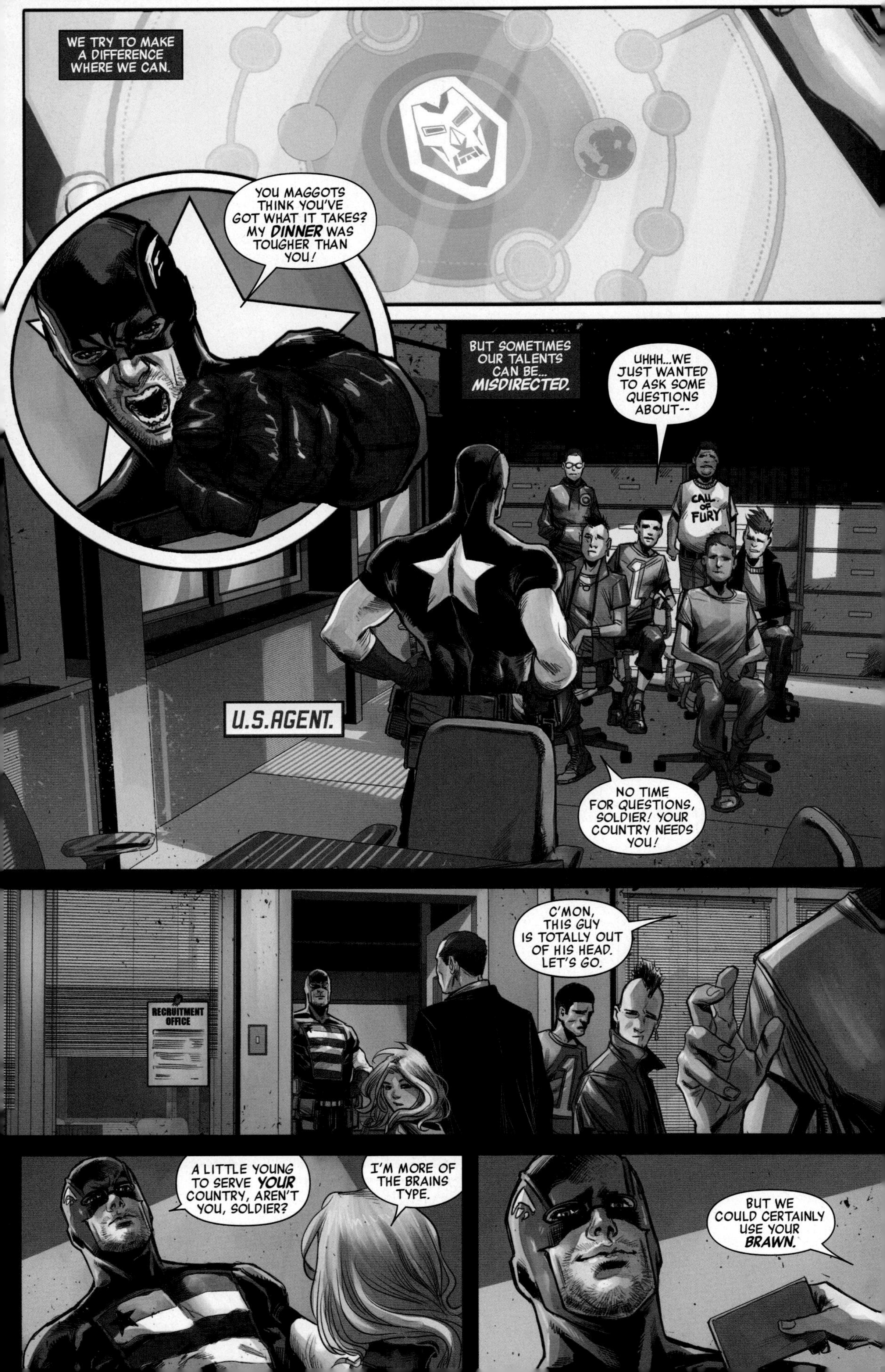
WE TRY TO MAKE A DIFFERENCE WHERE WE CAN.
YOU MAGGOTS THINK YOU'VE GOT WHAT IT TAKES? MY DINNER WAS TOUGHER THAN YOU!
BUT SOMETIMES OUR TALENTS CAN BE... MISDIRECTED.
UHHH...WE JUST WANTED TO ASK SOME QUESTIONS ABOUT--
CALL OF FURY
U.S.AGENT.
NO TIME FOR QUESTIONS, SOLDIER! YOUR COUNTRY NEEDS YOU!
C'MON, THIS GUY IS TOTALLY OUT OF HIS HEAD. LET'S GO.
RECRUITMENT OFFICE
A LITTLE YOUNG TO SERVE YOUR COUNTRY, AREN'T YOU, SOLDIER?
I'M MORE OF THE BRAINS TYPE.
BUT WE COULD CERTAINLY USE YOUR BRAWN.

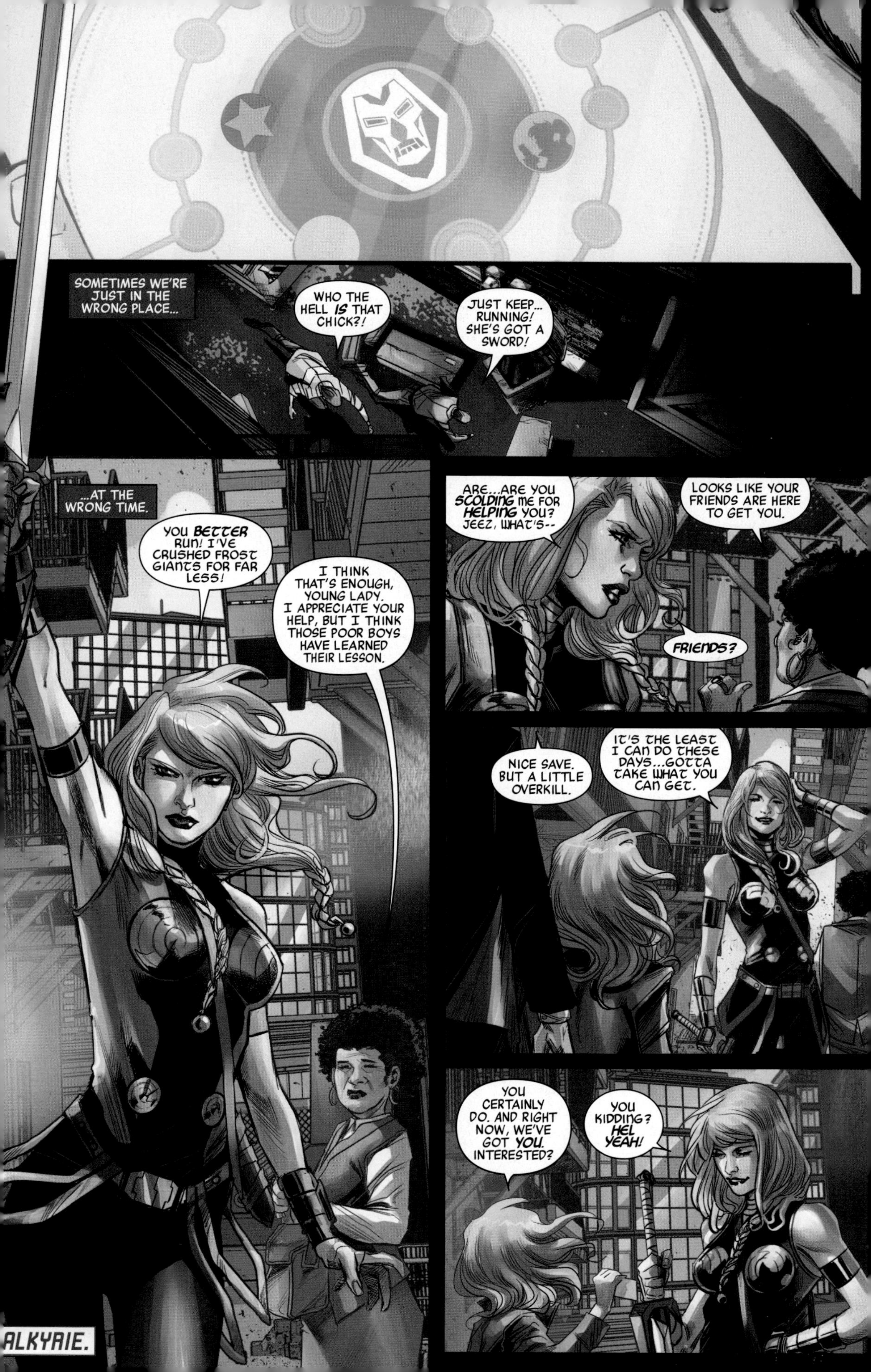
SOMETIMES WE'RE JUST IN THE WRONG PLACE...
WHO THE HELL IS THAT CHICK?!
JUST KEEP... RUNNING! SHE'S GOT A SWORD!
...AT THE WRONG TIME.
YOU BETTER RUN! I'VE CRUSHED FROST GIANTS FOR FAR LESS!
I THINK THAT'S ENOUGH, YOUNG LADY. I APPRECIATE YOUR HELP, BUT I THINK THOSE POOR BOYS HAVE LEARNED THEIR LESSON.
ARE...ARE YOU SCOLDING ME FOR HELPING YOU? JEEZ, WHAT'S--
LOOKS LIKE YOUR FRIENDS ARE HERE TO GET YOU.
FRIENDS?
NICE SAVE. BUT A LITTLE OVERKILL.
IT'S THE LEAST I CAN DO THESE DAYS...GOTTA TAKE WHAT YOU CAN GET.
YOU CERTAINLY DO. AND RIGHT NOW, WE'VE GOT YOU. INTERESTED?
YOU KIDDING? HEL YEAH!
ALKYRIE.

WE'RE ALL JUST WAITING FOR OUR MOMENT.

BRIMMING WITH POTENTIAL, READY TO SHINE.

YOU'RE SURE ABOUT THIS ONE?

HUH. NEVER EVEN HEARD OF HIM.

YEP. HE'S GOT A LOT OF POTENTIAL.

MAKE WAY, SLOWPOKES! WOO!

3-D MAN.

NICE RACE. WELL, IF YOU COULD CALL IT THAT.

IMPORTANT TO STAY IN SHAPE. YEAH?

WE THINK YOU COULD DO A LOT MORE.

THE AVENGERS NEED SOMEONE WITH YOUR SKILLS. CARE TO TRY OUT SOME NEW COMPETITION?

OH MAN BACK TO BIG LEAGU WHERE C I SIGN U

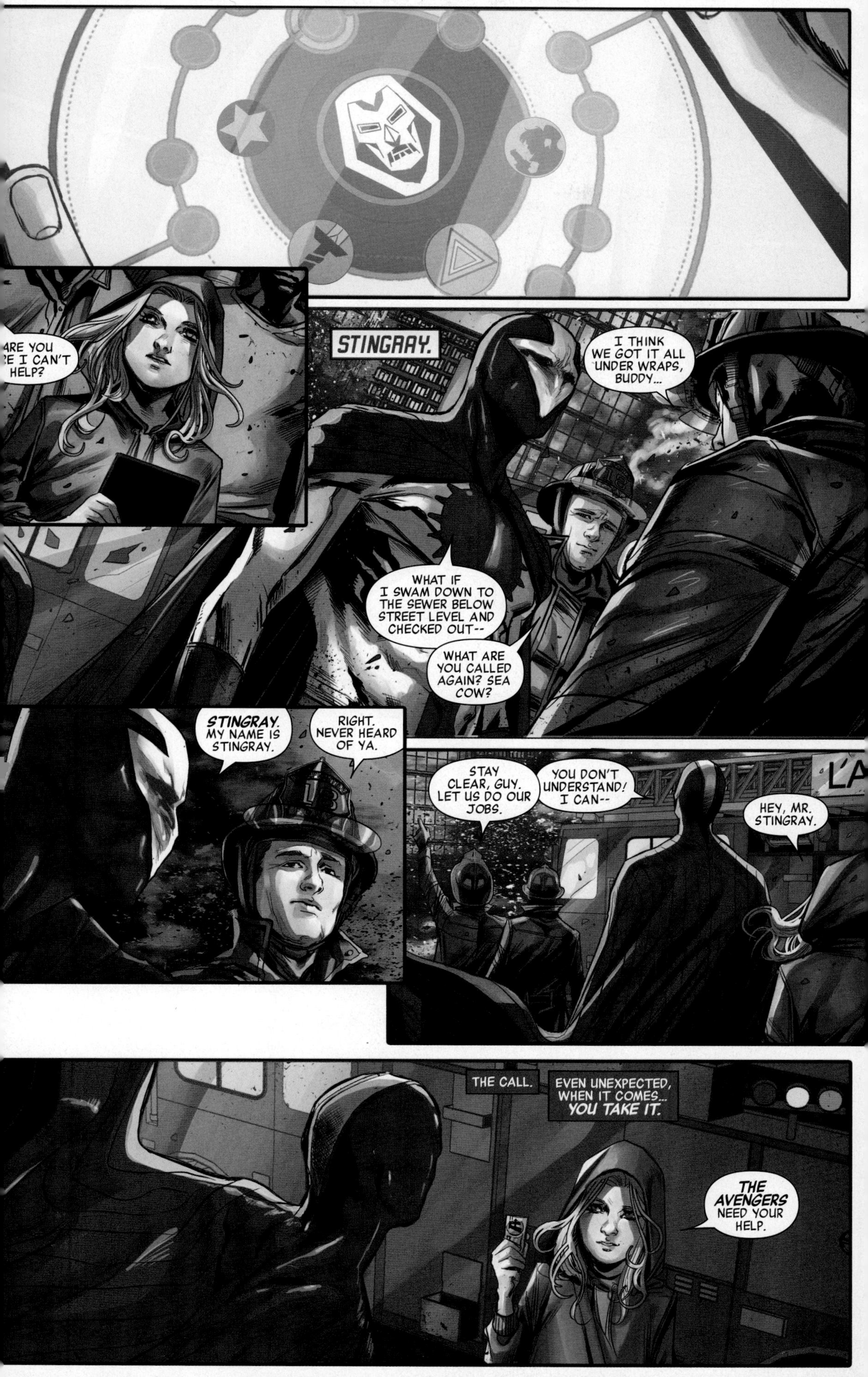
ARE YOU
E I CAN'T
HELP?
STINGRAY.
I THINK WE GOT IT ALL UNDER WRAPS, BUDDY...
WHAT IF I SWAM DOWN TO THE SEWER BELOW STREET LEVEL AND CHECKED OUT--
WHAT ARE YOU CALLED AGAIN? SEA COW?
STINGRAY. MY NAME IS STINGRAY.
RIGHT. NEVER HEARD OF YA.
STAY CLEAR, GUY. LET US DO OUR JOBS.
YOU DON'T UNDERSTAND! I CAN--
HEY, MR. STINGRAY.
THE CALL.
EVEN UNEXPECTED, WHEN IT COMES... YOU TAKE IT.
THE AVENGERS NEED YOUR HELP.

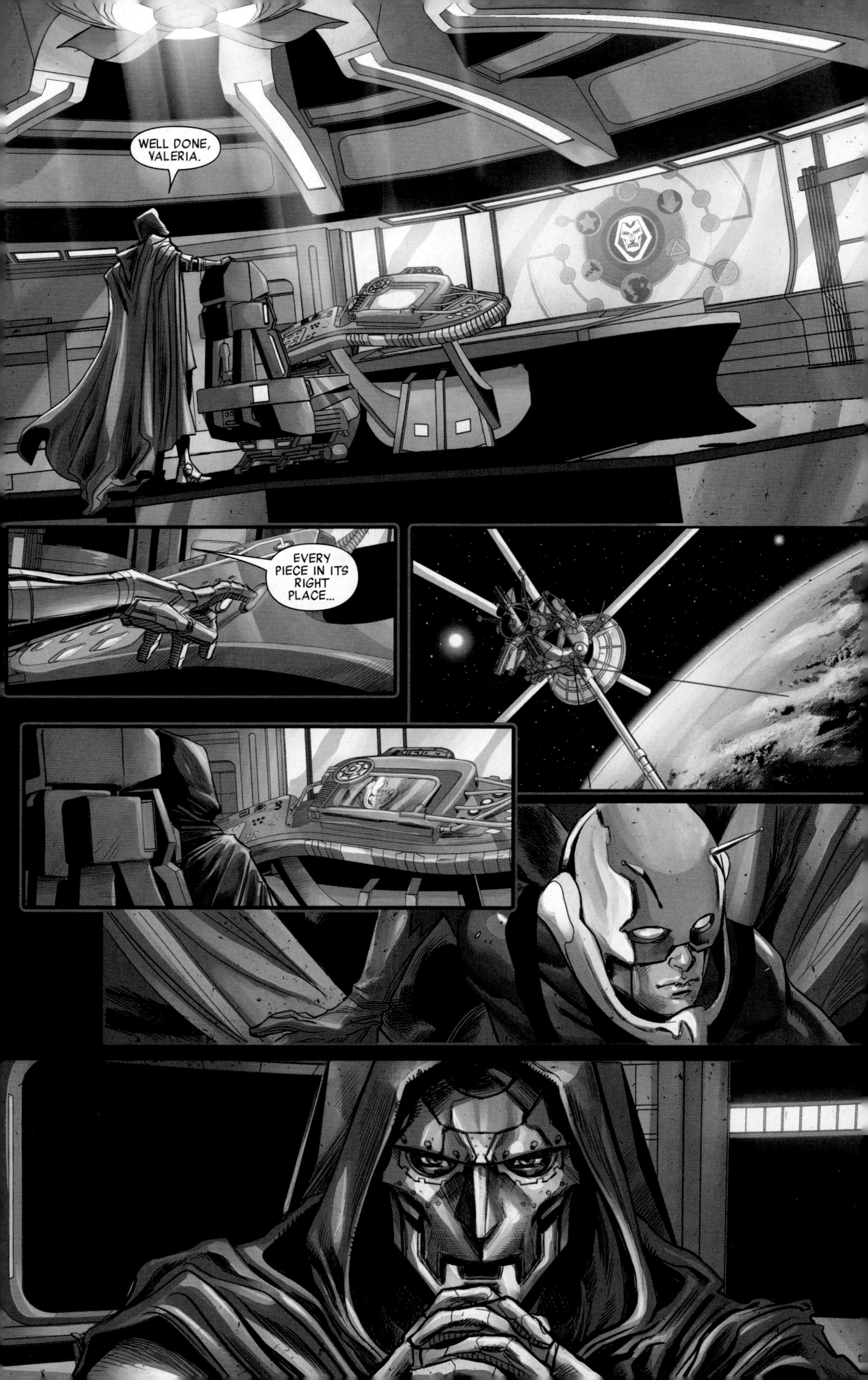
WELL DONE, VALERIA.
EVERY PIECE IN ITS RIGHT PLACE...

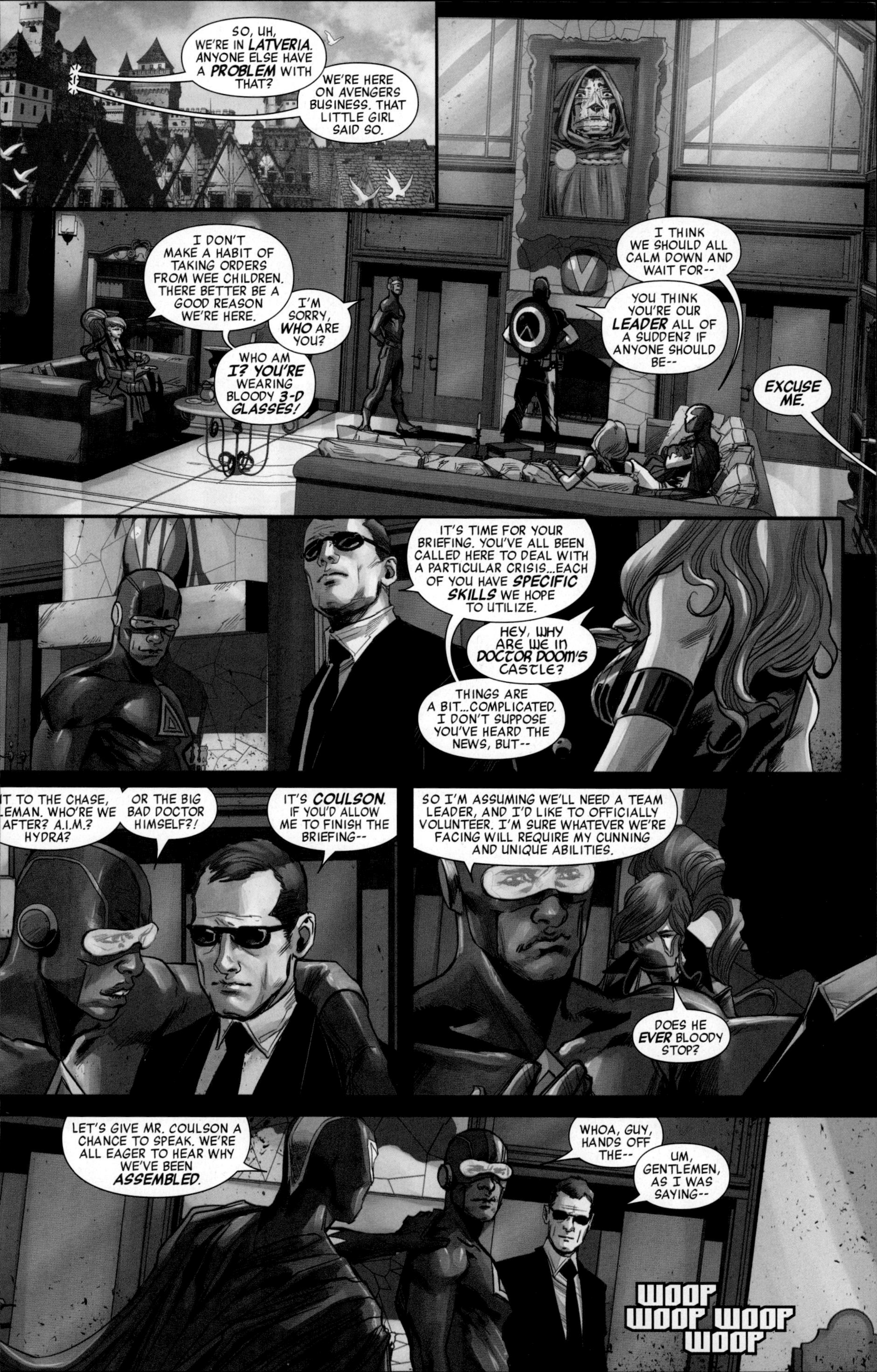
SO, UH, WE'RE IN LATVERIA. ANYONE ELSE HAVE A PROBLEM WITH THAT?
WE'RE HERE ON AVENGERS BUSINESS. THAT LITTLE GIRL SAID SO.
I DON'T MAKE A HABIT OF TAKING ORDERS FROM WEE CHILDREN. THERE BETTER BE A GOOD REASON WE'RE HERE.
I'M SORRY, WHO ARE YOU?
WHO AM I? YOU'RE WEARING BLOODY 3-D GLASSES!
I THINK WE SHOULD ALL CALM DOWN AND WAIT FOR--
YOU THINK YOU'RE OUR LEADER ALL OF A SUDDEN? IF ANYONE SHOULD BE--
EXCUSE ME.
IT'S TIME FOR YOUR BRIEFING. YOU'VE ALL BEEN CALLED HERE TO DEAL WITH A PARTICULAR CRISIS...EACH OF YOU HAVE SPECIFIC SKILLS WE HOPE TO UTILIZE.
HEY, WHY ARE WE IN DOCTOR DOOM'S CASTLE?
THINGS ARE A BIT...COMPLICATED. I DON'T SUPPOSE YOU'VE HEARD THE NEWS, BUT--
IT TO THE CHASE, LEMAN. WHO'RE WE AFTER? A.I.M.? HYDRA?
OR THE BIG BAD DOCTOR HIMSELF?!
IT'S COULSON. IF YOU'D ALLOW ME TO FINISH THE BRIEFING--
SO I'M ASSUMING WE'LL NEED A TEAM LEADER, AND I'D LIKE TO OFFICIALLY VOLUNTEER. I'M SURE WHATEVER WE'RE FACING WILL REQUIRE MY CUNNING AND UNIQUE ABILITIES.
DOES HE EVER BLOODY STOP?
LET'S GIVE MR. COULSON A CHANCE TO SPEAK. WE'RE ALL EAGER TO HEAR WHY WE'VE BEEN ASSEMBLED.
WHOA, GUY, HANDS OFF THE--
UM, GENTLEMEN, AS I WAS SAYING--
WOOP WOOP WOOP WOOP

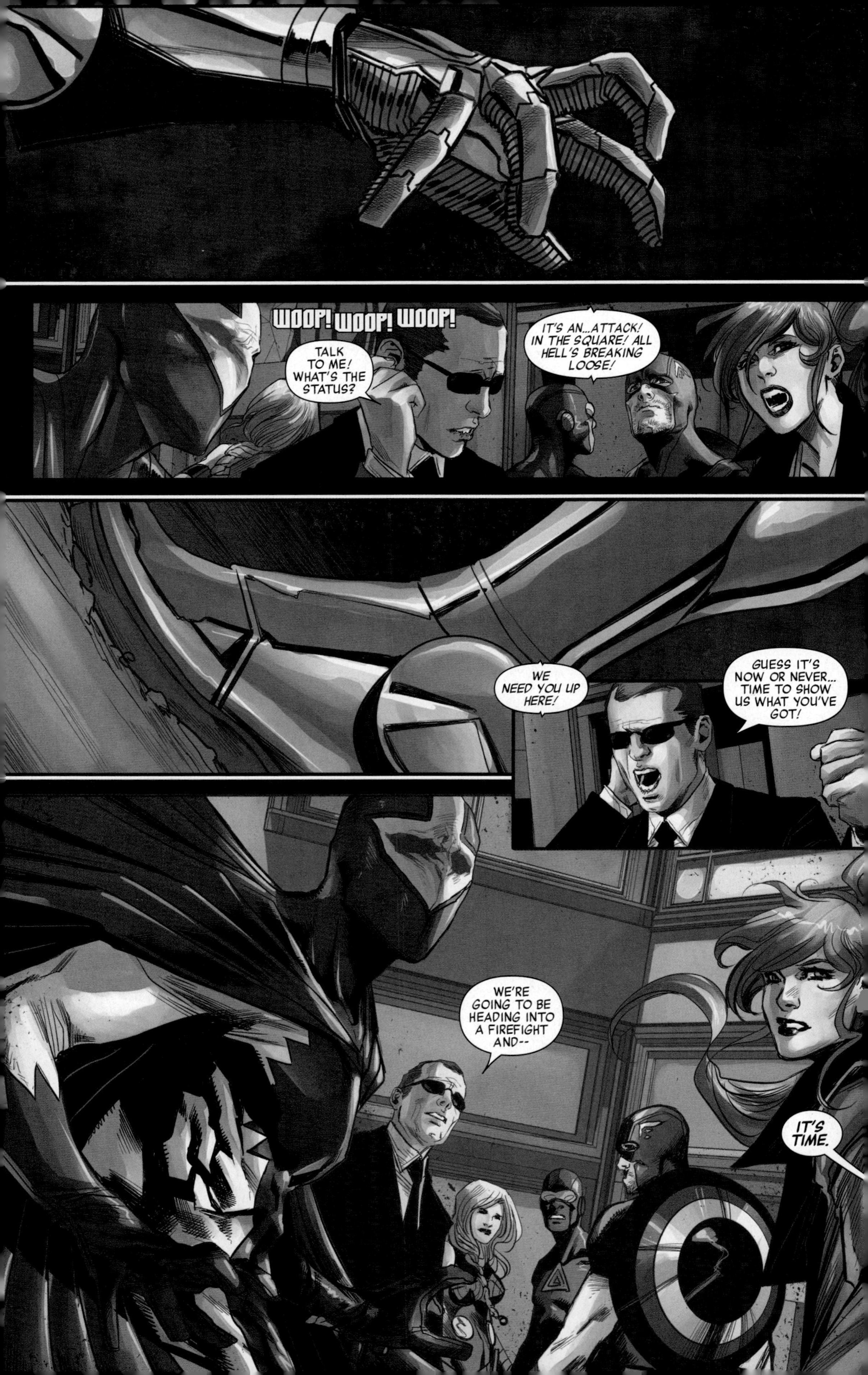
WOOP! WOOP! WOOP!
TALK TO ME! WHAT'S THE STATUS?
IT'S AN...ATTACK! IN THE SQUARE! ALL HELL'S BREAKING LOOSE!
WE NEED YOU UP HERE!
GUESS IT'S NOW OR NEVER... TIME TO SHOW US WHAT YOU'VE GOT!
WE'RE GOING TO BE HEADING INTO A FIREFIGHT AND--
IT'S TIME.

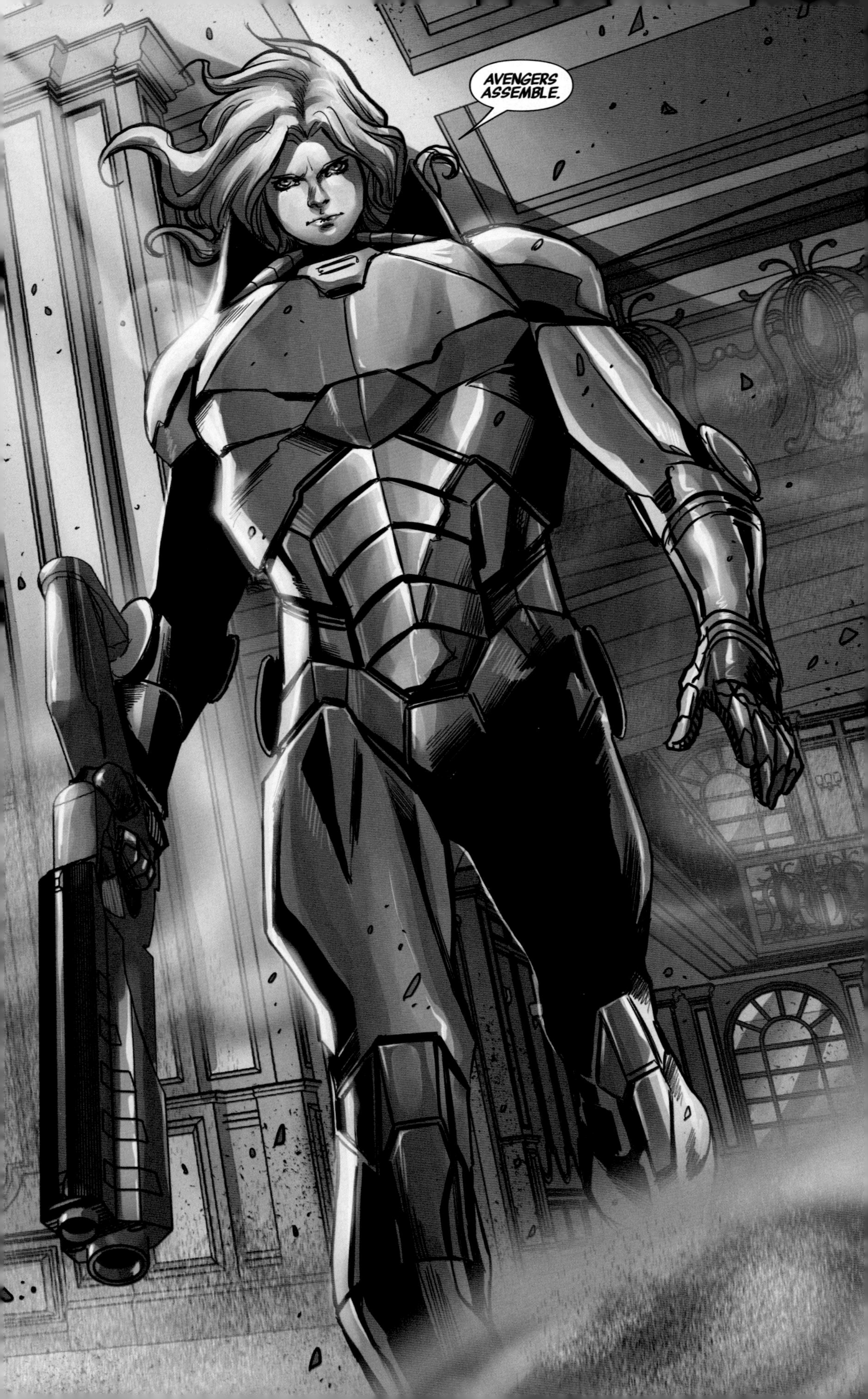
AVENGERS ASSEMBLE.

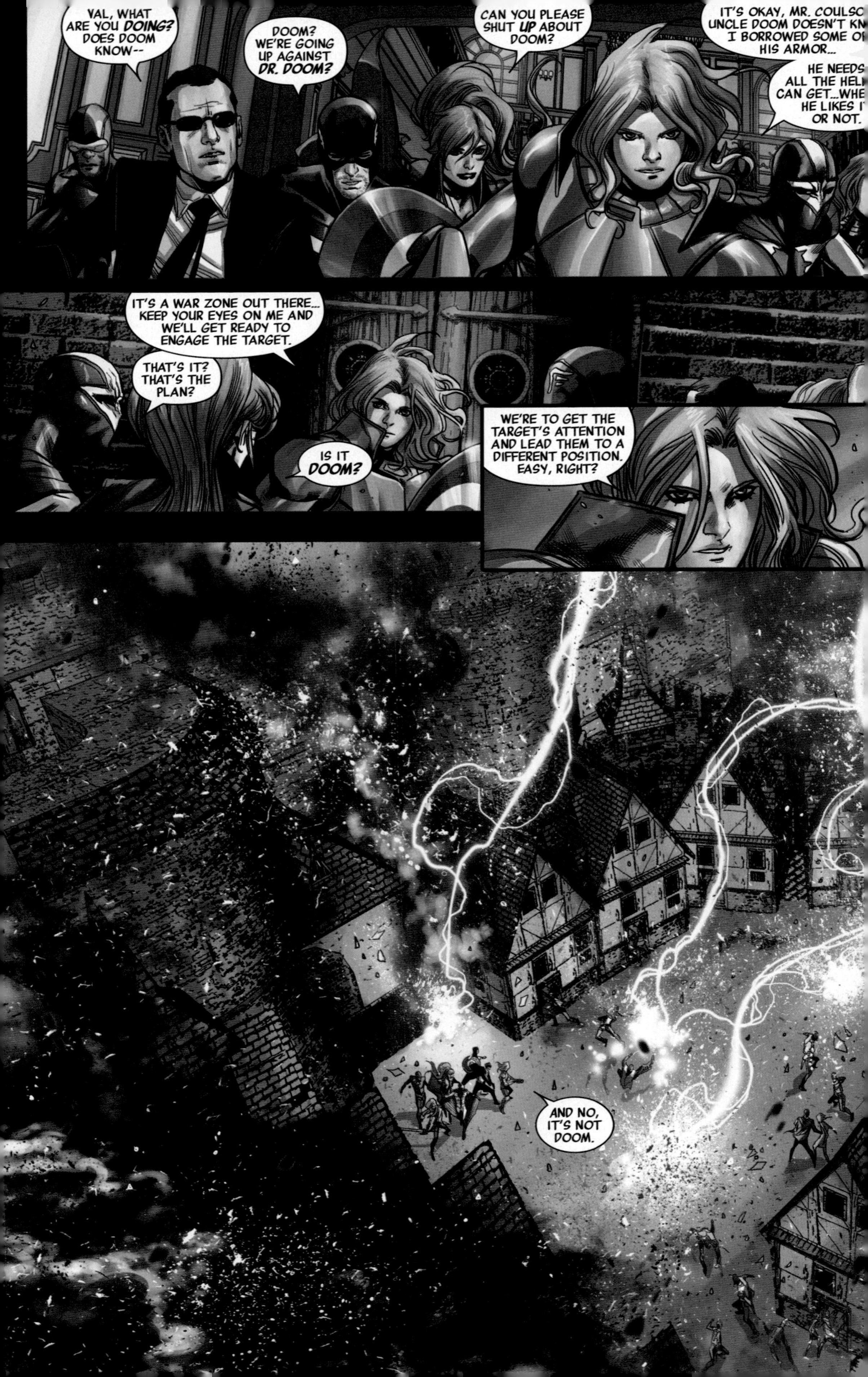
VAL, WHAT ARE YOU DOING? DOES DOOM KNOW--
DOOM? WE'RE GOING UP AGAINST DR. DOOM?
CAN YOU PLEASE SHUT UP ABOUT DOOM?
HE NEEDS ALL THE HEL CAN GET...WHE HE LIKES I OR NOT.
IT'S A WAR ZONE OUT THERE... KEEP YOUR EYES ON ME AND WE'LL GET READY TO ENGAGE THE TARGET.
THAT'S IT? THAT'S THE PLAN?
IS IT DOOM?
WE'RE TO GET THE TARGET'S ATTENTION AND LEAD THEM TO A DIFFERENT POSITION. EASY, RIGHT?
AND NO, IT'S NOT DOOM.

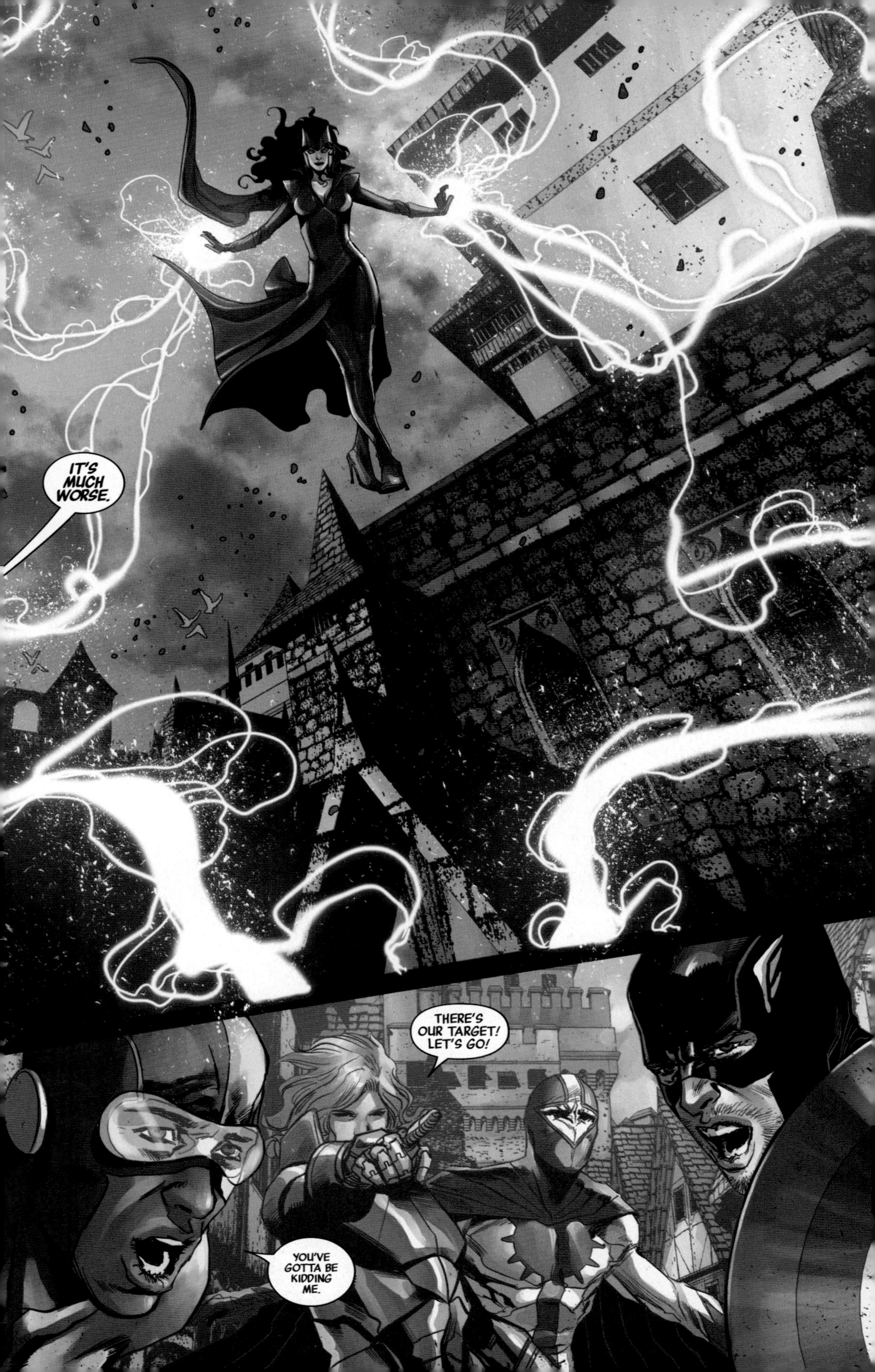
IT'S MUCH WORSE.
THERE'S OUR TARGET! LET'S GO!
YOU'VE GOTTA BE KIDDING ME.

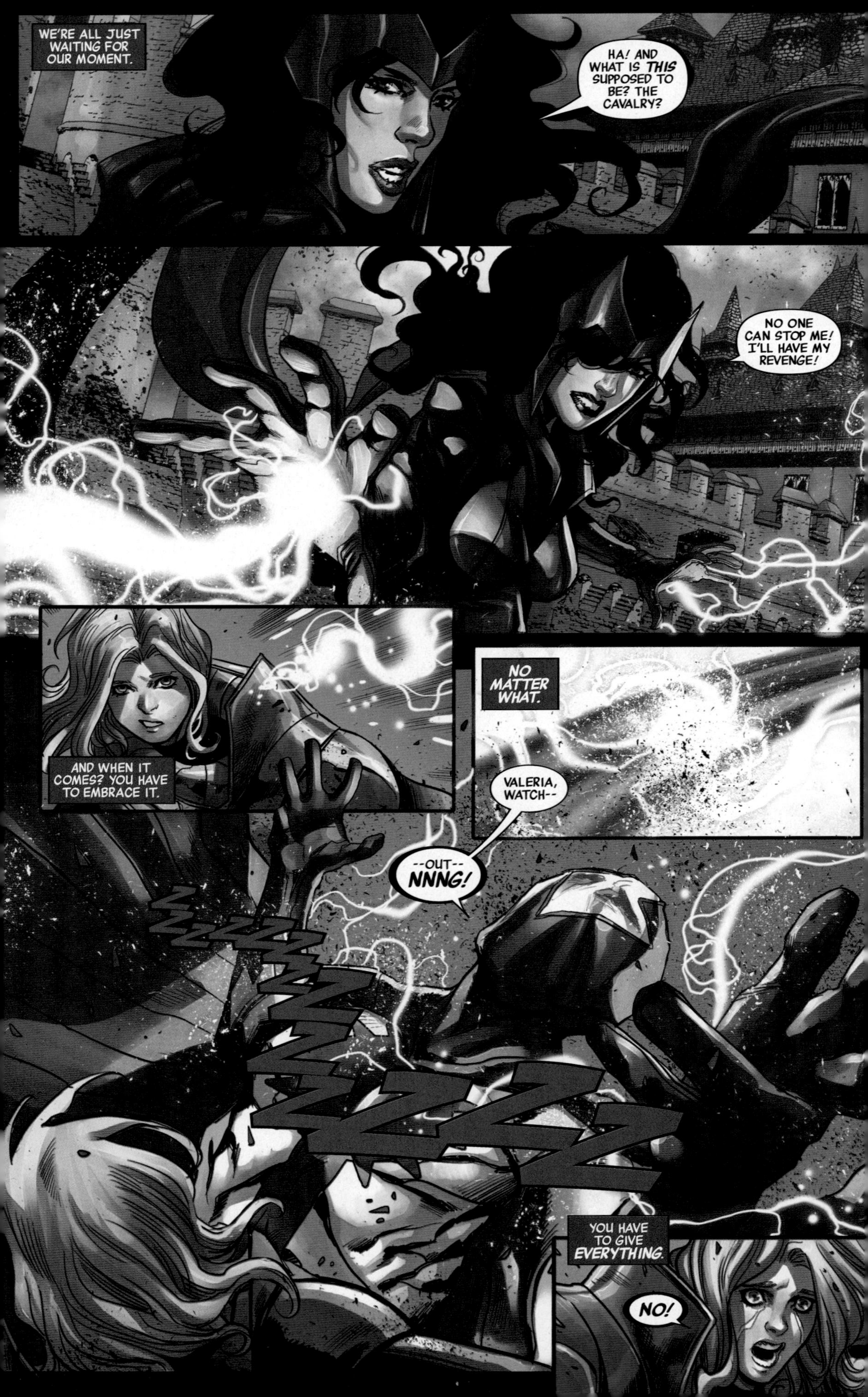
WE'RE ALL JUST WAITING FOR OUR MOMENT.
HA! AND WHAT IS THIS SUPPOSED TO BE? THE CAVALRY?
NO ONE CAN STOP ME! I'LL HAVE MY REVENGE!
AND WHEN IT COMES? YOU HAVE TO EMBRACE IT.
NO MATTER WHAT.
VALERIA, WATCH--
--OUT-- NNNG!
ZZZZZZZZZZZZ
YOU HAVE TO GIVE EVERYTHING.
NO!

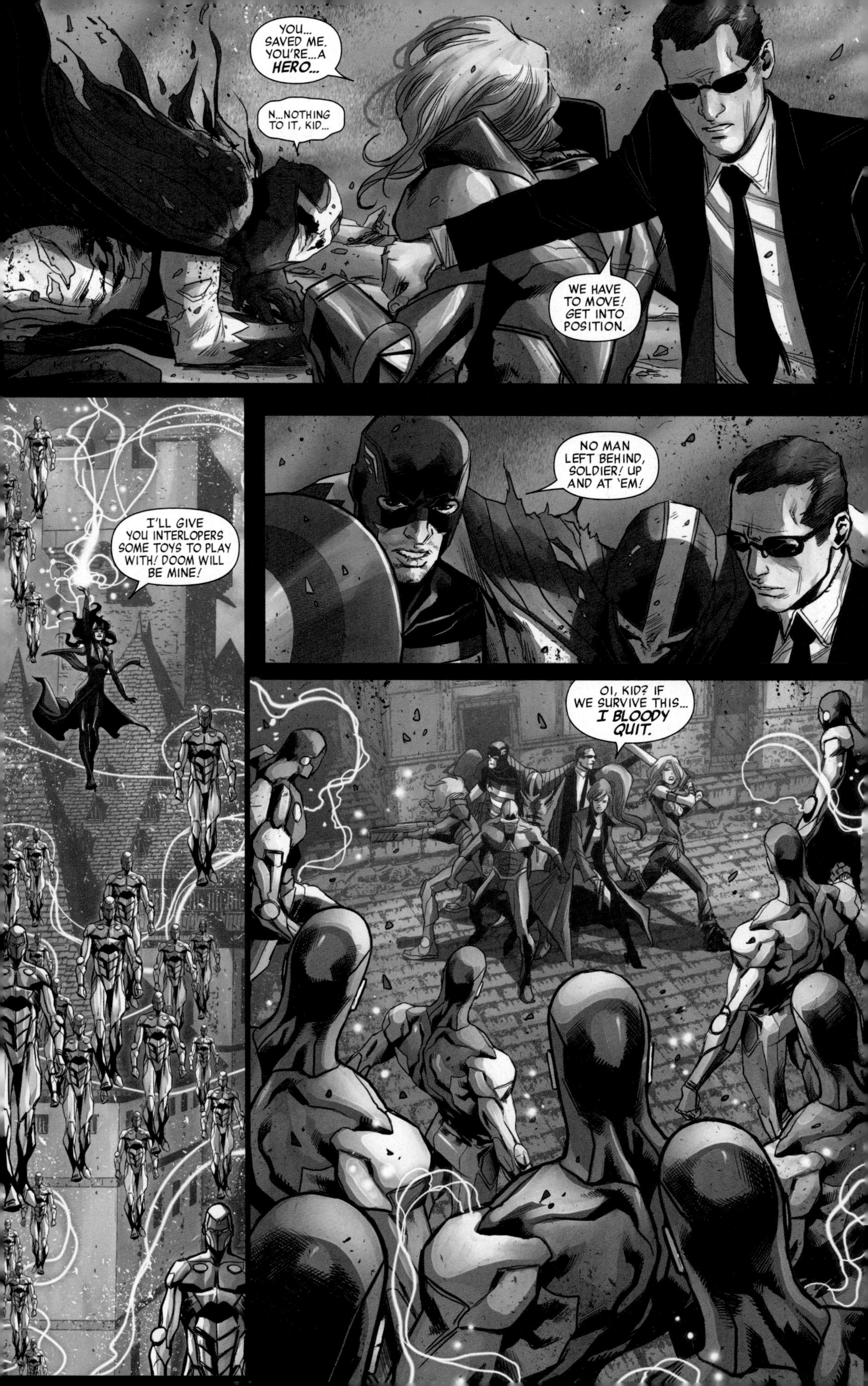
YOU... SAVED ME. YOU'RE...A HERO...
N...NOTHING TO IT, KID...
WE HAVE TO MOVE! GET INTO POSITION.
I'LL GIVE YOU INTERLOPERS SOME TOYS TO PLAY WITH! DOOM WILL BE MINE!
NO MAN LEFT BEHIND, SOLDIER! UP AND AT 'EM!
OI, KID? IF WE SURVIVE THIS... I BLOODY QUIT.

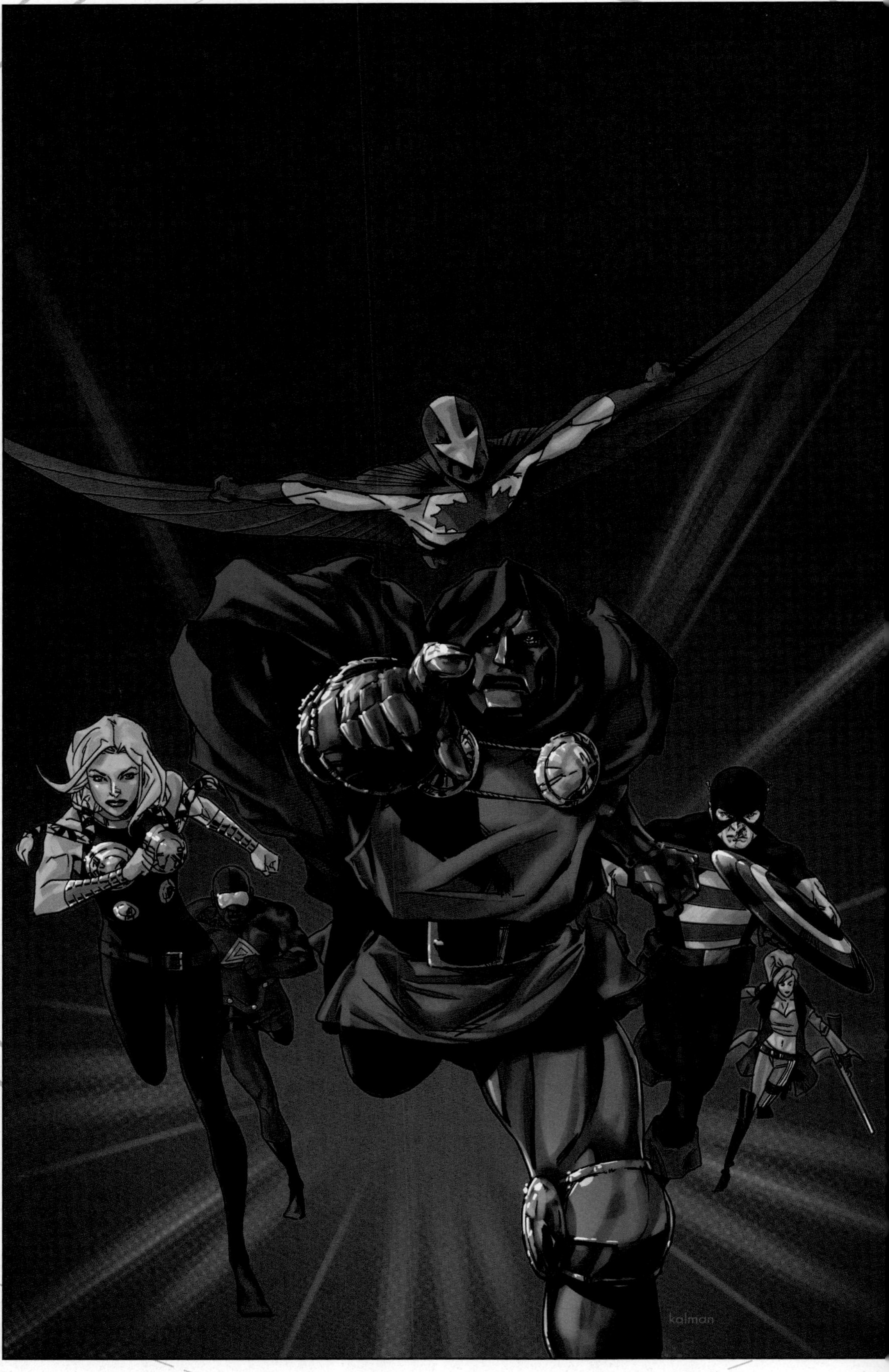
kalman

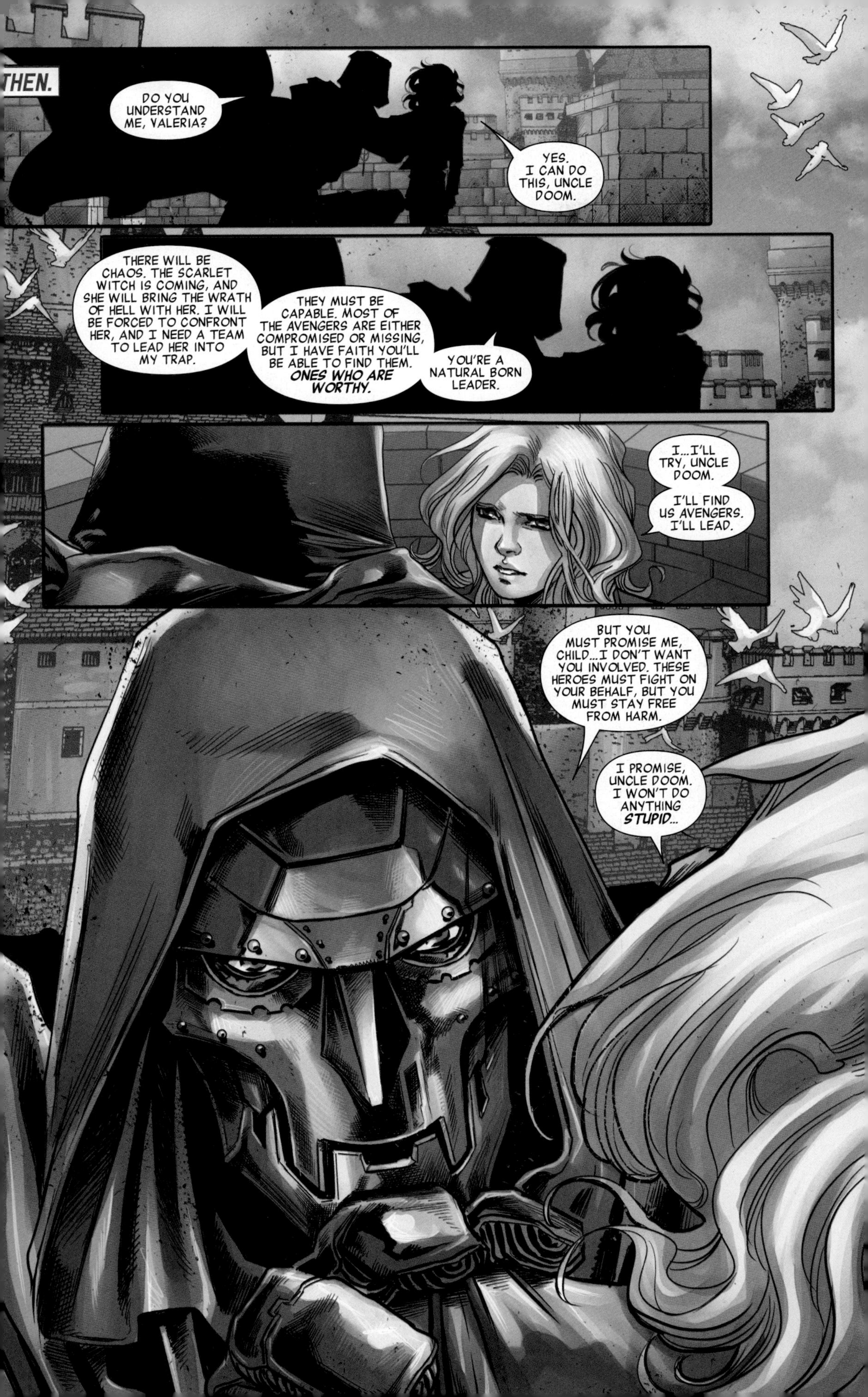
THEN.
DO YOU UNDERSTAND ME, VALERIA?
YES. I CAN DO THIS, UNCLE DOOM.
THERE WILL BE CHAOS. THE SCARLET WITCH IS COMING, AND SHE WILL BRING THE WRATH OF HELL WITH HER. I WILL BE FORCED TO CONFRONT HER, AND I NEED A TEAM TO LEAD HER INTO MY TRAP.
THEY MUST BE CAPABLE. MOST OF THE AVENGERS ARE EITHER COMPROMISED OR MISSING, BUT I HAVE FAITH YOU'LL BE ABLE TO FIND THEM. ONES WHO ARE WORTHY.
YOU'RE A NATURAL BORN LEADER.
I...I'LL TRY, UNCLE DOOM.
I'LL FIND US AVENGERS. I'LL LEAD.
BUT YOU MUST PROMISE ME, CHILD...I DON'T WANT YOU INVOLVED. THESE HEROES MUST FIGHT ON YOUR BEHALF, BUT YOU MUST STAY FREE FROM HARM.
I PROMISE, UNCLE DOOM. I WON'T DO ANYTHING STUPID...

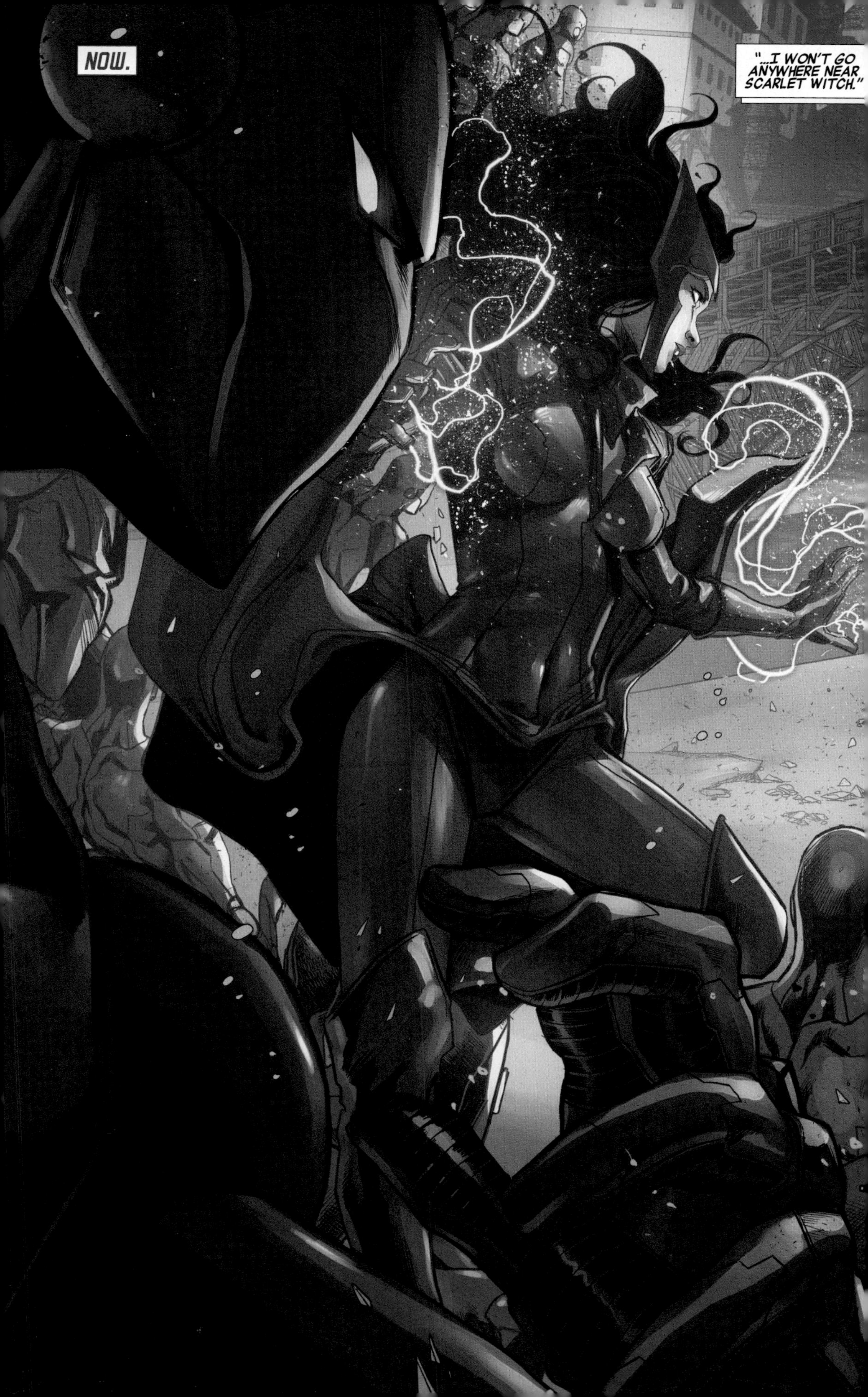
NOW.
"...I WON'T GO ANYWHERE NEAR SCARLET WITCH."

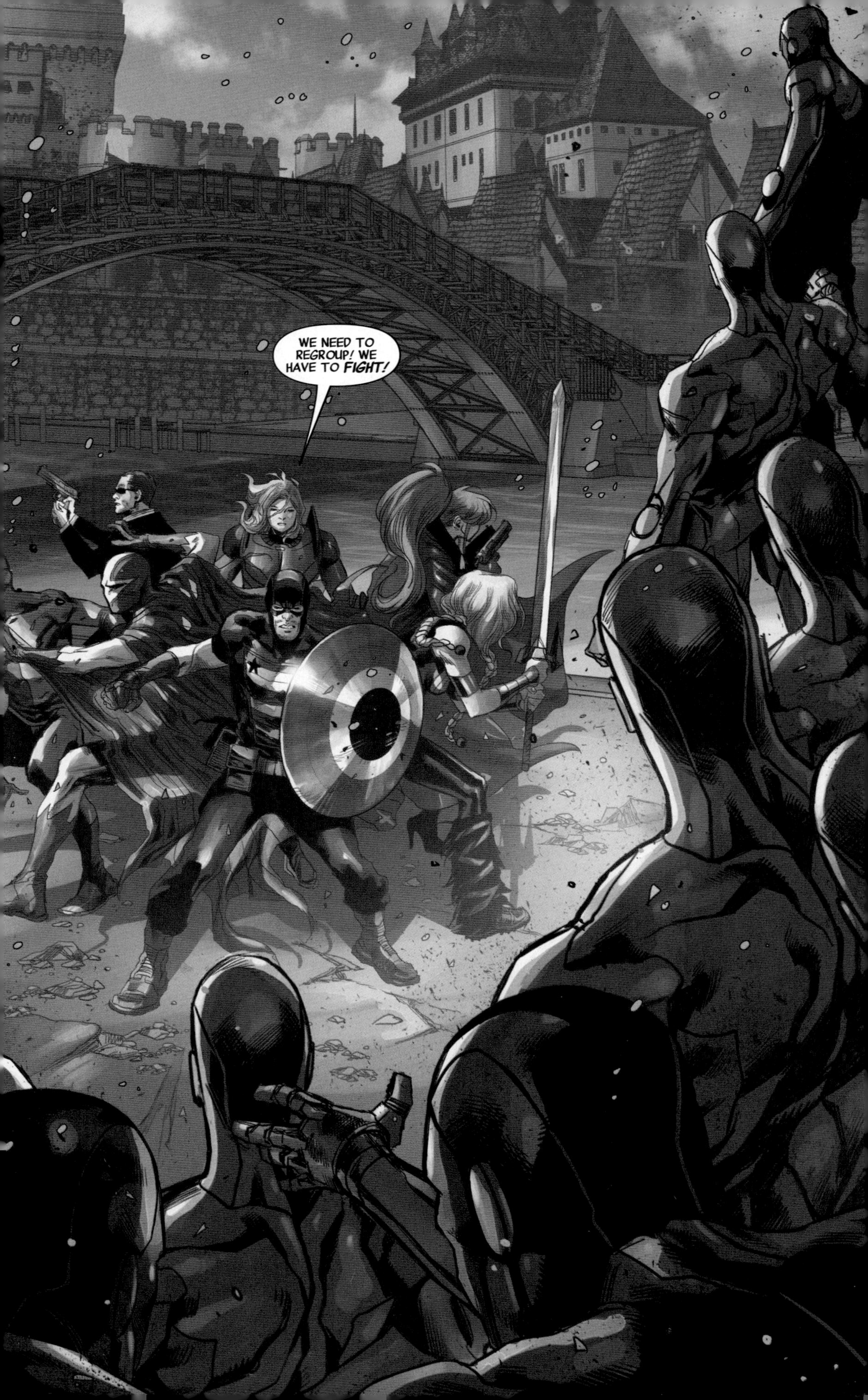
WE NEED TO REGROUP! WE HAVE TO FIGHT!

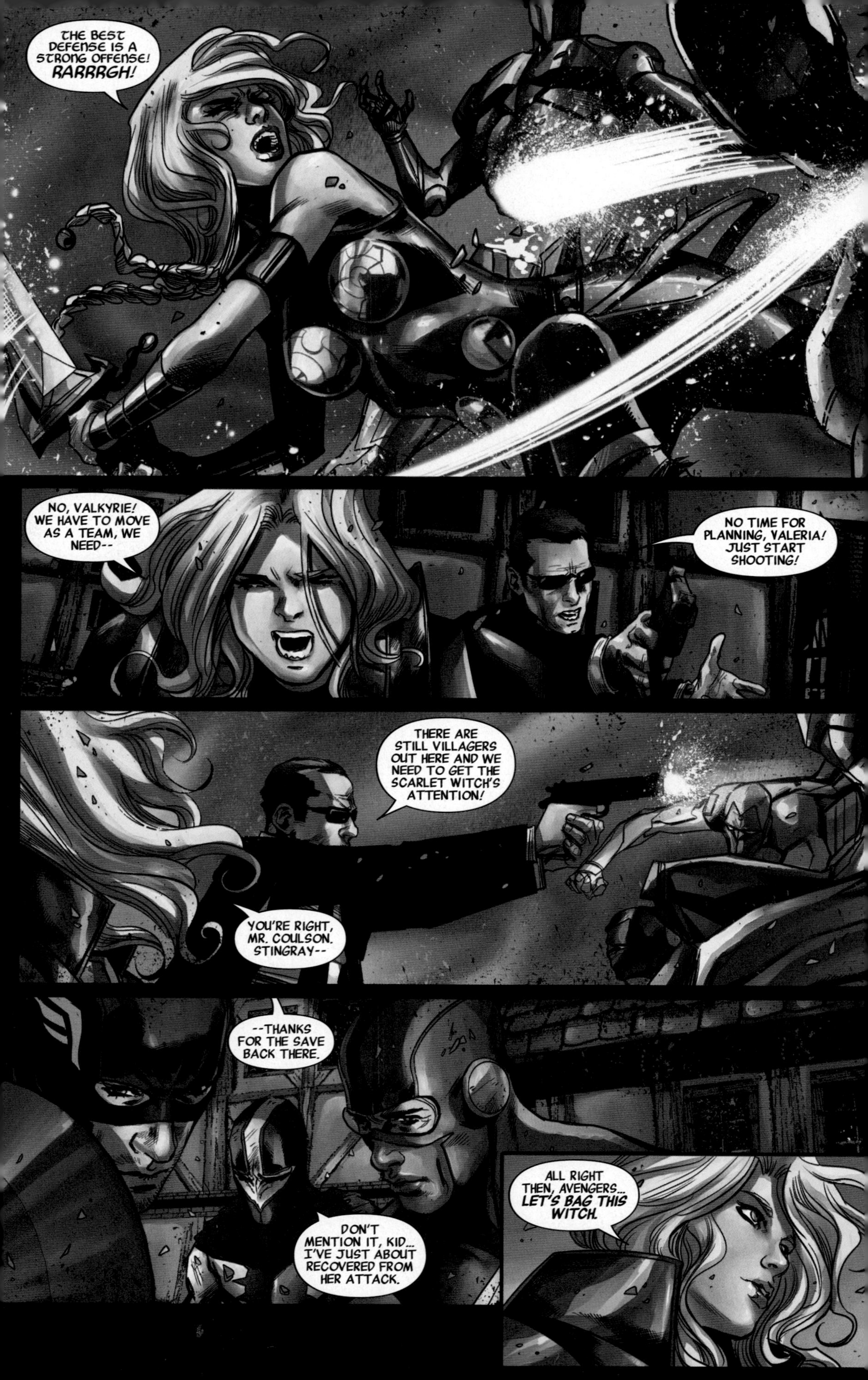
THE BEST DEFENSE IS A STRONG OFFENSE! RARRRGH!
NO, VALKYRIE! WE HAVE TO MOVE AS A TEAM, WE NEED--
NO TIME FOR PLANNING, VALERIA! JUST START SHOOTING!
THERE ARE STILL VILLAGERS OUT HERE AND WE NEED TO GET THE SCARLET WITCH'S ATTENTION!
YOU'RE RIGHT, MR. COULSON. STINGRAY--
--THANKS FOR THE SAVE BACK THERE.
DON'T MENTION IT, KID... I'VE JUST ABOUT RECOVERED FROM HER ATTACK.
ALL RIGHT THEN, AVENGERS... LET'S BAG THIS WITCH.

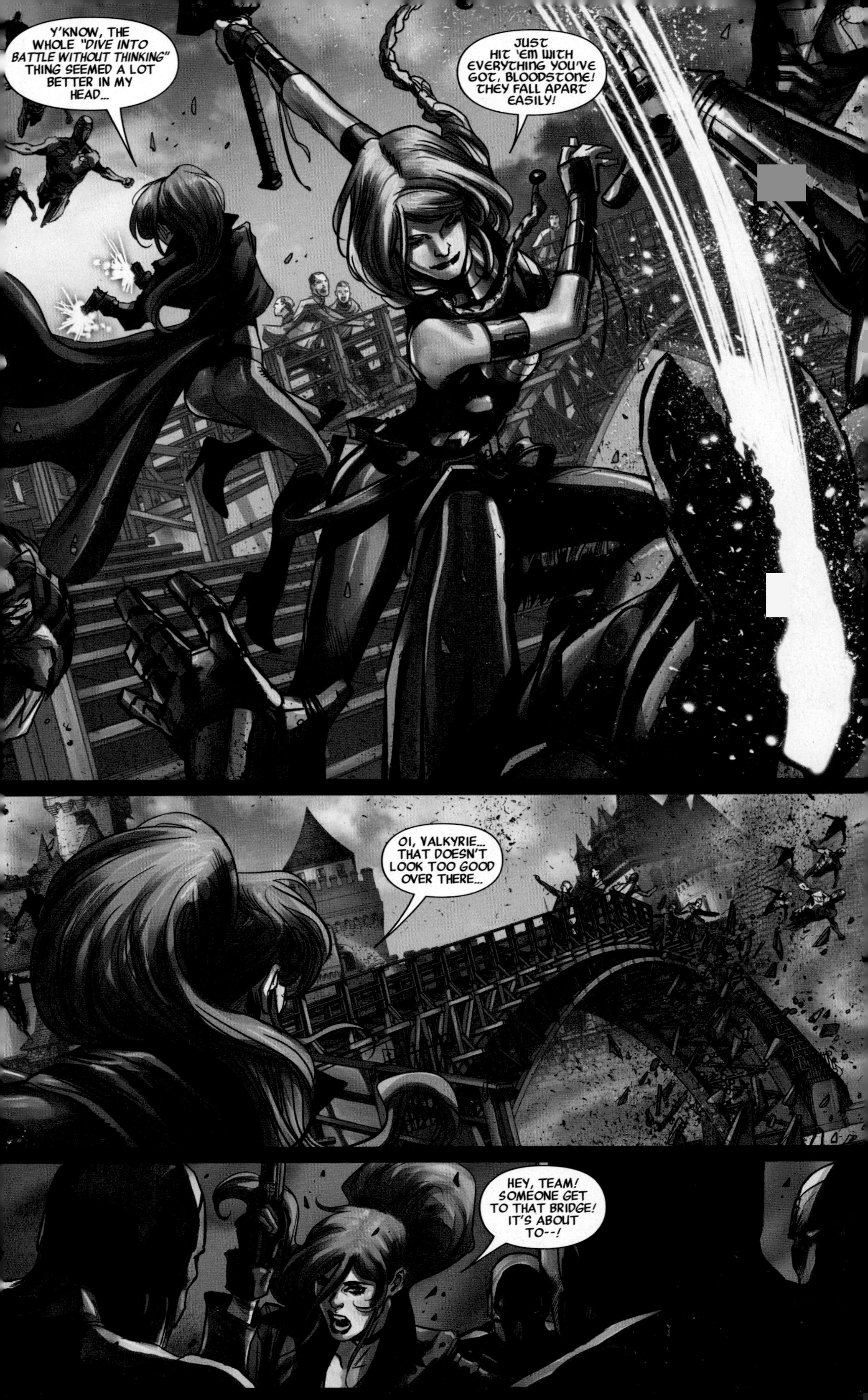
Y'KNOW, THE WHOLE "DIVE INTO BATTLE WITHOUT THINKING" THING SEEMED A LOT BETTER IN MY HEAD...
JUST HIT 'EM WITH EVERYTHING YOU'VE GOT, BLOODSTONE! THEY FALL APART EASILY!
OI, VALKYRIE... THAT DOESN'T LOOK TOO GOOD OVER THERE...
HEY, TEAM! SOMEONE GET TO THAT BRIDGE! IT'S ABOUT TO--!

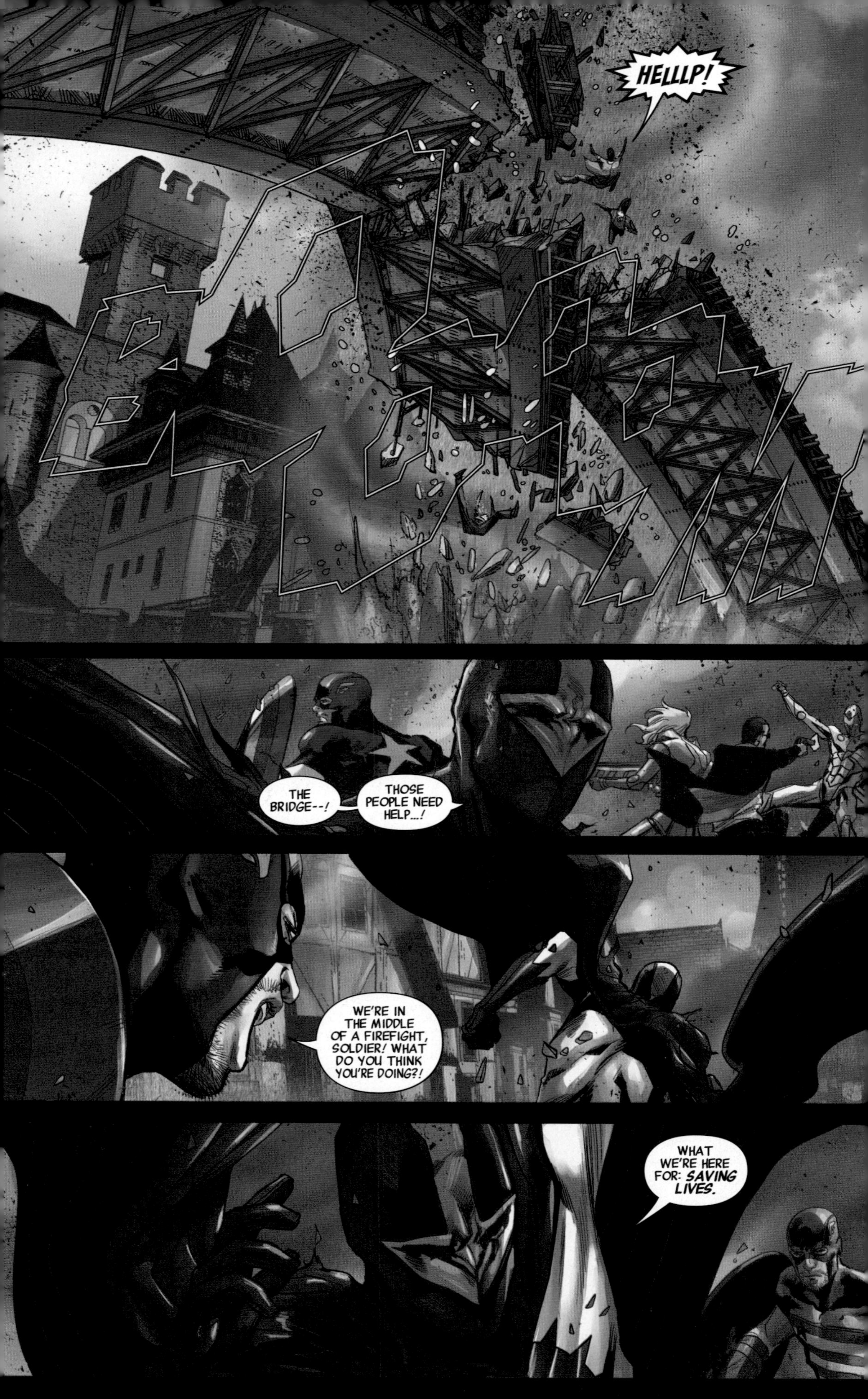
HELLLP!
THE BRIDGE--!
THOSE PEOPLE NEED HELP...!
WE'RE IN THE MIDDLE OF A FIREFIGHT, SOLDIER! WHAT DO YOU THINK YOU'RE DOING?!
WHAT WE'RE HERE FOR: SAVING LIVES.

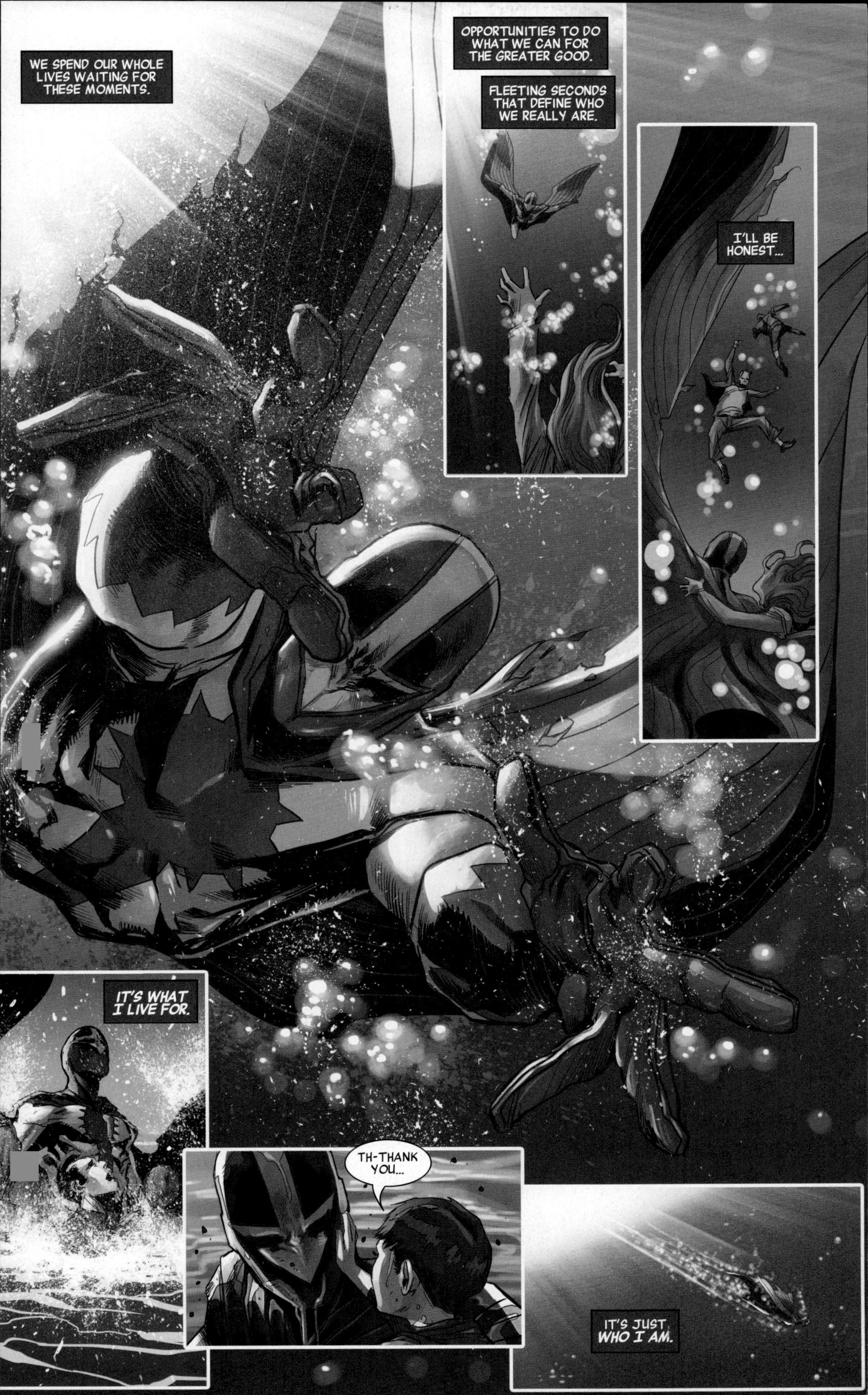
WE SPEND OUR WHOLE LIVES WAITING FOR THESE MOMENTS.
OPPORTUNITIES TO DO WHAT WE CAN FOR THE GREATER GOOD.
FLEETING SECONDS THAT DEFINE WHO WE REALLY ARE.
I'LL BE HONEST...
IT'S WHAT I LIVE FOR.
TH-THANK YOU...
IT'S JUST WHO I AM.

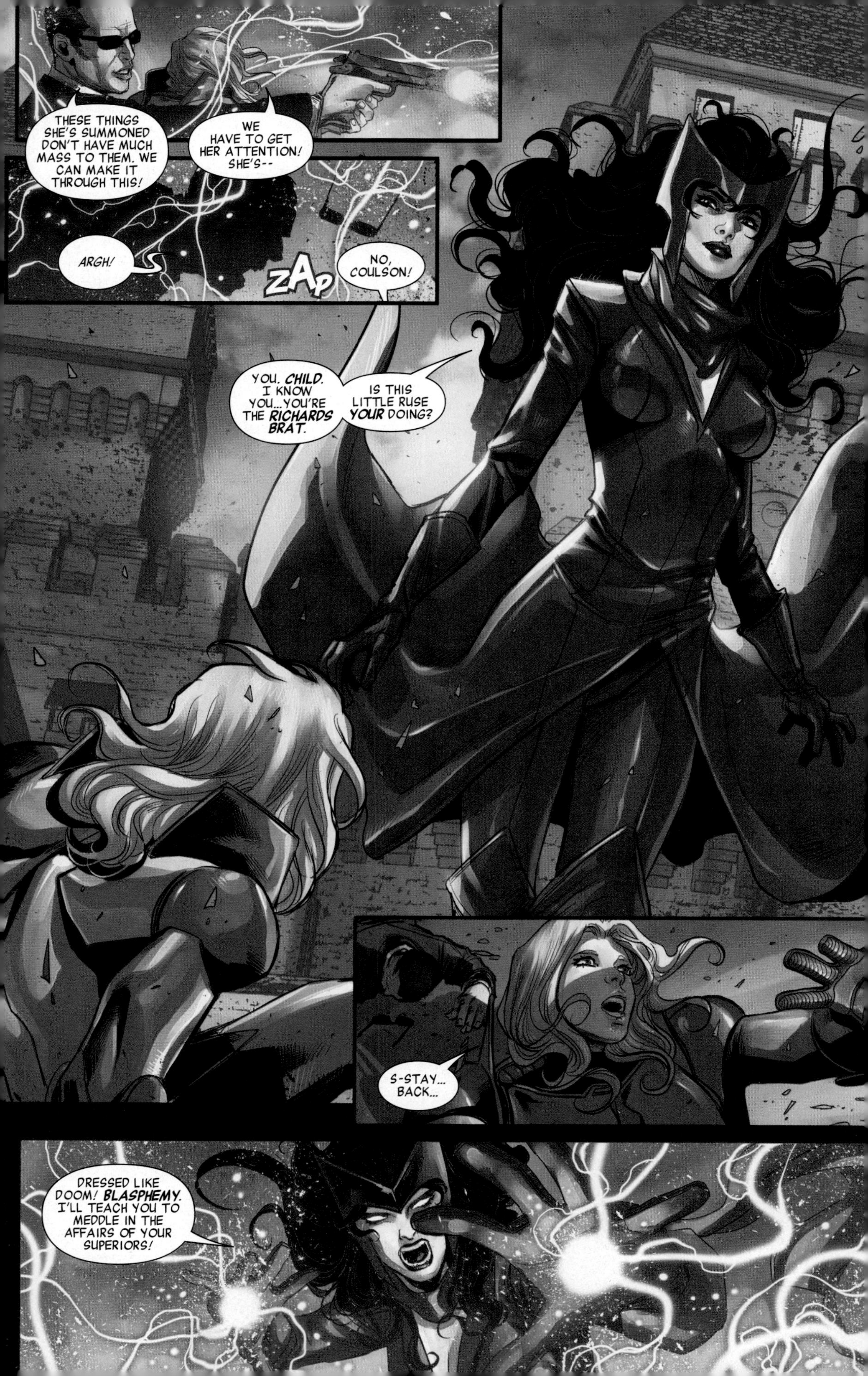

THESE THINGS SHE'S SUMMONED DON'T HAVE MUCH MASS TO THEM. WE CAN MAKE IT THROUGH THIS!
WE HAVE TO GET HER ATTENTION! SHE'S--
ARGH!
ZAP
NO, COULSON!
YOU. CHILD. I KNOW YOU...YOU'RE THE RICHARDS BRAT.
IS THIS LITTLE RUSE YOUR DOING?
S-STAY... BACK...
DRESSED LIKE DOOM! BLASPHEMY. I'LL TEACH YOU TO MEDDLE IN THE AFFAIRS OF YOUR SUPERIORS!

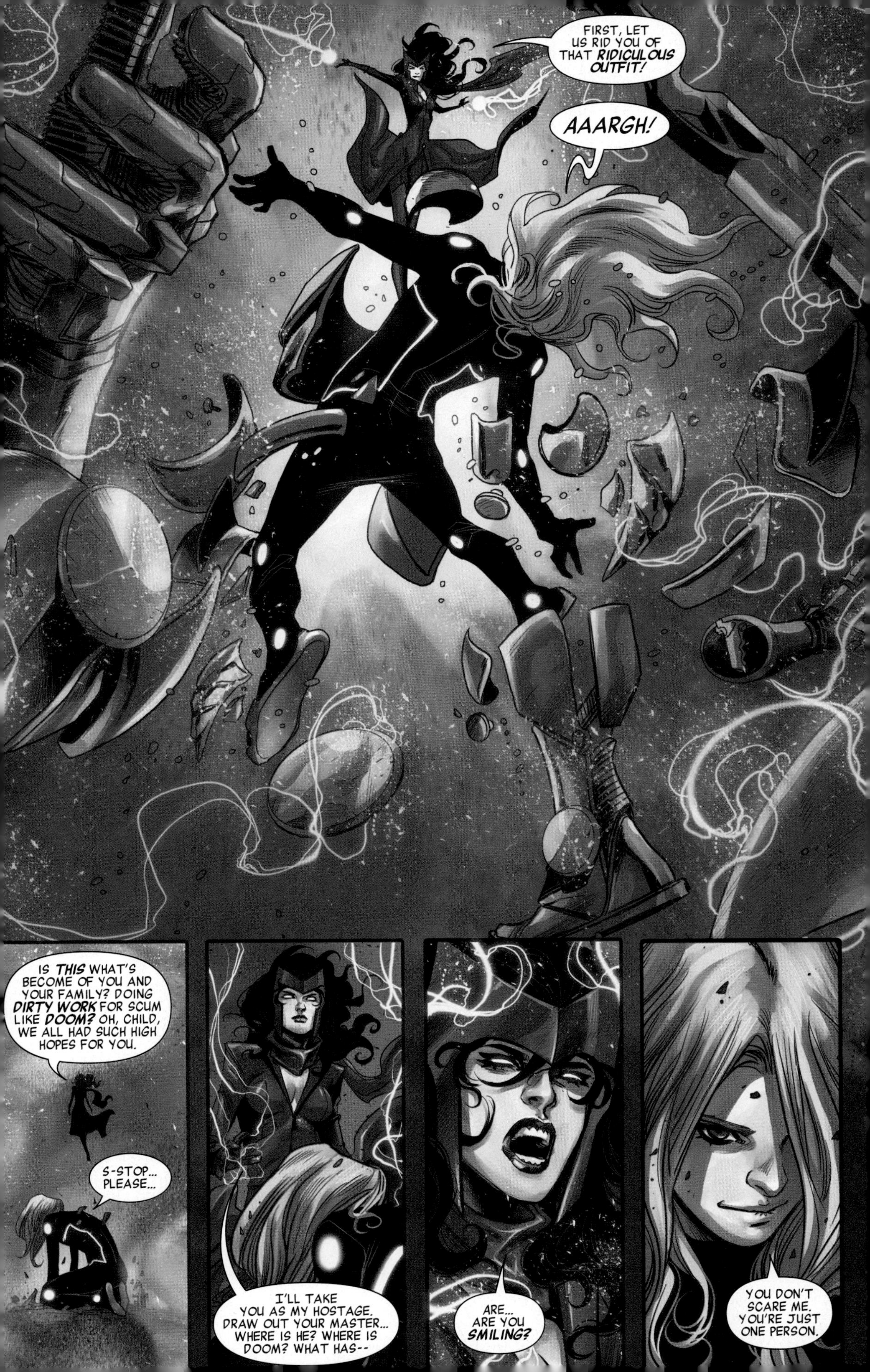

FIRST, LET US RID YOU OF THAT RIDICULOUS OUTFIT!
AAARGH!
IS THIS WHAT'S BECOME OF YOU AND YOUR FAMILY? DOING DIRTY WORK FOR SCUM LIKE DOOM? OH, CHILD, WE ALL HAD SUCH HIGH HOPES FOR YOU.
S-STOP... PLEASE...
I'LL TAKE YOU AS MY HOSTAGE. DRAW OUT YOUR MASTER... WHERE IS HE? WHERE IS DOOM? WHAT HAS--
ARE... ARE YOU SMILING?
YOU DON'T SCARE ME. YOU'RE JUST ONE PERSON.

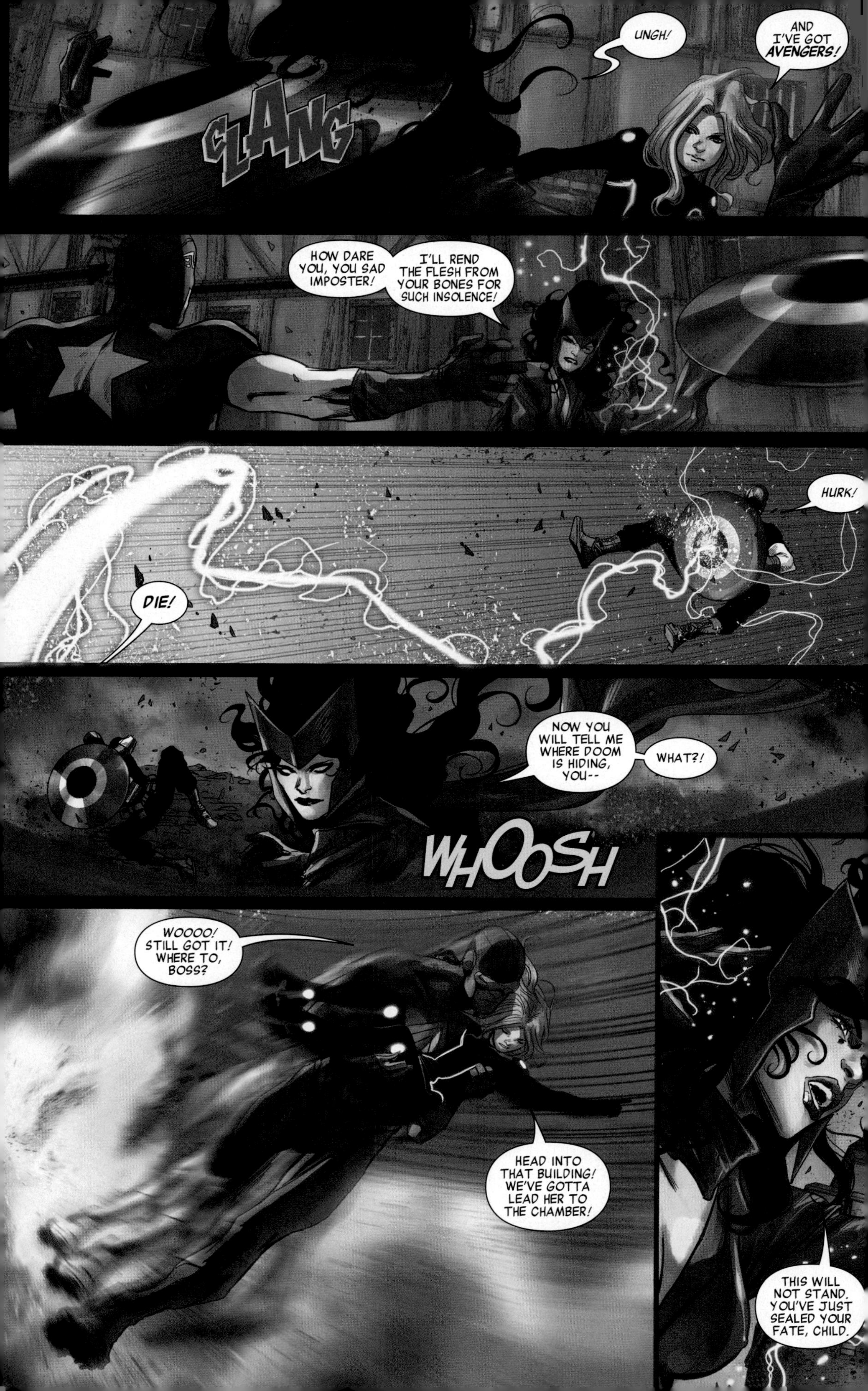
CLANG
UNGH!
AND I'VE GOT AVENGERS!
HOW DARE YOU, YOU SAD IMPOSTER!
I'LL REND THE FLESH FROM YOUR BONES FOR SUCH INSOLENCE!
DIE!
HURK!
NOW YOU WILL TELL ME WHERE DOOM IS HIDING, YOU--
WHAT?!
WHOOSH
WOOOO! STILL GOT IT! WHERE TO, BOSS?
HEAD INTO THAT BUILDING! WE'VE GOTTA LEAD HER TO THE CHAMBER!
THIS WILL NOT STAND. YOU'VE JUST SEALED YOUR FATE, CHILD.

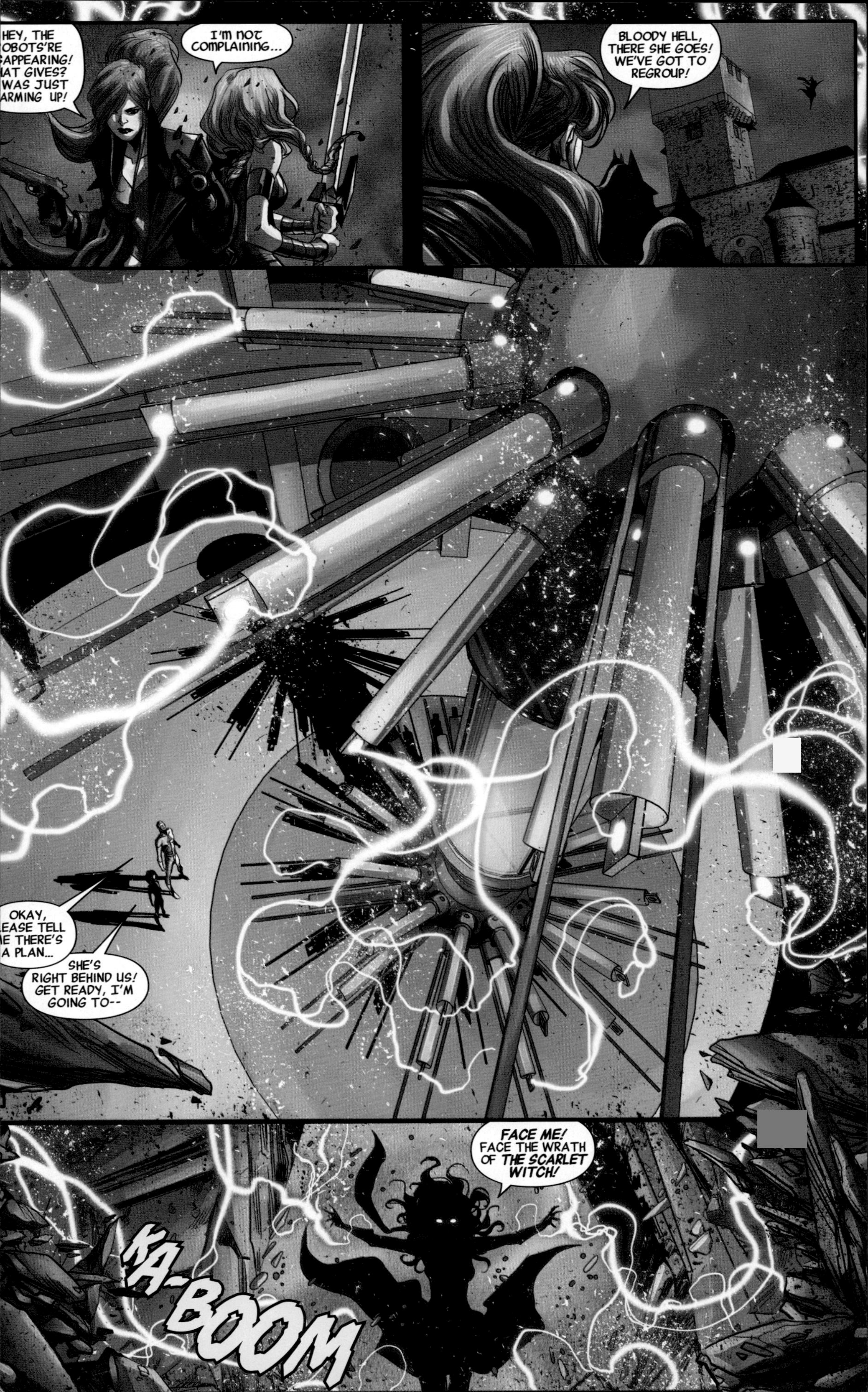
HEY, THE ROBOTS'RE DISAPPEARING! WHAT GIVES? I WAS JUST WARMING UP!
I'M NOT COMPLAINING...
BLOODY HELL, THERE SHE GOES! WE'VE GOT TO REGROUP!
OKAY, PLEASE TELL ME THERE'S A PLAN...
SHE'S RIGHT BEHIND US! GET READY, I'M GOING TO--
FACE ME! FACE THE WRATH OF THE SCARLET WITCH!
KA-BOOM

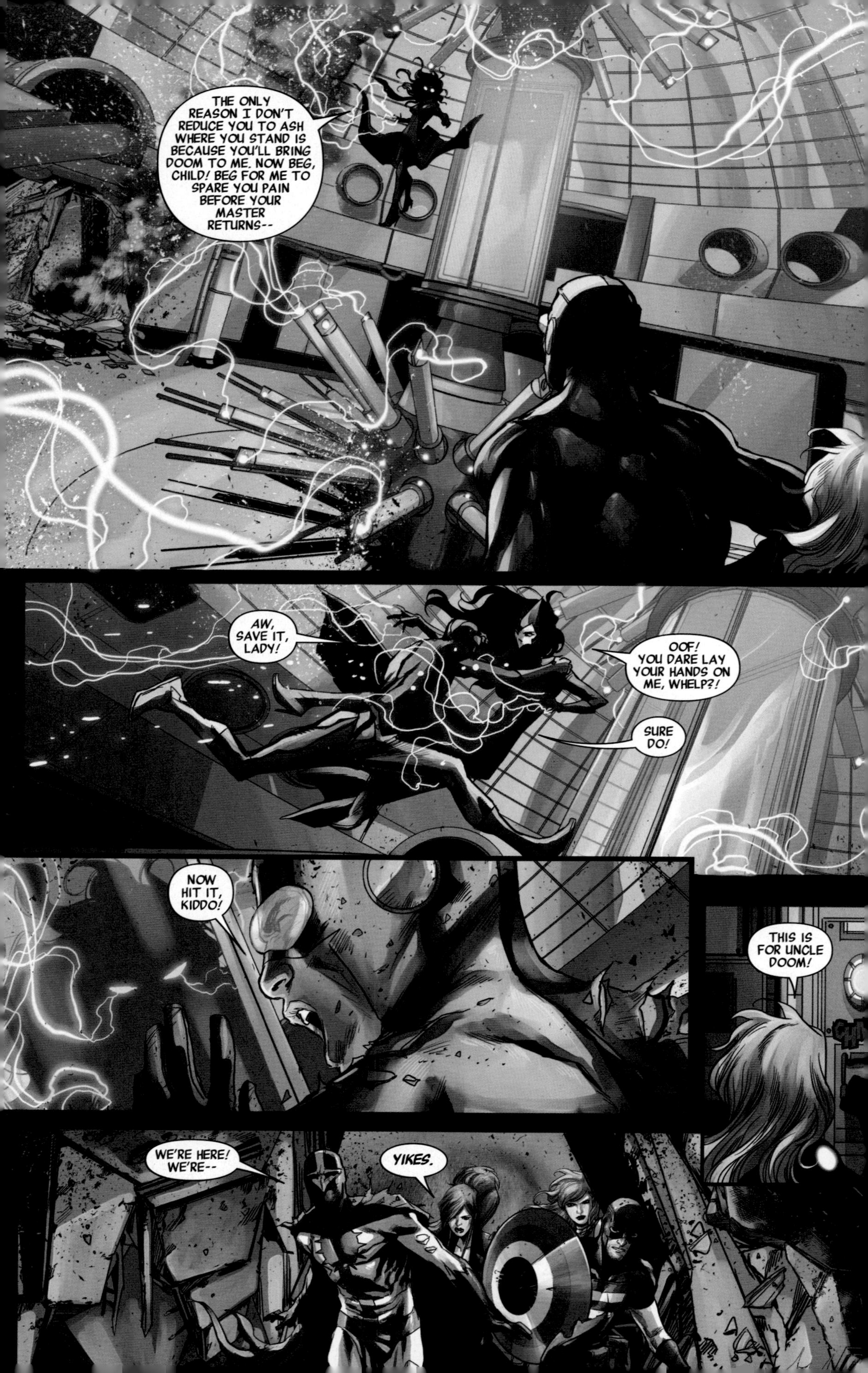
THE ONLY REASON I DON'T REDUCE YOU TO ASH WHERE YOU STAND IS BECAUSE YOU'LL BRING DOOM TO ME. NOW BEG, CHILD! BEG FOR ME TO SPARE YOU PAIN BEFORE YOUR MASTER RETURNS--
AW, SAVE IT, LADY!
OOF! YOU DARE LAY YOUR HANDS ON ME, WHELP?!
SURE DO!
NOW HIT IT, KIDDO!
THIS IS FOR UNCLE DOOM!
WE'RE HERE! WE'RE--
YIKES.

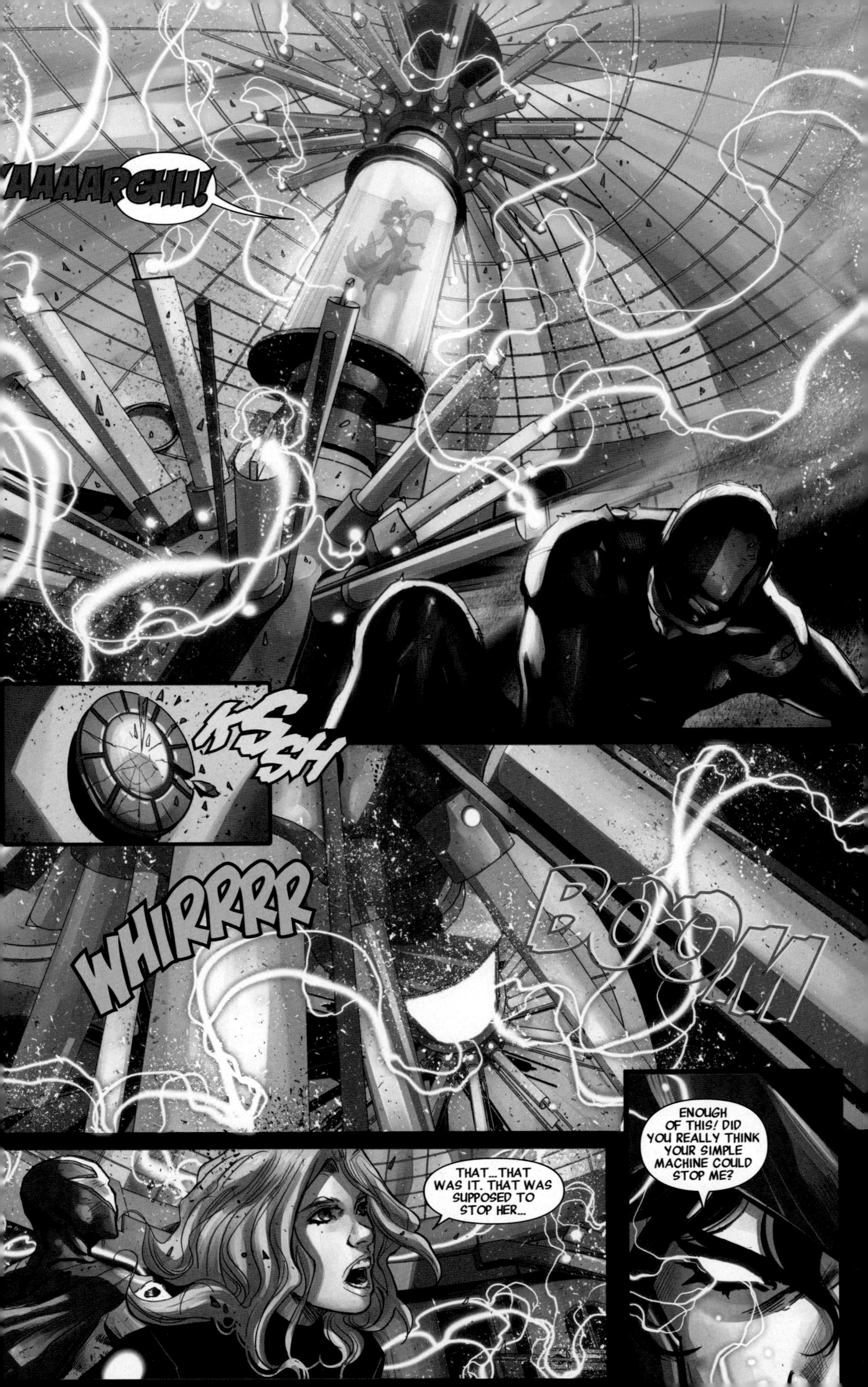
AAAARGHH!
KSCH
WHIRRRR
BOOM
THAT... THAT WAS IT. THAT WAS SUPPOSED TO STOP HER...
ENOUGH OF THIS! DID YOU REALLY THINK YOUR SIMPLE MACHINE COULD STOP ME?

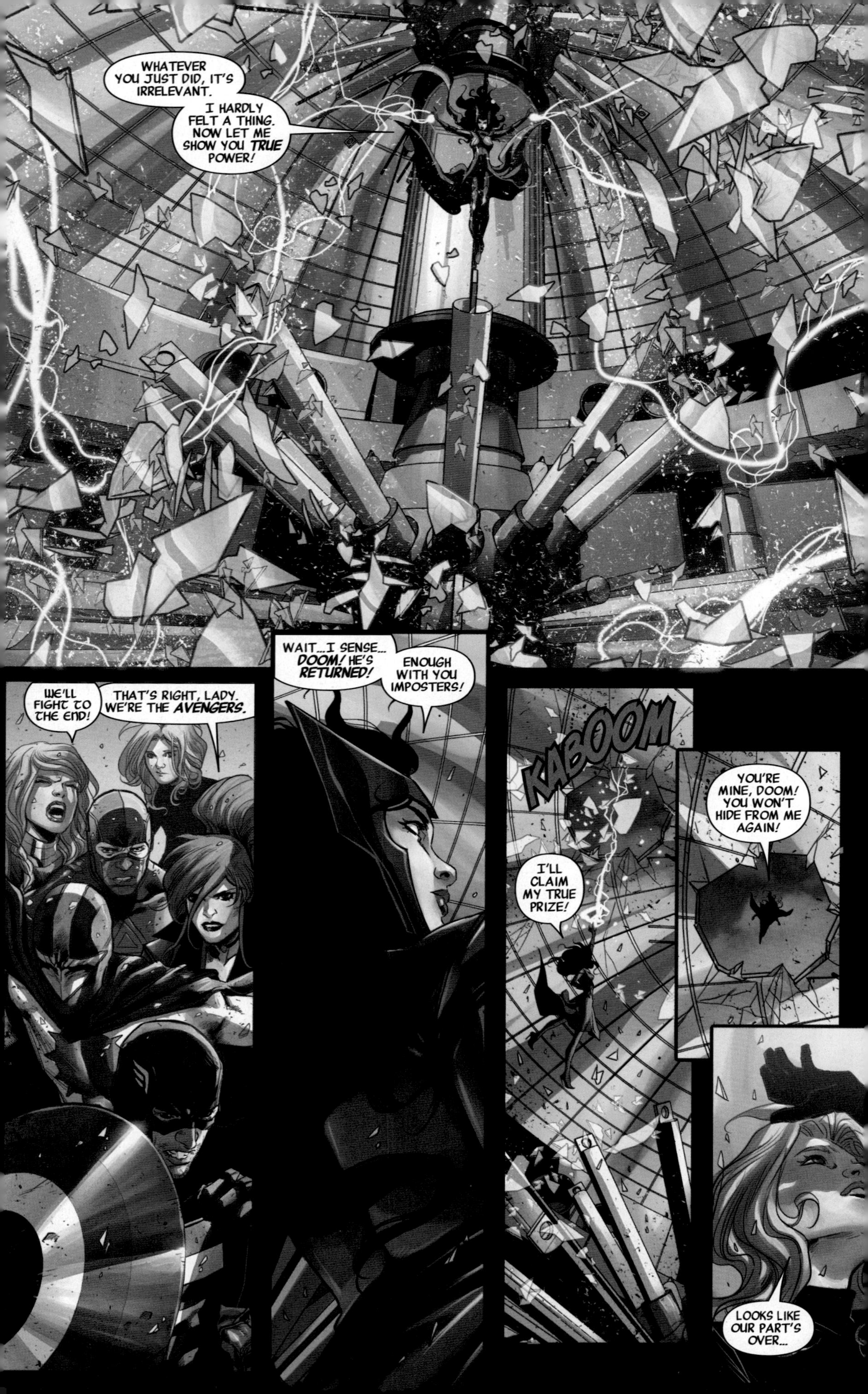
WHATEVER YOU JUST DID, IT'S IRRELEVANT.
I HARDLY FELT A THING. NOW LET ME SHOW YOU TRUE POWER!
WE'LL FIGHT TO THE END!
THAT'S RIGHT, LADY. WE'RE THE AVENGERS.
WAIT...I SENSE... DOOM! HE'S RETURNED!
ENOUGH WITH YOU IMPOSTERS!
KABOOM
I'LL CLAIM MY TRUE PRIZE!
YOU'RE MINE, DOOM! YOU WON'T HIDE FROM ME AGAIN!
LOOKS LIKE OUR PART'S OVER...

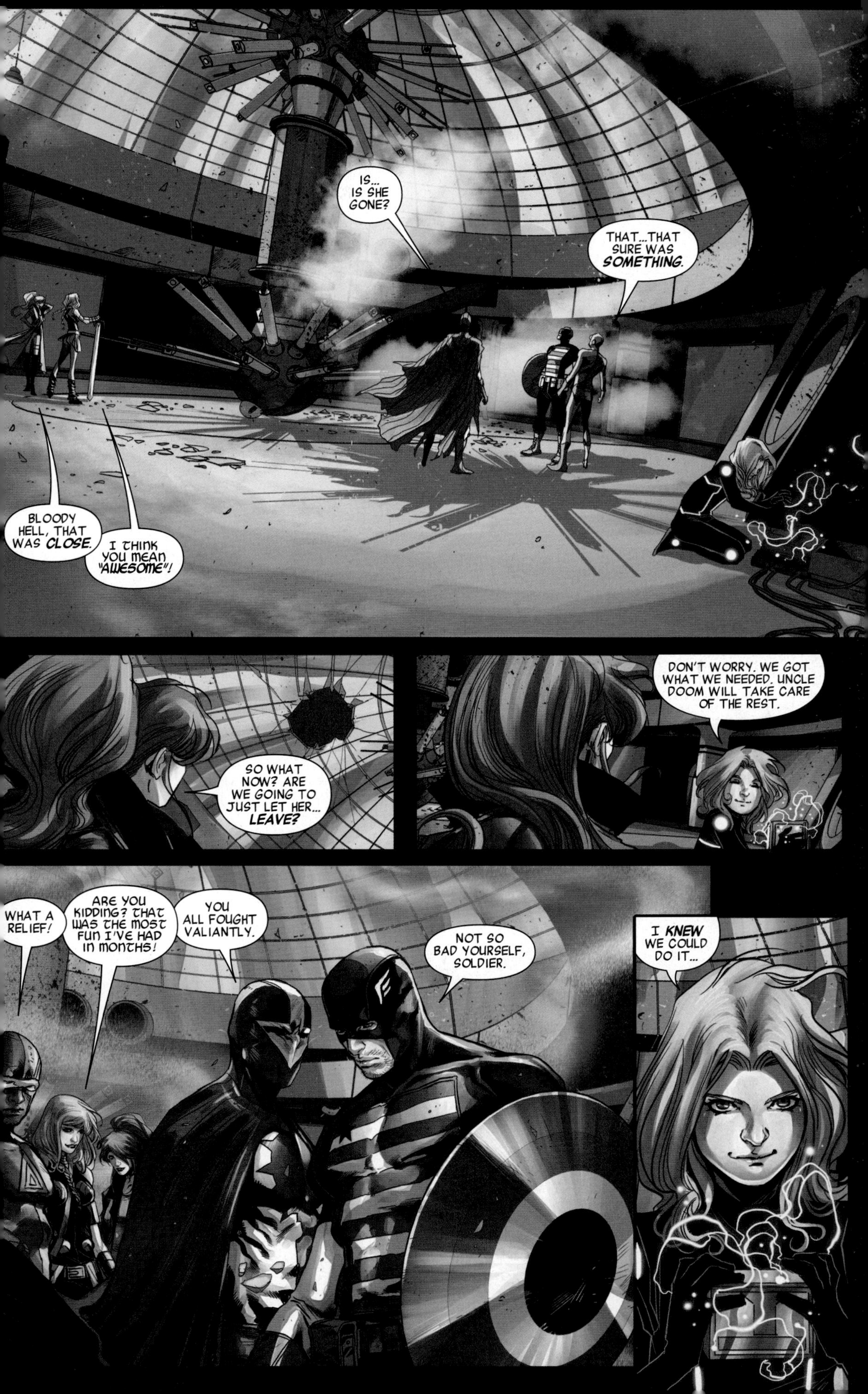
IS... IS SHE GONE?
THAT...THAT SURE WAS SOMETHING.
BLOODY HELL, THAT WAS CLOSE.
I THINK YOU MEAN "AWESOME"!
SO WHAT NOW? ARE WE GOING TO JUST LET HER... LEAVE?
DON'T WORRY. WE GOT WHAT WE NEEDED. UNCLE DOOM WILL TAKE CARE OF THE REST.
WHAT A RELIEF!
ARE YOU KIDDING? THAT WAS THE MOST FUN I'VE HAD IN MONTHS!
YOU ALL FOUGHT VALIANTLY.
NOT SO BAD YOURSELF, SOLDIER.
I KNEW WE COULD DO IT...

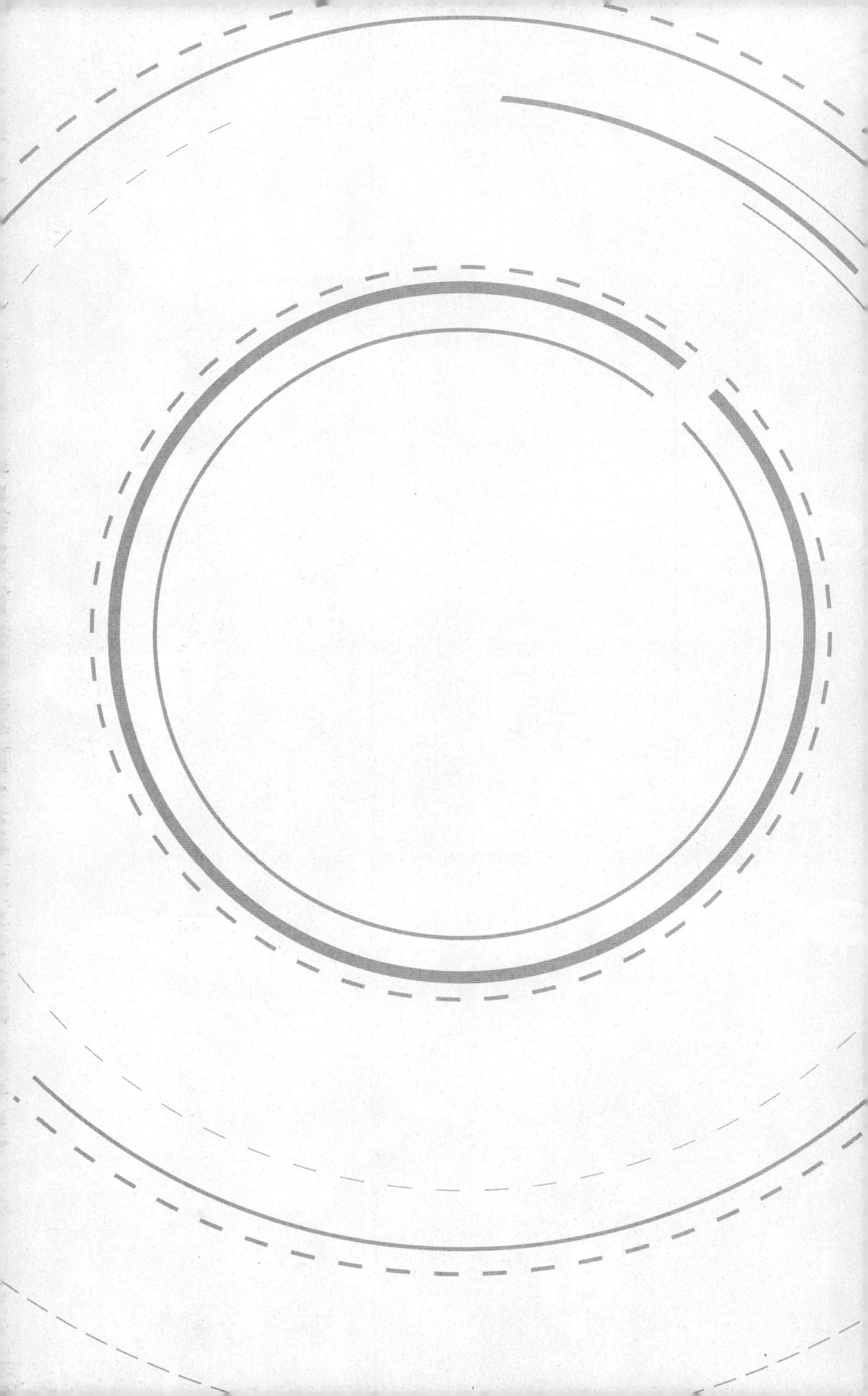

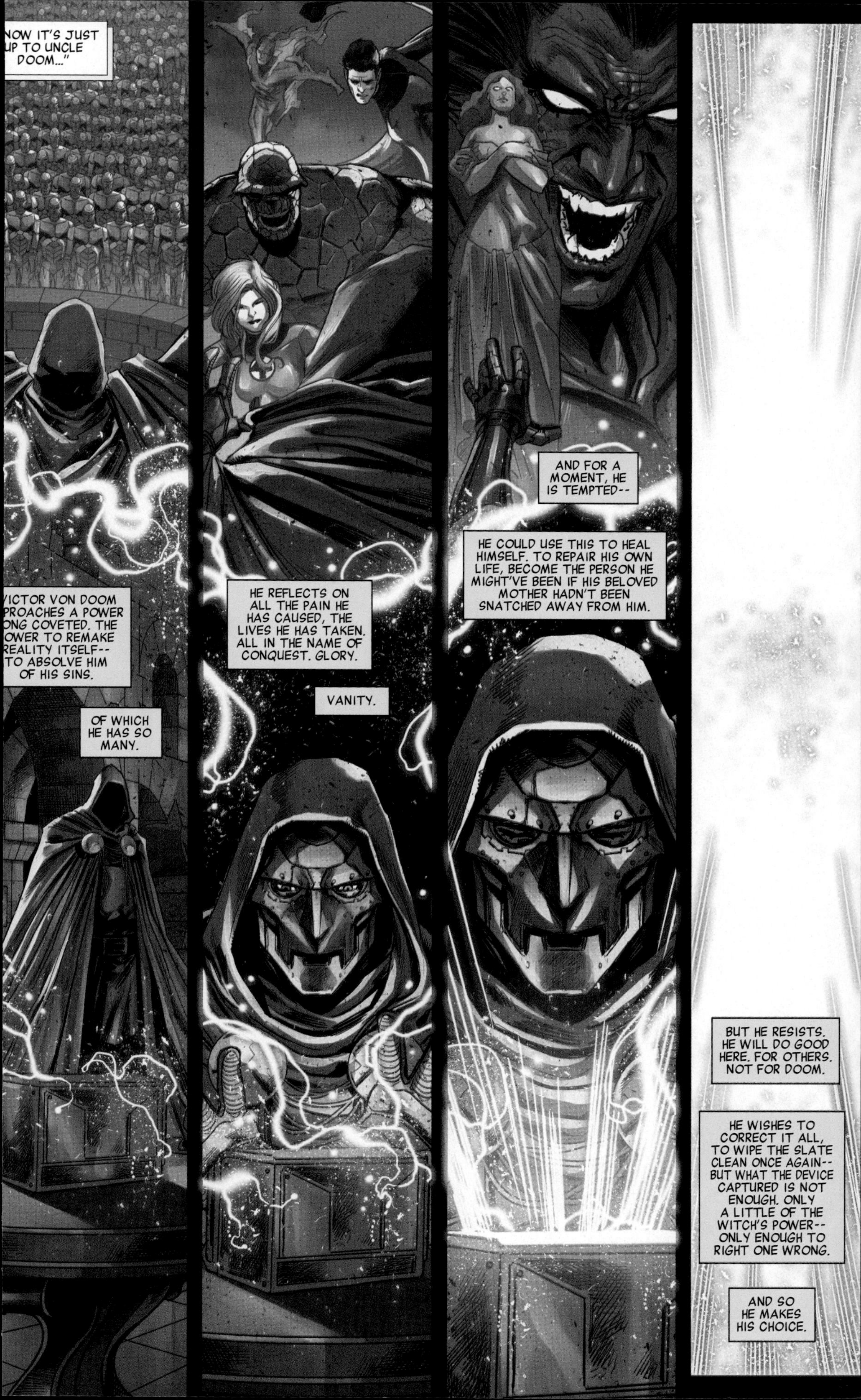
NOW IT'S JUST UP TO UNCLE DOOM..."
VICTOR VON DOOM PROACHES A POWER ONG COVETED. THE OWER TO REMAKE REALITY ITSELF-- TO ABSOLVE HIM OF HIS SINS.
OF WHICH HE HAS SO MANY.
HE REFLECTS ON ALL THE PAIN HE HAS CAUSED, THE LIVES HE HAS TAKEN. ALL IN THE NAME OF CONQUEST. GLORY.
VANITY.
AND FOR A MOMENT, HE IS TEMPTED--
HE COULD USE THIS TO HEAL HIMSELF. TO REPAIR HIS OWN LIFE, BECOME THE PERSON HE MIGHT'VE BEEN IF HIS BELOVED MOTHER HADN'T BEEN SNATCHED AWAY FROM HIM.
BUT HE RESISTS. HE WILL DO GOOD HERE. FOR OTHERS. NOT FOR DOOM.
HE WISHES TO CORRECT IT ALL, TO WIPE THE SLATE CLEAN ONCE AGAIN-- BUT WHAT THE DEVICE CAPTURED IS NOT ENOUGH. ONLY A LITTLE OF THE WITCH'S POWER-- ONLY ENOUGH TO RIGHT ONE WRONG.
AND SO HE MAKES HIS CHOICE.

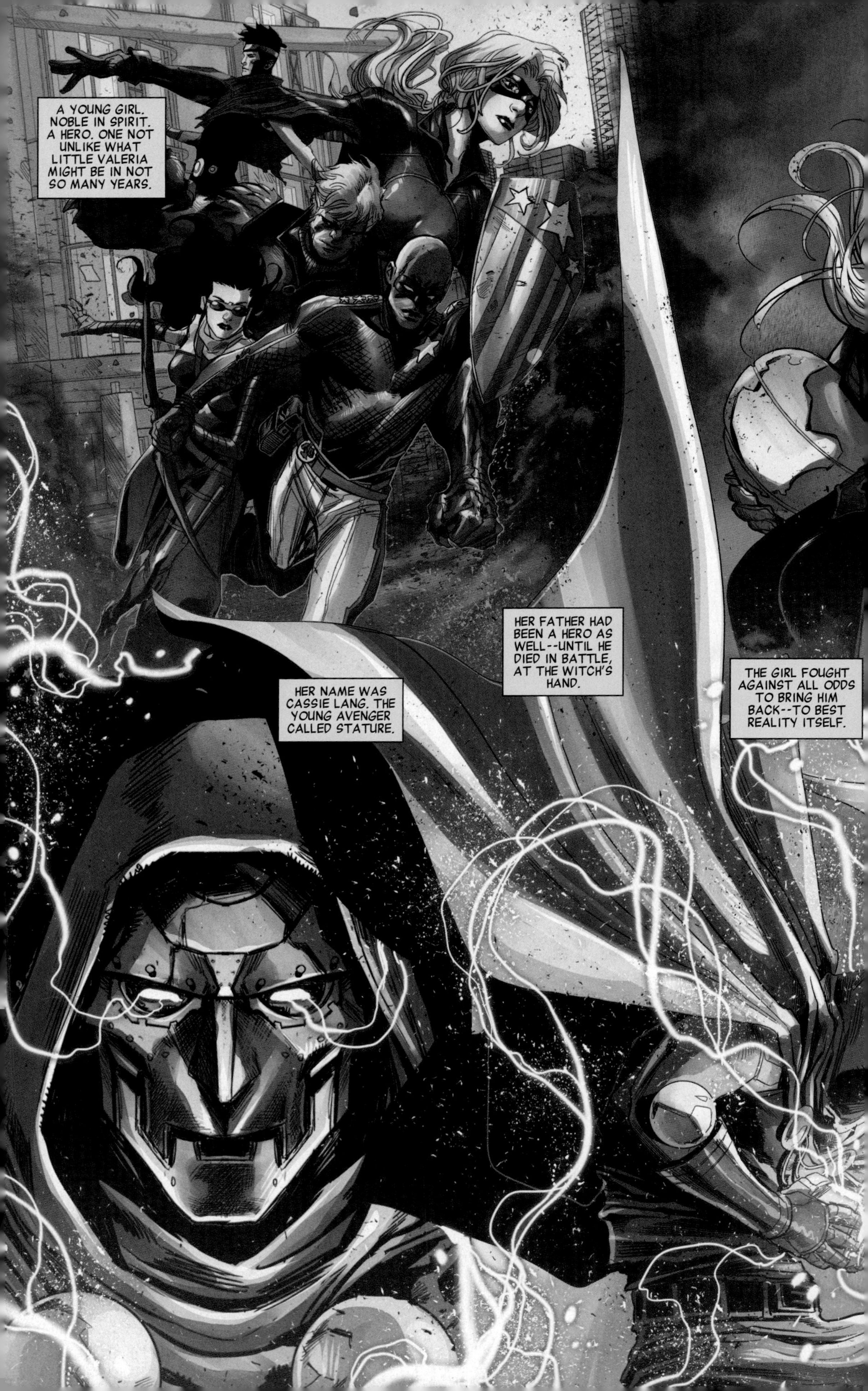
A YOUNG GIRL. NOBLE IN SPIRIT. A HERO. ONE NOT UNLIKE WHAT LITTLE VALERIA MIGHT BE IN NOT SO MANY YEARS.
HER NAME WAS CASSIE LANG. THE YOUNG AVENGER CALLED STATURE.
HER FATHER HAD BEEN A HERO AS WELL--UNTIL HE DIED IN BATTLE, AT THE WITCH'S HAND.
THE GIRL FOUGHT AGAINST ALL ODDS TO BRING HIM BACK--TO BEST REALITY ITSELF.

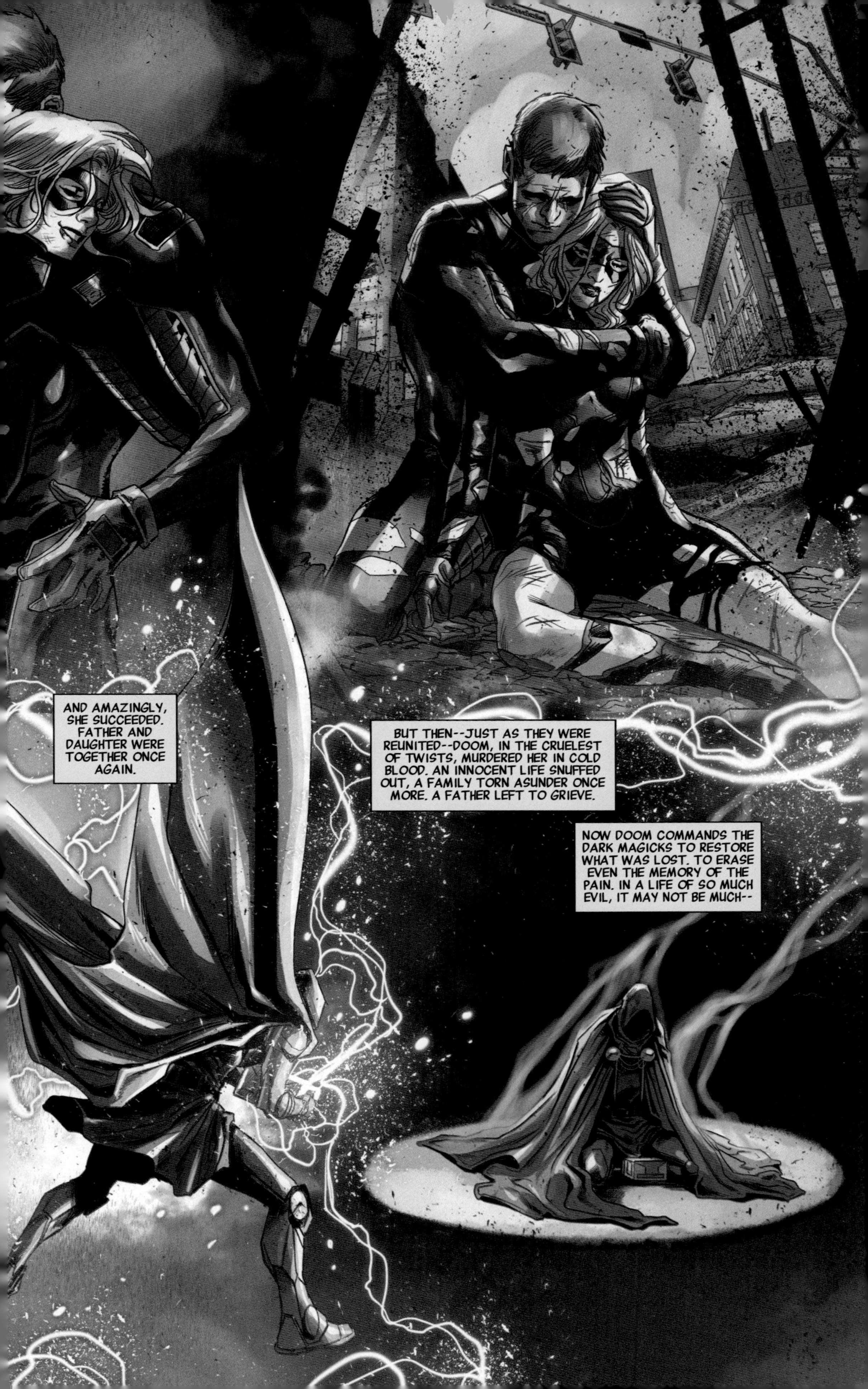
AND AMAZINGLY, SHE SUCCEEDED. FATHER AND DAUGHTER WERE TOGETHER ONCE AGAIN.
BUT THEN--JUST AS THEY WERE REUNITED--DOOM, IN THE CRUELEST OF TWISTS, MURDERED HER IN COLD BLOOD. AN INNOCENT LIFE SNUFFED OUT, A FAMILY TORN ASUNDER ONCE MORE. A FATHER LEFT TO GRIEVE.
NOW DOOM COMMANDS THE DARK MAGICKS TO RESTORE WHAT WAS LOST. TO ERASE EVEN THE MEMORY OF THE PAIN. IN A LIFE OF SO MUCH EVIL, IT MAY NOT BE MUCH--

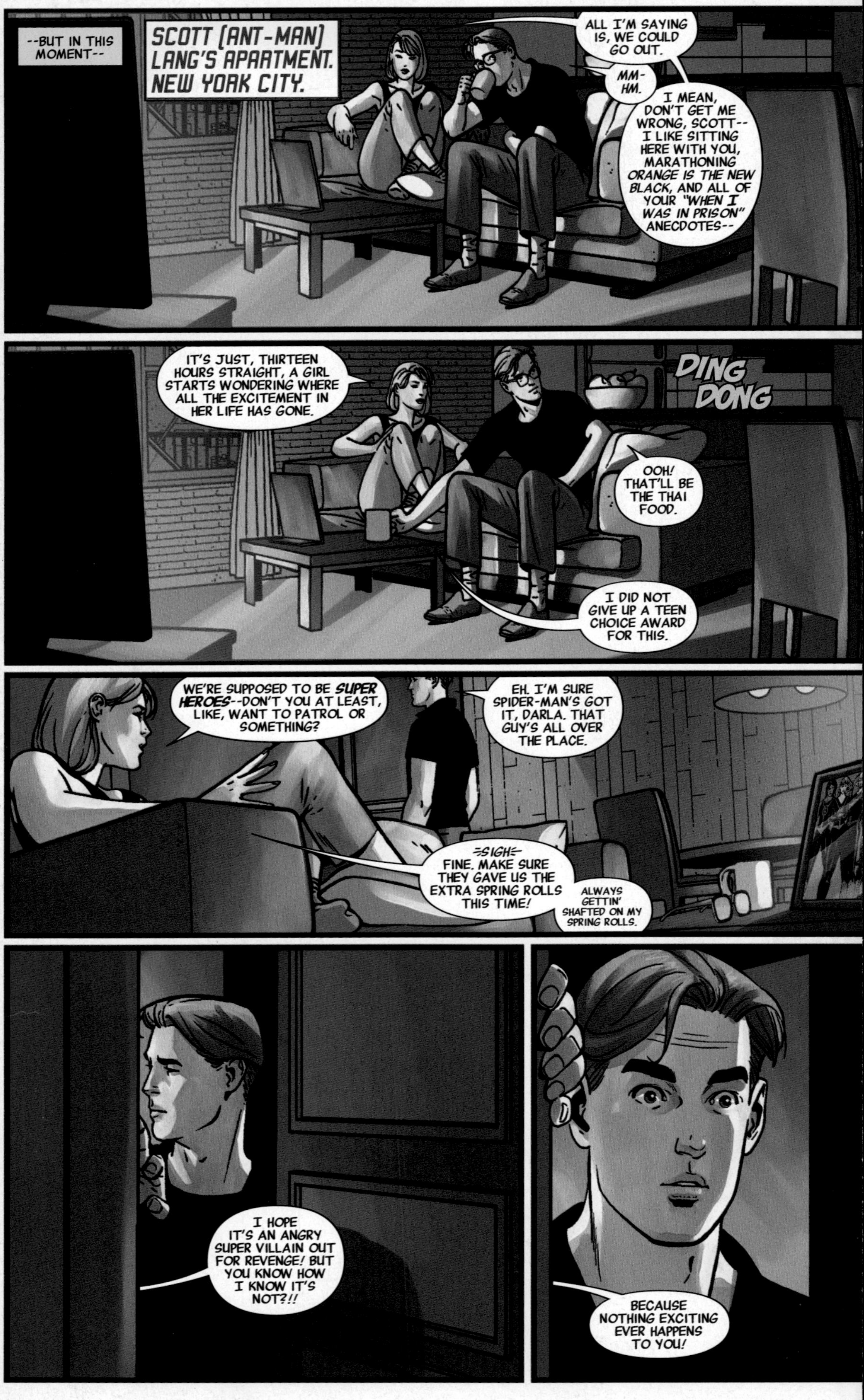
--BUT IN THIS MOMENT--
SCOTT (ANT-MAN) LANG'S APARTMENT. NEW YORK CITY.
ALL I'M SAYING IS, WE COULD GO OUT.
MM-HM.
I MEAN, DON'T GET ME WRONG, SCOTT-- I LIKE SITTING HERE WITH YOU, MARATHONING ORANGE IS THE NEW BLACK, AND ALL OF YOUR "WHEN I WAS IN PRISON" ANECDOTES--
IT'S JUST, THIRTEEN HOURS STRAIGHT, A GIRL STARTS WONDERING WHERE ALL THE EXCITEMENT IN HER LIFE HAS GONE.
DING DONG
OOH! THAT'LL BE THE THAI FOOD.
I DID NOT GIVE UP A TEEN CHOICE AWARD FOR THIS.
WE'RE SUPPOSED TO BE SUPER HEROES--DON'T YOU AT LEAST, LIKE, WANT TO PATROL OR SOMETHING?
EH. I'M SURE SPIDER-MAN'S GOT IT, DARLA. THAT GUY'S ALL OVER THE PLACE.
=SIGH= FINE. MAKE SURE THEY GAVE US THE EXTRA SPRING ROLLS THIS TIME!
ALWAYS GETTIN' SHAFTED ON MY SPRING ROLLS.
I HOPE IT'S AN ANGRY SUPER VILLAIN OUT FOR REVENGE! BUT YOU KNOW HOW I KNOW IT'S NOT?!!
BECAUSE NOTHING EXCITING EVER HAPPENS TO YOU!

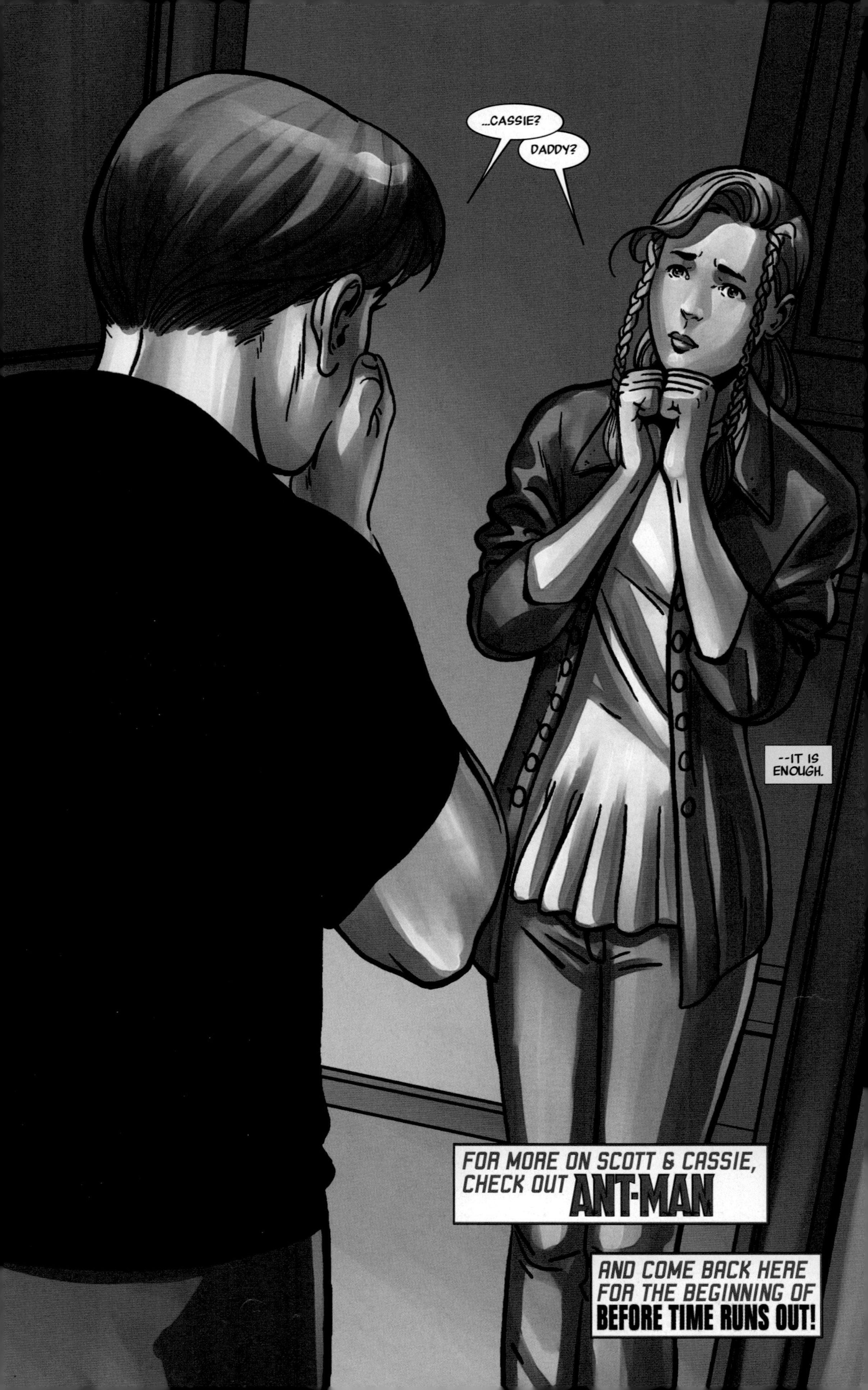
...CASSIE?
DADDY?
--IT IS ENOUGH.
FOR MORE ON SCOTT & CASSIE, CHECK OUT ANT-MAN
AND COME BACK HERE FOR THE BEGINNING OF BEFORE TIME RUNS OUT!

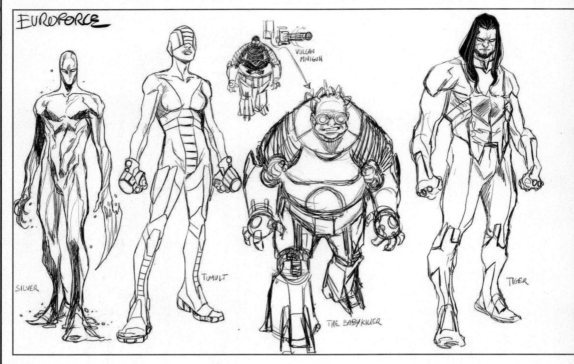

EUROFORCE

VULCAN MINIGUN

SILVER

TUMULT

THE BABYKILLER

TIGER

SWORDWOMAN

CHARACTER DESIGNS by Marco Checchetto

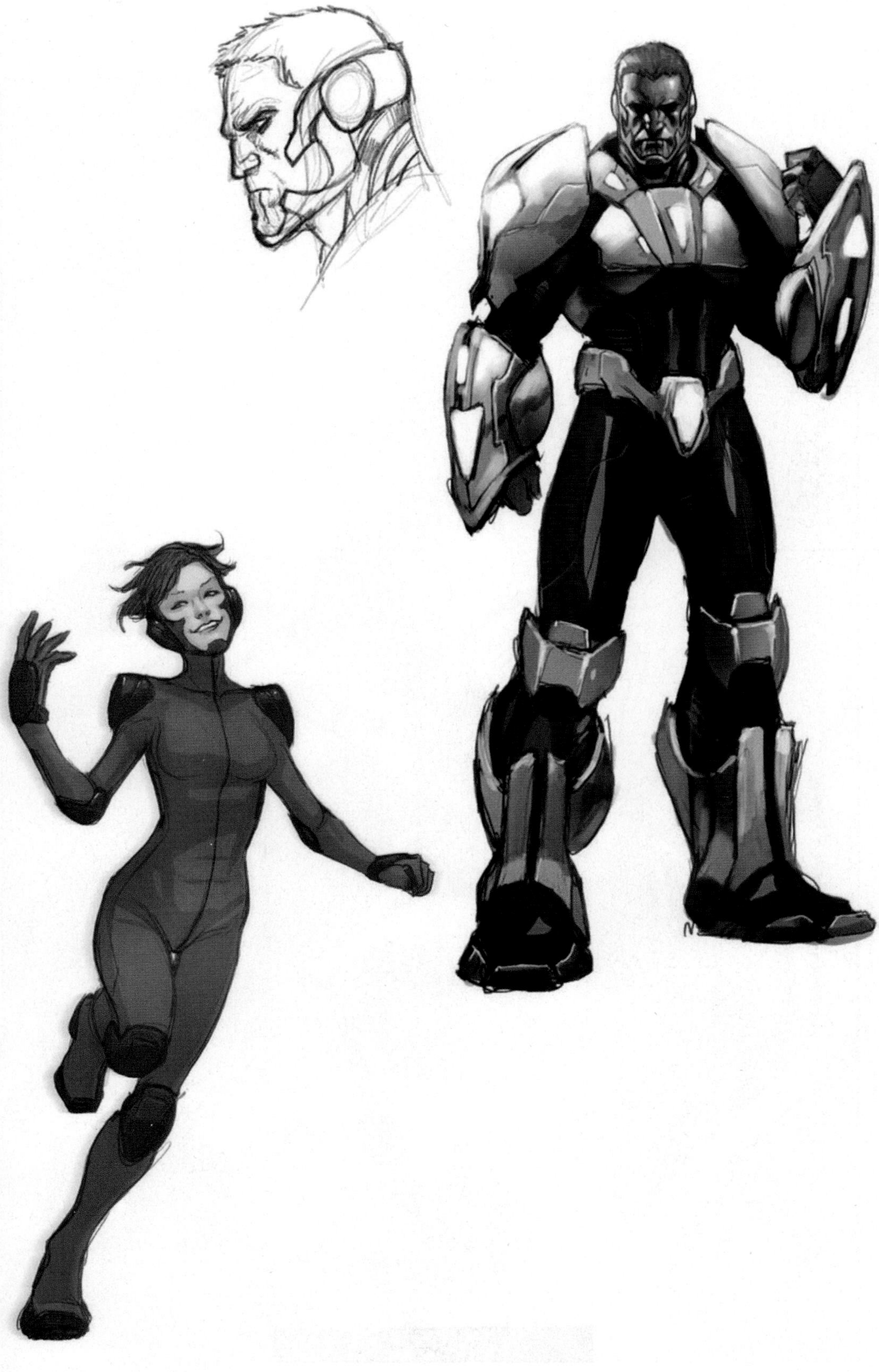

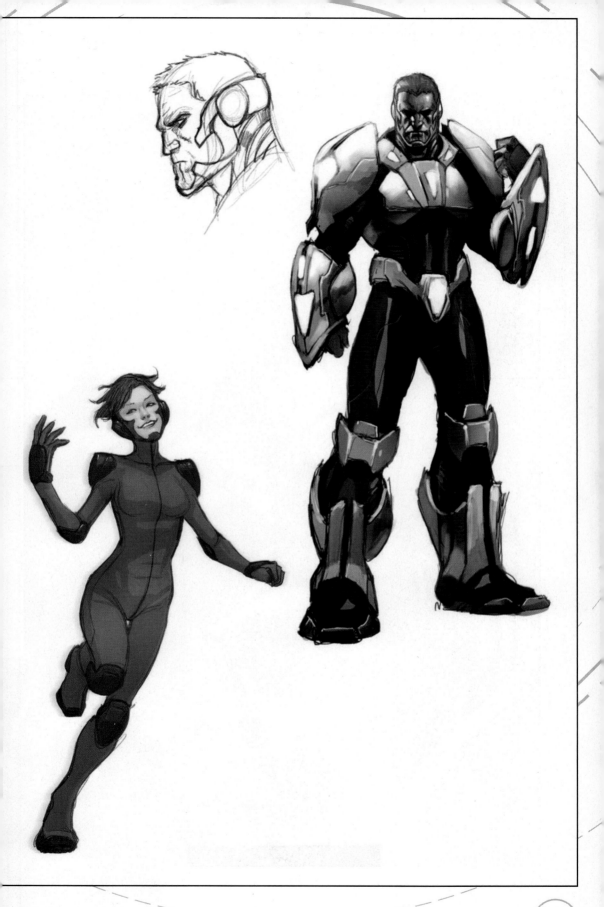

CHARACTER DESIGNS by Stefano Caselli

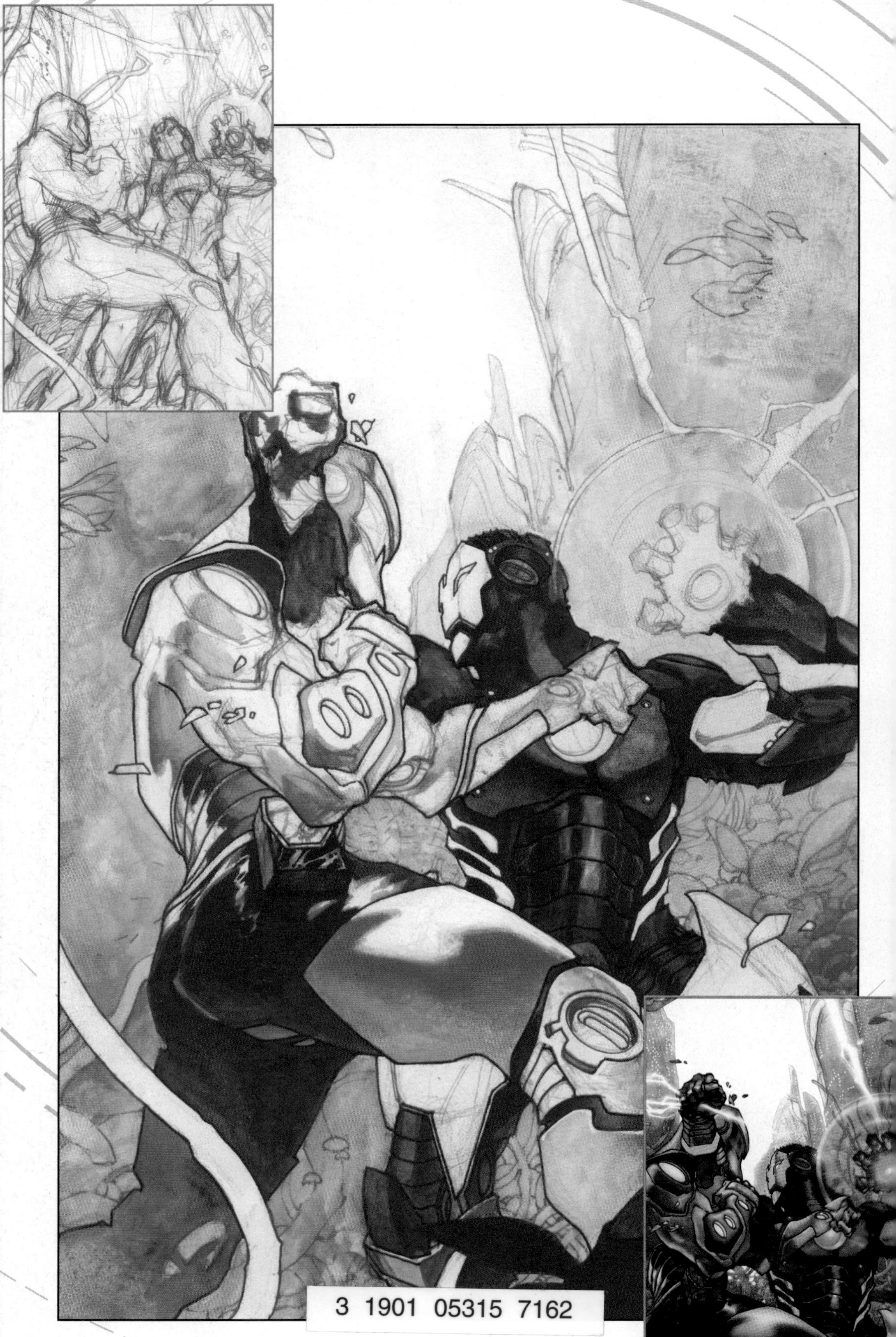

COVER PROCESS by Simone Bianchi